THE BATTLE OF BRETTON WOODS

THE
BATTLE
of
BRETTON
WOODS

John Maynard Keynes,
Harry Dexter White,
and the Making of a
New World Order

BENN STEIL

A COUNCIL ON FOREIGN RELATIONS BOOK

PRINCETON UNIVERSITY PRESS
PRINCETON AND OXFORD

339.53
STE

Requests for permission to reproduce material from this work should be sent to Permissions, Princeton University Press

Published by Princeton University Press, 41 William Street, Princeton, New Jersey 08540

In the United Kingdom: Princeton University Press, 6 Oxford Street, Woodstock, Oxfordshire OX20 1TW

press.princeton.edu

Library of Congress Cataloging-in-Publication Data

Steil, Benn.
   The battle of Bretton Woods : John Maynard Keynes, Harry Dexter White, and the making of a new world order / Benn Steil.
       p. cm.
   "A Council on Foreign Relations Book."
   Includes bibliographical references and index.
   ISBN 978-0-691-14909-7 (hbk. : alk. paper) 1. Monetary policy—History—20th century. 2. International finance—History—20th century. 3. United Nations Monetary and Financial Conference (1944 : Bretton Woods, N.H.) 4. Keynes, John Maynard, 1883-1946. 5. White, Harry Dexter, 1892–1948. I. Title.
   HG255.S837 2013
   339.5'3—dc23

                                                        2012035709

British Library Cataloging-in-Publication Data is available

The Council on Foreign Relations (CFR) is an independent, nonpartisan membership organization, think tank, and publisher dedicated to being a resource for its members, government officials, business executives, journalists, educators and students, civic and religious leaders, and other interested citizens in order to help them better understand the world and the foreign policy choices facing the United States and other countries. Founded in 1921, CFR carries out its mission by maintaining a diverse membership, with special programs to promote interest and develop expertise in the next generation of foreign policy leaders; convening meetings at its headquarters in New York and in Washington, DC, and other cities where senior government officials, members of Congress, global leaders, and prominent thinkers come together with CFR members to discuss and debate major international issues; supporting a Studies Program that fosters independent research, enabling CFR scholars to produce articles, reports, and books and hold roundtables that analyze foreign policy issues and make concrete policy recommendations; publishing *Foreign Affairs*, the preeminent journal on international affairs and U.S. foreign policy; sponsoring Independent Task Forces that produce reports with both findings and policy prescriptions on the most important foreign policy topics; and providing up-to-date information and analysis about world events and American foreign policy on its website, www.cfr.org.

The Council on Foreign Relations takes no institutional positions on policy issues and has no affiliation with the U.S. government. All views expressed in its publications and on its website are the sole responsibility of the author or authors.

This book has been composed in ITC Century Std

Printed on acid-free paper. ∞

Printed in the United States of America

10 9 8 7 6 5 4 3 2 1

To my precious Gloria and Ethan

CONTENTS

ACKNOWLEDGMENTS

I am extremely grateful and indebted to ten talented and highly motivated young people who provided critical research support in the writing of this book: Romil Chouhan, Demetri Karagas, Mark Holden, Nikolai Krylov, Ana Baric, Jess Seok, Maksymilian Czuperski, Parinitha Sastry, Ashley Lannquist, and Summer Lindsey. I was also privileged to have had ongoing feedback and sage advice from my Council on Foreign Relations study group, and would like to express my warmest thanks to each of the members who so generously dedicated their time and shared their expertise: Liaquat Ahamed, David Baldwin, David Beim, John Biggs, Michael Blumenthal, Karen Parker Feld, Richard Foster, Jeff Garten, Jim Grant, John Heimann, Jim Hoge, Harold James, Walter Russell Mead, Ernie Patrikis, Amity Shlaes, Paul Volcker, Shang-Jin Wei, and, in particular, the chairman of the group, Reuben Jeffery. I further benefited greatly from detailed comments on draft text from Andrew Wylie, Scott Moyers, Seth Ditchik, David Chambers, Dave Collum, and two anonymous referees. Finally, I would like to thank Richard Haass, president of the Council on Foreign Relations, and Jim Lindsay, CFR's director of studies, for their support and encouragement, as well as the Smith Richardson Foundation for its generous grant to fund the research. Errors and other failings in the book are, of course, mine and mine alone.

THE BATTLE OF BRETTON WOODS

CHAPTER 1

Introduction

In late 2008, with the world engulfed in the worst financial crisis since the Great Depression, French President Nicolas Sarkozy and British Prime Minister Gordon Brown each called for a fundamental rethinking of the world financial system. They were joined in early 2009 by Chinese central bank governor Zhou Xiaochuan, who pointed a finger at the instability caused by the absence of a true international currency. Each invoked the memory of "Bretton Woods," the remote New Hampshire town where representatives of forty-four nations gathered in July 1944, in the midst of the century's second great war, to do what had never been attempted before: to design a global monetary system, to be managed by an international body.

The classical gold standard of the late nineteenth century, the organically formed foundation of the first great economic globalization, had collapsed during the previous world war, with efforts to revive it in the 1920s proving catastrophically unsuccessful. Economies and trade collapsed; cross-border tensions soared. Internationalists in the U.S. Treasury and State Department saw a powerful cause and effect, and were determined in the 1930s to create, in the words of Treasury's Harry Dexter White, a "New Deal for a new world."

White, working in parallel and in frictional collaboration with his British counterpart, the revolutionary economist John Maynard Keynes, set out to create the economic foundations for a durable postwar global peace, one that would allow governments more power over markets, but fewer prerogatives to manipulate them for trade gains. Trade would in the future be harnessed to the service of political cooperation by ending shortages of gold and U.S. dollars. Speculators who stoked and profited from fears of such shortages would be shackled by strictures on the frenetic cross-border flows of capital. Interest rates would in each nation be set by government experts, schooled in the powerful new discipline of macroeconomics that Keynes had been instrumental in establishing. An International Monetary Fund (IMF) would ensure that exchange rates were not manipulated for competitive advantage. Most importantly, budding dictators would never again be able to use "economic aggression" to ruin their neighbors and fan the flames of war.

Robust economic recovery in the 1950s and '60s served to make Bretton Woods synonymous with visionary, cooperative international economic reform. Seven decades on, at a time of great global financial and economic stress, it is perhaps not surprising that blueprints for revamping the international monetary system from the likes of hedge fund guru George Soros, Nobel economist Joseph Stiglitz, and policy wonk Fred Bergsten all hark back to Bretton Woods, and the years of Keynes-White debate that defined it.

But can the story of Bretton Woods actually light the way?

To be sure, there were major flaws in the monetary framework that emerged from Bretton Woods, which contributed directly to its final collapse in 1971. Indeed, the life span of the Bretton Woods system was considerably shorter, and its operation more troubled, than is commonly reckoned. It was not until 1961, fifteen years after the IMF was inaugurated, that the first nine European countries formally adopted the required provisions that their currencies be convertible into dollars, by which point deep strains in the system were already manifest. Any successor system will bang up against the same difficult trade-offs between multinational rules and national discretion that bedeviled American and British negotiators in the 1940s. Since 1971 the world's economic statesmen have repeatedly called for the creation of "a new Bretton Woods": the Committee of Twenty in 1973–74, the Group of Twenty-Four in 1986, and the European members of the G7 in 2009, among others. They have all been disillusioned.[1]

Bretton Woods was embedded in a unique diplomatic context, surrounding the political and economic rise of the United States and precipitous fall of Great Britain. On the eve of the First World War the ratio of British debt to gross domestic product was a mere 29 percent;

by the end of the Second World War it had soared to 240 percent. A nation that had in the 1920s controlled a quarter of the earth's territory and population was, in Keynes's words, facing a "financial Dunkirk."[2] The story of the Faustian bargain Britain struck with the United States in order to survive the war would become an essential element in the Bretton Woods drama.

Central to that drama were the antipodal characters of Keynes and White: the facund, servant-reared scion of Cambridge academics, and the brash, dogged technocrat raised in working-class Boston by Lithuanian Jewish immigrants.

Keynes at Bretton Woods was the first-ever international celebrity economist. The American media could not get enough of the barbed, eloquent Englishman, who was both revered and reviled for his brash new ideas on government economic intervention. Keynes had assaulted the intellectual orthodoxy of the economics profession the way that Einstein had done with physics two decades earlier. In his monumental 1936 *General Theory*, Keynes had argued, with his unrivaled wicked wit and self-assuredness, that what governments thought was eternally sound policy was actually reckless when it came to confronting a depression. The key insight, he held, was that the very existence of money at the heart of the economy wreaked havoc with the self-stabilizing mechanisms that classical economists believed to be at constant work. Keynes would apply his insight in the design of a new global monetary architecture, built around a new international reserve currency—one that would be a threat to the global supremacy of the U.S. dollar and which White was determined to keep from seeing the light of day.

His visionary monetary schemes notwithstanding, Keynes had ultimately come to the United States with the mission of conserving what he could of bankrupt Britain's historic imperial prerogatives—what little room for maneuver it would be allowed in what seemed sure to be a dollar-dominated postwar world. His unlikely emergence as Britain's last-ditch financial ambassador—its chief voice in the Bretton Woods, Lend-Lease, and British loan negotiations—was grounded in the repeated failure of his country's politicians and mandarin class to make headway in what amounted to increasingly desperate begging operations in Washington.

A piece of British doggerel from the period neatly frames how the country's emissaries saw its plight: "In Washington Lord Halifax once whispered to Lord Keynes, it's true *they* have the money bags but *we* have all the brains."[3] Halifax having been one of many in the British political establishment who failed to loosen the strings on America's money bags, Keynes was sent off to the front lines in Washington and Bretton Woods in the vain hope that, if brains were to be the key to solvency, he might have more success.

No one grasped Britain's dire financial circumstances and needs more acutely than Keynes. He also had an effortless facility with words that might have made him a master diplomat, had he actually been more concerned with converting opponents than with cornering them logically and humiliating them. "That man is a menace to international relations," came one observation—not from an American interlocutor, but from a British war cabinet adviser, future Nobel economist James Meade, who considered Keynes "God."[4] "The lobbying for votes, the mobilisation of supporters, the politics of the lunch and the dinner table were not arts in which Keynes excelled," observed Treasury colleague Paul Bareau.[5]

Keynes struggled both mentally and physically to adapt to the strange circumstance of people, specifically denizens of Washington, D.C., who could be neither swayed by his superior command of facts and logic nor even compelled to get out of the way. The Americans never deviated from their hard-line geopolitical terms—at least until after the war, when Truman's team reshuffled the deck. Keynes frequently compounded the problems of the bad hands he was dealt by playing them inaptly. An astute, dedicated career diplomat would have played off the New York bankers, who were dangling loans in return for British opposition to the U.S. Treasury's monetary reform plans, against FDR's moneymen. But Keynes had a legacy to think of, and his place in the Bretton Woods pantheon was critical to it. The psychological price he paid for his persistence was bouts of a Stockholm syndrome variant, whereby he would persuade himself—and, with his unmatched rhetorical skills, the political class in London—that the American government, for all its intolerable legalism and defiance of reason, truly meant well and would do the right thing by Britain in the end.

The chief barrier to Keynes's blueprint for the postwar monetary order was, at the time of Bretton Woods, still a little-known U.S. Treasury technocrat, one who bristled at suggestions from the skeptical conference press that he might have few ideas save those fed to him by Keynes's *General Theory*. Yet Harry White had, in spite of his carrying no official title of consequence, by 1944 achieved implausibly broad influence over American foreign policy, having even played a critical role in the diplomacy leading up to war with Japan three years earlier.

Grudgingly respected by colleagues at home and counterparts abroad for his gritty intelligence, attention to detail, relentless drive, and knack for framing policy, White made little effort to be liked. "He has not the faintest conception how to behave or observe the rules of civilised intercourse," Keynes groused.[6] Arrogant and bullying, White was also nerve-ridden and insecure. Being wholly dependent on his ability to keep his boss, Treasury Secretary Henry Morgenthau, an FDR confidant with limited smarts, continually rearmed with actionable policies, he was always acutely conscious of his tenuous status in Washington. He often made himself ill with stress before negotiations with Keynes, and then exploded during them. "We will try," White spat out in one particularly heated session, "to produce something which Your Highness can understand."[7]

White's role as the chief architect of Bretton Woods, where he outmaneuvered his far more brilliant but willfully ingenuous British counterpart, marks him as an unrelenting nationalist, seeking to extract every advantage out of the tectonic shift in American and British geopolitical circumstances put in motion by the Second World War. White had a vision of a postwar order antithetic to long-standing British interests, particularly as they related to the empire. What even his closest colleagues were generally unaware of, however, was that White's vision involved a much closer American relationship with a new, rising European power, and that he was willing to use extraordinary means to promote it. Making sense of White's larger agenda is important, not only to grasp why the British found him such a difficult interlocutor, but also to understand why the lurch in American foreign economic policy was as sharp as it was after the war, when Truman shifted its control from the Treasury to the State Department.

White had a long-standing fascination with the Soviet Union, having decided in 1933, shortly after becoming an economics professor at Lawrence College in Wisconsin, to try to get a scholarship to go to Russia and study its economic planning system. He was diverted only by an invitation from Treasury adviser Jacob Viner in June of 1934 to come to Washington for a spell to help him with a monetary and financial reform study. It was there that he met George Silverman, Whittaker Chambers, and others working for the Soviet underground. By as early as 1935, White—idealistic, eager for influence, and dismissive of bureaucratic barriers to action—began the sort of dangerous double life that attracted many of his Washington contemporaries during the '30s and '40s.

Though White's official writings paint him squarely as a Keynesian New Deal Democrat, his private musings put him firmly further left. White envisioned a postwar world in which the Soviet socialist model of economic organization, while not supplanting the American liberal capitalist one, would be ascendant. An unpublished, handwritten essay of White's, newly uncovered in the course of this research, bears this out unambiguously. Written just prior to the end of the war, the piece contains highly provocative commentary on American attitudes toward the Soviet Union that undoubtedly would have led, had the piece been made public, to widespread calls for his dismissal.

"I have seen the future," wrote radical journalist Lincoln Steffens after a trip to Petrograd in 1919, "and it works." By the time of Bretton Woods a quarter century later, White believed that Soviet socialist economics had proven itself a success. "Russia is the first instance of a socialist economy in action," White writes. "And it works!" Much of the animus toward the Soviet Union within the American political establishment was, he argued, political hypocrisy born of an ideological inability to acknowledge the success of socialist economics.[8]

A critical question that must obviously be asked is whether White's Soviet connections actually had any impact on the outcome at Bretton Woods. The broad "White Plan" for postwar monetary reform certainly bore no imprint of Soviet monetary thinking, as there was none to speak of. To be sure, White was notably solicitous of the obstructionist Russians at the conference itself—more so than any of his American negotiating colleagues, and vastly more so than the Europeans, some of whom were angered by it. Yet this meant little in the end, as the Soviets never ratified the agreements. Had White become the first head of the IMF, his views might have been more consequential—we will never know. However, we will see that the primary reason White did *not* become the institution's head—and no American has ever since become its head—was emerging revelations of White's activities on behalf of the Soviets.

Winston Churchill once famously remarked that "we can always count on the Americans to do the right thing, after they have exhausted all the other possibilities." He was ultimately vindicated two years after Keynes's death, and a half year after White's, in the form of the Marshall Plan—an act of extraordinary American statecraft built on the epiphany that Britain was not actually a rival for power, as White had pegged it, but in fact a desperate ally to be bolstered in the face of a growing Soviet threat.

This is the story of the rise and fall of Harry White's blueprint for a new world order, and the vestiges of that fall that we wrestle with today.

The Mount Washington Hotel, location of the Bretton Woods conference, July 1944.
(Courtesy of the International Monetary Fund)

CHAPTER 2

The World Comes to the White Mountains

"The majestic beauty of the surroundings," wrote the *New York Times* correspondent, newly arrived in the remote and chilly northern New England mountains, is "in striking contrast to the temporary bedlam which broke out on this plateau in the shadow of Mount Washington."[1] It was July 1, 1944, and hundreds were descending on the hastily refurbished Mount Washington Hotel, the full postal address of which was Bretton Woods, New Hampshire. The town's only other landmark— there being no main street, or even store—was the Fabyan railway station, which received the unusual inflow of foreigners on trains dubbed "the Tower of Babel on wheels."

It was two and a half years since Treasury's Harry Dexter White had begun planning his international monetary conference, now aptly situated in the White Mountains. Yet management of the once-grand hotel, which had been closed for two years, had been given only a month to prepare for the inrush. The town's entire population had, just a few months earlier, consisted of a handful of hotel caretakers, the stationmaster, and the postmistress—his wife. Now, workers, soldiers, and government officials were frantically tidying up even as army buses ferried in the delegates and their advisers—among the latter being "an astonishing number of future prime ministers, finance ministers and central bank governors."[2] Hotel staff struggled to contend with shortages in everything from beds to hot water to fellow staff.

"Bretton Woods proves to be an extraordinarily beautiful spot," recorded just-arrived British delegate Lionel Robbins, yet "everything is in a state of glorious confusion."[3] The new manager himself had to be quickly replaced, having either resigned in despair or been fired for drunkenness—depending on whose account you believed.[4] The seventy-strong press, the conference secretariat, hundreds of delegation staff, and other assorted overflow bedded down in surrounding hostelries, some up to five miles away.

The curious remote locale for the most important international gathering since the Paris Peace Conference of 1919 owed its selection to Treasury Secretary Henry Morgenthau's desire for a large eastern resort facility, adequate for conferencing, far from the oppressive summer heat and busy wartime gloominess of Washington. Yet whereas better-known coastal spots might have done as nicely, Bretton Woods offered an attractive political amenity. It was to be found in a state whose Republican senator, Charles Tobey, a redoubtable opponent of international organizations, faced a tough November primary election. If the spotlight helped Tobey with the New Hampshire electorate, President Roosevelt expected the favor would be returned when the conference agreement came up for Senate approval. FDR was all too conscious of the fact that Woodrow Wilson's League of Nations had foundered in that chamber.

The name Bretton Woods was given to the mountainous New England tract by Sir Thomas Wentworth, after his ancestral home at Bretton Hall, near Bretton, England, in 1772—Wentworth and a few fellow noblemen having been awarded the land by King George III. It became a popular vacation retreat among the wealthy of Boston, New York, and Philadelphia in the early years of the twentieth century, following the construction of the Mount Washington.

Built in 1902 by coal-mining and railroad magnate Joseph Stickney using 250 Italian craftsmen, the massive four-hundred-room Y-shaped Spanish Renaissance–style hotel, notable on approach for its expansive white stucco façade and red-roofed turrets sitting atop five-story octagonal towers, nestled incongruously between low mountains and the million-acre White Mountain National Forest. Stickney christened it with a proud toast to "the damn fool who built this white elephant," the largest structure in New Hampshire.[5] Its interior featured a seven-hundred-seat-capacity great hall with stained-glass windows, an equally grand dining room, an indoor swimming pool, luxury shops, a post office, a barber's shop, two movie theaters, a bowling alley, and a

stock ticker. Tea was taken in an elegant, round, window-walled con-
servatory topped by an ornate painted cupola, while cocktails were
served outside on the long, columned veranda, measuring a full fifth of
a mile, looking out on the vista of forest and hills. The view toward the
summit of Mount Washington, the tallest peak in New England, looked
much like the Alps, and New Hampshire natives often referred to the
area as the Switzerland of North America.[6] The wooden mammoth had
played host to the likes of the Astors and Rockefellers, Babe Ruth,
and Winston Churchill, before the Great Depression pummeled its pull
(shutting it down for the 1930 season) and World War II pushed it to
the brink of bankruptcy.[7] Having by legend been routinely haunted by
ghosts, the Mount Washington was about to become one itself before
the Bretton Woods conference brought it back to life.

The delegates themselves numbered over seven hundred, from
forty-four countries. By all accounts this was, for David Stoneman,
president of the Mount Washington's corporate owner, nothing to
recommend them. New Hampshire had never been fond of strangers.
The thirty-three-strong Chinese contingent, second in size only to the
American, made a particularly suspicious sight in the secluded hills.
At one point several of them had to beat a hasty retreat off a hiking
trail after surprising "a trigger-happy hermit who mistook them for
Japanese bent on subverting the conference."[8] But the U.S. government ultimately won Stoneman over by convincing him that the conference was important to humanity and, more important, the hotel's
bottom line. Stoneman, misgivings notwithstanding, signed a contract
to play host for three weeks. The evening of the delegates' arrival, he
wandered through a "gathering of Colombians, Poles, Liberians, Chinese, Ethiopians, Russians, Filipinos, Icelanders, and other spectacu-
lar people," according to the cosmopolitan *New Yorker* magazine, in a
white linen suit, looking red-faced and shaken.[9] It was as if Martians
had invaded his stately refuge.

One of the hotel's newly arrived foreign guests, Russian-born Lydia
Lopokova, described the place as a "madhouse," complaining that
"[t]he taps run all day, the windows do not close or open, the pipes
mend and unmend."[10] Her room, 219, had a fine view overlooking
the rugged River Ammonoosuc and the cog railway that climbed up

Mount Washington, the base of which was typically shrouded in fog each morning. She swam daily in the frigid pool of water formed by the Ammonoosuc directly behind the hotel.[11] A prima ballerina in her younger years, Lydia herself contributed to the kinetic atmosphere of the traditionally tranquil resort by keeping the American Treasury Secretary awake each night with her dance exercises over his ceiling in room 119.

Lydia's own fame notwithstanding, her husband was the conference's media idol. As such, the British delegation head, John Maynard Keynes, was obliged to make the rounds of the cocktail circuit with an eager American press corps hanging on his every word and movement.[12] "Our unfortunate Chairman," Robbins wrote, "was photographed from at least 50 angles—Lord Keynes conversing with the Chairman of the Russian Delegation," though neither understood the other's language, "Lord Keynes warmly clasping [the hand of Chinese delegation head] Dr Kung, . . . Lord Keynes standing up; Lord Keynes sitting down . . . and so on and so forth."[13]

One issue that had consumed the American team's strategy session the previous day was what to do about the world's most celebrated and controversial economist. Too many in Congress were already convinced that the whole Bretton Woods agenda was a British trick to purloin American gold, and no one irked them more with his posh perorations than Lord Keynes. By dint of America's host-nation status and diplomatic tradition, Morgenthau laid claim to the conference presidency and the honor of delivering the opening address; he and his deputy were now determined to keep the spotlight off Keynes, and trained instead firmly on the American message.

"[The British] wanted Keynes to nominate me," Morgenthau told his team, but "I did not want it. I vetoed it."

Morgenthau's official convening of the conference at 3:00 p.m. on July 1 took place against a backdrop of dramatic developments on the battlefields of Europe. The massive Allied invasion of Normandy was now nearly a month into force. In four days time, German Field Marshal Gerd von Rundstedt would be relieved of the Western Command after advising Hitler to make peace. Delegates felt that the beginning of the end of the war was in sight: their deliberations therefore held real meaning. The message read out to them from President Roosevelt sought to forge an indelible connection between the economic matters before them and prospects for a durable peace.

"It is fitting that even while the war for liberation is at its peak, the representatives of free men should gather to take counsel with one another respecting the shape of the future which we are to win," the president said.

> The program you are to discuss constitutes, of course, only one phase of the arrangements which must be made between nations to ensure an orderly, harmonious world. But it is a vital phase, affecting ordinary men and women everywhere. For it concerns the basis upon which they will be able to exchange with one another the natural riches of the earth and the products of their own industry and ingenuity. Commerce is the life-blood of a free society. We must see to it that the arteries which carry that blood stream are not clogged again, as they have been in the past, by artificial barriers created through senseless economic rivalries.

> Economic diseases are highly communicable. It follows, therefore, that the economic health of every country is a proper matter of concern to all its neighbors, near and distant. Only through a dynamic and a soundly expanding world economy can the living standards of individual nations be advanced to levels which will permit a full realization of our hopes for the future.

Morgenthau's own speech elaborated the themes of war and peace, but adopted a starkly darker tone when it came to the roles of collapsing trade and currency disorder in paving the path to war in the 1930s. Morgenthau told the assembled that "competitive depreciation of currency" and "devices to hamper and limit the free movements of goods" had become the "economic weapons" with which "the Fascist dictators" of Europe had initiated the bloodshed. "Economic aggression," he said, "can have no other offspring than war. It is dangerous as it is futile."

Whereas Keynes would have shared Morgenthau's sentiments on the disastrous political progeny of bad economics, the most substantive part of the speech would surely have unnerved him—cutting straight to the heart of British angst over America's blueprint for the immediate postwar economic and political architecture.

"Our agenda is concerned specifically with the monetary and investment field," Morgenthau had started innocuously enough. "It should be viewed, however," he went on, "as part of a broader program contemplated in the Atlantic Charter and in *article VII of the mutual-aid agreements* concluded by the United States with many of the United Nations. Whatever we accomplish here must be supplemented and buttressed by other action having this end in view."[14] Article VII referred to a provision of the 1942 legislative bill, popularly known as Lend-Lease, through which the Americans pledged to aid the British war effort financially. Prime Minister Winston Churchill had famously heralded it as "the most unsordid act in the whole of recorded history." Yet the bill sent to Congress had been more self-interestedly titled "An Act Further to Promote the Defense of the United States," and Article VII spelled out what the Americans called the British "consideration" for the aid: a commitment by the British "to the elimination of all forms of discriminatory treatment in international commerce, and to the reduction of tariffs and other trade barriers."

Much of the British establishment considered this a mortal threat to British solvency and sovereignty. Reading an earlier draft wording of Article VII in July 1941, Keynes exploded in rage in front of the State Department's Dean Acheson: "the lunatic proposals of Mr. Hull," he later termed it, referring to Acheson's boss, Secretary of State Cordell Hull.[15] Keynes knew that Article VII was, in reality, code for an end to "Imperial preference," by which Britain secured privileged trade access to the markets of its colonies and dominions. In the war's aftermath, the Americans would be in a powerful position to supply the markets previously served by the British, and, stripped of its traditional export rights, war-ravaged Britain would remain wholly dependent on American succor to pay for imports vital to its survival.

Being left to the mercy of an all-powerful United States was intolerable, particularly as the U.S. government had been determined to show its people that American boys had not been sacrificed to perpetuate the moral abomination of empire. Yet here at Bretton Woods was the American Treasury Secretary tethering the historic event to the mast of his country's superpower ambitions. The British had been anxious to see themselves as partners with the Americans in creating the ground rules for the postwar order, yet at every step to Bretton Woods the Americans had reminded them, in as brutal a manner as necessary, that there was no room in the new order for the remnants of British imperial glory.

H. D. White, April 25, 1945. (Harris and Ewing, Courtesy of Harry S. Truman Library)

CHAPTER 3

The Improbable Rise of Harry White

By Harry White's reckoning, his life started in 1930, the year he received his doctorate from Harvard. He notes nothing before it in the biography he provided for *Who's Who*.

Harry's life had actually started across the Charles River thirty-eight years earlier, in much less refined surroundings. Yet Harvard represented a rebirth of sorts. The son of a peddler, he had an epiphany at age thirty, in his second attempt at an undergraduate degree. Having failed entrance exams in civics and American history the first time around, he was nonetheless incubating a growing passion for politics. Economics was a means to that end. "[P]retty soon I realized that most governmental problems are economic," he told a friend years later, "so I stayed with economics."[1] Harry was onto something.

The youngest of seven children, Harry was born on October 29, 1892, four months after his father, Jacob, had become an American citizen. Jacob and his wife Sarah had come to the United States in 1885, part of the immigration wave of Lithuanian Jews escaping tsarist pogroms. The family name Weit appears to have attached to them courtesy of an enterprising American immigration officer, who thought it an improvement on Weiss.[2] Jacob was twenty-five at the time. He made a hardscrabble living in the Boston hardware and crockery business, eventually saving enough to open his own stores. The family settled at 57 Lowell Street, at the foot of Beacon Hill, in the heart of a bustling tenement district and just below the roaring elevated train line. Jacob anglicized the family name to White in 1897.[3]

Harry was a nervous boy, who went largely unnoticed except by the neighborhood bullies.[4] Though raised with a respect for education—he was part of a Webster Literary Club school group that met weekly to discuss compositions each boy wrote—he showed no particular early signs of brilliance. He entered the Old Eliot public grammar school in 1901, just shy of his ninth birthday, by which time the family had moved to 7 Salem Street, removed from the noise and shadow of the El. His mother Sarah tragically died that year. But his father's business was beginning to prosper, and they moved again, this time to the Boston suburb of Everett, where Harry entered Everett High School in 1906. Though his grades were far from exemplary (a 79 in French, an 85 in chemistry), he completed a four-year course in three years. The *Boston Globe* reported on June 25, 1909. that Harry "Dexter" White—the first recorded appearance of Harry's mysterious middle name—was, at sixteen, the youngest of that year's Everett graduates. High school classmates described him as shy, but witty and smart. Despite being puny, he was also an avid tennis and baseball enthusiast.[5]

Two months after Harry's graduation and eight years after his mother passed away, Harry's father Jacob also died. By this time, the family owned four hardware stores, and Harry spent the next two years clerking for the business, sometimes acting as a store manager. In September 1911, he enrolled at the Massachusetts Agricultural College, now the University of Massachusetts at Amherst. Though he failed his civics and American history entrance exams, he passed in English and was admitted conditionally. He implausibly registered his future profession as "farming." Harry passed the civics and history exams a few months later, but left college to return to the family business in February 1912. His grade point average was 80.8, comfortably above failing only because of a 99 in military science.

For the next five years, Harry worked long hours at J. White Sons. But he also showed a strong civic-mindedness, spending each Sunday morning teaching the senior boys class at the Home for Jewish Children in Dorchester as well as leading them as a Boy Scout troop.[6] Harry was nonetheless on the lookout for a life-changing opportunity. A big one came on April 6, 1917, when Congress passed President Woodrow Wilson's declaration of war on Imperial Germany. Now twenty-five, Harry did not wait to be drafted, enlisting in the U.S. Army six days later. He applied and was admitted to the officers' training course in Plattsburg, New York, and at the end of the summer was commissioned as an infantry first lieutenant. Among a group of five men in his company he was selected to receive advanced training with several hundred other officers for a so-called Iron Battalion, and was then assigned to train recruits at Camp Deven in Massachusetts.[7] Just before being sent overseas, Harry, as was common among his generation of soldiers, got married. His new wife was a twenty-two-year-old Ukrainian-born student named Anne Terry, who would eventually go on to become a successful author of children's books.

By all appearances, White's military career was largely uneventful. Stationed in France in training and supply camps, his units saw no combat. He returned home after the armistice in November 1918, fleetingly reentering the family hardware business. The life of a small local businessman no longer satisfied him. From 1919 to 1922, he directed organizations aiding orphans of servicemen and the poor, relocating to New York City in 1920. It was in New York that White, now aged thirty, decided to make a go at an academic career, entering Columbia University to study government in 1922. After three terms, he uprooted himself again, this time to cross the country and enroll in Stanford University as a junior. It was here, in 1923, that he had his epiphany.

In October 1924, White graduated Phi Beta Kappa "with great distinction" in economics. He received his master's the following June. A professor later described him as "aggressive and brilliant," set on pursuing a PhD at Harvard and a subsequent academic career.[8] He also began displaying the passion for progressive politics that was to mark his later career in Washington. In February 1924, White wrote a letter to the fiery liberal Wisconsin Senator Robert La Follette, Sr., claiming to represent a group of mature Stanford graduates urging "Fighting Bob" to run for president. The men "yearn to serve your cause," White wrote. "Most earnestly they urge upon you the fact that at no time has our country been more in need of a leader, and that at no time since Lincoln's has there been a man more fitted to lead than you. They await instructions as to how they can best further your cause."[9] In the end, La Follette, who ran on a Progressive Party platform pledging nationalization of the water and railroad industries, finished third in the election, behind Republican Calvin Coolidge and Democrat John W. Davis, with a respectable 17 percent of the popular vote. In fulfillment of his earlier ambition, White headed back across the country in 1925 to start his PhD studies at Harvard.

White's dissertation, prepared under the supervision of noted economist Frank Taussig, who regarded White as one of his most promising students, won Harvard's David A. Wells Prize and was published as a book in 1933 under the title *The French International Accounts 1880–1913*. The research marked the beginning of White's fascination with policy questions surrounding the relationship between the workings of the international monetary system and the performance of the real economy.

Though the historical period White studied had ended only two decades before the release of White's book, it might as well have been eons prior. The years 1880–1913 constitute the great era of laissez-faire in world economic history—the reign of the classical gold standard, in which governments around the globe had allowed an unprecedented degree of economic activity within and between their nations to be regulated by the market-driven transfer of gold claims across borders (the physical stuff itself just shifted around in central bank vaults). The year 1933, in stark contrast, saw the world mired in the Great Depression, with the gold standard in tatters, trade decimated, and unemployment at previously unimagined levels. Yet White had been pondering and writing about international economics during the late 1920s, when there was still a powerful popular belief in finding the path back to "the Golden Age of Security," as the celebrated Austrian Jewish writer Stefan Zweig called the three decades prior to the Great War.[10]

White's thesis shows him to be neither a defender of the past nor a prophet of a new future. As an economist, he appeared to be a tinkerer, an engineer. He admired the economic machine, but was looking for the dials government might fiddle with to make it run better. He began by describing the traditional, so-called neoclassical, theoretical account of how cross-border movements in capital affected, in turn, exchange rates, gold flows, interest rates, credit, prices, and trade, showing how this remarkable watch-like system continuously regenerated equilibrium. It was this dynamic of ceaseless change and systemic stability that was held to underlie the prewar gold standard. But White set out to see whether the data testified to such elegant simplicity. He returned to France, this time as a civilian rather than a soldier, and plowed through trade figures. Though neither White nor his book's reviewers were satisfied with the quality of the statistical raw material he worked with, White melded his numbers with logic to tell a reasoned story of a French economy that was not quite synchronized with neoclassical equations.

It was hardly a riveting read. There was none of the passion that marked his letter to Fighting Bob. "[T]he assumption that the capital exports benefit both the country and the world at large is not unassailable," was typical of his sober conclusions. "[S]ome measure of intelligent control of the volume and direction of foreign investments is desirable. . . . The ramifications of exporting a large portion of a country's savings are too complex, and the consequences too important to permit the continuance of capital exports without making some attempt at evaluating their effects on the well being of the country at large."[11] Though the sentiments were pure Keynes, the prose had none of the master's barbed eloquence.

Despite White's modest success with his thesis, he rolled from one annual teaching appointment to the next, for six years, without making progress toward a tenured faculty position. Promotion from within has always been challenging at Harvard, but it would seem that White was held back by an impression that he was academically unexceptional and temperamentally challenging. A student described him as an excellent teacher, but a fellow instructor saw him as unhappy and "not outstanding" in ability. Now forty years old, White grew frustrated with his limbo status, and accepted an assistant professorship at a small campus far from Cambridge—Lawrence College, in Appleton, Wisconsin. In 1933, after only a year in Appleton, White was promoted to full professor, but remained frustrated. His colleagues thought him smart and a fine teacher, but abrasive and opinionated. As at Harvard, his economics were considered plain-vanilla. But his progressive politics made him a natural to embrace newly elected president Franklin Roosevelt and his New Deal agenda, and White was anxious to get his own hands on the dials.

An undated draft of a letter from White to his Harvard mentor Taussig, probably written in 1933, shows that White clearly had no intention of remaining an academic worker bee in Appleton:

My interest has been aroused by the growing claims that our domestic economy must be insulated against critical disturbances, and that a greater (degree) restriction of imports could supply the insulation. This plea for virtual economic self-sufficiency needs, I believe, more critical treatment than has been forthcoming. I am wondering whether it may not be possible to develop feasible means of rendering our domestic affairs less sensitive to forcing disturbances without sacrificing either stabilizing influences of int[ernational] econ[omic] relations or the gains from for[eign] trade. The path, I suspect, may lie in the direction of centralized control over foreign exchanges and trade.

White would hew closely to this technocratic vision—of an open American economy buffered against disturbances by government control of exchange rates and regulation of trade—throughout his subsequent career in Washington.

White then goes on to tell Taussig where he believes the answers lie—curiously, in Soviet Russia:

I have been spending the spring and summer reading and thinking about the problem but my opinion is as yet unsettled. I am also learning Russian in the hope that I may get a fellowship which would enable me to spend a year chiefly in Russia. There I should like to study intensively the technique of planning at the Institute of Economic Investigation of Gosplan. I expect to apply for a Social Science Research fellowship tho my hopes of an award are not high.[12]

It is interesting to speculate on the intellectual and career path White might have taken had he gotten his fellowship and moved to Moscow. Would he have come back an ardent central planner? A disillusioned anti-Stalinist? The only thing that seems clear is that he would have missed a much bigger opportunity to change the world.

This came in the form of a letter dated June 7, 1934, from University of Chicago economics professor Jacob Viner, a highly respected and respectful intellectual opponent of Keynes and a teacher of the young Milton Friedman. Viner was at the time advising Treasury Secretary Henry Morgenthau, and he invited White to come to Washington for three months to assist him in conducting a study of the U.S. "monetary and banking legislation and institutions . . . with a view to planning a long term legislative program for the Administration." White telegraphed his acceptance two days later—"Will be very glad to come to work with you"—without knowing or asking what he would be paid, which Viner suggested by return telegraph would be only a third of White's Appleton salary, plus a $200 pension allowance. White began his work in Washington on June 20, and never saw Appleton again.

White labored away on his report for Viner during the hot Washington summer, submitting it on September 22. The sweeping title, "Selection of a Monetary Standard for the US," clearly suggests that its author had no intention of getting sidetracked with fringe issues. He now wanted to make, not just shape, policy at the highest level, and he was not about to let the opportunity afforded by an economic crisis go to waste.

White began by laying out his bleak vision of an economic future marked by growing national political rivalry, rolling back many of the gains built up during the prewar gold standard era:

> The stabilizing influence exerted by the interdependence of nations is not likely in the future, however, to be so great as it has been in the past. Other countries are awake to the disturbing forces coming from abroad. They also are concerned over their domestic stability, and are less hesitant about adopting restrictive measures to ward off disturbances. Bumper export crops in the United States are more likely in the future to be met by specially imposed import restrictions designed to check 'dumping', rising discount rates will be met with more effective measure[s] for protecting gold, and so on. Increased government control by numerous important countries over their international trade and finance will be used more and more to wrest competitive advantage away from competing countries; and the struggle for competitive advantage in trading relations will, as a result, become keener and more prolific of sudden important shifts in the movements of international goods and capital. These developments in the direction of more intense economic nationalism obstruct the path of such stabilizing influences as the free exchange of goods, services, and capital might be expected to have.[13]

White concluded that any new monetary standard would have to have "promotion of trade and finance" as a key criterion, but that it would also have to allow "sovereignty in shaping domestic policies."[14] What was needed was a system that would "combine the best features of both the gold standard and a national monetary standard while avoiding the chief disadvantages of each." It would be "a 'managed' currency standard."[15]

When a country confronted an adverse balance of payments with the world (more imports and bond purchases than exports and bond sales), it faced, White said, a choice "between two evils": a fall in the exchange rate or a fall in the domestic price level. Both were disruptive. Both were undesirable. But a choice had to be made.

Under the gold standard, exchange rates were fixed, so that the balance of payments had to adjust through domestic deflation. White, like Keynes, concluded that it should be the other way around. "I believe there is definitive evidence," White wrote, "that alterations in the domestic price level are far more costly to the nation than frequent alterations in the exchange rate would be." The United States "would be courting trouble to place ourselves in a position similar to that which we found ourselves between 1929 and 1933," a period of persistent deflation.[16]

White therefore wanted to rewrite the rules of the American monetary system to give a revamped Federal Reserve far more discretionary powers than the gold standard could accommodate, and then convince the rest of the world to help make such a new system stick internationally. This was an even more herculean task than it seemed, given that no one had actually "created" the gold standard. It had emerged in Britain in the early nineteenth century by dint of trial and error over centuries, and governments around the world signed on much later only when it became clear that the system served to boost both local and global commerce.

But in 1934, the world was mired in depression. U.S. gross domestic product was 28 percent lower than it had been at the start of the decade.[17] Trade had plummeted 29 percent.[18] Unemployment had soared to 22 percent.[19] White argued that U.S. economic recovery demanded trade expansion opportunities for American business, and that such expansion in turn required a new model for international monetary stabilization. This was to be White's bedrock position as his responsibilities and power expanded over the next ten years.

The fraying relic of the gold-exchange standard that remained at the end of the 1920s had collapsed entirely by 1934. Britain, its inspiration and foundation in the nineteenth century, abandoned it with great reluctance and bitterness in September 1931. Twenty-five nations followed in short order. The United States refused to throw in the towel until April 1933, shortly after Roosevelt took office. President Herbert Hoover had tried to preserve the gold standard by means of trade restrictions; Roosevelt maneuvered in the other direction, moving away from multilateralism in money while trying to preserve it in trade.

The drama of the final collapse of the gold-exchange standard would poison Anglo-American relations for decades. To the British way of thinking, Britain had been ignominiously forced off gold by selfish and short-sighted American and French policies: the Americans with their abominable import tariffs, and the French with their wretched devaluations. The Americans, for their part, saw themselves as innocent victims of an odious British default.

To be sure, gold was still imbued in the minds of the public and central bankers alike with special properties that made it important to sustaining confidence in the integrity of paper money and base-metal coins. But the classical gold standard as such was a system in which national claims on gold flowed according to rules, not the panic-induced hoarding motives that now drove gold flows in its stead. In ditching the gold-exchange standard, Roosevelt also banned hoarding of the metal by private citizens, while mandating it at the national level. He signed an executive order on April 5 requiring all domestic gold coins, bullion, and certificates to be delivered up to the Federal Reserve Banks, and forbade its export. On June 5, Congress took the dramatic step of abrogating the gold payment clause in public and private contracts, legally severing the dollar from its gold mooring—a highly controversial step that was barely upheld in a five-to-four Supreme Court decision in February 1935.

In June of 1933, after weeks of behind-the-scenes negotiations between American banking experts and their British and French counterparts, Roosevelt became convinced that the British and the French were seeking competitive advantage through undervalued currencies. He was determined not to have his plans for domestic economic revival wrecked by falling prices and a hobbled export sector, and he used a major international political gathering to crush any doubts in the currency markets. On July 3, Roosevelt, an internationalist by background who had strongly supported the League of Nations as a vice presidential candidate in 1920, shocked the sixty-six-nation London Economic Conference by sending a dyspeptic public message denouncing "the old fetishes of so-called international bankers," and insisting that "the sound internal economic system of a nation is a greater factor in its well being than the price of its currency in changing terms of the currencies of other nations." The president's harshly worded attack on the utility of currency coordination among the major monetary powers dashed European hopes of restabilizing exchange rates on agreed grounds. British Prime Minister Ramsay MacDonald was said to have been devastated by the speech; French Monetary Commission rapporteur Georges Bonnet enraged. The conference collapsed. A cable back to the White House from London revealed an American delegation very much on the defensive owing to the perceived "harshness and untimeliness" of the president's language[20]— which Roosevelt later acknowledged as excessive.

At the time, however, the president had no qualms about tweaking the British, whom he thoroughly distrusted. "[W]hen you sit around with a Britisher he usually gets 80 per cent of the deal," the president tartly remarked to Henry Morgenthau, his longtime confidant and then-head of the Farm Credit Administration. And of Chancellor of the Exchequer and future Prime Minister Neville Chamberlain, Roosevelt was convinced that "he thoroughly dislikes Americans." The British, for their part, were convinced that FDR had double-crossed them, and this poisoned all subsequent discussions on exchange rate matters during his presidency.[21]

Even though FDR's missive was anathema to London and riddled with contradictions in economic logic, it was hailed as "magnificently right" by none other than J. M. Keynes, who, in addition to being fond of barbed prose, strongly approved of its sentiments regarding the primacy of national economic management.[22] Harry White, on the other hand, was already laboring behind the scenes to make his mark on American international economic policy by arguing that currency stability was essential to achieving domestic economic stability, contradicting the president's message.

Back at home, Roosevelt was equally blunt and mercurial with his monetary tactics. Treasury experimented with numerous schemes, such as gold buying, to push down the dollar and push up domestic goods prices. From his bed each morning, Roosevelt would, after briefly conferring with his advisers, set a daily target for bumping up the gold price, not always through scientific methods. One day, November 3, the president suggested that gold should go up twenty-one cents. "It's a lucky number," he explained, chuckling, "because its three times seven."[23]

"If anybody ever knew how we really set the gold price through a combination of lucky numbers, etc.," observed Morgenthau, "I think they would be frightened."

New York Federal Reserve Bank President George Harrison asked the president to let him inform the British government before beginning to buy up gold abroad. "Every time we have taken the British into our confidence," FDR objected, "they have given us a trimming."[24] But he relented. On receiving the news from Harrison, Bank of England governor Montagu Norman—"old pink whiskers," the president called him—was apoplectic. "The world will be put into bankruptcy!" he insisted. But Roosevelt delighted in the real and imagined reaction of foreign financiers, chuckling with Morgenthau over the images of befuddled bankers they conjured up.[25]

Acting Treasury Secretary Dean Acheson, who had effectively replaced the long-ailing actual Secretary William Woodin, insisted that FDR's gold-buying operation was illegal. The attorney general concurred that the president lacked the authority to buy gold above the $20.67-an-ounce price fixed by statute. Roosevelt was incensed by press reports that some in his administration considered the program unconstitutional, and wrongly laid the blame on Acheson. (The culprit was likely budget director Lewis Douglas, who would resign in frustration over currency and budget policy the following August.)[26] After a breakfast conference on November 13, FDR told the "dumbfounded" forty-three-year-old Morgenthau that he was to replace Acheson.[27] Currency policy was hardly Morgenthau's strong suit, but his fealty to the president and his program more than made up for it. He was sworn in on January 1, 1934, only the second Jewish cabinet Secretary in the country's history.[28]

Despite the president's fondness for setting the dollar's daily value by whim, the process proved unsustainable. It generated increasingly frenzied domestic lobbying, as well as foreign protests. So on January 31, 1934, Roosevelt, using the powers granted to him under the

Gold Reserve Act passed by Congress the previous day, fixed the dollar at a level 59.06 percent below its previous official price: down from $20.67 per ounce to $35 dollars per ounce (where it would remain, at least in a highly circumscribed legal sense, until 1971). Morgenthau announced that the Treasury would thereafter buy gold at $34.75 and sell it at $35.25, transactions being limited to governments on the gold-exchange standard and their central banks.[29] The act transferred title to all gold held at the Federal Reserve to the government, thus shifting the locus of power over the country's monetary system from New York to Washington. This effort would be a persistent theme of administration policy right through to the Bretton Woods conference in 1944.

Harry White was determined to stay in Washington after his work with Viner was complete, and took another temporary appointment, beginning October 5 of that year, as a special expert and chief economic analyst with the U.S. Tariff Commission. He resigned that post three weeks later when given the opportunity to take a temporary appointment with the Treasury Department's Division of Research and Statistics, with the title principal economic analyst, on November 1. This "emergency work" was slotted to end eight months later, in June 1935. But it turned out to be only the beginning of a dramatic twelve-year Treasury career.

White began elaborating his policy views with an "Outline Analysis of the Current Situation," completed in March 1935. He emphasized the pressing problem of the ten million unemployed. But he also expressed concern about the growing popularity of extreme anticapitalist figures such as Senator Huey Long, a persistent thorn in the president's side, and radio priest Father Coughlin. They were "rapidly gaining support for extremely radical programs."

Much of the memo, together with a sharper-edged one calling for a much more aggressive "Deficit Spending Policy," has a distinctly modern ring, and could easily have been written by contemporary American liberal economists:

The cry of "loss of confidence" is largely a smokescreen let loose by certain conservatives who are traditionally opposed to almost any

Government expenditure, who object to any increase in taxes, and are too shortsighted to know that the perpetuation of the present level of unemployment constitutes the most dangerous threat to their own interests. . . . The statement that the bond market could not absorb Government bonds has been made ever since the first unbalanced budget, yet today Government bond prices in the United States are higher than ever.[30] . . . If [companies] do not employ the potential purchasing power [of the unemployed], the Government can do so at virtually no expense to the community.[31]

"Can we operate under a deficit of 8 billion in 1936 also?" White then asked. "The only answer is that if business has not improved sufficiently to warrant a reduction in Government expenditure . . . then certainly private industry cannot be depended upon to restore prosperity unaided."[32]

But was further large-scale deficit spending the "only answer" to anemic business investment? If "loss of confidence" did, in fact, flow from large and persistent deficits, then more spending could be harmful rather than helpful. Gauging precisely whose confidence is affected how and by what is naturally challenging, which explains why passionate arguments between proponents and opponents of "fiscal stimulus" do not die away.

White never achieved significant direct influence on domestic policy, but he did begin to carve out a critical role on international policy by effectively tying the two together. Never mentioning the president's London "bombshell," as it had become known, White stressed the critical importance of "reestablish[ing] international economic equilibrium," and doing so "without jeopardizing our long run program of stabilizing domestic business at a high level of real income." The domestic approach "is dependent upon" the international approach, and each "influences the other. The program must be viewed as a whole rather than two separate programs."[33] No division could be drawn, White insisted in a third memo, "between domestic and international monetary problems, or between domestic business activity and foreign trade."[34]

Here was White aligning himself wholeheartedly with the president's domestic agenda while insisting that it would be effective only if tethered to a new program for international monetary stabilization, which White himself would develop. His logic was that "restoration of international monetary equilibrium [would] increase foreign trade, [and] an increase in foreign trade constitutes an important factor in recovery." He was vexed by the problem of British and French competitive devaluations. "Given the choice," White argued, "every country prefers to have its currency under-valued rather than over-valued." Therefore, without efforts to restore equilibrium exchange parities by international agreement, countries would act to protect their domestic industries by erecting import barriers and would protect their export markets through "bilateral trade and exchange arrangements," all of which would act to reduce global trade and hamstring recovery.[35]

Roosevelt was not yet budging from his London stance, but he was anxious to see Morgenthau find a way to avoid another round of competitive devaluation among the major economic powers. This created a huge opportunity for White. Already recognized in the Treasury as "an able young economist [and] a man of extraordinary energy and quick intelligence,"[36] he was doing his work on monetary stabilization at a time when the White House was waking up to its domestic benefits, which made him the right man, in Morgenthau's eyes, to visit Europe for some fact-finding and exploratory talks in April.

The first of many major spats between FDR's departments of State and Treasury arose over who would lead the new monetary diplomacy, Secretary of State Cordell Hull or Treasury Secretary Morgenthau. A brief truce took hold after Morgenthau approved the wording of a State Department telegram to the Dutch government stating that White would be coming to study monetary conditions and was "not in any way authorized to negotiate on military matters or enter into discussions of policy."[37]

The most important part of White's trip was his stay in London, from late April through mid-May, during which he held a constant stream of meetings with industrialists, bankers, economists, civil servants, and elected representatives. His personal report on the trip, filed on June 13, reveals that it began with a meeting at the U.S. Embassy, during which he told the skeptical American ambassador that he hoped to get the cooperation of British officials by telling them that the discussions would be "on an academic, theoretical basis," and that he would make it clear he "had no connection with administration policy, but was merely there to observe economic phenomena."[38] This, of course, was nonsense. But it was no barrier to White getting appointments, as British officials, who naturally kept mum on UK policy, were anxious to pick White's brain on U.S. dollar policy. White reported being discreet, which would have been challenging for a man as passionate and voluble on the subject as he was.

The industrialists, White found, were broadly against any refixing of the price of sterling in terms of gold, holding it chiefly responsible for Britain's economic troubles from 1925 to 1931. With the huge contraction in world trade after 1929, they now exported mostly to Britain's sterling-based dominions, and therefore showed little concern over sterling's gyrations. He found their lack of interest in exchange problems curious, particularly the little-Englander notion that "when the price of sterling changed in terms of other currencies, it was the other currencies that moved and not sterling."[39] Ruling Labour Party figures, such as Hugh Dalton and George Lansbury, similarly expressed no interest in fixing exchange rates, and were strongly opposed to any return to the gold-exchange standard. They shared Roosevelt's belief that domestic price stabilization was far more important to economic recovery. Among economists, London School of Economics professors Lionel Robbins and T. E. Gregory took a very different position, advocating Britain's return to gold "as soon as possible" at a rate of about $4.80 to the pound. The risk of not doing so, they believed, was a further decline in trade, a collapse of the sterling bloc owing to falling confidence in the currency, and a continued wave of beggar-thy-neighbor devaluations around the world. But the most consequential meeting White was to have was with Robbins' then intellectual rival, J. M. Keynes.

Keynes spoke broadly in favor of exchange stabilization, belying his reputation for opposing it, and raised mainly practical problems with achieving it: in particular the British government's stance that the dollar was undervalued, and that sterling should only be stabilized at a lower rate; and the likelihood, in his view, that "certain groups in Congress" would override any arrangement the Roosevelt administration might agree to. He did show a keen prescience, and may even have influenced events, in suggesting that cooperation among the British, American, and French treasuries might serve to avoid parliamentary or congressional obstruction—an idea that White, never one to be deterred by legal or bureaucratic obstacles, found congenial, and which in fact took shape the following year. But the primary significance of their meeting lay in the fact that each man would subsequently become his country's primary interlocutor in the Anglo-American financial drama that came to define Bretton Woods.

The European trip was immensely important to White's subsequent career. It marked the beginning of his decade-long tenure as the intellectual bedrock of Henry Morgenthau's ever-expanding power base. A longtime friend of the president, whose Hyde Park estate was near Morgenthau's farm in Dutchess County, New York, Morgenthau could still outmaneuver Hull and the State Department only to the extent that his ideas were compelling, practical, and forcefully implemented. Yet the Treasury Secretary was not of particularly nimble mind nor robust constitution.[40] White was his perfect complement. He was highly ambitious, but needed a powerful patron to advance. What he brought to Morgenthau was a coherent vision of an internationalized New Deal, incessant energy, command of detail, and "a flair for converting economic theory into administrative practice."[41]

The immediate question of finding a practical way to stop the poisonous devaluation tit for tat, at least until a more permanent replacement for the tattered gold-exchange standard could be established, came to a head in the summer of 1936. Following the formation of the French left-wing Popular Front government led by Léon Blum, gold outflows forced a major devaluation of the franc. This pushed the Roosevelt administration and the British Conservative government led by Stanley Baldwin into action. Following weeks of tense negotiations, on September 25 a Tripartite Agreement was concluded aimed at producing a truce in the currency wars.[42] Morgenthau characterized it as a "gentlemen's agreement," fearing anything that might smell like a formal treaty. The Americans and the British reluctantly swallowed a 30 percent French devaluation, undertaking not to retaliate with devaluations of their own. The three governments agreed to use their respective exchange stabilization accounts to limit gyrations among their currencies. The French had wanted a much firmer commitment, pledging the three powers to working toward restoration of the international gold standard. But Roosevelt would have none of it, insisting that his London conference statement asserting American freedom of action "should be our text and bible," according to Morgenthau.[43] The president had further demanded the removal of any reference to "central bank" cooperation—associating central banking with "private finance," as did his Treasury Secretary, whereas monetary policy was wholly a matter for governments.[44]

Over the next two months, the U.S. Treasury also initiated a major policy shift. Following passage of the 1934 Gold Reserve Act, the Treasury would sell gold only to countries on the gold-exchange standard. But in October of 1936, Morgenthau changed the policy to allow gold sales to the British and French treasuries at a price to be set daily. "The responsible governments of the people," Morgenthau announced at a press conference, "will now cooperate to assure a minimum of exchange fluctuation. . . . The international speculator, responsible to no one, and recognizing no flag in the conduct of his business, will in the future not be able by rapidly shifting his funds from market to market, to reap private advantage through stimulating chaos in foreign exchange."[45] Though it was a far cry from the classical gold standard of yore, the combination of the Tripartite Agreement and the resumption of U.S. gold sales brought some modest stability to the international economy. Belgium, the Netherlands, and Switzerland signed on to the Agreement in November, and were granted the right to trade in gold with the United States on the same terms as Britain and France. The United States stuck with the policy even as it allowed the pound to fall gradually against the dollar after 1937.

But the faint signs of economic stabilization proved ephemeral. The stock market collapsed in October '37. The French devalued again in the spring of '38, after which the franc was pegged to the pound. The pound stayed on a managed float right up to the eve of the Second World War, when it was fixed to the dollar at $4.03. The U.S. economy was back in recession; the New Deal was faltering.

Nonetheless, by 1936 the U.S. Treasury, if not yet the president, had become wedded to the objective of monetary stabilization, and had established the American government's dollar price of gold as an essential international monetary benchmark and anchor. To be sure, the gold standard was dead and buried. Monetary rules were out; autonomous national government discretion was in. Keynes was triumphant. Still, by making a credible promise to keep the dollar convertible into gold at a time when the European democracies were starved for stability but powerless to provide it, the United States managed to re-create the semblance of an international monetary system without the politically intolerable domestic policy discipline the gold standard demanded.

White was now cementing his role as one of Morgenthau's most important advisers, in spite of his tenuous Treasury existence. His appointment as special economic analyst was renewed for one year in July 1935, and in October of '36 he was made an assistant director of the Division of Research and Statistics. He still had to be paid through an internal Treasury appropriation out of the devaluation profits of the Exchange Stabilization Fund set up by the '34 Gold Reserve Act—an ad hoc procedure that would, remarkably, go on until 1945, when he finally became a full-fledged civil servant.

Now in his midforties, White was on the tall side of short (five feet six), stocky, and moonfaced, with round rimless spectacles, blue eyes, and a trim, black mustache not infrequently likened to that of Germany's dictator, Adolf Hitler. His gait was quick and jerky, his manner similar. Though colleagues, including Hull, greatly respected his work ethic and command of detail, "He could be disagreeable," Morgenthau reflected years later. He was "quick-tempered, overly ambitious, and power went to his head."[46] He was also impatient, blunt, and sardonic. The Secretary's son and namesake, who periodically sat in on morning staff meetings, observed that White's "rapid-fire comments sounded disdainfully critical," except when he addressed the Secretary directly—White always knew on which side his toast was buttered. He "was meticulously civil to anyone in a position to afford him access to the powerful."[47] White's principal assistant at Bretton Woods, Edward Bernstein, described him as "temperamental" and "foul tempered." Professionally, White "really wasn't a top-notch technician, but if you could think of somebody having a mind for economic policy, he had it."[48] White's memos reveal a preternatural ability to explain technical subjects clearly and carefully, and to relate economic principles to actual international political circumstances. Though White's meeting schedule was busy and interruptions frequent, his memos often give the feel of having been crafted in cloistered serenity. It is easy to see how he became the influential adviser he did: what busy cabinet Secretary would not have considered such a man invaluable, if not indispensable?

Yet White could not take orders, and "often tried to circumvent [opposition] by going outside of ordinary bureaucratic channels," observed Morgenthau biographer John Morton Blum, "a habit that could be identified with furtiveness or even confused with subversion."[49] Given what we now know about White's freelance diplomacy, however, charges of subversion aimed at him may not always have been the result of confusion.

White's colleagues generally knew little about his personal life, other than that he had a wife and children and an interest in chess and music.[50] In 1936, White moved his family, which included two daughters aged ten and seven, from a District of Columbia suburb near Silver Spring, Maryland, to an apartment on Connecticut Avenue. In 1938 they made another move to an eight-room house on Fairfax Avenue, in Bethesda, Maryland, where they remained until after the war.

In the Connecticut and Fairfax Avenue homes, White had a Bokhara rug, probably worth over $3,000 in present dollar terms. What made the rug interesting was not its workmanship or artistic value, but the link it represented to a critical aspect of White's life—a murky existence situated dangerously between his personal life and his official life in Washington.

According to the most detailed account of the rug story, White received it in early 1937 as an anonymous Christmas gift, delivered by George Silverman, an official at the Railroad Retirement Board who later moved to Treasury under White.[51] A visitor to White's home some years later is said to have remarked to White knowingly that it "looks like one of those Soviet rugs." White, a nervous man to begin with, became very visibly nervous. When the friend visited subsequently, the rug was gone.

Silverman, the rug deliveryman, would eventually be fingered by Whittaker Chambers, a courier between Soviet intelligence and its secret sources within the U.S. government, as being part of an American spy ring run by Nathan Gregory Silvermaster, an economist with the Treasury and the War Production Board. The unnamed visitor who spooked White by calling attention to its source was, according to Chambers, part of "Elizabeth Bentley's apparatus," Bentley having also been a courier who turned U.S. government informant in 1945.

White was "clearly impressed" with his gift, according to Chambers. The rug was one of four that he had asked an expert middleman, Columbia University art professor Meyer Schapiro, to buy wholesale, having received orders and cash from Soviet Military Intelligence (GRU) agent Colonel Boris Bykov to get "big, expensive rugs" for his valuable American sources, White among them.[52] Bykov, who spoke little English and whom Chambers knew only as "Peter," had initially wanted to give them "a big sum of money," but Chambers told him this was stupid. "They are Communists on principle. If you offer them money, they will never trust you again." Bykov was baffled by this, but relented. He told Chambers to inform White and the others that the rugs "had been woven in Russia and were being given to them as gifts from the Russian people in gratitude to their American comrades."[53] And "on the four rugs," Chambers concluded triumphantly, "we marched straight into active espionage."[54]

By Chambers' account, White's clandestine work began in 1935. An idealist who envisioned a future in which world affairs were managed by enlightened technocrats such as himself, White appeared to welcome the chance to hasten its coming through secret foot soldiers like Chambers. Yet unlike Chambers, White would take orders from no one. He worked on his own terms. He joined no underground movements. If those who did found his knowledge and access valuable, he relished the means they afforded to put both to productive use. His official status in government being beneath what he knew his talents merited, he also craved the recognition such outsiders accorded him.[55]

Working through intermediaries close to him, White secured official Treasury documents for Chambers which, after Chambers photographed them in his Baltimore workshop, he returned through the same channel.[56] White also prepared weekly or biweekly memos for Chambers summarizing what he considered useful information.[57]

As White deepened his freelancing efforts, Treasury's official relations with the Soviets deteriorated. On Saturday, September 26, 1936, the day after the Tripartite Agreement was announced, Treasury was forced to step into the foreign exchange markets and support sterling against the dollar, owing to a large Russian sterling sell order placed through Chase National Bank. Morgenthau was livid when he learned the details from the New York Fed. Convinced that the Russians were trying to wreck the agreement, he called a press conference to reveal the Russian actions and to show American resolve in using the Stabilization Fund. The Russians, in turn, were furious over the Secretary's statement, implausibly claiming that the funds had been needed to meet a dollar payments obligation in Stockholm, and that the timing was incidental.

Chambers took great efforts to protect White, ditching one go-between, code-named "Wilton Rugg," for violating the underground principle of strict punctuality. Silverman, who was a close friend and confidant of White's, took over Rugg's role in 1936. He did not introduce Chambers to White until he was convinced that Chambers "could handle that odd character." White enjoyed the covert element of their meetings, though not to the extent that he would inconvenience himself to keep them secret: he usually picked a spot right near his Connecticut Avenue apartment.

"I had never liked Harry White," Chambers wrote bluntly. "I see him sauntering down Connecticut Avenue at night, a slight, furtive figure. . . . [H]e is nervous at the contact, idles along, constantly peeping behind him, too conspicuously watchful." In their meetings, White was edgy but curiously ingenuous. He talked "endlessly about the 'Secretary,'" Morgenthau, whose moods, as White described them, were mirrored in White's own cheery or glum demeanor with Chambers.[58] White was painfully aware that his influence in the world depended entirely on his personal relationship with Morgenthau, who in turn owed his standing to his friendship with the president. Morgenthau certainly made no effort to raise White's independent profile within the White House: "I really don't think [the president] knows," the Secretary observed as late as August 1942, "who Harry White is."[59] If White's cord to Morgenthau, or Morgenthau's to the president, were severed,

White would be no more than an energetic bureaucratic temp whose tenure in Washington could end in a heartbeat. Instead of enjoying the thrill of secretly refashioning U.S.-Soviet relations on the streets of Washington, he could at any moment be headed back to academic obscurity in Appleton.

White was introduced directly to Bykov by Chambers in early 1937, after the Russian complained that White was the least productive of his sources. Chambers credits this meeting with stimulating an enthusiasm previously lacking in White, owing to White's need for the attention of "big important people."[60] Chambers sought out the assistance of Hungarian Communist Josef Peters (known as "J. Peters") in identifying a Treasury Department Communist to "control" White and get more out of him. Peters suggested Harold Glasser, whom White had helped bring into the Treasury. In short order, Glasser assured Chambers that "White was turning over everything of importance that came into his hands."[61]

In terms of the work for which White was employed by the U.S. government, he continued to expand his official roles. In February 1936, he was appointed as Treasury representative on the interdepartmental Committee on Foreign Trade Agreements. In December 1937, Morgenthau designated White to represent the department in meetings of the National Munitions Control Board.[62] But in his spare time, White also took the initiative to work on reform of the Soviet monetary structure, an effort that he naturally kept quiet from the administration.

In his private street walks with Chambers, White bored him with what Chambers considered monetary gibberish. "I had told White that I knew nothing whatever about monetary theory, finance or economics," Chambers recounted. "Nevertheless, in our rambles, when he was not complaining that the Secretary was in a bad humor, or rejoicing that he was in a good humor, White engaged in long monologues on abstruse monetary programs." White pressed Chambers to get his ideas on Soviet monetary reform to the Soviet government. Chambers went to Bykov, who shared his lack of interest. But to Bykov's surprise, there was much enthusiasm in Moscow at the idea of having its monetary matters guided by an expert at the U.S. Treasury. Bykov quickly shifted gears, and told Chambers to get White's full plan to him immediately. But White had gone on summer vacation near Peterborough, New Hampshire, obliging Chambers to drive up after him.

White gave Chambers his plan for Soviet monetary reform, yet displayed no particular excitement over the details of it. This flummoxed Chambers. "I had assumed that his eagerness was the evidence of a disinterested love for monetary theory and concern for the Soviet Union. But I sometimes found myself wondering why he worked for the apparatus at all. His motives always baffled me."[63]

As regards the economics White advocated, they were hardly Marxist. They were by this time what would be described as thoroughly Keynesian. He insisted that government should take an active role in supporting economic activity; certainly more so than was orthodox before the Great Depression, but he never pushed for broad government control of the means of production. His writings on international monetary affairs express a concern with the need to fashion a system that "reduces the necessity of . . . restrictions on private enterprise."[64] As for White's domestic politics, these were mainstream New Deal progressive, and there is no evidence that he admired communism as a political ideology.

It is this chasm between what is known publicly of White's economic and political views, on the one hand, and his clandestine behavior on behalf of the Soviets, on the other, that accounts for the plethora of unpersuasive profiles of the man that have emerged over more than half a century.[65] "Who Was Harry Dexter White?" asked *Life* magazine five years after his death—a question it signally failed to answer. Accounts tend to fall uncomfortably into one of two polar camps. There are those in which White emerges as an unquestioning servant of Moscow, laboring in the shadows over many years to undermine American policy.[66] And there are those in which White emerges as a committed New Dealer and internationalist who occasionally crosses the line in his well-intentioned efforts to forge harmony with the Soviet Union.[67] Neither camp paints a compelling portrait.

The closest thing to a missing link between the official White and the secret White is an undated, unpublished, handwritten essay on yellow-lined notepaper buried in a large folder of miscellaneous scribblings in White's archives at Princeton. Apparently missed by his chroniclers, it provides a fascinating window into the grand schemes of this intellectually ambitious overachiever at the height of his stature, toward the end of World War II.

The essay, tersely titled "Political-Economic Int. of Future," begins by arguing that the United States, as a result of the "rude awakening" afforded by the Second World War, was perhaps "for the first time in its 170 years of nationhood . . . moving consciously toward the adoption of a policy of permanent international alliances, commitments, and responsibilities." Key to maintaining world peace would be "a tight military alliance" among the United States, the United Kingdom, the Soviet Union, and possibly China "designed to uphold int[ernational] law. . . . [N]o combination of powers outside these four would have the slightest chance of victory against them."

Such an alliance was essential, White maintains, describing a world ten years hence in which "The defeated countries regain some of their economic strength, and more of their pride. They again feel the stirrings to become a powerful nation—possibly to erase their status of a defeated, second rate power. . . . Who can doubt that powerful elements in defeated Japan and defeated Germany will again thirst for resumption of their former states of greatness? What evidence is there in Japanese and German history that would support the belief that either of these two nations will docilely accept a permanent status of impotence?"

The biggest threat to the successful establishment of the alliance was U.S. "isolationism" and "its twin brother rampant imperialism"—a jarring phrase that would surely have led to widespread calls for his dismissal had the document become public. Such imperialism, he charges, "urges the U.S. to make [the] most of our financial domination and military strength and become the most powerful nation in the world."

As White pursued U.S. global financial domination with a zeal not witnessed before or since in the Treasury, it is more than curious that he should here express objection to using such domination to "become the most powerful nation in the world." With whom did White intend the United States to share power? The essay is clear. Half of it focuses on the Soviet Union, referring critically throughout to American views of the rising rival power.

In the United States, White charges, there existed a "very powerful Catholic hierarchy who may well find an alliance with Russia repugnant; and other groups which are fearful that any alliance with a socialist economy cannot but strengthen socialism and thereby weaken capitalism." His attack on an unidentified "Catholic hierarchy" would, again, surely have landed his head on the block had the document's existence become known.

White goes on to develop the theme that the United States and its Western allies were hypocritical in their attitudes toward the Soviet Union. "[T]he virulent opposition between capitalist and socialist ideology . . . constitutes a dangerous source of disunity," he laments, arguing that the actual economic and political differences between capitalist and socialist countries were exaggerated. The United States had many prominent examples of public ownership, such as the Tennessee Valley Authority, the national park system, and oil reserves. Prices were fixed by law in areas such as transportation, telephone service, water, gas, and electricity. Private market competition "is subject to innumerable restrictions and qualifications." Meanwhile "in Russia, hundreds of thousands of small farms are leased and operated by individuals; carpenters, cobblers, and all means of services are sold to consumers in the same manner as in cap[italist] countries; people receive royalties on publications, and own govt. bonds and receive interest there on; wage rates though determined by govt. are influenced by the principle of supply and demand almost just as much as in capitalist countries." Critically, though, White foresees change in capitalist countries after the war, "and in every case the change will be in the direction of increased govt. control over industry, and increased restrictions on the operations of competition and free enterprise." Thus there would be convergence in the direction of the Soviet model.

Why, White then asks, do the capitalist countries see themselves in opposition to the Soviet Union? Is it the form of government? No, he concludes, as capitalist countries can practice "democracy such as we have in the U.S. and England, or dictatorship such as in Spain, or Portugal or Nicaragua [or] Honduras. The fact that Italy, Spain, Brazil, and Poland and China had very little of what we should call democracy did not give rise to any basic antagonism to these countries, nor did it interfere in the slightest with our trade and financial arrangements with them." Alternatively, "under a socialist economy it is possible to have a dictatorship such as existed in Russia prior to the war (political patterns during war-time are not a fair basis of comparison), or it could have a high degree of democracy such as called for by the Russian constitution adopted in 1936 but never put wholly into effect. . . . Thus it is clear that differences in political structure are not the basis of the opposition to Soviet Union."

The strikingly understated observation that "a high degree of democracy" was "never put wholly into effect" in Soviet Russia more than hints at the writer's rose-tinted view of Stalin's domestic political regime. And what about religious freedom? "Contrary to popular opinion the right of a person to worship as he pleases has never been abrogated in Russia," White insists. "The constitution of U.S.S.R. guarantees the right." Furthermore, "Germany from 1933 on conducted a much more virulent attack against religious freedom," yet the capitalist countries took no issue with Germany until they felt militarily threatened. And of Russia's instigation of socialist revolutions abroad? "The demise of the Third Int[ernational], and the policy pursued by present day Russia of not actively supporting such movements in other countries should greatly help eliminate that source of friction."

Having swept away internal politics, religion, and foreign policy as honest sources of Western opposition to Russia, White concludes that the true source of the conflict must be economic ideology: "It is basically opposition of capitalism to socialism. Those who believe seriously in the superiority of capitalism over socialism," among whom White appears not to number himself, "fear Russia as the source of socialist ideology." He then ends his essay with what, coming from the U.S. government's most important economic strategist, can only be described as an astounding conclusion: that "Russia is the first instance of a socialist economy in action. And it works!"[68]

White's conclusion that Soviet socialist economics "works," and that capitalist countries were moving in the direction of more state control of industry and competition, lends credibility to a controversial account of White's economic views provided by journalist Jonathon Mitchell before the Internal Security subcommittee of the Senate Judiciary Committee in 1954. Mitchell, whom Morgenthau had commissioned to write speeches in 1939, recounted a lunch meeting with

White in August 1945, shortly before the Japanese surrender in World War II, in which White allegedly argued that the system of government-controlled trading that had emerged during the war would continue into the postwar period, owing to a lack of capital (dollars and gold) that would oblige governments to maintain tight controls on cross-border private trade. The International Monetary Fund would fail to rectify this problem—a stunning viewpoint for a man who could rightfully claim the fund's paternity. The United States, White continued, would, with its huge domestic market, be able to carry on a system of private enterprise for five to ten years, but could not ultimately survive as a capitalist island in a world of state trading. According to Mitchell, White pointed to British socialist Harold Laski's book *Faith, Reason, and Civilization*, which argued that Russia had created a new economic system that would replace capitalism, as "the most profound book which had been written in our lifetime," and one that "had foreseen with such uncanny accuracy and depth the way in which the world was going."[69]

Laski's book celebrated Soviet communism as a new faith that could fill the spiritual as well as material gap left by an obsolete Christianity and a morally bankrupt capitalism. "[S]ince the October Revolution," Laski pronounced, "more men and women have had more opportunity of self-fulfilment than anywhere else in the world."[70] Though such views may appear eccentric today, several decades after the end of the cold war, Laski was in 1945 chairman of the British Labour Party, and therefore a figure well within the Western political mainstream. White's essay, though lacking the patina of Laski's scholarly historical sweep, clearly shared elements with Laski's polemic—in particular the notion that the capitalist Allied countries were guilty of hypocrisy. The capitalists had no problem, both argued, accommodating themselves to the crushing of democracy in Germany and Italy—it was only when Hitler and Mussolini turned their aggression outward that the capitalists manufactured the urge to defend political and religious freedom. In the case of Russia, it was actually the success of socialist economics that they could not abide.

White's brother, Nathan, blasted Mitchell's credibility in a book-length defense of his sibling published in 1956; and indeed, given

White's known intellectual footprint at the time, Mitchell's account sounded incredible. But this newly unearthed essay of White's suggests that Mitchell's story is, in fact, wholly credible.

"There's no doubt that Harry was close to the Russians," Bernstein reflected on White decades later. And "it was just like Harry to think he could give advice to everybody."[71] But why would White have strayed so far beyond merely giving advice?

During the Second World War, a surprising number of American government officials, who would never have considered themselves disloyal to the United States, provided covert assistance to the Soviets. "They were," in Elizabeth Bentley's reckoning, "a bunch of misguided idealists. They were doing it for something they believed was right . . . they felt very strongly that we were allies with Russia, that Russia was bearing the brunt of the war, that she [Russia] must have every assistance, because the people from within the Government . . . were not giving her things that we should give her . . . that we were giving to Britain and not to her. And they felt . . . it was their duty, actually, to get this stuff to Russia."[72]

White, by Chambers' account, began his efforts before the war, in the years just after the Soviet Union secured U.S. diplomatic recognition in 1933 and joined the League of Nations in 1934. By all appearances, White believed that U.S. policy should and would in the coming years move in the direction of deeper engagement with the newly legitimated Soviet regime. Silverman and Chambers in essence afforded White the occasion to establish his bona fides with the still-mysterious foreign power years before any official opportunity would present itself.

Bykov's decision to send White a rug was not the only time the Soviets appeared to be clumsy in showing their appreciation for his efforts. Chambers claimed to have come across the following story many years later, while a writer at *Time* magazine.

One day (likely in 1945) a carpenter in Washington received a container of caviar at his house. Then a case of vodka was delivered. Then came an engraved invitation in the mail to attend a social event at the Soviet embassy. The carpenter was dumbfounded. Finally came a telephone call from a Harry Dexter White at the U.S. Treasury. The carpenter was also named Harry White. The Treasury-White had traced his misdirected presents. He proposed that carpenter-White send him half the goods and keep the other half. "I was going to send them all back to him," the carpenter told a reporter. "But I thought," after reflecting on his talk with Treasury-White, that "he's the kind of fellow, that if I send them all back, will still think that I kept half. So I did."[73]

In early 1938, increasingly troubled by what he was learning of Stalin's purges and fearful for his own safety, Chambers made the fateful decision to break from the Communist Party. He now had to frighten his informants into silence. In White's case, Chambers figured that could best be accomplished by marching into his office at Treasury. That plan he quickly abandoned after reaching the building and realizing that he had no way of talking himself beyond the guard's post: White had known him only as "Carl." So he called White from a nearby store. Expecting White to be shocked by this breach of protocol, he instead found White curiously happy to hear from him.

White met Chambers near the Treasury, and the two started walking. "Back on a little trip to inspect the posts?" White asked cheerfully. They went into a soda shop and ordered coffee. White was unusually garrulous, meandering on about "the Secretary" and Silverman before asking Chambers whether he was "coming back to Washington to work." Chambers was blunt; White was to break from "the apparatus" or Chambers would denounce him. White slumped over his coffee. "You don't really mean that," he protested. Chambers assured him otherwise. The two left in a state of mutual embarrassment, at which point Chambers spotted a street photographer and quickly spun White around. As Chambers steered the stunned White in a new direction, White looked over his shoulder and saw the camera, grateful for what he had avoided. That was the last time the two would meet.[74]

Following Chambers' defection, White, according to Elizabeth Bentley, promised his wife, "who was not a Communist and disliked his revolutionary activities, that he would stay out of espionage in the future."[75] This promise he may actually have kept—for several years.

There has been much debate over many decades about the value of the information White passed to the Soviets through Chambers. Some consider it important, some unimportant. But this was never the critical point. As Chambers himself concluded, though White and his other sources were "pathetically eager to help," the "secrets of foreign offices are notoriously overrated."[76] A little knowledge of history and some basic political imagination would yield at least as much as political espionage.[77] What was critical was having agents of a hostile foreign power operating at the heart of a nation's domestic and foreign policy machinery. "In the persons of Alger Hiss and Harry Dexter White," Chambers' two star recruits, "the Soviet Military Intelligence sat close to the heart of the United States Government."[78] Hiss went on to become director of the Office of Special Political Affairs at the State Department, and White an assistant secretary of the Treasury with enormous influence over policy and personnel. He was privy to the Treasury Secretary's conversations and thoughts and on many issues shaped them. And as we will see, White's Soviet sympathies were not incidental to some important policy positions he pursued over many years.

Keynes's *General Theory* had been published in 1936, and his ideas spread to Washington quickly. In particular, the view that governments should not hesitate to use deficit spending to counteract a recession—mainstream today, but widely considered irresponsible pre-Keynes—had gained influential supporters within the administration, including Harry Hopkins, director of the Federal Surplus Relief Administration and the Works Progress Administration (becoming Secretary of Commerce in 1938); Herman Oliphant, general counsel in Treasury; and Marriner Eccles (whose ideas predated Keynes), chairman of the Federal Reserve Board. White himself was forthright in opposing balanced-budget orthodoxy. "It would be wrong," he argued in a meeting with Morgenthau and Viner in October 1937, "to balance the budget by deflationary measures such as increasing taxes or reducing government expenditures."[79] But Morgenthau was unswayed on the benefits of raising federal spending—a position from which he never deviated, even years later. He continued to advocate monetary solutions to the crisis, to which White responded with specific proposals, ranging from reducing bank reserve requirements to greater Federal Reserve Bank

buying of securities (both of which would put more cash into the financial system) to further devaluing the dollar.[80]

Morgenthau lost his case with FDR, who decided it was time to try
to spend the country out of recession. This boosted White's stature.
The year 1938 was a brutal one, with the economy shrinking, for the
first time since 1933, by 3.5 percent. Morgenthau, seeing his influence
ebbing, thereby became more dependent on White for policy guidance,
and in March of that year promoted him to director of the Division
of Monetary Research. In April he added White to the so-called 9:30
Group of his senior advisers. That month, the president announced
a $4 billion emergency spending program, which included large pub-
lic works projects. With the Treasury now projecting a deficit of $4–5
billion for fiscal year 1939, Morgenthau briefly wrestled with the idea
of resigning before deciding it would cause too much damage to the
president's efforts.

For his part, FDR, however passionately he wished to stay focused
on domestic affairs, was under increasing pressure from both at home
and abroad to respond to spreading global military aggression: in particular, Germany's massive rearmament, Germany and Italy's intervention in the Spanish Civil War, Italy's invasion of Ethiopia, and Japan's
occupation of China. On October 5, 1937, he responded with his
famous "Quarantine the Aggressors" speech, in which he positioned
the United States as a partisan against the Axis powers, without actually naming any nation, while simultaneously trying to avoid stoking
American isolationist sentiment by emphasizing his government's
commitment to peace. The speech was also notable for its linking of
peace with commerce and trade, an increasingly prominent theme in
American political thinking after the Great War of 1914.

Morgenthau, in parallel, steadily expanded Treasury's remit in foreign affairs, creating new responsibilities and opportunities for White.
China was an early such case. The 1934 Silver Purchase Act—passed
under relentless political pressure from a lobby composed of silver
producers, banker bashers, and inflation proponents—had obliged the
Treasury to buy up the metal and boost its price. The practice wreaked
havoc on the Chinese currency, which was tied to silver—long trea-
sured in the country, even though there was no indigenous supply.[81]

Chinese silver stocks were smuggled out of the country and sold abroad, reducing the money supply and triggering deflation, credit contraction, and a slump.

For the Japanese occupiers, this was a welcome source of profit and an effective means of undermining the Chiang Kai-shek government, which pleaded to the United States to change its policy. Morgenthau was sympathetic, as he considered the Silver Act a major headache. But he had little room for maneuver. Hull was raising economic and political objections to Treasury's suggestions, prompting Morgenthau to accuse State of being unduly sensitive to Japanese opinion. For his part, the president refused either to change U.S. silver policy or to condone Treasury getting enmeshed in Chinese currency reform.

In October 1935, Chinese ambassador Alfred Sze told Morgenthau that his country was abandoning its silver standard, and offered to sell its stock of the metal to the United States in lieu of dumping it on the world market. Morgenthau saw this as an opportunity to end-run State by labeling it a monetary matter. Yet he still had to tread delicately, given that the Silver Act committed the United States to supporting silver's monetary role, and not weakening it, as the Chinese were doing.

White backed the idea of buying the Chinese silver, but with China undertaking a reciprocal commitment to peg the yuan to the dollar. China conducted the greater portion of its trade in sterling, which, as sterling fell against the dollar, dragged the yuan down with it. White hoped to stop this, to the benefit of U.S. exporters and manufacturers.[82]

Then, as now, China resisted American pressure to change its currency policy. Morgenthau fired back at Sze,

> We have our politicians and our public and our future to think of. We are not going to invest $65,000,000 and you tie your money to sterling. . . . You made this move and we want you to succeed. We feel that it is best for both countries to have the yuan quoted in terms of dollars instead of in terms of sterling. You people are playing poker and you are bluffing.[83]

Yet China still would not budge. With the president's approval, it was Morgenthau who finally blinked. But instead of acquiescing to China's request that the United States buy 100 million ounces of silver, he tried to save face by offering to take only half. The deal was done.

Morgenthau remained concerned that China would do a similar deal with Britain in return for a yuan link with sterling. Back and forth monetary diplomacy continued through May 1936, with Chinese emissary K. P. Chen importuning Morgenthau to buy more silver, and Morgenthau repeatedly complaining that the yuan was moving in lockstep with sterling. The Treasury Secretary emphasized that the United States "feel[s] it is very important to the world peace to help China strengthen her currency."[84] Chen promised to end the system of quoting the yuan in terms of sterling, which, he acknowledged, gave the appearance of there being a sterling peg. Anxious to sideline the State Department, Morgenthau finally agreed to an arrangement between the American and Chinese treasuries whereby the former would buy a further 75 million ounces of silver at market prices in monthly installments through January 1937, with proceeds to remain in New York and to be used by the Chinese exclusively to stabilize the yuan's external value. Details were to be kept confidential.

The Chinese monetary deal, together with the Tripartite Agreement, cemented Treasury's role as not only the foreign policy arm of the New Deal, but also the economic arm of U.S. foreign policy. It furthermore afforded White the opportunity to expand his personal portfolio into the heart of foreign policy making. In a forty-four-page single-spaced typed memo to Morgenthau on the economic situation in China in 1936, White ranged widely and confidently on political issues, marking Chiang Kai-shek as "a virtual dictator" (even though "his actual power is more limited than either Hitler or Mussolini"). U.S. trade competitiveness being a central concern of White's throughout his tenure at Treasury, he went into numbing detail on the causes of the sharp reversal in 1935 of the long-standing U.S. trade surplus with China. Not surprisingly, he reserved the better part of his analysis for currency matters, framing the yuan-link question as an important component of the wider sterling-dollar global rivalry. The United Kingdom, he argued, needed a China sterling peg more than the United States needed a dollar peg, "partly because of England's greater need for foreign trade, and her traditional role in international finance, and partly because the United States is a coming nation and England is a going one." White was thinking eight years ahead toward U.S. positioning at

Bretton Woods, observing that "the more sterling countries there are, the stronger will be England's position around a conference table with the gold countries should an international conference take place."[85] The question of how to ensure that the dollar permanently supplanted the pound as the global trade, financing, and reserve currency was to occupy him for the remainder of his time at Treasury.

On the European front, 1938 was to prove a pivotal year in boosting White's profile in foreign affairs. Concluded on September 30, the Munich Agreement—now a byword for shameful appeasement of aggression—saw Britain and France accede to Germany's annexation of the Czech Sudetenland, paving the way for Hitler's occupation of Prague the following March.

In early October, Morgenthau instructed White to draft a letter to the president on the international situation. White's enthusiasm was unbounded: "I'd rather work on this than anything else I have."[86] Whether Morgenthau intended for White to range as far as he did is uncertain, but much of the stark prose White penned formed almost verbatim Morgenthau's "strongest statement on foreign policy he had yet ventured."[87]

White took an unvarnished hard line on Germany, Japan, and Italy, repeating the words "aggressor" and "aggression" over and over, and urging the president, "whose record has never been besmirched by even a trace of appeasement," to act with "iron firmness." The letter sets out the Treasury's legitimate interest in the subject by focusing initially on the havoc the aggressors were wreaking with international trade and monetary affairs, which was severely damaging America's export interests, driving up the dollar, and undermining the administration's programs to promote trade and dollar competitiveness. But it quickly moves on to urge the president to take much more assertive political action—short of war, for as long as war can be avoided—to aid the victims of aggression: particularly China. The letter is scornful of British diplomacy—"Who would have expected . . . that the Premier of England would hurry to Hitler to plead that he be not too demanding or impatient, and plead, moreover in humble tones lest the dictator take umbrage and demand more?"—and disdainful toward Britain and France for the collapse of their independence and influence brought on by their weakness of will. "Let it not be necessary,"

White implores the president through his boss, "for the President of the United States to fly to Tokyo and in humble manner plead with the Mikado that he be content with half the Philippines rather than wage war for the whole."[88]

The letter was sent to the president on October 17. On November 14, at a "momentous White House meeting," as Morgenthau characterized it, FDR laid out in historic terms the need for America to prepare for war. The president "pointed out that the recrudescence of German power at Munich had completely reoriented our own international relations; that for the first time since the Holy Alliance in 1818 the United States now faced the possibility of an attack on the Atlantic side in both the Northern and Southern Hemispheres. . . . [S]ending a large army abroad," however, "was undesirable and politically out of the question."[89] The international situation having been framed by the president as a security threat to the United States that, however momentous, could not be met by sending troops back onto the European battlefield, other tools had to be applied to neutralize it. White, who had set out to become an economist at Stanford in 1923 only after concluding "that most governmental problems are economic," now had the perfect opportunity to prove himself right.

Departmental boundaries were to be no obstacle. The State Department, White thundered in a memo of August 1940, was filled with "budding Chamberlains, Daladiers, and Hoares," the primary British and French appeasers at Munich. "I am convinced that the time has come when a strong, clear cut foreign policy must be formulated and endorsed for the State Department to execute."[90] American diplomatic efforts were "pathetic," consisting of "a nineteenth century pattern of petty bargaining with its dependence on subtle half promises, irritating pinpricks, excursions into double dealing and copious pronouncements of good will alternating with vague threats—chiefly to hide the essential barrenness of achievement. Our diplomatic maneuvering is proving as futile in strengthening our international position or in keeping us out of a difficult war as was the equipment and strategy of the Polish army in the task of defending Poland." He thought little of any of the foreign ministries of the democracies, blasting the "half measures, miscalculation, timidity, machinations or incompetence of the State Departments of the United States, England, and France" in a memo drafted in late May 1941 and presented to Morgenthau on June 6. "An 'all-out' effort involves in diplomacy as in military strategy the fullest use of every economic and political advantage."[91]

That such language could emanate from a mere Treasury research division head seems startling, but by this time White's standing with Morgenthau vastly exceeded his official civil service status. With the War Department having been placed on standby and the State Department showing no alacrity, Morgenthau was eager to step into the breach and give substance to the president's call to action. White had both the zeal and the ideas.

One of his more robust early themes, developed in a March 1939 memo, was the need for the United States to work closely with "the other most powerful country in the world," the Soviet Union.[92] White painted an underlying commonality of interest between the United States and the Soviets that was not nearly so apparent to his president. The Chamberlain government in Britain, White argued, needed to be pressured into military collaboration with Russia in order to counter German aggression. He advocated a $250 million ten-year loan to Russia ($4 billion in current dollars), the funds to be used to purchase American cotton, machinery, and manufactures. Even after the Russians occupied the Baltic states in 1940 and the Treasury froze Baltic assets in response, White pushed hard in the opposite direction, backing a tripartite cooperation arrangement whereby the United States would buy $200 million worth of strategic commodities from Russia, which would in turn sell military materials to China on credit. Russia had to be distinguished from aggressors like Germany and Japan, White argued, sounding much like anti–Cold Warriors of the 1970s and '80s, as Russia "was not interested in the near future in territorial expansion. . . . Russian aggression takes the form of ideological propaganda rather than military aggression."[93] Contrast this with Roosevelt four months earlier, to an American Youth Congress convention:

> I, with many of you, hoped that Russia would work out its own problems, and that its government would eventually become a peace loving, popular government with a free ballot, which would not interfere with the integrity of its neighbors. That hope is today either shattered or put away

in storage against some better day. The Soviet Union, as everybody who has the courage to face the fact knows, is run by a dictatorship as absolute as any other dictatorship in the world. It has allied itself with another dictatorship and it has invaded a neighbor so infinitesimally small that it could do no conceivable possible harm to the Soviet Union, a neighbor which seeks only to live at peace as a democracy, and a liberal, forward-looking democracy at that.[94]

The president's Treasury Department would over the years continue, however, to pursue foreign policy initiatives consistent with a much more optimistic view of Soviet intentions. Harry White would increasingly become the driving force behind these efforts.

On Sunday, December 7, 1941, just before 8:00 a.m. Hawaii time, 366 Japanese bomber and fighter planes attacked the enormous, and inexplicably vulnerable, American war arsenal at Pearl Harbor. The results were catastrophic. Four American battleships were blown up or sunk. Four more were badly damaged. Eleven other warships were sunk or disabled. One hundred eighty-eight military aircraft were destroyed on the ground. Two thousand three hundred thirty Americans were dead or dying; 1,177 of these were killed on one battleship alone, the *Arizona*. The following day President Roosevelt delivered his famous war message to Congress, declaring December 7, 1941, to be "a date that will live in infamy. . . . No matter how long it may take us to overcome this premeditated invasion, the American people in their righteous might will win through to absolute victory."

Churchill, when informed by the president of the horrendous casualties, responded "What a holocaust!"[95] But in private he called the Japanese assault "a blessing. . . . Greater good fortune has never happened to the British Empire." He had finally gotten what he had so desperately sought. America was in the war. "I went to bed and slept the sleep of the saved and thankful."[96] Over in Moscow, sentiments were similar. "We sighed a deep sigh of relief," recalled the head of the American desk of the NKVD Intelligence Directorate, Vitali Pavlov.[97] Yet this was not merely cheerleading from the sidelines. Pavlov had, secretly, been part of the game.

The Japanese decision to attack Pearl Harbor was the culmination of a series of critical political developments and, clearly, no single event, no single action, and no single individual can be said to have triggered it. Nevertheless, the most proximate cause has a curious connection with Pavlov and his most important American contact, Harry Dexter White.

On November 20, Japanese ambassadors Nomura and Kurusu transmitted to Hull a proposed "modus vivendi" from Tokyo—a temporary working arrangement focused on easing political, military, and economic tensions. Negotiations proceeded over the next several days, during which U.S. intelligence intercepted and decoded Japanese cables to the ambassadors indicating, in no uncertain terms, that differences had to be resolved by November 29, Tokyo time. The U.S. Navy Department thought that a Japanese attack on the Philippines or Guam was possible, but Pearl Harbor not, as a strike on American territory would be a clear "strategic blunder" that would inevitably bring the United States into all-out war with Japan.

At that point, White, improbably, emerged as a key player in the drama. On November 17 he had submitted a long memo to Morgenthau titled "An Approach to the Problem of Eliminating Tension with Japan and Insuring the Defeat of Germany," which quickly became part of the frantic endgame diplomatic maneuvering. Morgenthau had not been a key player on matters Japanese to this point, but once again White emerged to fill the Secretary's intellectual void. After deleting the diplomatically unhelpful criticisms of U.S. foreign policy in the introduction, Morgenthau forwarded White's "very amazing memorandum of suggestions" to Hull and Roosevelt.

White wanted the president to propose a deal with specific terms. If the Japanese were to accept it, he claimed tantalizingly, "the whole world would be electrified by the successful transformation of a threatening and belligerent powerful enemy into a peaceful and prosperous neighbor. The prestige and the leadership of the President both at home and abroad would skyrocket by so brilliant and momentous a diplomatic victory."

Hull worked together with a small group of top U.S. military and administration officials, in conjunction with representatives of key friendly governments, to craft an alternative American "modus vivendi," which incorporated White's key requirements: that Japan withdraw all forces from China and Indochina, and cease all support for any Chinese government or regime other than the Nationalist Kuomintang Government of the Republic of China. Secretary of War Henry Stimson doubted the Japanese would cooperate because it was "so drastic." White, however, was pushing against any relaxation of terms. He drafted a fiery letter for Morgenthau to send to the president, warning against a "Far Eastern Munich" that would sell China "to her enemies for thirty blood stained pieces of gold" and "dim the luster of American world leadership in the great democratic fight against fascism." Morgenthau never sent it. But White pressed on other fronts. He telegrammed Edward C. Carter, a former secretary-general of the Institute of Pacific Relations, who had an FBI-documented record of support for Soviet positions and causes, asking him to come to Washington to lobby against concessions to Japan.[98]

The tide turned White's way when FDR learned from Stimson of a Japanese expeditionary force making its way south from China toward Indochina. The president "blew up," according to Stimson, saying that it changed the whole situation. He wanted the "modus vivendi" replaced by "broad basic proposals." He authorized Hull to present the Japanese with what became known as the Ten-Point Note. Hull summoned Nomura and Kurusu on November 26 to deliver the austere ultimatum, incorporating White's demands on China, without concessions. An alarmed Kurusu told Hull that the Japanese government would "throw up its hands" if presented with such a response to their truce proposal. Hull did not waver. The collision course had been set.

That White was the author of the key ultimatum demands is beyond dispute. That the Japanese government made the decision to move forward with the Pearl Harbor strike after receiving the ultimatum is also beyond dispute. Though Army Chief of Staff General George C. Marshall posited after the war that the Japanese might not have attacked had discussions not broken down before the end of 1941, an attack may by that point have been inevitable. But it is notable that the Soviets, American allies in the European war, were anxious to ensure that such an attack *did* take place. "The war in the Pacific could have been avoided," wrote retired GRU military intelligence colonel and World

War II "Hero of the Soviet Union" Vladimir Karpov in 2000, nearly sixty years after Pearl Harbor. "Stalin was the real initiator of the ultimatum to Japan," he insisted.

How was that possible? "Harry Dexter White was acting in accordance with a design initiated by [NKVD intelligence official Iskhak] Akhmerov and Pavlov," Karpov argued. "[White] prepared the *aide-memoire* for signature by Morgenthau and President Roosevelt." The Soviets had, according to Karpov, used White to provoke Japan to attack the United States. The scheme even had a name: "Operation Snow," snow referring to White. "[T]he essence of 'Operation Snow' was to provoke the war between the Empire of the Rising Sun and the USA and to insure the interests of the Soviet Union in the Far East. . . . If Japan was engaged in war against the USA it would have no resources to strike against the USSR."[99]

How did they carry out their operation? This is where Pavlov comes in. Pavlov was a mere twenty-seven years old when he was sent to Washington in the spring of 1941—the product of a Soviet intelligence service whose older ranks had been decimated by Stalin's purges. His mission was to activate an "agent of influence," Harry White; to discern whether he was still in a cooperative mood in spite of the Nazi-Soviet Pact; and, if so, to secure his advocacy within the upper ranks of the U.S. foreign policy apparatus for an ultimatum to Japan that would trigger a war. Pavlov published his account fifty-five years later in a book titled *Operatsia Sneg*—Operation Snow.[100]

Pavlov called White in late May of 1941, saying he had a message to pass on to him from "Bill" in China. Bill was the name by which White knew Akhmerov, who had presented himself to White as a sinologist on his way to China when the two had been introduced in 1939 by Lithuanian émigré and Soviet intelligence liaison agent Joseph Katz.[101] Pavlov asked White to lunch at the Old Ebbitt Grill, where White had previously met with Bill.

White greeted Pavlov at the restaurant after spotting the *New Yorker* magazine that Pavlov had placed on the table in front of him, to signal his identity. Pavlov explained that he had recently been in China, where Bill had asked him to carry back a message to White outlining his concerns about Japanese expansionism in Asia. Apologizing for his poor English, Pavlov placed Bill's note in front of White, who read it and expressed his surprise at how similar Bill's thoughts were to his own. White tried to put the note in his pocket, but Pavlov extended his hand in a gesture to stop him, and White returned it instead.

Pavlov said he would be returning to China soon, and that Bill was anxious to learn White's views. Did the United States recognize the Japanese threat, and was it determined to do something to counter Japanese aggression? White thanked Pavlov, assuring him that Bill's ideas corresponded with his own convictions and understanding of matters in the region. Having had his views bolstered by an expert such as Bill, with profound knowledge in the area, he would be able to undertake the necessary efforts in the necessary direction. White had been speaking slowly, and concluded by asking Pavlov to confirm that he had understood him correctly. Pavlov reassured him by repeating his message for Bill virtually word for word. White nodded. He paid for the lunch, and the two departed.

Very shortly after the meeting, White drafted his thunderous June 6 memo to Morgenthau, described earlier. In addition to his broad-based assault on American diplomatic timidity, White laid out specific pro- posals relating to two countries: Japan and Russia. The Russian por- tion focused on economic inducements to break up the Nazi-Soviet Pact. The Japanese portion laid out a comprehensive accommodation with Tokyo, whereby the United States would provide some modest political and economic concessions in return for Japan withdrawing its forces from China and Indochina, and forswearing extraterrito- rial rights in the latter. Whatever White believed, these demands were unrealistic; the Japanese would never accept them.[102] This, at least, was what Soviet intelligence was counting on.

Bill's note—that is, Akhmerov's note—had indicated three demands that the Soviets wanted the Americans to make of the Japanese: to stop their aggression in China and on its borders; to pull back their forces from the continent; and to withdraw their forces from Man- churia. White unambiguously laid out the first two.[103] Curiously, how- ever, he proposed that Manchuria be recognized as part of the Japanese Empire, only to reverse that position a few months later.

White's vacillation on Manchuria shows that he was no puppet of Soviet intelligence, contrary to Karpov's claims, and that Akhmerov could have influenced only the contours and timing of White's intervention. The significance of Operation Snow lay not in White acting as he did *because* he was so prodded, and certainly not in acting against what he believed to be American interests; rather, it is that the Soviets *believed* that White was influential and impressionable enough, and that conflict between the United States and Japan was important enough, that they chose to use him in pursuit of their aims. In any case, White's intervention was to have great consequence in the autumn.

Morgenthau was in June not ready to inject himself into Japan negotiations, and he simply filed the memo. But it did motivate the overloaded Secretary to hand over the keys on Asia policy to his eager aid. "I am not interested [in China]," Morgenthau told White in July 1941. "I want somebody—one person who's going to look after it."

"You don't want me to raise any of the issues . . . [?]" an incredulous White began to ask.

"No, you settle them," the Secretary shot back.[104]

White decided to reassert himself on Japan in his November 17 memo, this time taking a tougher stance. Instead of recognizing Manchuria as part of the Japanese Empire, the United States should now, White proposed, demand that Japan withdraw its troops from Manchuria. The Secretary was in a much more receptive frame of mind than he had been when White presented his June 6 memo, the geopolitical stakes in Asia having since risen markedly.

Germany had broken its pact with the Soviet Union and invaded on June 22. A critical question then became whether Japan would move north against the Soviets or south against the Americans. Pavlov and Akhmerov had been confident that White would follow through on the lunch discussion, and it appeared that he had. By November, Japan had leapt to the top of the president's priorities, and Morgenthau now saw White's proposal as actionable and potentially game changing. The rest is history: history in which White played an influential role well beyond his official brief.

That brief was about to change. On December 8, 1941, the day after the Pearl Harbor attacks, Morgenthau announced at his morning meeting that he was giving White the status of an assistant secretary (a made-up title not to be confused with the formal position "Assistant Secretary of the Treasury," to which White would not ascend until 1945). This informal promotion recognized the foreign policy role

White had carved for himself over the past half year, particularly with relation to China and Japan.[105] "He will be in charge of all foreign affairs for me," Morgenthau explained. "I want it in one brain and I want it in Harry White's brain. . . . When it is some question of foreign matters, Harry will come in and see me and I will give him a decision and when the decision is made he will tell you about it."[106]

Harry White was now one of the most powerful men in Washington.

J. M. Keynes, 1929. (Copyright Bettmann/Corbis/AP Images)

CHAPTER 4

Maynard Keynes and the Monetary Menace

Harry White's American journey was as winding and obstacle-strewn as Maynard Keynes's rise in England seemed effortless and preordained. White felt his life truly started nearly four decades after his birth, with a doctorate from his country's most famed university. Keynes never bothered with one; he hadn't even a degree in economics. Yet chosen as a teaching assistant by the storied Cambridge economist Alfred Marshall in 1908, Keynes was elected to a life fellowship at his alma mater—Kings College, Cambridge—at age twenty-six.

Keynes's academic success would have been a surprise to no one. His father, Neville, spent four decades as a lecturer in moral sciences and then registrar at Cambridge, having been in Marshall's mind one of the two or three best students he had ever taught.[1] Keynes's mother, Florence, educated at Cambridge's Newnham College, became the city's first woman mayor. She was twenty-two when Maynard was born on June 5, 1883, and outlived him by twelve years. Like his father, Maynard was called by his middle name (Neville and Maynard shared the first name John, which likely went unused because Neville's father was also a John).

Raised comfortably with his younger sister Margaret and brother Geoffrey in a family of cultured upper-middle-class intellectuals, attended to by a cook, a parlor maid, a nursery maid, and later a German governess, Maynard nonetheless had a weak constitution that would plague him for life. He further suffered from a "fixed, constant, unalterable obsession" with what he considered his ugliness.[2] But he began showing superior ability in abstract reasoning very early on. By age twelve it even infused the family prayers: "Let Mother equal x," he implored, "and let Geoffrey equal y."[3] His particular facility with algebra would later show itself in his favored mode of mathematical argumentation, although by the 1910s he would become a caustic opponent of the overuse of mathematical methods in economics.

As a schoolboy, and decades later the most innovative and iconoclastic economist of his age, if not of all time, Maynard worked quickly and displayed impatience with details, preferring to conquer big problems with bold-brush techniques and bursts of vivid intuition. "When you adopt perfectly precise language," he would say in 1933, "you are trying to express yourself for the benefit of those who are incapable of thought."[4] In today's age, in which young economists are typically better rewarded for being precisely wrong with higher math than roughly right with reasoned approximations, it is questionable whether such a brilliant young man could even become tenured at a top American economics faculty.

Maynard entered the elite Eton College in September 1897, age fourteen, having scored first in mathematics on his entrance examination. From there he went on to Cambridge's Kings College via competitive scholarship, graduating behind eleven other mathematicians but well within the top 10 percent. It was only after graduation that he formally studied economics for a brief period—Marshall agreeing to tutor the boy an hour a week for two months, thanks to Maynard's paternal connection with the great professor. Maynard would later reflect proudly on his chosen profession that the economist "must be mathematician, historian, statesman, philosopher."[5] He would never display a rare gift as any one of these alone, but he amalgamated them with a genius that no economist has ever matched.

It is a long-standing matter of contention among Keynes's chroniclers the degree to which his personal life should be held to inform his development as a public intellectual, scholar, and statesman. Famed economist Joseph Schumpeter, for example, cuttingly pronounced Keynes's famous aphorism "in the long run we are all dead" to be a natural perspective for a childless thinker. Keynes and his future wife, it should be noted, had tried to have a child in the late 1920s; but more to the point, to dismiss important elements of Keynes's thinking on the grounds that they were artifacts of alleged hidden impulses is to fail to give his reasoning its due.

To ignore major elements of Keynes's private life, however, as does his first major biographer, Roy Harrod—particularly Keynes's homosexuality, despite its featuring in nearly two decades of passionate and poignant personal correspondence from the early 1900s—is to underplay the importance of Keynes's associations outside official college and government circles, in particular with members of the Cambridge "Apostles" male secret society and the iconoclastic Bloomsbury group of London intellectuals and aesthetes. Keynes would famously write of the Apostles "We were . . . in the strict sense of the term, immoralists," by which he meant willing to break with conventions in pursuit of worthy public motives.[6] Keynes's personal attachments had an undeniable impact on his ethical worldview and the sharp-edged rhetorical habits he practiced in official settings. Both were consequential in terms of how he was perceived in the 1930s and '40s by critical American observers and interlocutors.

In 1906, age twenty-three, Keynes decided to enter the civil service, aiming at the top prize: a place in Her Majesty's Treasury, of which only one was available, via competitive examination in subjects ranging from logic and philosophy to mathematics and economics. He placed second overall, to his bitter disappointment, and chose the India Office as his consolation prize. Like most British mandarins running the empire, he had little firsthand knowledge of the subjects whose national affairs he was charged with managing: his lifelong experience with Indians was limited to those whom he met in London and Cambridge.[7] Given his dislike of early mornings and late nights ("I snuff the candle at both ends," he quipped), the hours—11:00 a.m. to 5:00 p.m., with two months' holidays a year—suited him fine.[8] However, "bored nine tenths of the time and rather unreasonably irritated the other tenth whenever I can't have my own way,"[9] he resigned on his twenty-fifth birthday in 1908 to take up a coveted lectureship back in Cambridge. At that point, he was drawn more by wanting to return to Cambridge than wishing to start a career as an economist. His background in the emerging discipline of economics was still sketchy at this point; he only began plowing through Adam Smith in 1910, the year after he won the university's Adam Smith prize.[10]

No one, it seemed, was a quicker study than Keynes, particularly when his passions were piqued. He published his first academic article,

"Recent Economic Events in India," in the *Economic Journal* in 1909. This perhaps marked the true beginning of his lifelong intellectual love affair with matters of money. Generating "statistics of verification" linking Indian price movements with gold inflows and outflows put him into a "tremendous state of excitement," he wrote to his lover, painter Duncan Grant. "Here are my theories—will the statistics bear them out? Nothing except copulation is so enthralling."[11] By October 1911, age twenty-eight, he was editor of the journal—a position he would hold, and to which he would remain intensely devoted, for the rest of his life.

Another happy by-product of his first experience in government was the publication of his first book, *Indian Currency and Finance* (1913). Though published five years after Keynes left the India Office, just after his thirtieth birthday, he actually wrote most of it over a Christmas vacation in 1912. The book was primarily a defense of India's brand of gold-exchange standard, in which the currency was maintained at a fixed value against gold by way of sterling credits held in London. Keynes countered supporters of a full, classical gold standard for India, arguing that the country's much looser system economized on the use of gold and made its money more elastic to the actual needs of business. Those who insisted that a reserve currency need take the form of a physical commodity were misguidedly backing "a relic of a time when governments were less trustworthy in these matters than they are now, and when it was the fashion to imitate uncritically the system which had been established in England and had seemed to work so well during the second quarter of the nineteenth century."[12] Today, of course, popular debate is often heated over whether governments are insufficiently trustworthy in monetary matters or, alternatively, overly hidebound in their response to financial market breakdowns. Keynes further offered some acerbic observations on banking that would ring strikingly apt to many today, asking "how long it will be found necessary to pay City men so entirely out of proportion to what other servants of society commonly receive for performing social services not less useful or difficult."[13]

Two broad themes emerged in the book that would be constants in Keynes's thinking. First, rational monetary reform consisted in the progressive diminution of the role of gold. Second, London was the natural global financial center upon which such reform could and should be built (half the world's trade at the time was financed by British credit). The catastrophic war into which Europe would plunge the following year would, however, upset the assumption, so widely shared among the British establishment, that London and the pound sterling would indefinitely be able to play their foundational nineteenth-century international roles.

At this stage in his career, Keynes was hardly a "Keynesian" on monetary matters. In 1912, for example, he was arguing that falling prices were better than rising ones because the former benefited wage earners and creditors over entrepreneurs and debtors: this led to a more equal distribution of wealth, he said, and was therefore more just.[14] However, he was foreshadowing his later full-frontal attacks on the gold standard, arguing in a 1914 *Economic Journal* article that it interfered with the rational management of monetary policy, "the intellectual and scientific part [of which] is solved already." If "gold is at last deposed from its despotic control over us and reduced to the position of a constitutional monarch," he pronounced with his trademark acerbic wit, "a new chapter of history will have opened. Man will have made another step forward in the attainment of self-government."[15] He was also becoming an accomplished popular commentator, writing regularly on monetary and financial matters for newspapers and weeklies.

Despite fundamental shifts and reversals through time in his thinking on matters such as the virtues of free trade and price and currency stability, Keynes's writing sustained one supreme constant: biting disdain toward those who remained wedded to either old heresies, as he saw them, or old orthodoxies. "The community as a whole cannot hope to gain," he wrote in his Cambridge Union speaking notes in 1910, "by making artificially scarce [through tariff protection] what the country wants."[16] As Secretary of the Cambridge University Free Trade Association, Keynes at that time considered opposition to free trade a mark of unfitness for anyone wishing to be considered an economist.

Keynes took an early and abiding interest in British Liberal politics—his father having been an antisocialist, conservative-leaning Liberal, his mother a more instinctual, spiritual, "do-gooding" sort.[17] He was drawn particularly by the party's eclectic mix, in its early-twentieth-century heyday, of support for free trade abroad and social insurance at home. Keynes decided to reenter government service in January 1915, age thirty-one, when former Under-Secretary of State for India Edwin Montagu, now Financial Secretary to the Treasury, secured his wartime appointment to a coveted Treasury position. Keynes was immediately taken by the atmosphere: "very clever, very dry and in a certain sense very cynical; intellectually self-confident and not subject to the whims of people who . . . are not quite sure they know their case." He later proudly contrasted it with the American Treasury, which had "very little authority beyond looking after the collection of taxes."[18]

Harry White had enthusiastically enlisted in the U.S. Army and served in France during the war. Keynes, who was able to qualify for exemption as long as he worked at Treasury, remained at home. He lodged a curious—on the face of it, superfluous—official conscientious objection, however, in February 1916, on the grounds that conscription per se violated his freedom of choice: "I am not prepared on such an issue as this to surrender my right of decision, as to what is or is not my duty, to any other person, and I should think it morally wrong to do so."[19] Why did he do this? Keynes was under enormous personal pressure from friends in the Bloomsbury set, such as Duncan Grant and Lytton Strachey, and his Cambridge coterie, in particular Bertrand Russell and D. H. Lawrence, to resign his Treasury position and oppose the war. He never opposed it in principle, though by January 1916 he was wobbling over its conduct. The conscientious objection application was, by all appearances, an insurance policy to cover himself if he lost his Treasury exemption through resignation.[20]

Keynes became Liberal Chancellor Reginald McKenna's most trusted adviser. He took the successful conduct of the war to be a personal, intellectual challenge, becoming immersed in the complex tasks of financing Britain's efforts. Responsible for external finance, he grappled with the risks Britain was obliged to run in borrowing vast sums of U.S. dollars in New York, a portion of which it funneled to less creditworthy Allies to buy munitions, food, oil, and metals. By September of 1916 Britain was spending about $200 million a month ($4.15 billion in current dollars) in the United States, roughly half financed by running down gold reserves and sales of American and Canadian securities, the rest by borrowing.[21] Making matters worse, relations with the United States were deteriorating as British financial dependency on the country was rising. Washington was chafing at British naval interference with U.S.-German trade, and Britain's primary New York banker, J. P. Morgan, was opposing Woodrow Wilson's presidential reelection campaign. In November, the U.S. Federal Reserve Board instructed its member banks to reduce their credit exposure to foreign borrowers and warned private investors against taking Allied Treasury bills as collateral. The aim was political as well as prudential: to prod the Allies to end the war. On January 22, 1917, Wilson, facing growing domestic pressure from anti-British and anti-tsarist constituencies, would call publicly for a "peace without victory."

Keynes concluded that British foreign policy needed to "be so directed as not only to avoid any form of [American] reprisal or active irritation but also to conciliate and please." Wilson, he noted uncomfortably, would, once private financing dried up, "be in a position, if he wishes, to dictate his own terms to us."[22] Though Britain was losing gold at an alarming rate, Keynes supported the Treasury line that the dollar-sterling exchange rate needed to be defended. Over two decades later he would reflect that "to have abandoned the peg would have destroyed our credit and brought chaos to business; and would have done no real good."[23] Part of the aim had clearly been to avoid signaling to the Germans that Britain was reaching the end of its resources.[24]

Had the German government seen this clearly, it might not have made the fateful decision to resume unrestricted submarine warfare to block off the American supply line to the Allies in February. The U.S. ambassador in London, Walter Page, cabled home the observation that it was "not improbable that the only way of maintaining our preeminent trade position and averting a panic is by declaring war on Germany."[25] Such declaration came, mercifully for Britain, on April 6.

This seemed to guarantee continued British war financing, but it also injected a new and worrisome political element. The New York bankers looked on Allied war financing as an opportunity to supplant their London counterparts as the dominant players in the international market, and looked at Washington as a hindrance rather than an ally. Benjamin Strong's New York Fed, barely two years old, had its sights set on supplanting the Bank of England as the leading force in international monetary affairs. In Washington, however, many in Congress viewed the bankers with outright hostility for having, in their view, dragged the country into the war. Treasury Secretary William Gibbs McAdoo, Wilson's son-in-law, for his part viewed Britain, New York, and Congress all as rival political powers, and was determined to keep them in check.

The British had succeeded in borrowing $400 million from J. P. Morgan before the United States entered the war, and now turned their attention on Washington. Treasury Financial Secretary Sir Samuel Hardman Lever asked McAdoo on April 9 to advance Britain $1.5 billion for the coming six months. McAdoo, who suspected the money would be used mainly to pay back Morgan and sustain the sterling-dollar peg, rather than purchase American goods, greeted the proposal with ill-tempered dismissal.

In Britain, the government infighting was worse than in America. Bank of England Governor Walter Cunliffe tried to force Keynes's firing over Treasury's handling of the sterling-dollar rate, in July going so far as to block Lever in New York from accessing the bank's gold stock in Ottawa. McKenna's successor as chancellor, Bonar Law, hit back by forcing Cunliffe's early retirement.

All this domestic intrigue masked the much larger question of the degree to which the American government would be in a position to dictate the postwar political settlement. Britain's Treasury was here on the diplomatic front lines, having to secure adequate financing without ransoming its imperial prerogatives or vital interests in the European balance of power.

With Keynes drafting the critical letters explaining the dire circumstances to McAdoo, the latter drip-fed funds to the British in a manner allowing the U.S. Treasury to control its use. On July 20, Law sent McAdoo a cable, again drafted by Keynes, saying that British "resources available for payments in America are exhausted," and that unless Washington could fill the gap "the whole financial fabric of the alliance will collapse. This conclusion will be a matter not of months but of days." On the twenty-eighth, Keynes drew a line under Britain's commitment to the sterling-dollar peg, successfully arguing internally that it should be defended only so long as dollars remained; once the British dollar stash had been exhausted, convertibility should be dropped to protect the Bank of England's remaining gold. He drafted another cable to Washington explaining the exchange predicament, which prompted McAdoo to release further funds.

Keynes proved more effective as a diplomatic ghostwriter than as a player on the ground in Washington. He accompanied Lord Chief Justice Reading (Rufus Isaacs) on a begging mission to McAdoo in September, making an immediate impression on the British ambassador, who told his wife that Reading's Treasury clerk, Keynes, was "too offensive for words." He is "a Don and . . . also a young man of talent. . . . I presume the rule for such nowadays is to show his immense superiority by crushing the contemptible insignificance of the unworthy outside."[26] Washington Treasury Financial Representative Sir Basil Blackett wrote that Keynes, who had been "rude, dogmatic, and disobliging" with the Americans in London, was now making "a terrible impression for his rudeness out here."[27] In this regard, little would change during the next world war. As for Keynes's impressions of Washington, "the only really sympathetic and original thing in America," he wrote home to Duncan Grant, "is the niggers, who are charming."[28]

Keynes rebelled against having to reason with the war's parvenu paymasters in Washington. Starting in late 1917 he was required to submit to monthly Inter-Ally Council financial oversight meetings, alternatingly in London and Paris, over which U.S. Assistant Secretary to the Treasury Oscar Crosby presided to weed through competing claims on American resources. Keynes derided the council as a vast "monkey-house"—a term he would apply frequently to the non–Anglo Saxon elements that would gather at Bretton Woods a quarter century later. Though Keynes loathed being subjected to "vain, mendacious and interminable French and hateful Yankee slang" at the gatherings, he conceded that "flourishing the name of Crosby" in Whitehall proved highly effective in bringing "recalcitrant departments" into line.

London had long thrived as the center of world finance, but the war changed everything. Britain was now building up enormous liabilities to the United States, much of which involved underwriting French and Italian dollar debts that would never be paid back. Keynes contrived clever schemes to reverse the situation, even possibly allowing Britain to profit from its conduit role. He set out in March of 1918 to persuade the U.S. Treasury to "take over all the future obligations of France and Italy" while leaving Britain to do the actual global procurement—this might allow it to dominate world commodity markets, such as wheat, and act as a monopoly supplier to neutral countries. That the Americans declined to be so duped was a constant source of irritation to him. They seemingly delighted, he fumed, "in reducing us to a position of complete financial helplessness and dependence."[29]

Though America's entry into the war in April 1917 seemed to ensure an ultimate Allied victory, it would clearly be one in which the old financial and monetary order, with Britain at its head, would not survive. The experience sensitized Keynes to the enormous geopolitical costs of British dollar dependence, and would color his front-line financial dealings with the American Treasury during the Second World War.

Keynes had greatly admired, and even had a warm personal relationship with, former Prime Minister H. H. Asquith. Much changed when Asquith resigned in December 1916 in favor of then–Secretary of State for War (and McKenna's predecessor as chancellor) David Lloyd George, a far more determined and cunning political operator, who thought little of Keynes's capacity as a wartime adviser. Keynes was, the new prime minister said, "much too mercurial and impulsive a counsellor for a great emergency. He dashed at conclusions with acrobatic ease. It made things no better that he rushed into opposite conclusions with the same agility."[30] Lloyd George personally struck Keynes's name from the final royal honors list in February 1917 (Keynes would get the CB in May with Law's intervention). Keynes returned the PM's sentiments: "I work for a government I despise," he told Duncan Grant in December, "for ends I think criminal." To his mother he lamented that the "prolongation of the war . . . probably means the disappearance of the social order we have known hitherto." Though he added that "the abolition of the rich will be rather a comfort and serve them right anyhow," the sentiment was a rather narrowly targeted one: he himself had spent the war comfortably attended to by servants. As regards world affairs, "In another year's time," he opined, "we shall have forfeited the claim we had staked out in the New World and in exchange this country will be mortgaged to America."[31]

Keynes's despair over the conduct of the war was exceeded by his bitterness over the terms of the peace. After the conclusion of the armistice with Germany on November 11, 1918, he stayed on at Treasury to become its principal voice at the Paris Peace Conference, which began in January 1919. He resigned in "misery and rage" three weeks before the signing of the Treaty of Versailles on June 28. He would not rejoin the Treasury until 1940—the next time Britain would need American cash to survive a European war.

Three questions related to German reparations melded in a scalding political cauldron that even the most pellucid economic reasoning could not contain: what damages should Germany be held liable for, what was Germany's capacity to pay, and how should the Allies divide the takings? Keynes would later that year pen a vivid and devastating memoir of the negotiations, *The Economic Consequences of the Peace*, that would bring him immediate and widespread international acclaim, as well as more than a fair measure of angry opprobrium in the United States, Britain, and—particularly—France. His withering portraits of the three main protagonists—American President Woodrow Wilson, British Prime Minister David Lloyd George, and French Prime Minister Georges Clemenceau—established Keynes's credentials as one of Europe's most brilliant and incisive polemicists.

Keynes mocked the "slowminded and bewildered" Wilson, a "blind and deaf Don Quixote," reflecting the Englishman's broader views of malleable, hypocritical, and dim-witted American religiosity. Wilson, Keynes said, "would do nothing that was not just and right; he would do nothing that was contrary to his great profession of faith. Thus, without any abatement of the verbal inspiration of [his] Fourteen Points, they became a document for gloss and interpretation and for all the intellectual apparatus of selfdeception, by which, I daresay, the President's forefathers had persuaded themselves that the course they thought it necessary to take was consistent with every syllable of the Pentateuch." He had been outfoxed by old European "wickedness"; that is, the "cynical" and "impish" Clemenceau, and the "goat-footed bard," Lloyd George, "rooted in nothing, . . . void and without content," with a "flavour of final purposelessness [and] inner irresponsibility."[32]

Keynes's main aim in writing the book was not to lampoon the Big Three, however, but rather to explain—more precisely, to drive home with concise historical and logical analysis—why the treaty's economic terms were deeply misguided and dangerous. His account of the development of Europe's economy from 1870 to the start of the war was remarkable, given his later thinking on the importance of national economic planning and, in particular, monetary management, for its emphasis on the immense and widespread material benefits that sprang from Europe's organic economic integration. Most striking was his observation that "[t]he various currencies, which were all maintained on a stable basis in relation to gold and to one another, facilitated the easy flow of capital and of trade to an extent the full value of which we only realize now, when we are deprived of its advantages."[33] The Great War had brought this to an end—the franc and pound both plummeted, ending a hundred years of fixed exchange rates, in February after American official aid to Britain was cut off.[34] Keynes also noted, sounding almost libertarian, that "the immense accumulations of fixed capital which, to the great benefits of mankind, were built up during the half century before the war, could never have come about in a Society where wealth was divided equally."[35]

Keynes, who labored with enormous passion and endurance at the conference to convince the principal players that Germany if it "is to be 'milked' . . . must not first of all be ruined,"[36] produced a clever and farsighted scheme to solve, in one grand package, the problems of the European Allies' debts to each other and to the United States together with those of establishing what Germany could reasonably be required to pay in reparations, given its resources and export capacity. The key innovation was to reduce Allied claims on Germany to a level that Keynes, and the Americans, thought manageable, in tandem with a reduction in Britain's debt to the United States. Keynes emphasized that without some means of scaling down its American obligations Britain would be exposed to "future pressure by the United States of a most objectionable description," and Keynes's scheme would have accomplished this.[37] Lloyd George embraced the idea, which he rarely did when Keynes was the source, but the Americans would not bite. "I realize the efforts that are being made to tie us to the shaky financial structure of Europe," Wilson wrote to financier Bernard Baruch, one of his primary advisers, "and am counting upon your assistance to defeat the efforts."[38]

The economic apparatus that Keynes applied to arrive at an estimate of Germany's capacity to make annual reparations payments much lower than his own government, and that of France, were demanding did not go unchallenged by fellow economists. He took the greatest pains in trying to refute, in particular, the arguments of French economist Jacques Rueff, published in Keynes's own journal, that he was in a logical muddle over the impact of German transfers on exchange rates and the balance of payments.[39] Rueff would nearly two decades later challenge Keynes's most celebrated scholarly text, *The General Theory*, on parallel grounds: that Keynes mistakenly attributed observed economic dislocations to flaws inherent in the monetary system, rather than to readily identifiable and correctable policy errors.

In any case, the tremendous international success of *The Economic Consequences of the Peace* owed little to Keynes's technical apparatus and much to his uncanny ability to capture the narrow and grotesque political shortsightedness behind the treaty terms. Although much of his early profits from the book would be dissipated in his new hobby of foreign exchange speculation, he had now become a celebrity public intellectual and lived like one. In 1925 he married acclaimed Russian ballerina and divorcée Lydia Lopokova, whom he had first met at a party in London during her tour in 1918. (It had not been love at first sight: "She is such a rotten dancer," he said to financier Oswald Falk, "she has such a stiff bottom.")[40] Lydia was charmingly ingenuous and free-spirited in Keynes's eye, but too jarringly undereducated for his literati circle. Though the seemingly curious marriage added to Keynes's popular cachet, it injected a permanent irritant into his Bloomsbury friendships. He loved her truly and deeply, all the same, for the remainder of his days.

Almost all who achieve the status of noted scholar and public intellectual make their names as scholars first. Not Keynes. He would not produce a truly great work of economic theory until 1930, the year he turned forty-seven. Yet by 1923 he was publishing fifty-one newspaper articles in a year (his highest output), and turning a very handsome living from it. He lived well, and became a generous patron of the arts.

What were boom years for Keynes were bust years for the British economy, which was mired in a depression from 1920 to 1922. When the economy bottomed out in 1923 unemployment was still near 10 percent, and would remain stubbornly high throughout the decade (before getting much worse in the 1930s). Was this the result of slow adaptation to the disruption of prewar trade networks? Misguided policy choices in the monetary sphere? Or did economists perhaps have unfounded faith in certain myths of the self-regenerating marketplace? At this stage, Keynes was not ready to take the full intellectual leap required to ground a full frontal assault on classical economics, but he was ready to launch a steady war of intellectual attrition.

His main target was the Bank of England, which through interest rate rises was putting heavy downward pressure on the war-inflated British price level in an effort to make feasible the restoration of the venerated prewar dollar-sterling parity of $4.86. British unit labor costs, though they did fall, did not do so nearly as rapidly as prices, leaving them roughly 25 percent too high by the end of 1922. Keynes publicly attacked the bank's belief that wages were sufficiently flexible that the old dollar parity was still feasible and worth the short-run pain. Though Keynes felt the policy was bringing Britain to the "verge of revolution," and that the government should let "the dollar exchange go hang," he as yet offered no revolutionary insights as to why the policy should be considered hopeless and misguided.[41] His belief that wages were "stickier" than prices was widely shared, but in itself did not tell against policies aimed at unsticking them.

In fact, he still at this point believed that unemployment would eventually come down, owing to pent-up demand, irrespective of whether the bank loosened monetary policy, as he was urging. He was also still a conventional free trader, arguing against "the protectionist fallacy" that tariffs and import barriers could cure unemployment. He argued that protectionism could only *temporarily* increase employment by pushing up prices, but this concession begged the question as to why he was then arguing for lower interest rates and a cheaper pound to do just this—push up prices.[42] It is clear that his old intellectual convictions had not yet aligned themselves coherently with his new, more radical ones, but the broad path was becoming evident: "The more troublous the times," he said in a lecture to the National Liberal Club in December 1923, "the worse does a *laissez-faire* system work."[43] The germs were clearly forming for the novel ideas he would later propound on the puzzle of persistent underemployment.

Keynes's first major attempt to synthesize his postwar ideas on money was *A Tract on Monetary Reform*, published in December 1923. Milton Friedman, Keynes's most famous critic on the use of activist government fiscal policy, considered it Keynes's best work, which would surely have suggested to Keynes that he had not gone nearly far enough in breaking with classical thinking on monetary management —a conclusion he did in fact reach within a few months of the *Tract*'s publication. The book was nonetheless a sparkling reflection of Keynes's unique intellectual style, mixing abstract economic analysis with witty and biting commentary on contemporary affairs.

The central theoretical argument of the book—not wholly original, built on earlier work by prominent economists such as Irving Fisher and Knut Wicksell—was that it was the demand for money, rather than its supply, that the monetary authorities should aim to stabilize. The most important implication of his theoretical argument, Keynes argued, was that the authorities, in order to stabilize prices, which should be the primary aim of monetary policy, needed to intervene actively and continuously to vary the supply of currency notes and the ratio of bank cash reserves to bank deposits. This was in marked contrast with the gold standard, the central villain of the peace in Keynes's telling, wherein the authorities behaved much more mechanically in response to movements in the monetary gold stock across borders: when gold flowed in they loosened credit, and when it flowed out they tightened credit.

The acerbity of Keynes's assault on the gold standard, at the time still widely considered central to any sound international monetary system, was intendedly shocking to readers, accounting for many of the critical reviews of the book. "Words ought to be a little wild," Keynes would say in 1933, "for they are the assaults of thoughts upon the unthinking."[44] Keynes acknowledged that the gold standard had performed admirably in the late nineteenth century, but insisted that conditions were decidedly different now. In particular, one of the many awful effects of the war was to transfer much of the world's monetary gold to the United States. There was more than a tinge of jealous nationalism in Keynes's assertion, however justified, that attempts to restore the gold standard, a "barbarous relic," would lead to a "surrender [of] the regulation of our price level and the handling of the credit cycle to the hands of the Federal Reserve Board," which had set up "a dollar standard . . . on the pedestal of the Golden Calf."[45] The shift in financial power from London to New York and Washington was to be a constant concern of Keynes, reflected even in his theoretical work, for the remainder of his career.

The *Tract* made many subtle and insightful points about the nature of the trade-offs between inflation and deflation, exchange stability and flexibility, and the short run and the long run (in which "we are all dead"),[46] yet its blaspheming Bloomsbury-cultivated tone limited its practical force insofar as it offended many of those it needed to convert. And though Keynes's scorn was generally aimed at conservatives, his growing influence was also a thorn in the side of prominent socialists such as H. G. Wells, who saw in Keynes's anti-Bolshevist Middle Way–ism a barrier to the far more thoroughgoing economic policy changes they wished to see.[47]

In any case, the domestic policy debate in Britain quickly narrowed to whether the government should pursue further deflationary measures to reestablish the old dollar parity or wait passively for parity to reemerge and then take measures to anchor it. Keynes, seeing that his attack on the platonic image of the gold standard had missed its mark politically, shrewdly retreated. Appearing before a parliamentary committee in July 1924, he now argued that the American economic boom would inevitably boost dollar prices and restore the parity with no necessity for a decline in sterling ones. At that point, he would favor restricting gold imports by license in order to block a further rise in the pound's dollar value. He studiously avoided profaning the holy parity itself.

Yet when Chancellor of the Exchequer Winston Churchill made the fateful decision to return Britain to the gold standard at the prewar rate on April 28, 1925, Keynes shifted gears again and blasted the principle of committing to *any* parity. "I hold that in modern conditions," he wrote in a letter to *The Times* of London on August 1, "wages in this country are, for various reasons, so rigid over short periods, that it is impracticable to adjust them to the ebb and flow of international gold-credit, and I would deliberately utilise fluctuations in the exchange as the shock-absorber." Though this might appear a defense of floating exchange rates, he would far more often than not in his career defend the desirability of "stable" rates. This continuous finessing of so fundamental an issue in monetary management would flummox his supporters and enervate his detractors.

Simultaneous with his *Times* letter Keynes published *The Economic Consequences of Mr. Churchill*, playing on the commercial success of his earlier attack on the Versailles Treaty. It sold well in Britain, though, much unlike his earlier *Consequences*, poorly in the United States. Churchill, Keynes knew, had agonized over the decision, and the latter was careful, notwithstanding the book's mischievous title, to pin the blame on the chancellor's "experts." Churchill did not, and never would, have a sophisticated grasp of monetary issues, but he was ultimately swayed by the widely held view that a renunciation of the prewar parity would have been a "repudiation" of Britain's solemn obligation to maintain the convertibility of the pound.[48] This would, in his mind, have had serious geopolitical ramifications. "If we had not taken this action," he said in announcing it, "the whole of the rest of the British Empire would have taken it without us, and it would have come to a gold standard, not on the basis of the pound sterling, but a gold standard of the dollar." As it turned out, a "gold standard of the dollar" would result anyway, but with Britain bearing great economic costs in maintaining what was clearly an overvalued exchange rate from 1925 until 1931, when the country was ignominiously driven off gold again. With hindsight, it is extraordinarily difficult to argue with Keynes's verdict on Churchill's decision; where reasoned disagreement still exists is over whether Churchill should have sought to establish *any* parity, even a much lower one.[49]

Keynes had by the mid-1920s developed and articulated an historically informed and institutionally sensitive *framework* for thinking about the elements of good economic policy, yet nothing groundbreaking in terms of *theory*—that is, a set of clearly defined general principles on which a capitalist economy could be said to work. In sharp contrast with those who continued to believe in a nineteenth-century laissez-faire approach, Keynes thought it vital that government actively manage the monetary system, with the aim of avoiding the injustices meted out to different groups in society by inflation or deflation, and not leave such matters to the vagaries of the gold market. Central banking, he believed, should now "be regarded as a kind of beneficent technique of scientific control such as electricity and other branches of science are."[50]

He further believed that energetic fiscal policy, mainly in the form of capital spending, needed to be applied as a means of filling the gap left by flagging private investment. His views on the private sector and market competition were ambivalent. On the one hand, he viewed business confidence as being of primary importance to economic performance. On the other, he wrote approvingly of the supplanting of the entrepreneur by the large corporation and the steady encroachment of the state into the way the latter operated. Anything that assisted the "aggregation of production" under the interconnected elites distributed throughout the business enterprises, the civil service, and the universities was to be welcomed.[51]

In contrast to socialists, Keynes was never motivated by a desire to redistribute wealth. He thought unemployment a distinct social evil, as were income declines suffered disproportionately by specific groups of workers, such as miners, owing to misguided deflationary policies; but he never agitated for policies designed to reduce the rewards of the market for some groups in order to increase them for others. Despite his disenchantment with the Liberal Party, he remained almost as hostile to the Labour Party as the Conservatives: the Labour Party "is a class party," he wrote, "and the class is not my class. If I am going to pursue sectional interests at all, I shall pursue my own . . . the *class* war will find me on the side of the educated *bourgeoisie*."[52]

Keynes was, in his time, a radical in terms of his thinking about the role of government in achieving specific objectives; he had no patience with those who counseled restraint on the grounds of either tradition or fear of unintended consequences. But he was a Burkean conservative in the sense that he believed that the aims and methods of economic policy had to be built around society as it was, at any given point in time, and that society should never be forced to bend itself to abstract economic principles, irrespective of whether such principles might have been effective in grounding policy in the past. "We have to invent new wisdom for a new age," he wrote. "And in the meantime we must, if we are to do any good, appear unorthodox, troublesome, dangerous, disobedient to them that begat us."[53] Though he was a deep skeptic on the benefits of trying to engineer social change, he had almost unbounded faith in the ability of experts to engineer the proper fixes for whatever economic ailments might afflict the nation at any point in time. "It is fatal for a capitalist government to have principles," he wrote in his characteristic bracing style. "It must be opportunistic in the best sense of the word, living by accommodation and good sense."[54]

The question of money—its function, its history, its management, and its psychology—became an ever-deeper fascination of Keynes. This was clearly as much visceral and emotional as it was intellectual. In an essay titled "Economic Possibilities for Our Grandchildren," which emerged from a presentation at Winchester College in March 1928, he famously condemned the "love of money [as] a somewhat disgusting morbidity, one of the semi-criminal, semi-pathological propensities which one hands over with a shudder to specialists in mental disease."[55] Reflecting views that were not uncommon among his class at the time, he also saw this love as a particular pathology of a particular group: Jews. "I still think the race has shown itself, not merely for accidental reasons," he wrote to a polite American critic of his views, "more than normally interested in the accumulation of usury."[56]

Keynes himself was "more than normally" partial to speculation, which would cost him dearly that year. Long on commodities such as rubber, corn, cotton, and tin, he was forced to sell securities to cover margin calls when the market turned against him. His net worth plummeted from £44,000 at the end of 1927 (about $3.5 million in current dollars) to £7,815 at the end of 1929, following the Wall Street crash in October, in spite of his having no holdings of U.S. stocks.[57] Keynes would in 1930 insist that falling commodity prices were the result of policy-induced insufficient demand rather than overinvestment—a perhaps not altogether surprising view from one whose commodities punts had turned out so disastrously.[58]

October of that year would see the publication of his first, and second-to-last, major tome: the two-volume *Treatise on Money*. He had been writing and rewriting the book since 1924, five years before the crash, and the text reflects, at times jarringly, the author's changing concerns as the decade progressed. Keynes acknowledged immediately that it was not a literary masterpiece; the onset of the Great Depression would convince him that he also needed to make a much greater leap intellectually.

Like the earlier *Tract* and the later *General Theory*, the *Treatise* cannot be read—though its title implies otherwise—purely as an explication or refinement of abstract theoretical ideas. All three books are efforts to explain the specific underlying dynamics of the British economy, particularly as they relate to money and monetary policy, in a period of years preceding their publication. The *Treatise* is concerned in particular with what Keynes saw as his country's deeply misguided effort to return to the gold standard, which he characterized as an outworn, primitive basis for managing the pound—it had had its day in the late nineteenth century, but society had changed, Britain's role in the world had diminished, and economic science had advanced in ways that now made informed, discretionary control by central banking experts the only defensible means of monetary management.

A critical message of the *Treatise*, as Keynes saw it, was that a central bank—or, more specifically, the Bank of England, now that its dominant international role had been arrogated by the Fed—operating monetary policy so as to avoid gold reserve losses inflicted severe and lasting damage to domestic profits and employment owing to the endemic stickiness of certain prices, mainly labor. This stickiness might be due to "the power of the trade unions or the mere human inclination to think in terms of money"—that is, because of institutional blockages to labor market adjustment or mere psychological quirks.[59] One of the critical differences between Keynes and the so-called classical economists is that whereas the latter believed that blockages could be overcome politically, and quirks through market forces, Keynes believed that it was *monetary policy itself* that needed to adapt to the "natural tendencies" of society and "the earnings system as it actually is."[60] This debate renewed itself with great force in the 1970s, a period of so-called stagflation: high unemployment *and* high inflation, a combination that puzzled many Keynesian-schooled economists at the time.

The *Treatise* is an eclectic—at times tedious, at others sparkling or impish—threading of theory, statistics, history, and psychology to support ideas Keynes had been incubating in much less articulated form for years. Most prominent among these is the idea that it is not to the saving behavior of our thrifty ancestors that we owe our present wealth and heritage of great cultural monuments, but rather to the animal spirits of their more spendthrift and enterprising kin. "Were the seven wonders of the world built by thrift?" Keynes asked rhetorically. "I deem it doubtful."[61] This judgment he supports with a dashing and controversial "Historical Illustrations" chapter—a monetary reading of world history—as well as a much tougher-going chapter explicating Keynes's theory of the radical separability of savings and investment behavior, and the failure of market interest rates to play the balancing role accorded to it by classical economics.

The *Treatise* ends with an important chapter on the management of international monetary affairs. Both wonky and visionary, it develops ideas that Keynes would later champion at Bretton Woods. In particular, there was the concept of "Supernational Bank-money" (S.B.M.)—an international reserve asset to be issued by a new Supernational Bank, which Keynes hoped would come to supplant gold as the ultimate such reserve asset. Keynes would refashion S.B.M. in the 1940s as "bancor," with the aim not just of supplanting gold but of preventing what seemed to be the inexorable march toward global dollar hegemony.

Keynes was in November 1929, just following the crash, appointed to the government's Macmillan Committee on Finance and Industry, which conducted a sustained inquiry into the relationship between banking and industry. Devoting an enormous amount of time to its meetings and testimony-taking over the course of 1930, Keynes dominated the proceedings, repeatedly putting luminaries from the Bank of England and the Treasury on the defensive and laying the intellectual foundations for a new, vastly more aggressive approach to monetary policy and government spending in a business downturn—an approach that came to define for many the core of Keynesianism.

The central bank, Keynes argued, had to "dose the system with money" and "feed the hoarder" in order to force down interest rates and revive private investment.[62] But this was far from sufficient. If business would not invest enough, the government had to do the job itself. Generating deficits to finance large-scale public investment should not be a worry; the new expenditure would pay for itself through lower unemployment benefits and revived business activity. This was an early statement of the now widely invoked "fiscal multiplier," a concept Keynes adopted from the work of his favorite student, Richard Kahn. Prominent critics such as former pupil Hubert Henderson argued that the primary effect of Keynes's schemes would be to lead businessmen to expect higher taxes in the future, thereby reducing incentives for private investment even further and, in consequence, necessitating ever more of Keynes's dangerous medicine. Keynes accused Henderson of "lack of fundamental analysis"; Henderson accused Keynes of rejecting sound conservative approaches, such as bringing British industrial costs into line, because it was "inconsistent with your self-respect."[63]

Keynes was, confusingly, of many minds on unemployment and wages. In February of that year he had said that his "reading of history is that for centuries there has existed an intense social resistance to any matters of reduction in the level of money income."[64] Yet just a few days later he was arguing that unemployment benefit "diminishes the pressure on the individual man to accept a rate of wages or a kind of employment which is not just what he wants or what he is used to" and that the dole was blocking the adjustment of wages to falling prices and rising unemployment that would have prevailed "in the old days."[65] Meanwhile he also criticized minimum-wage legislation, arguing that tax-financed wealth redistribution was a "wiser" way to help "the poorer part of the community" than "fixing the wages of individuals at a higher figure than it pays their employers to give them."[66]

In the end, though, his main conclusions were clear: policy should serve to push up prices rather than reduce money wages because it involves "less social resistance" and is fairer in that "the *rentier* class and other recipients of fixed money incomes" share the pain of adjustment with wage earners.[67] Perhaps most controversially, Keynes argued that if government could not drive up prices sufficiently to offset the cost disadvantage under which British business now operated—and British "wages policy is definitely set to a more liberal remuneration of the worker relatively to his efficiency than prevails in a good many other countries"—then protectionism, particularly import tariffs, and blocks on foreign investment were necessary.[68] Keynes now found not only defensible but necessary policy views he had in earlier times ascribed to cranks. Lionel Robbins of the London School of Economics, who served with Henderson and Arthur Pigou under Keynes on Prime Minister Ramsay MacDonald's committee of economists, later reconciled himself to Keynes's views on public spending but never to his heresies on free trade.

The committee's report, marked as it was by fierce dissent from Henderson, Robbins, and Pigou on critical questions, had no direct policy impact. The same intellectual standoff reprises in each financial crisis. To what degree is the slump that follows financial crises a product of structural imbalances that require sound, patient, structural repairs? Or can an injection of fiscal adrenaline revive business optimism and bring the economy quickly back to life, irrespective of what brought about the patient's collapse? Keynes unambiguously backed the second approach. He condemned "the enormous anomaly of unemployment in a world full of wants," a stirring phrase that simply left buried the question of causes and their removal.

Keynes, though he had not yet articulated in a coherent theoretical form why he should believe so strongly that all economic problems should have short-term solutions, was repulsed by the idea that crisis should require grinding suffering and slow redemption for the sin of uncompetitiveness. He was in the process of staking out a radical intellectual middle ground between the Marxist view that capitalism was doomed to die of crisis and the classical nineteenth-century liberal view that it needed to be freed of political impediment so that it could do its good work. He condemned "the pessimism of the revolutionaries who think that things are so bad that nothing can save us but violent change," as well as that "of the reactionaries who consider the balance of our economic and social life so precarious that we must risk no experiments."[69]

Yet in the meantime Keynes, always politically attuned, recognized that even if his stimulus ideas were a nonstarter his tariff suggestions, which he had earlier put forth without great conviction, had legs. By early 1931, he had dropped his vocal advocacy of public works and was backing import barriers—arguing, somewhat curiously, that passionate free traders, of which he had certainly been one in the early 1920s, should they get their way would induce a crisis of confidence that would bring into the cabinet ministers pledged to more protectionism.[70] What is striking is that Keynes did not, at this point in time, support his position with economic theory. It was purely a matter of political viability: "Now free trade, combined with great mobility of wage-rates, is a tenable intellectual proposition," he wrote in March, but those options "do not exist outside the field of pure hypothesis."[71]

Yet Keynes would later argue in *The General Theory* that lower wages, in the circumstances in which Britain found itself in the early 1930s, were, in fact, bad economics. It is a staple of Keynes's career that he was incessantly in search of reasons—economic or political, theoretical or practical—to back what his intuition told him was the right path.

Keynes can arguably take some modest background credit, or blame, for passage of the Import Duties Act later that year. He also took to the airwaves urging British housewives to stop saving and go shopping—for British goods: "whenever you save five shillings," he told them by radio in January 1931, "you put a man out of work for a day . . . [whereas] whenever you buy goods you increase employment—though they must be British, home-produced goods if you are to increase employment in this country. . . . Therefore, O patriotic housewives, sally out tomorrow early into the streets and go to the wonderful sales."[72]

Perhaps surprisingly, Keynes was not, at this point, advocating devaluation, which would be among the least controversial policy prescriptions today. As late as September 10, just eleven days before Britain's exit from the gold standard, Keynes was still arguing publicly, in the *Evening Standard*, for import controls as an alternative. This was the most conspicuous example of Keynes trying to have it both ways: cultivating his status as a freethinking public intellectual, while staying within the bounds of what the government, which assured him the constant limelight, considered responsible public commentary on the most delicate issue of economic policy—Britain's commitment to sustaining the international status of the pound sterling and the City of London. Thus he remained circumspect on the exchange rate in public while believing privately that Britain needed to sever the link with gold and regain control over domestic interest rates.[73]

Keynes was, of course, surprised at how quickly the pound came crashing down—he would not have flogged the expedient of trade protection otherwise. On September 16, a mutiny of sailors at Invergordon, enraged by news that they faced wage cuts of up to 25 percent, triggered a run on the pound. Two days later the Bank of England informed the government that it could not sustain convertibility beyond a few days. On September 21, Chancellor Philip Snowden took Britain off the gold-exchange standard—the pound would fall by 30 percent against the dollar by the end of the year. Economics writer Graham Hutton recalled Keynes as being almost giddy with excitement. This was "a wonderful thing," Keynes said in rare still-available filmed footage from October 1931. Now, he insisted, British businessmen and unemployed workers "must not allow anyone to put them back in the gold cage, where they have been pining their hearts out all these years."[74] Britain had, "at one stroke . . . resumed the financial hegemony of the world," he offered, somewhat optimistically.[75] Over twenty countries dependent on exports to the empire devalued with Britain, spontaneously creating a "sterling bloc" on which Keynes believed that the Bank of England and City of London could ground a continuing central international role. He publicly abandoned his support of tariffs.[76]

If Keynes was looking somewhat like a political animal, changing his stripes as the tides of political necessity ebbed and flowed, it was because he desired passionately to stay relevant. In the 1940s, when he would enter into the realm of international diplomacy, this need would at times become painfully apparent as he sought to persuade the British cabinet and House of Lords that he was succeeding, even when he was clearly not, in critical financial and monetary negotiations with the Americans. For the time being, however, Keynes found himself politically marginalized. A Conservative-dominated national government was overwhelmingly elected on October 27, and the Liberal Party, to which Keynes had formerly had a passionate attachment, was now a fringe grouping. Though Keynes might have been expected to support Labour on the grounds that its policies meshed with his priorities of more government investment and working-class spending power, he objected to the party's hostility to capitalism and obsession with redistribution for its own sake. The leading advocate for his ideas within the party, Oswald Mosley, had resigned in February, launching the British Union of Fascists in 1932; Keynes remained unfairly stained within the Labour Party by Mosely's endorsement of his ideas.

Keynes's political marginalization afforded him the time and intellectual freedom to refine—or more accurately, fundamentally rethink—the economic underpinnings of his concern with persistent unemployment and the role of money in abetting it. Critical reviews of the *Treatise* from the likes of Friedrich Hayek, the young, rising Austrian economist at the London School of Economics, and former student Dennis Robertson convinced Keynes not that he was misdiagnosing the problem but that he needed a radically different theoretical approach to defend his diagnosis. In spite of the pound's devaluation and a fall in interest rates, unemployment reached 17 percent in 1932. Something, he was sure, was awry in the classical view of the self-correcting market, and that something, he was equally sure, had to do with the very nature of a money-based economy. But he had not yet put his finger on it. "We have been opposing the orthodox school more by our flair and instinct than because we have discovered in precisely what respects their theory is wrong," he confessed in November 1934.[77] But in a New Year's Day 1935 letter to George Bernard Shaw, in response to Shaw's urgings that he take Karl Marx more seriously, Keynes wrote that he was "writing a book on economic theory, which will largely revolutionise—not, I suppose, at once but in the course of the next ten years—the way the world thinks about economic problems." As for Marx, his economic value, "apart from occasional . . . flashes of insight" is "*nil.*"[78]

Proving to his fellow economists that the free market lacked an autoregenerative device consumed much of his intellectual energy, but he continued to push his case for deficit-financed government spending through popular publications—most notably his widely debated pamphlet *The Means to Prosperity*, which applied Kahn's idea of the fiscal multiplier to the depressed British and American economies.[79] Keynes concluded that a dollar of new public spending would generate at least two dollars of additional output—a truly bounteous harvest. Despite its bold economic claims, the pamphlet was strikingly sober in tone compared with Keynes's earlier popular writings, eschewing barbed swipes at knavish politicians. Nonetheless, Conservative Chancellor Neville Chamberlain very publicly rejected Keynes's urgings, declaring bluntly that "no Finance Minister ever deliberately unbalanced his budget."[80] Chamberlain balanced the 1933/34 budget; the economy recovered well, growing 3.3 percent in '33 and 8.7 percent in '34.[81] Keynes postulated defensively that growth was "slower and on a smaller scale than it would have been if there had been more government loan expenditure."[82] We will never know.

The Means to Prosperity was widely read in the United States; newly sworn-in President Franklin Roosevelt received a copy, though what he did with it or made of it is unknown. We do know, however, that the United States supported a scheme for international public works at the 1933 World Economic Conference, though such an idea would likely never have come to light this early in a world without Keynes. (His own government rejected it.)[83] Keynes's influence over Roosevelt's New Deal is a matter of some debate: its supporters and opponents alike often highlighted Keynes's influence, but Keynes himself—who met Roosevelt for the first time on a private visit to Washington in May of 1934—was a public critic of the president's centerpiece National Recovery Administration ("a programme of reform, disguised as recovery, which probably impeded recovery," in Skidelsky's words).[84] We can certainly speculate with some confidence that the pamphlet's argument for expanding central bank reserves globally through newly conjured international "gold-notes"—which played on the public's attachment to gold without conceding any meaning to its actual presence or absence—was studied and absorbed by a certain economics professor in Appleton, Wisconsin: Harry Dexter White.

Keynes's economic thinking was changing along many lines, sometimes significantly. He made his strongest-ever statement in support of economic "National Self-Sufficiency" in a famous Dublin lecture on April 17, 1933. No longer was protectionist thought, it seemed, evidence of a poor education and lack of wits. Keynes had come to recognize the growing "advantages of gradually bringing the producer and the consumer within the ambit of the same national, economic and financial organisation." The benefits of an international division of labor, he now believed, were overrated. Moreover, he "sympathise[d] . . . with those who would minimise . . . economic entanglement between nations" on the grounds that this led to fewer "strains and enmities." So "let goods be homespun whenever it is reasonably and conveniently possible," he concluded in an oft-quoted line, "and, above all, let finance be primarily national." That is, international capital flows, of all the various economic entanglements, had the most pernicious effects.[85] Oswald Mosely sent Keynes a letter of congratulations on the lecture, much to the latter's embarrassment.

Keynes's protectionist idyllicism would hardly be his last word on the subject; indeed, Keynes's pronouncements on the net costs and benefits of various economic policies tended to be much influenced by his emotional state and the prejudices of his audience (which he liked to challenge). In any case, Keynes certainly did not to take to heart his own pleading that finance stay at home. He began enthusiastically buying shares on Wall Street in 1932; U.S. stocks made up 40 percent of his personal portfolio by 1936, the year he finally published his magnum opus.[86]

The General Theory of Employment, Interest and Money is one of the most influential works of economic thought, and arguably the most intellectually audacious, ever published. As a critique of the classical nineteenth-century liberal belief in the social solidity of the free market, it was, given its vastly superior analytical rigor, far more devastating than Marx's *Das Kapital.* Yet its message could not have been more different; whereas Marx and Keynes both saw in capitalism the seeds of its own demise, Keynes was convinced that it could— and indeed for the good of society must—be saved through judicious government intervention, particularly in the form of timely large-scale public investment.

It is difficult to overestimate the impact *The General Theory* had on the economics profession, particularly in the United States. It virtually established macroeconomics as a discipline; the term only started being used in the 1940s. But the unusual style of *The General Theory* also made it difficult for even expert readers to separate out its "true" substance. It is only slightly outlandish to liken the book to the Bible: powerful in its message; full of memorable, mellifluous passages; at times obscure, tedious, tendentious, and contradictory; a work of passion driven by intuition, with tenuous logic and observation offered as placeholders until disciples could be summoned to supply the proofs. As Keynes himself said of his masterwork, "I am more attached to the comparatively simple fundamental ideas which underlie my theory than to the particular forms in which I have embodied them, and have no desire that the latter should be crystallized at the present stage of the debate. If the simple basic ideas can become familiar and acceptable, time and experience and the collaboration of a number of minds will discover the best way of expressing them."[87]

The central argument of the book was revolutionary (at least to economists): the economy had no natural tendency toward full employment. High unemployment could persist indefinitely if governments did not intervene forcefully to boost consumption demand. Cheap money provided by the central bank was not enough. This was wholly contrary to classical economics, which held that protracted involuntary unemployment was a result of some interference in the workings of the price mechanism. Classical economics showed that full employment required flexible wages; Keynes showed why, with different assumptions, falling wages could actually worsen unemployment. These different assumptions were related to the nature of money, human psychology, and conventions of contemporary society. Each of these on its own would do for his argument, and he was not that particular.

Such a brazen treatise would have gotten a much colder reception during the American boom years of the 1920s, but in the midst of a Great Depression, with unheard-of levels of unemployment, it was compelling even to economists who disagreed with Keynes's logical apparatus. In the United States the book held particular appeal as an intellectual justification for controversial New Deal policies. If today it seems natural to most policy makers that governments should run deficits in recessions to stabilize the economy, it was far from a natural notion in the 1930s; it was Keynes who made the prescription intellectually respectable.

Like another great mind of his time, Albert Einstein, Keynes had a preternatural ability to see relationships between complex phenomena entirely differently than generations of experts before him. Though mathematics was the primary analytical tool for both physics and economics, neither Einstein nor Keynes was exceptionally gifted in, nor fascinated by, higher mathematics. They had an utterly rare gift of intellectual intuition; both thought through problems which obsessed them using the vehicle of analogy, like riding on a light beam (which sparked Einstein's theory of special relativity) or living in an economy that produces and consumes only bananas (through which Keynes "proved" that thrift was deadly). A great admirer of Einstein, whom he had met in Berlin in 1926, Keynes, it would surely seem, quite consciously emulated Einstein's approach of turning on their heads eternal mechanisms the world thought it understood. "Einstein actually did for Physics what Mr Keynes believes himself to have done for Economics," observed Arthur Pigou, one of the old school that Keynes sought not merely to overturn but to embarrass with his book.[88]

Isaac Newton had claimed that time was absolute and fixed, and who but a madman questioned this? Einstein did. Time was relative, he believed, and he subsequently proved it. Keynes's controversial claim of having erected a new *General Theory* was a transparent mimicking of Einstein's "general" (as contrasted to his merely "special") theory of relativity.[89] Classical economists—that is, the only ones who were reputable in the 1920s—believed in Say's Law, expressed by Keynes as "supply creates its own demand," and Keynes set out to prove that this was false.[90]

Say did not write the precise words Keynes ascribed to him, and there is endless controversy over what *exactly* "Say's Law" comprises. Say did write that "a glut can take place only when there are too many means of production applied to one kind of product and not enough to another." This does imply that demand cannot fall short of potential supply; supply the right sort of goods and services, and the demand will be there. This owes to the fact that "the mere circumstance of creation of one product immediately opens a vent for other products"; the creator supplies *because* he demands.[91] Keynes argued that Say's Law had everything the wrong way around; in fact, it was "expenditure [that] creates its own income."[92] It was demand, not supply, that determined the level of economic activity. It was investment that called forth the requisite savings, through its boosting of income; not the other way around. The result, in Keynes's theoretical apparatus, was that demand, given the psychological factors that tended to depress it, could at any given time be insufficient to ensure full employment. Classical economics was wrong on this central issue, with terrible consequences when its prescriptions were followed.

It was "a peculiarity of Keynes's work," FDR economic adviser Lauchlin Currie wrote in a review of *The General Theory*, "that he appears always to think of an increase in income as being generated by an increase in investment and never by an increase in consumption." Currie thought it "would make it more acceptable" to the president, however, if he placed the emphasis on *consumption* rather than investment, while still branding his analysis "Keynesian." This emphasis on using the federal budget to manipulate consumption levels became a hallmark of American fiscal Keynesianism.[93]

The most fundamental analytical question that has divided economists since publication of *The General Theory* is whether a situation of persistent mass unemployment can be characterized as an "equilibrium," meaning that it can exist *even if* all prices are perfectly flexible. This is where high theory and hard reality intersect, because the answer has important implications for policy. If the answer is yes, this was indeed a revolutionary insight, as it meant that there was no self-correcting mechanism in the market—a slump could go on forever unless government investment stepped in for what would otherwise be permanently deficient private investment. If the answer is no, however, then rather than initiate a self-sustaining recovery through the multiplier effect such intervention would mute the price signals calling for a shift in productive capacity toward more desired uses. The Keynesian solution addresses symptoms rather than causes, in the classical view, and thereby delays sustainable recovery.

This debate has never been resolved, as the same evidence is cited by each side to support its position. Thus the Japanese economic malaise of the 1990s was, in the Keynesian view, the result of premature termination of "fiscal stimulus," or, in the classical view, the result of an excessive reliance on it. The same debate repeated itself following the collapse of the U.S. housing market in 2007.

Keynes had struggled for years since his repudiation of the intellectual apparatus of *The Treatise* to induce a compelling theoretical cause for his burning belief that investment could, even under flexible prices, fail to harmonize with savings in a way that would maximize aggregate income. In *The General Theory*, he believed he had found it. It was the concept of "liquidity preference," or the idea that people might choose to hoard inert cash rather than consume or invest the fruits of their labor. The conviction that "money is the root of all evil," Skidelsky observed, "is almost a sub-text of the *General Theory*."[94] Liquidity preference was the theoretical kernel that seeded Keynes's new thinking about global monetary reform. For Keynes's French nemesis during the debate on German war reparations, Jacques Rueff, who would go on in the 1960s to be a leading critic of both Keynes's and White's Bretton Woods blueprints, it was not only the nub but the fatal flaw of *The General Theory* edifice. Critiques of *The General Theory* are many and disparate, but Rueff was surely right to see Keynes's account of the workings of the monetary system as the crux of his case against classical economics.[95]

In a *Quarterly Journal of Economics* article published three years after Bretton Woods and a year after Keynes's death, Rueff showed why, logically, "the demand for additional cash holdings," or what Keynes called derisively "the propensity to hoard," had to be "equivalent in its economic effects to demand for consumption goods or investment goods." If Rueff was right, Keynes had failed in his attempt to move beyond the *Treatise* and to establish a theoretical foundation for his bold policy prescriptions.

Rueff's defense of classical economics was most readily grasped in a commodity-based monetary system, such as the prewar gold standard, in that the demand for money was necessarily equivalent to the demand for mining, moving, and monetizing gold. Yet it held just as well, Rueff argued, in a fiat money system in which central banks issued cash in return for securities—securities representing "wealth which is either stored up or, more generally, on its way through the process of production." To demand money is not to demand nothingness, as Keynes would have it, but rather to demand real wealth capable of being monetized within the framework of the existing monetary system. So just as an increased demand for gold does not itself diminish the purchasing power impinging on the market, an increased demand for money does not itself do so.

Did it matter whether Keynes was right or wrong about money? "Had Keynes begun . . . with the simple statement that he found it realistic to assume that modern capitalistic societies had money wage rates that were sticky and resistant to downward movements," the great economist Paul Samuelson argued in 1964, "most of his insights would have remained just as valid."[96] This is the logical basis on which much Keynesian analysis today is undertaken—not on Keynes's theorizing about the unique menace of money (to which Keynes clung tenaciously). "Most people who admire Keynes," Joseph Schumpeter wryly observed, "take from him what is congenial to them and leave the rest."[97]

For his part, Rueff argued that Keynes's monetary and fiscal policy prescriptions had no sound basis. On the contrary, their inevitable result down the road would be inflation and a private productive apparatus less able to supply the goods and services people actually want.[98] Hubert Henderson and others had shared this view, but it did not become widespread until the stagflation of the 1970s and the consequent anti-Keynesian blowback. At that point, the implication of *The General Theory* that government could always, and predictably, improve on the laissez-faire outcome no longer seemed tenable. The revival of the book following the 2008 economic crisis was largely based on the notion that it was a reliable tract on depression economics, if not in fact a "general theory" that could be applied in boom times as well, as Keynes had held.

In early 1937, though, it was far from clear that *The General Theory* had much to offer in the way of immediate policy guidance. The British economy had been growing since 1932, with balanced budgets, low interest rates, and solid private-sector investment, particularly in building. Growth was 4.9 percent in 1936, 3.5 percent in 1937; unemployment, though still high at 8.5 percent, had fallen steadily year on year since 1932.[99] Economic orthodoxy appeared to be alive and well. But after the seemingly revitalized American economy went into a nosedive in the summer, Britain's downturn followed.

Keynes's own health also deteriorated markedly that year, with bouts of severe chest pain and exhaustion overcoming him. The diagnosis was subacute bacterial endocarditis, and resulting heart damage; antibiotics would be prescribed today, but they had not yet been invented. His Hungarian doctor, Janos Plesch, treated him with injections of a recently discovered antibacterial drug, which helped but never cured him. He would in the coming years show intermittent signs of recovery, yet he was now on a permanent downward trajectory.

Had it not been for the reemergence of the dark clouds of war, Keynes would likely have lived longer and died less notable. Though a liberal cosmopolitan like Einstein, Keynes was not a nationally uprooted one, which disposed him differently toward politics. Keynes was thoroughgoingly British, and it was the British problems of his day that drove his theorizing—problems of deflation and depression, paying for war and surviving the perilous transitions to peace. And when war came to Britain once again, Keynes, in spite of his delicate and deteriorating health, was ready to man the front lines of its critical financial engagement.

Keynes had believed passionately that the Versailles Peace Treaty had sown the seeds of future European conflict, and the rise of Hitler's Germany bore this out. Unlike Neville Chamberlain, who had become prime minister following Stanley Baldwin's resignation in May 1937, Keynes did not believe in a policy of chasing agreement with Hitler. But such objection did not extend to Britain resisting Hitler's provocations against the continental status quo. In a *New Statesman* article in March of 1938, Keynes urged that the Czechoslovakian government reach an accommodation with Germany over the Sudetenland, even if this required "a rectification of the Bohemian frontier."[100] When Chamberlain returned from Munich on September 30 declaring "peace in our time"—with German troops preparing to march past Czechoslovakia's frontier fortifications, rendering the country defenseless—Keynes called it "a tremendous relief." His criticism of Chamberlain at Munich was grounded in the fantastic belief that since "H[itler] was totally against war," the PM could somehow have done better by the Czechs had he been rhetorically tougher earlier.[101]

Though Keynes was unsparingly critical of Chamberlain in his private correspondence, there is more that unites the two men's outlook than Keynes would ever have conceded. Chamberlain saw war with Germany as a threat to the survival of the empire; Keynes was not attached to the empire as such, but understood better than anyone that the fraying economic ties of the empire were, given the immense cost of prosecuting another European war, the only bulwark against outright economic dependence on the United States.

Hitler, of course, made short shrift of his promises to respect the revised Czech borders. In March 1939, German troops occupied Prague, and the *Führer* quickly declared Bohemia and Moravia German protectorates. Chamberlain abruptly changed course and threw up a cordon sanitaire around Poland, guaranteeing its borders and independence. Such a pledge was even less credible than the idea of one for Czechoslovakia, which he had rejected the previous year.

Though the prime minister had grave doubts about the ability of the Red Army, reeling from Stalin's purges, to make any useful contribution to his belated efforts to halt further Nazi advances, negotiations were opened with Moscow. Hope vaporized, however, with the shocking signing of a Treaty of Non-Aggression, the so-called Molotov-Ribbentrop Pact, between the great ideological enemies, the Soviet Union and Nazi Germany, on August 23. Hitler invaded Poland on September 1. Britain declared war on Germany two days later. On the seventeenth, Soviet troops invaded Poland from the east. The Great War would thereafter be known as the First World War; the Second World War had begun.

British defense spending, which had previously not exceeded 7 percent of gross domestic product, reached 18 percent in 1939, before soaring to 46 percent in 1940.[102] This was the background against which Keynes returned to the Treasury.

Once war had started, Keynes focused, as he had during the First World War, on devising the right economic strategy for winning it. Fifty-six years old, in poor health, and too uncontrollable a force to be woven into Whitehall, he was not among the economists initially drafted into service. That did not stop him from forcefully stating his views, on paper and in person, on every subject from price controls (which he strongly opposed) to disrupting Romanian oil refining, with anyone in government who was in a position to push through policy.

He continued to speak out publicly as well. Demonstrating the flexibility of his *General Theory* approach, he explained in *The Times* of London why controlling excess demand, rather than overcoming inadequate demand, was now, in wartime, going to be the critical domestic problem.[103] His emphasis on the whys and hows of preventing inflation endeared him (temporarily) to Hayek while infuriating Labour Party mandarins, not least its leader Clement Attlee. The publicity the piece generated prodded Keynes to pen a pamphlet titled *How to Pay for the War*. Published in February 1940, it incorporated working-class supports to dampen attacks from the left, but stayed true to Keynes's classical-liberal conviction that the price system should be allowed to function as normally as possible—this even as the government restricted private purchasing power, through means such as compulsory savings, in order to ensure that war needs were met without consequent inflation.

Britain's first military intervention on the Continent came in April 1940, with a humiliating unsuccessful attempt to oust German forces from Norway. The political result was overwhelming political pressure on Chamberlain to give way either to Lord Halifax (Edward Wood), who carried more Conservative support, or to Churchill, who could garner more cross-party backing. Chamberlain went with Churchill, who was summoned on May 10 by King George VI and asked to take over as prime minister. Among his five-strong cross-party war cabinet Churchill appointed as chancellor fellow Conservative Kingsley Wood, who in June asked Keynes to join a Consultative Council. Keynes thought it a "super-dud Committee," but congenial insofar as it involved minimal formal obligations while affording direct access to the chancellor.[104] In August, however, he was also back where he truly longed to be: at Treasury, where he began serving on various committees as an unpaid adviser. Yet the appointments just kept coming; in January 1941 he was named economic adviser to the chancellor and in October a director of the Bank of England. The enfant terrible of the economics profession was now, remarkably, firmly entrenched within the British political establishment.

How to Pay for the War had less of a direct impact on specific elements of British war financing than Keynes would have wished; Wood's 1941 budget, for example, relied much more on taxation (particularly of the wealthy), price controls, and rationing than it did on Keynes's ideas for deferred pay. Yet Keynes's claim to his mother that he had brought about "a revolution in public finance" was not clearly an exaggeration.[105] For the first time, national income accounting was being used as a tool to regulate aggregate demand, which was indeed revolutionary. And though Keynes had written the pamphlet specifically to address the British war effort, it generated considerable interest across the Atlantic; the *New Republic* in July published an article titled "The United States and the Keynes Plan," applying Keynes's analysis to American conditions.[106]

Keynes was convinced from the outset of the war that American collaboration, if not necessarily troops, would be vital to Britain's war effort. In November 1939 he penned some tactless "Notes on the War for the President," advising Roosevelt among other things to "break off diplomatic relations with Germany and declare a state of nonintercourse."

Germany's "lapse," he noted, "is partly our fault. For twenty years we have behaved like asses."[107] The United States, Keynes further suggested, should provide credits to the Allies for the war effort, repayable after the victory over fascism to a reconstruction fund to save Europe from communism.[108] Having the previous year received a chilly presidential response to his first letter of unsolicited advice, and apparently none to his second, Keynes in the end judiciously decided against sending his "Notes."

Keynes would throughout the war continually overestimate American sympathies with Britain and underestimate the importance of public and congressional resistance to U.S. aid or involvement. To American eyes, the wickedness of German and Italian fascism was just one side of the debased western European coin; the abomination of British imperialism was the other. The British were, further, economic rivals who managed their empire so as to interfere with American exports, whose bankers and governments had conspired to undermine monetary stability, and who had shamefully walked away from their Great War debts.

By late 1940, Keynes had pivoted from domestic finance concerns to foreign ones, injecting himself into the inner circle of Treasury strategy making. He noted that Roosevelt would "ask in return [for aid] certainly some political concessions or agreements and perhaps economic ones," and therefore defined "the most pressing problem [as] retention by us of enough assets to leave us capable of independent action"—that is, to avoid becoming a satellite of the United States.[109] In an October 27 memorandum to Sir Frederick Phillips, who with David Waley was responsible for Overseas Finance at Treasury, he laid out his plan for preserving Britain's capacity to harvest dollars, vital to financing British purchases of overseas supplies, from its foreign trade and investments. Key to this plan was American financing of British military purchases in the United States, which he insisted must be in the form of grants rather than loans. Britain could not once again be forced to bear "the dishonour and the reproaches of default" while allowing the United States to sell at its convenience to foreign markets supplied by the British, thereby cutting off British means of repayment. The government had to guard "against the present emergency being used as an opportunity for picking the eyes out of the British Empire."[110]

The underlying assumption of the memo was that the United States was an ally in the war, though one that needed to be trained to behave like one. Such an assumption suffered from two key weaknesses: the United States was not yet at war with anyone, and was not about to be lectured as to what it was allowed to do in playing the role Keynes assigned to it. This he was about to learn in May 1941, on his first official visit to Washington since World War I.

CHAPTER 5

"The Most Unsordid Act"

In 1939 the United States was under the spell of isolationist senti-ment—or more accurately, sentiments, as the spectrum of views represented by those determined to keep the country out of war was enormous. It ranged from pacifists to pro-communists to pro-fascists, from those sympathetic to Germany to those who believed French and British resistance hopeless. Fewer than 3 percent sup-ported the United States entering the war at once on the side of France and Britain, whereas 30 percent were against even trade with any warring country.[1] Isolationist sentiments were reflected in a series of Neutrality Acts designed to keep the country from becoming entan-gled with belligerents on one side or the other. Legislation in 1935 insti-tuted an embargo on trading in arms and other war materials. The fol-lowing year Congress added a ban on loans or credits to belligerents, reflecting the findings of the so-called Nye Commission, which held that bankers had pushed the nation into World War I.

FDR, deeply concerned that Britain and France would be unable to defend themselves against German aggression without Ameri-can assistance, went before Congress on September 21 to argue for a relaxation of the embargo. He was convinced that if Britain fell it was only a matter of time before Germany, with all the shipbuilding facilities of Europe under its control, took the war to the Western Hemisphere. The secretaries of war and navy, the chief of staff of the army, and the chief of naval operations all concurred that Britain was holding positions vital to American defense, and that the only accept-able alternative to fortifying the British was to send American forces to occupy the positions. In the words of Roosevelt biographer Robert

Sherwood, FDR "knew that with Britain and her Navy gone all of our traditional concepts of security in the Atlantic Ocean—the Monroe Doctrine, the principle of freedom of the seas, the solidarity of the Western Hemisphere—would become mere memories, and the American people would be living constantly 'at the point of a Nazi gun.'"[2] A negotiated peace would equally have been a disaster, as it would have given Hitler valuable time and resources to consolidate his position and to rearm, while enhancing the influence of those against preparation for war in Britain, France, and, most importantly, the United States. "In my opinion," Roosevelt ventured with utmost political delicacy, the embargo was "most vitally dangerous to American neutrality, American security and, above all, American peace."[3]

The president chipped away at the embargo by persuading Congress to amend the '35 act on November 4. While still banning American ships from transporting American goods to belligerent ports, the act now allowed munitions sales on a "cash-and-carry" basis—that is, with the recipients paying in cash and providing transport on their own ships. Tweaking the act this way allowed the United States to direct material aid to Britain while still maintaining the guise of neutrality, as a lack of German funds and British control of the Atlantic sea lanes effectively prevented Germany from collecting goods under cash-and-carry.

The scheme proved tragically inadequate, however, to the needs of Germany's victims. Beginning with the invasions of Norway and Denmark in April 1940, and Holland, Belgium, Luxembourg, and France in May, Hitler snuffed out one democracy after another with horrifying efficiency. Civilians in the Low Countries were systematically machine-gunned and bombed as they tried desperately to flee the onslaught.[4] On May 10, the day German forces overran the Low Countries, British Prime Minister Neville Chamberlain, now forever disgraced by the Munich Agreement, resigned, and Winston Churchill was summoned to Buckingham Palace to succeed him.

The fighting in Belgium and France was, in Churchill's words, "a colossal military disaster." "The whole root and core and brain of the British Army" narrowly escaped complete annihilation at Dunkirk, with the heroic evacuation of over 338,000 British and French troops on a hastily assembled fleet of 850 boats between May 27 and June 4.

Nonetheless, almost the entirety of the British Army's equipment was lost, and there was no longer any doubt that Britain's survival hinged on the ability and willingness of the United States to produce and deliver enormous amounts of vital supplies. Britain could finance the purchases on a cash-and-carry basis for no more than a few months, after which British dollar and gold reserves would be exhausted.

Roosevelt knew he had to stretch his legal authority and, where he could not, he had to prod Congress to expand it if the United States were going to provide Britain with the large-scale and timely aid it needed to stay in the war. On June 10, the day Italy attacked France from the south, the president horrified his own custom-wedded conservative State Department with a speech thundering that "the hand that held the dagger"—referring to Italy's dictator Benito Mussolini—"has plunged it into the back of its neighbor." He then pledged that "[i]n our American unity, we will pursue two obvious and simultaneous courses; we will extend to the opponents of force the material resources of this nation; and at the same time, we will harness and speed up the use of those resources in order that we ourselves in the Americas may have equipment and training equal to the task of any emergency and every defense." Thus, with no congressional authority, FDR committed the United States both to aiding Germany and Italy's opponents and to preparing his own country for war.

Using highly questionable legal pretexts contrived by Treasury lawyers, the administration proceeded immediately by flying 150 war planes to Canada, where they were then loaded aboard a French aircraft carrier. But France surrendered before the carrier reached its destination, and the ships wound up waiting out the war in the Caribbean island of Martinique. The administration then raided the depleted U.S. arsenals for 500,000 rifles, 80,000 machine guns, 130,000,000 rounds of ammunition, 900 75-mm guns, 1,000,000 shells, and some bombs and TNT—again, with dubious legal authority—and shipped them to Britain, where their arrival was welcomed as manna from heaven. But many around the president argued that he was committing political suicide, or worse—as the weapons would fall into Hitler's hands soon enough, and then be turned against America.[5]

In Britain, the financial situation was going from bad to dire. Before the war, Britain had about $4.5 billion in reserves. Now, even after expropriating and liquidating the U.S. holdings of British citizens, the coffers were virtually empty. On November 25, British Ambassador Lord Lothian told American reporters that Britain was "beginning to come to the end of her financial resources," angering Roosevelt and Morgenthau, who surmised that his comments would make it even more difficult politically for the administration to continue providing assistance. "If Senator Nye or any other senator called me on the Hill," Morgenthau complained to the ambassador, "they would say, 'Well, on such and such a date Ambassador Lothian said the English were running short of money. By what authority did you let them place additional orders in this country?"[6] Nonetheless, Morgenthau understood the gravity of the situation, his own department having estimated that the British deficit would be $2 billion by June the following year. At the same time, he knew Congress would expect him to have drained the British dry before offering them assistance. This he set out to do, demanding of British Treasury official Sir Frederick Phillips a complete list of British holdings, securities, gold, and direct investments, each classified according to estimates of their liquidity.

Not everything, however, would do as payment. "There is one thing I know I can say for Mr. Roosevelt," the Secretary told him: "that we don't want any of those islands. . . . I know he doesn't want Jamaica, I know he doesn't want Trinidad, and I know he doesn't want British Guiana."[7]

On December 9, while officially inspecting new base sites in the West Indies, but in reality on a cruise aboard the *Tuscaloosa*, FDR received by navy seaplane a letter from Churchill of over four thousand words, going into remarkable detail about the war fronts in Europe, Africa, the Middle East, and Asia, emphasizing the critical problems of production and shipping. He argued that, in Britain and America's common interest, it was the British duty "to hold the front and grapple with the Nazi power until the [war] preparations of the United States are complete." In the meantime, Britain needed shipping, particularly destroyers, and supplies. He was candid in telling the president that "[t]he moment approaches when we shall no longer be able to pay cash" for such items. But, he suggested with palpable hesitancy, "I believe that you will agree that it would be wrong in principle and mutually disadvantageous in effect if, at the height of this struggle,

Great Britain were to be divested of all saleable assets so that after victory was won with our blood, civilization saved and time gained for the United States to be fully armed against all eventualities, we should stand stripped to the bone. Such a course would not be in the moral or economic interests of either of our countries. . . . Moreover I do not believe the government and people of the United States would find it in accordance with the principles which guide them, to confine the help which they have so generously promised only to such munitions of war and commodities as could be immediately paid for."[8] The contrast between the high-minded sentiments that Churchill ascribed to America, in the hopes that it might soon live up to them, and the global garage sale that Morgenthau was demanding of the British in order to avoid congressional defeat could not have been more stark.

Harry White estimated that British orders already placed in the United States, at least $5 billion, were vastly in excess of Britain's capacity to pay. Morgenthau wanted to know whether it was in America's interest to fill these orders, given that Britain might well not survive even with the matériel. Army Chief of Staff General George Marshall argued strongly that it was, given that the airplanes, tanks, and ordnance the British needed would be essential to American defense if Britain fell, as would the ramped up production capacity entailed. Secretary of War Henry Stimson concurred, urging no delay. The issue was getting the president on board; but he was on board a ship, and insisted that no action be taken before he had the chance to discuss the matter with Morgenthau on his return.[9]

Roosevelt had been genuinely moved by Churchill's letter—if not specifically by Britain's plight, then certainly by the consequences for the United States should Britain succumb. He knew that "cash-and-carry" and bootlegging behind Congress's back was no longer a viable basis on which to funnel supplies to Britain, and he was determined to find a new political formula to replace it. "We must find some way," he said, "to lease or even lend these goods to the British."

What he contrived was a political masterstroke. Returning to Washington on December 16, tanned and energized, he held a press conference the next day at which he asserted that "there is absolutely no doubt in the mind of a very overwhelming number of Americans that the best immediate defense of the United States is the success of

Britain in defending itself." Having established as fact a public sentiment that was, at that point, far from factual, he then erected a straw
man for himself to demolish. Some people, he said, thought we should
lend money to the British, while others thought we should give the
money as a gift. Few such people actually existed on either side, but
the image of the two polar camps served the president's rhetorical purpose, as he then went on to lay out his own ingenious middle ground:

> Now, what I am trying to do is eliminate the dollar sign. That is something
> brand new in the thoughts of everybody in this room, I think—get rid of
> the silly, foolish, old dollar sign. Well, let me give you an illustration. Sup-
> pose my neighbor's home catches fire, and I have a length of garden hose
> four or five hundred feet away. If he can take my garden hose and con-
> nect it up with his hydrant, I may help him to put out his fire. Now, what
> do I do? I don't say to him before that operation, "Neighbor, my garden
> hose cost me $15; you have to pay me $15 for it." What is the transaction
> that goes on? I don't want $15—I want my garden hose back after the fire
> is over. All right. If it goes through the fire all right, intact, without any
> damage to it, he gives it back to me and thanks me very much for the use
> of it. But suppose it gets smashed up—holes in it—during the fire; we
> don't have to have too much formality about it, but I say to him, "I was
> glad to lend you that hose; I see I can't use it any more, it's all smashed
> up." He says, "How many feet of it were there?" I tell him, "There were
> 150 feet of it." He says, "All right, I will replace it." Now, if I get a nice
> garden hose back, I am in pretty good shape.
>
> In other words, if you lend certain munitions and get the munitions back
> at the end of the war, if they are intact—haven't been hurt—you are all
> right; if they have been damaged or have deteriorated or have been lost
> completely, it seems to me you come out pretty well if you have them
> replaced by the fellow to whom you have lent them.
>
> I can't go into details; and there is no use asking legal questions about
> how you would do it, because that is the thing that is now under study;
> but the thought is that we would take over not all, but a very large num-
> ber of, future British orders; and when they came off the line, whether
> they were planes or guns or something else, we would enter into some
> kind of arrangement for their use by the British on the ground that it was

the best thing for American defense, with the understanding that when the show was over, we would get repaid sometime in kind, thereby leaving out the dollar mark in the form of a dollar debt and substituting for it a gentleman's obligation to repay in kind. I think you all get it.

Britain, as Roosevelt framed it, was asking America to borrow a garden hose in a dire emergency, and it would be foolish and dastardly of America to try to sell the hose instead. Had the president simply asked Congress for a blank check to aid the British war effort he would have faced certain overwhelming defeat, with catastrophic consequences for the remaining European resistance to Hitler's onslaught. But the garden hose analogy struck a chord with the American public, and gave the president a fighting chance for passing what became known as the Lend-Lease Act.

Roosevelt assigned the job of drafting "Lend-Spend, Lend-Lease—whatever you call it"[10] to Treasury, and Morgenthau delegated it to General Counsel Edward Foley and his associate Oscar Cox. Treasury took every precaution to make sure the bill would survive not just hostile congressional scrutiny, but subsequent judicial review, with Morgenthau going so far as to solicit judicious rewordings from Supreme Court Justice, and close Roosevelt friend, Felix Frankfurter—to whom the "Bill Further to promote the defense of the United States, and for other purposes" owed its shrewd, if inelegant, title. The Democratic House and Senate majority leaders John McCormack of Massachusetts and Alben Barkley of Kentucky put the icing on the cake by introducing the bill in their respective chambers with the patriotic number "H.R. 1776."

Nonetheless, passage was far from smooth sailing. Republicans on the House Foreign Affairs Committee put Morgenthau, Hull, and Stimson through bruising testimony. For the British, it was abject humiliation to have the U.S. Treasury Secretary, armed with figures prepared by White, testifying on the depths of British penury and speculating on what little might remain to be picked off the empire's carcass in return for American support.

Resistance to the plan was bolstered by the forced resignation of the U.S. ambassador to Britain, Joseph Kennedy, a hated figure in Downing Street, who admonished Congress that this was "not our war." Charismatic aviation hero Charles Lindbergh also took up the opposition cause. "We are in danger of war today, not because Europeans attempted to interfere in our internal affairs," Lindbergh insisted, "but because Americans attempted to interfere in the internal affairs of Europe. . . . If we desire peace, we need only stop asking for war."[11] Lend-Lease was widely painted as a measure likely to bankrupt America and drag it into a hopeless conflict remote from the nation's vital interests.

House Democrats made clear to Hull and Morgenthau that the bill would not survive without amendment. One such amendment limited the time during which the president might authorize Lend-Lease agreements but, significantly, did not restrict the period during which the agreements might be carried out. Another placed a cap of $1.3 billion on the value of existing military supplies or those on order that might be transferred to foreign governments but, again significantly, did not restrict the value of future aid. On February 8, 1941, two days after Hitler signed his Directive No. 23 calling for stepped-up operations on the British war economy, particularly sea attacks on merchant shipping and air attacks on armaments factories,[12] the Lend-Lease bill passed in the House by an impressive majority of 260 to 165, with 24 Republicans voting in favor.

The seas were stormier in the Senate, where Ohio Republican Robert A. Taft, who would later prove a formidable opponent of Bretton Woods, was joined by Democrats James Byrnes of South Carolina and Harry Byrd of Virginia in adding an amendment specifying that Lend-Lease assistance could only be supplied out of funds provided by Congress specifically for that purpose. With the president incapacitated with the flu, Morgenthau and Stimson led the fight to restore presidential authority in doling out the aid. Foley drafted a revision that flipped the amendment on its head, giving Congress the power to impose specific restrictions on the president's ability to dispose of defense articles abroad, but not the power to define in advance what the president could do. This did the trick, and the bill passed the Senate by a vote of 60 to 31. It became the law of the land on March 11, 1941.

Notwithstanding the tethers Congress placed on presidential Lend-Lease authority, it was a remarkable legislative victory for the White House, sweeping aside the formidable isolationist barriers erected by the Neutrality and Johnson (Foreign Securities) acts. In doing so, Roosevelt had had no wellspring of public affection for the British that he could summon to his aid. "In the 1940s," observed British historian Michael Howard, "the Americans had some reason to regard the British as a lot of toffee-nosed bastards who oppressed half the world and had a sinister talent for getting other people to do their fighting for them."[13] Memories were also fresh of Britain's failure to repay its Great War debts. Yet a wary Congress had nonetheless acceded, by a substantial majority, to making the United States a partisan and patron to the British in yet another European war.

Lend-Lease was greeted with enormous relief in London. The weekend following its passage saw two German warships sink sixteen British merchant ships in the Atlantic, adding to the urgency of American aid.[14] Churchill spoke in the House of Commons of Britain's "deep and respectful appreciation of this monument of generous and far-seeing statesmanship."[15] And in a famous line that many have mistakenly associated with the postwar Marshall Plan, Churchill later praised Lend-Lease as "the most unsordid act in the whole of recorded history."[16] Yet Churchill was painfully aware of just how grudging the assistance was. He was simply unable politically to vocalize it in the way one of his Tory colleagues did: "The idea of being our armoury and supply furnishers seems to appeal to the Yanks as their share in the war for democracy. . . . They are a quaint lot—they are told that if we lose the war they will be next on Hitler's list . . . and yet they seem quite content to leave the actual fighting to us; they will do anything except fight."[17]

What Churchill had certainly not understood at the time was how costly Lend-Lease assistance would turn out to be after the war. The Act to Promote the Defense of the United States, as its official name made clear, was not intended as an act of generosity. Roosevelt, who had promised the electorate in 1940 that American "boys [would not] be sent into any foreign wars,"[18] contrived it as a stopgap means of keeping Germany and Japan at bay; that it happened also to be essential to Britain's survival was largely incidental.

More importantly, Roosevelt's garden hose analogy was deeply warped during the legislative process. "Laws, like sausages," observed poet John Godfrey Saxe seventy-two years earlier, "cease to inspire respect in proportion as we know how they are made."[19] Though the title of the act suggested that lending hoses to the British brought a direct reciprocal benefit to the United States, the text of the act, as it emerged from the sausage grinder, recognized no such benefit. In fact, Congress required that the president secure "payment or repayment in kind or property, or any other direct or indirect benefit which the President deems satisfactory." The hoses would then, after all, only be lent at a price. The "dollar sign" was back. If the wording nonetheless seemed to leave room for the president to be generous, as Churchill wanted to believe he was, FDR's economic advisers chose to take none of it. Though Roosevelt played only fleeting direct roles in the subsequent bargaining over the price of the hoses, Morgenthau, White, and Hull would for years use Lend-Lease to press the British relentlessly for financial and trade concessions that would eliminate Britain as an economic and political rival in the postwar landscape.

Henry Morgenthau was, in the words of his official biographer, John Morton Blum, "a good friend to the British." Yet "in his negotiations with them [he] was also a dogged protagonist of American interests." Recognizing the critical importance of, and greatly admiring, Britain's lonesome and courageous stand against Hitler in 1940 and 1941, he worked harder than anyone to push Lend-Lease through Congress. "Yet no one was more certain than Morgenthau that British and American interests were not identical, however much both peoples were dedicated to destroying Nazism."[20] Morgenthau saw the financiers of the City of London, like those of Wall Street, as a force hostile to the aims of the New Deal. Knowing that the British saw in Lend-Lease not just a means of securing vital wartime supplies, but also a means of conserving precious gold and dollar balances that would prove essential to preserving their empire and influence after the war, the Secretary was determined not to let these balances grow beyond the minimum necessary for Britain to survive the war.

In gauging and monitoring these balances, he was wholly dependent on White, who in Blum's words was "an ardent nationalist in his monetary thinking," and "sought openly, with the Secretary's approval, to make the dollar the dominant currency in the postwar world." White therefore also resisted, even "more vigorously than Morgenthau, any deliberate expansion of England's gold and dollar holdings."[21]

On the issue of British balances, Morgenthau and White were themselves vigorously opposed by the State Department—specifically Secretary Hull and the arch-Anglophile Dean Acheson, who had reemerged in 1941 as his assistant secretary after a hiatus from government following his Treasury resignation in 1933. Hull, who believed passionately that free trade was essential to international peace, considered a solvent Britain to be indispensable to reconstituting such trade after the war. Morgenthau and White, however, had the vital advantage of being aligned with a Congress that jealously guarded its Lend-Lease appropriations authority, which had to be renewed every six months.

In fact, "Congress was spontaneously more generous toward China than toward England, perhaps because no one envisaged China as a postwar rival for power or commerce."[22] Even the Soviet Union was treated more leniently, as the British bitterly noted.[23]

What drove Harry White to take his hard line on British reserves and trade policy? In 1938 and 1939, memo after memo in White's archives reveals a Treasury Department obsessed with the sterling-dollar exchange rate, and what a further decline in sterling might mean for America's competitive position. Prepared for White and Morgenthau by White's deputies, they provide detailed analyses of Britain's accounts, estimating the likelihood of, and anticipating possible justifications for, significant sterling depreciation. The underlying economic concern was that, as one such memo put it, "most currencies drop with sterling and a decline in sterling really involves the appreciation of the dollar in terms of most currencies. This makes a decline in sterling more important for the United States and less important to England."[24]

"If sterling declines," explains another memo, " . . . increased pressure would be placed upon practically all currencies in the world. . . . Japan and Germany would be stimulated to resort on a greater scale to various devices for maintaining their markets . . . [and] it might create a public demand for a revision of the [U.S.-UK] Trade Agreement. The consequence of such unsettlement in the international monetary sphere cannot aid world recovery and may initiate resumption of a downward trend."[25] Another memo quantifies the loss of U.S. trade competitiveness from foreign currency depreciation at 8 percent, versus a gain of 3 percent for the United Kingdom, in the year to February 1939, and lays blame on "the instability of the sterling-dollar rate, particularly the expectation in financial circles of the intentions of the British authorities with regard to the sterling rate."[26] The bitterness toward Britain in the memos is palpable. Retaliation is proposed in the form of publicly rebuking Britain for violating the Tripartite Agreement, taking action against British imports, raising the Treasury buying price for foreign gold to offset any sterling fall, or dumping sterling for gold (which might involve U.S. exchange losses, but trigger a much bigger British reserves crisis).[27] Against this background, it is clear why Treasury would seek to use Lend-Lease leverage to put a permanent end to sterling's international role. This would necessarily involve dismantling the structural supports of the empire.

No Briton read the U.S. Treasury's intentions better, and resented them more bitterly, than Maynard Keynes. While his prime minister was extolling American generosity before parliament, Keynes was blasting Morgenthau for exploiting Britain's vulnerability as it was struggling for physical survival in common cause. Acknowledging the Secretary's need "to placate opposition in Congress," Keynes accused him nonetheless of trying to maximize "his future power to impose his will on us." Morgenthau was "stripping us of our liquid assets to the greatest extent possible *before* the Lend Lease Bill comes into operation, so as to leave us with the minimum in hand to meet during the rest of the war the numerous obligations which will not be covered by the Lend Lease Bill." And in a parting shot nicely capturing the milieu in which he had been raised, Keynes charged the Secretary with "treat[ing] us worse than we have ever ourselves thought it proper to treat the humblest and least responsible Balkan country."[28]

With Lend-Lease passed, Congress still had to approve a $7 billion appropriation bill to make it operational. But the House Appropriations Committee was demanding that none of that money be used to cover materials ordered before March 11, 1941. Given that Morgenthau had previously assured Congress that Britain could pay for whatever it had ordered, this was a logical requirement. The administration therefore pressed Britain to liquidate further assets quickly. This included major companies. Courtaulds' American Viscose Corporation, a fiber producer representing Britain's largest and most profitable U.S. holding, was sold to an American banking group for $54 million, roughly half its actual value.[29] Were we "to sell by hook or by crook every direct investment which can conceivably find even a bad market in the course of the next six months or so?" Keynes demanded incredulously. "If so, this is capitulation. . . . Surely, we cannot contemplate that without a struggle."[30]

Keynes had one powerful American ally in London: ambassador John Gilbert Winant. Tall, dark, angular, and soft-spoken, he was warmly regarded in England after the tenure of his acerbic Anglo-phobe predecessor, Joe Kennedy. Today, Winant is best known for his affair with Churchill's second daughter, Sarah, as well as for killing himself with a gunshot to the head in 1947.

Keynes vented to Winant over the lack of understanding in America of Britain's tremendous sacrifice. Winant urged Keynes to travel to Washington and put his case in person. It was quickly agreed in the UK Treasury that he should go as the chancellor's personal representa-tive. Keynes's mission, the press was informed, would be "to establish a clearer definition of what is to be included in Lend Lease." After an arduous series of flights lasting nearly a week, he and Lydia arrived in New York on May 8, 1941, with flashing press cameras awaiting them. This was the first of Keynes's six official Treasury trips to the United States during the 1940s, four of them during the war.[31]

The choice of Maynard Keynes for such a critical diplomatic mis-sion was a calculated gamble by the British government. He had no official government title. Even his peerage was still a year away. He was not a diplomat: though he mastered the English language like no economist before or since, he was congenitally undiplomatic. Faced with the choice between stroking his host and turning a phrase, he typically chose the latter. But Lothian had failed. Halifax, his replace-ment, had failed. The Americans were unmoved by their titles or sta-tus or experience or connections. Like the pound sterling, their value was now purely domestic. What Keynes had that still commanded genuine regard in America was celebrity status. Brilliant, controver-sial, and eminently quotable, Keynes provided an endless stream of good copy for fascinated journalists. For his part, Keynes was struck by the power and maliciousness of the American press. The only group in the country he may have loathed more was lawyers: "Surely the plague of lawyers . . . is a worse plague of Egypt than the Pharaoh ever knew."[32]

Keynes was briefed in New York and Washington on the American personalities and attitudes he was soon to face; of White he was warned that the statistician was "deeply suspicious of us."[33] More precisely, White revered Keynes as an economist, but was acutely aware of the United States' overwhelmingly favorable bargaining position and was determined not to be bested by mere clever words, unsupported by dollars or gold. One would imagine that Keynes had White in mind when he reported back to the chancellor on June 2 that "the younger Civil Servants and advisers strike me as exceptionally capable and vigorous (with the very gritty Jewish type perhaps a little too prominent)."[34]

As for Morgenthau, Keynes was woefully unprepared for their inaugural encounter, which could hardly have gone worse for the British. Appearing to settle in for an amiable dialogue in which he, Keynes, would sort out all previous misunderstandings and illogicalities in Lend-Lease arrangements, the British special envoy was instead met with a stony, probing Treasury Secretary whose only concern was to ensure that nothing would upset his hard-won accommodation between the president and Congress.

Keynes had no appreciation for the complexities of the American separation of powers—he had never visited and would never visit Congress, and knew few congressmen. While he took it virtually for granted that he could show Morgenthau the sense of limiting Lend-Lease to armaments and agriculture, leaving Britain to build up dollar reserves "to meet unforeseen situations," he succeeded only in piquing the Secretary's suspicions that the British would try to exploit Lend-Lease to spruce up their finances. Morgenthau shot back terse queries about British intentions, which Keynes defensively put down to the Secretary's "method of protection until he is quite sure what you are after. It is . . . most difficult to get him to see one's real point, and misunderstandings peep out at every corner."[35]

Keynes could not fathom that the Americans did not share British interests. He acted as if the Americans simply did not comprehend that Lend-Lease, as structured, would wreck Britain's room for maneuver beyond the immediate task of repelling the Nazis. Morgenthau, for his part, understood this just fine, however dim his ken for details, and thought it rudely unbusinesslike of the British to reopen a transaction.

Keynes made it worse with a subsequent May 16 memo to Morgenthau, in which he proposed an alternative scheme under which Britain would formally ask the United States to Lend-Lease it fewer politically difficult items, in return for which the Americans would take over existing British financial commitments, leaving Britain with more dollars and therefore more independence of action. Even if Morgenthau had been sympathetic, which he was not, his authority was severely circumscribed by a mulish Congress and a president who intentionally played off domestic power centers one against another, and Keynes's relentless flow of ideas threatened to embarrass him by revealing his impotence. This, more than any personal animus against Keynes, exasperated the Secretary.

Morgenthau discovered that Keynes, not at all surprisingly, had been operating through multiple channels, trying to minimize distress sales of British companies through, among other methods, loans from the New Deal Reconstruction Finance Corporation, headed by Secretary of Commerce and Morgenthau rival Jesse Jones. Keynes's efforts to get his mission sponsored by Winant backfired, as the Secretary suspected the ambassador of acting in consort with Jones. Unmoved by Keynes's efforts to humanize Britain's plight in his cover letter, Morgenthau read passages out to Sir Frederick Phillips, the UK Treasury representative in Washington, "in derisive tones," concluding "that the sole purpose [of Keynes's U.S. mission] is to sabotage the Viscose deal."[36] He called Halifax from the White House, demanding angrily to know who represented the British Treasury in Washington and what the nature of Keynes's mission was. (Phillips was in charge, replied Halifax, and Keynes was in Washington on Lend-Lease business only.)

On June 17, Keynes sent a follow-up memo to Roosevelt's close friend, soon-to-be personal envoy to London, and Lend-Lease czar Harry Hopkins, containing yet more ideas for extending and improving Lend-Lease. "I've got a long letter from Keynes—a long-winded letter from Keynes," Hopkins told Morgenthau. "I don't like his style and approach. My own opinion is that except from the point of view of the British Treasury, he'd just be well off at home."

"You and me, both," replied the Secretary.

"Here's the point about Keynes," continued Hopkins. "If he hangs around here until we get mixed up in a new Lend-Lease bill, he's apt to pull something and he'll be telling us how to write a Lend-Lease bill and people will get madder than hell here about it."

"Well, now God damn it, if he's here for the Treasury . . . his business is to be writing you letters and sending me copies," the Secretary concluded. "You see what he's going to do, he's going to move on any front he thinks he can move on . . . if I'd got a two line note or copy of a note from Phillips, which . . . would have said, well, now, we're in quite a jam and wish you would help us out—personally, I undoubtedly would stir my stumps far more than getting a six page letter from Keynes, you see? . . . He's one of those fellows that just knows all the answers, you see?"[37]

Just as Churchill failed in his incessant efforts over many years to woo Roosevelt into an emotional commitment to Britain's cause, Keynes likewise never succeeded in engaging Morgenthau at this level. "Everybody agrees that he is jealous and suspicious and subject to moods of depression and irritation," Keynes wrote of the Secretary, sounding more like a scorned lover than a professional envoy.[38] Nonetheless, Keynes was able to persuade himself—as Churchill did with Roosevelt—that Morgenthau's flashes of good humor were signs of true warmth and deep feeling. While one must "make allowance for the extreme jealousy of colleagues," Keynes concluded of Morgenthau's rivalry with Jones, the Secretary "is one of Great Britain's best and truest friends in the Administration."[39] This was accurate. The White House had nothing more congenial on offer.

As for Roosevelt himself, Keynes met him twice in the course of his eleven-week sojourn (and only once thereafter, in 1944). As was his wont, Keynes found his interlocutor "in grand form" when FDR was engaging toward him, as in his first visit on May 28, and "fundamentally weak and tired" as in his second on July 7, when he was not. "The President was in good form," Halifax observed, "though Keynes thought he was tired. . . . The truth I think was that he was not greatly interested in the detail of Keynes's subject."[40]

Whereas Keynes had seized the initiative in the spring with a fruitless effort to make Lend-Lease more friendly to British concerns about financial independence, the Americans took control of the discussion and turned it on its head in late June. It was time to put flesh on "the consideration" that Britain would provide the United States in return for Lend-Lease.

Keynes was caught between the rock of Morgenthau and the hard place of Hull. Morgenthau and the Treasury team were determined to control Britain's dollar and gold reserves by policing its exports, thereby minimizing the country's financial independence—the opposite, naturally, of what Keynes was seeking. But to add grievous insult to such injury, Hull's State Department, which Roosevelt had in May designated to lead the consideration negotiations, had a separate and sometimes conflicting priority: to dismantle Britain's "imperial preference" trading system. The grand principle behind this demand was that the postwar world needed to be grounded in nondiscriminatory multilateral trade—a longtime obsession of Hull's.

Bitterness toward the economics of empire had been growing for decades. "Excluded nations cannot be expected to accept the fiction of empire," wrote American diplomat and Hull ally William Culbertson in 1925, "in justification of their exclusion from extensive areas of the earth's surface."[41]

The currency and trade issues melded in the pot of imperial preference, which became more of a "mandate" than a "preference" under wartime practices. By the summer of 1940, Britain was dangerously short of dollars, and all "hard currency" transactions by British residents were made subject to exchange control and imports minimized through licensing. Inhabitants of "sterling area" countries could use the British pounds they accumulated from exports within the area, but as British exports plunged, so the "sterling balances"—that is, British debts—owed to these countries grew. By agreement, the precious dollars they fetched from exports were pooled in London, and only drawn on to buy essential American exports. As regards nonsterling countries, Britain negotiated agreements with neutrals in Europe and Latin America to pay them for exports in "area pounds sterling," which could only be used for goods and services bought within the sterling area.[42]

The net effect was that Britain kept the global demand for American exports artificially low by blocking the conversion of pounds into dollars (the issue referred to as "blocked balances"), and by controlling its dominions' spending of the dollars they earned directly. This naturally mobilized American exporters and congressmen to clamor for full and equal access to Britain's traditional export markets. Keynes was constantly on the defensive in Washington, at one point publicly having to rebut congressional and media charges that Britain was using Lend-Leased goods specifically to undercut the United States in Latin America. Hopkins' Lend-Lease administration responded to the clamor by proposing that British exports be limited to historical specialties like whiskey and Harris tweed, provoking Keynes to suggest sarcastically that it might consider adding haggis.[43]

The State Department presented its British Lend-Lease proposal to Keynes on July 28. Hull's free-trade principle was summed up in the famous Article VII, which stated that

> the terms and conditions upon which the United Kingdom receives defense aid from the United States of America and the benefits to be received by the United States in return therefore, shall be such as not to burden commerce between the two countries but to promote mutually advantageous economic relations between them and the betterment of world-wide economic relations; they shall provide against discrimination in either the United States of America or the United Kingdom against the importation of any produce originating in the other country; and they shall provide for the formulation of measures for the achievement of these ends.

As innocuous as such a statement might appear, it was sufficient to tip Keynes into a rage. "The lunatic proposals of Mr. Hull," he called them.[44]

British business was alarmed. "It is easy to talk of Anglo-American co-operation, but we must be realistic and face the difficulties," insisted the London Chamber of Commerce:

> After the war we shall not be in the same favourable position as in the past. Instead of being a creditor, we shall be a debtor nation.. . . . In such circumstances the view is widely held in industrial circles in this country that we must, at any rate for some considerable period, rely on a policy of directive imports, on the assumption that we only import from overseas countries those essential commodities for which such overseas countries are prepared to accept payment by the only means which will be open to us—i.e., by the export of our own produces and such services as we can render. In effect, almost a system of barter, or, at any rate, a system of

bilateral trade which will regulate our imports by our capacity to pay for them. This involves import and export controls, possibly by quota, preferential treatment of the imports of those countries which are prepared to assure us of the means of paying for them, and exchange control.[45]

What lay behind Hull's idea, in Keynes's mind, was an abolition of all rational trade regulation and exchange controls—all manner of sound national economic management. These would be particularly vital prerogatives for Britain after the war, faced, as it surely would be, with a vast balance-of-payments problem. Keynes further saw Hull's free-trade "principle" as disingenuous, since it could accommodate many clever forms of American import tariffs.

Keynes's most important American ally, Dean Acheson, strongly opposed the Treasury agenda, which "envisage[ed] a victory where both enemies and allies were prostrate—enemies by military action, allies by bankruptcy,"[46] while defending the State Department's agenda against what he considered to be Keynes's dark imaginings. But Keynes was hardly alone in his view. While he himself was concerned with Britain's economic welfare, and not the empire as such, compatriots in Churchill's cabinet such as Leo Amery, secretary of state for India, and Lord Beaverbrook, minister of supply, were staunch imperialists and unflinching in their political opposition to Article VII demands.

Keynes actually hurt his country's cause by articulating the logical necessity of postwar British trade discrimination so fulsomely. Harry Hawkins, then head of the State Department's Division of Commercial Policy, shot him back a counterwarning that such action would inevitably provoke a trade war with the United States: a war Britain could not win. Keynes, Hawkins said, "wholly fails to see that after the sacrifices the American people are called upon to make to help Great Britain in the present emergency (even though we are thereby helping ourselves), our public opinion simply would not tolerate discrimination against our products in Great Britain and, at Great Britain's insistence, other countries." Keynes's intellectual footprint did not help his case: Britain had to remain "as free as possible of interference from economic changes elsewhere, in order to make our own favourite experiments toward the ideal social republic of the future," he had written in 1933.[47] This reinforced Hawkins in his view that "specific provisions for postwar economic policy [had to be] in the Consideration Agreement." As for Keynes himself, Hawkins said, he should, once he returned to London, stay there. His "well-known obstinacy" was bound to scuttle an agreement.[48]

"Few lovers expended as much ink and thought upon wartime correspondence as did the prime minister on his long letters to Roosevelt," reflected Churchill biographer Max Hastings, "sometimes dispatched twice or thrice weekly." Though at times near bursting with frustration over his unrequited affection for FDR, Churchill persisted in the hopes that the president would, before it was too late, come to see the unity of Anglo-American purpose that the prime minister tried to manufacture for him. Thus the PM's "hopes were unbounded" when the president finally proposed a secret August 9 rendezvous aboard the U.S. cruiser *Augusta* in Placentia Bay, off the coast of Newfoundland. "I must say," Churchill excitedly wrote to the queen, "I do not think our friend would have asked me to go so far for what must be a meeting of world-wide notice, unless he had in mind some further forward step."[49]

Roosevelt was in fine form: "unfailing geniality, matched by the opacity which characterised his conversation on every issue of delicacy."[50] Yet the president was still in no position politically to make military commitments. Instead, he wanted commitments from the British; commitments to common principles that would show the world, and particularly Congress and the American people, that the British were fighting, with American support, for a better postwar world. The United States could not be seen simply sticking its nose into yet another bloody Old World power squabble.

The Russians—who on August 11 launched their first air raid on Berlin, and would nine days later suffer the beginnings of the horrific nine-hundred-day German siege of Leningrad—apparently saw the Anglo-American meeting in a distinctly threatening light; this despite the fact that Roosevelt and Churchill agreed on board to provide Russia with immediate aid "on a gigantic scale."[51] Thirty years later, a Soviet biographer of Churchill wrote that "plans were worked out [at Placentia Bay] to establish Anglo-American domination of the post-war world."[52]

Whereas FDR himself, in common with Churchill, had little interest in pushing economic principles, his advisers would not pass up the opportunity to nail down their Article VII aims—particularly given Keynes's forthright objections to them. State Department Under-Secretary Sumner Welles brusquely told his British counterpart, Sir Alexander Cadogan, that postwar reconstruction would require "the freest possible economic interchange without discriminations, without exchange controls, without economic preferences utilized for political purposes and without all of the manifold economic barriers which had in my judgment been so clearly responsible for the present world collapse," taking aim at those in Britain who were looking to forge "exactly the same kind of system which had proved so fatal during the past generation."[53]

Churchill was anxious for the opportunity afforded by FDR to set down their common vows in public. He produced a draft overnight, which suggested it had been sketched earlier, anticipatorily. "Considering all the tales of my reactionary, Old World outlook, and the pain this is said to have caused the President," Churchill reflected years later, "I am glad that it should be on record that the substance and spirit of what came to be called the 'Atlantic Charter' was in its first draft a British production cast in my own words."[54]

The primary principles enumerated were self-determination, freedom of the seas, and freedom "from fear and want." These created little fuss. The hornet's nest was in the economics.

Churchill proposed that the United States and United Kingdom would "strive to bring about a fair and equitable distribution of essential produce, not only within their territorial boundaries, but between nations of the world." This produced in Welles only a slightly milder allergic reaction than the American Article VII elicited in Keynes. Churchill's pabulum, Welles harrumphed, "meant precisely nothing. They were reminiscent of the pious hopes expressed in a thousand and one economic conferences that 'a fair equitable international distribution of commodities' would come into being, during the very years when tariffs were being built up in the United States, and when every variety of discriminatory trade barrier was being erected in an increasingly autarchic world." But it was "the United Kingdom [that] had placed the final stone upon the grave of . . . liberal trade policies" through the 1932 Ottawa Agreements, which "were designed to force every component part of the British Empire, covering a quarter of the globe, to trade solely within that area." Therefore, "Unless the declaration now to be issued contained the firm commitment that the British government would join the United States after the war in trade policies which would eliminate all such fatal impediments to international trade . . . there would patently exist no assurance of any new and better world economic order to come."[55] Keynes, now back in London, would, if in a charitable mood, have dismissed this as ignorant free-trade blubber.

Welles rewrote Churchill's fourth principle. The United States and United Kingdom would now

> strive to promote mutually advantageous economic relations between them through the elimination of any discrimination in either the United States of America or the United Kingdom against the importation of any product originating in the other country; and they will endeavor to further the enjoyment by all peoples of access on equal terms to the markets and to the raw materials which are needed for their economic prosperity.

This was essentially Keynes's hated Article VII.

Recognizing brevity as the soul of wit, and discrimination as the bugbear of his State Department, Roosevelt simply struck out everything before the semicolon and scribbled in a few key words after: the U.S. and UK would, according to this third rendering, "endeavor to further the enjoyment by all peoples of access, *without discrimination and* on equal terms to the markets and to the raw materials *of the world* which are needed for their economic prosperity" (italics added).

Churchill was not slow to pick up on the target of the text. Upon reading it, he immediately inquired of Welles whether it was meant to apply to the Ottawa Agreements. Welles affirmed that "of course it did." The PM masterfully held himself out as a well-known opponent of the agreements, while insisting that it would take "at least a week before he could hope to obtain by telegraph the opinion of the Dominions with regard to this question."[56]

Hopkins wanted Welles and Cadogan quickly to draw up new phraseology that Churchill could sign without delay, to which Welles objected that "further modification of that article would destroy completely any value in that portion of the proposed declaration." His memoirs claim the president to have been "strongly of the same opinion," leaving him to grump that Hopkins must have persuaded FDR that the matter was not "of sufficient importance to warrant any delay in reaching agreement upon the final text."[57] FDR memoed to Welles that "time being of the essence" he would eliminate "the only [subject] in conflict: discrimination in trade," disassociating himself from Hull and Welles's anti-imperial trade agenda. Thus, over Welles's objections, the fourth principle of the Atlantic Charter ultimately pledged the two countries to "endeavor, *with due respect for their existing obligations*, to further the enjoyment by all States, great or small, victor or vanquished, of access, on equal terms, to the trade and to the raw materials of the world which are needed for their economic prosperity" (italics added). Churchill cabled London triumphantly that the "Phrase about 'respect for existing obligations' safeguards our relations with Dominions."[58]

The Charter was released in a communiqué on August 14. It was never signed, in order to avoid having to have it ratified as a treaty by the U.S. Senate. Still, the document aroused bitter opposition from isolationist congressmen, obliging the administration to insist that it involved "no moral obligation of any sort during or after the war."[59]

Welles and Hull were buoyant in public—"The age of imperialism is ended," announced Welles—but fuming in private. In his memoirs, Hull said the existing-obligations clause "deprived the article of virtually all significance." In a desperate act of petulance, he even proposed weeks after the conference adding to the fourth principle an unqualified commitment to the elimination of imperial preference. Winant reported back from London that Churchill, unsurprisingly, was not keen on presenting such an amendment to his cabinet or to the dominion governments.[60] Hull retreated.

The British had won a round, but would inevitably lose the fight. The Atlantic Charter was a statement, and words were cheap. But Lend-Lease was a contract between a desperate buyer and a monopoly seller. While Lend-Lease supplies continued to flow to Britain, the settlement terms had yet to be agreed, and the State Department was still determined to get its "consideration."

Negotiations between the State Department and the British embassy over Article VII dragged on into the autumn. Though State was immovable on the elimination of imperial preference, British negotiators made headway on two fronts. First, they persuaded State that the achievement of this aim should be determined by "agreed action," and that such action would be determined "in the light of governing economic conditions." Second, they achieved a vague American "consideration" for their own consideration on trade in the form of an American commitment to take "appropriate . . . domestic measures, of production, employment, and the exchange and consumption of goods," in the case of an economic slump. This addressed Keynes's concern that the United States would transmit recessions abroad by failing to take countervailing monetary and fiscal action, while simultaneously hog-tying other countries' freedom of action to do so.

Still, some three-quarters of Churchill's war cabinet opposed any reference to trade preferences in Lend-Lease. Even those not afflicted with sentimental attachment to imperial preference, such as the prime minister himself, found offensive the impression that Britain was bartering away the foundations of its empire in return for war goods.

As was so often the case during the war, the British were ultimately compelled to submit themselves to the calculated, fugacious goodwill of the American president. In February 1942, Roosevelt, at Hull's urging, cabled Churchill asking for quick approval of the new Article VII draft. But Britain's war efforts were faltering—Singapore had fallen to the Japanese on February 15—and the president was responsive to Churchill's concern that further Article VII wrangling could provide fodder for enemy propagandists who were claiming that the United States was exploiting Britain's war emergency to seize control of the empire. Roosevelt, rejecting the State Department's formal draft reply, cabled back "in his own intensely personal and considerate manner" that "nothing could be further from his mind than an attempt to use Lend-Lease as a trading weapon over the principle of imperial preference."[61] This was sufficient to mollify the British cabinet, and the British-American Lend-Lease Agreement was finally signed on February 23.

It was not, however, sufficient to bind the administration. Roosevelt told Congress a few weeks later that a "direct benefit received in return for our aid is an understanding with Britain (and prospectively with others of our allies) as to the shape of future commercial and financial policy."[62] What would that commercial and financial policy comprise?

"We informed British Ambassador Halifax," Hull wrote, "that we had expressed Article VII in general terms so as to avoid specific reference to preferential arrangements, which reference might cause political embarrassment to the British Government. . . . [If] asked to explain what did fall within the term [preferential arrangements], we proposed to say it was all-inclusive."[63]

Churchill, for his part, would be bludgeoned relentlessly in Parliament to justify his acceptance of Article VII, which he could defend on no firmer ground than Roosevelt's fleeting and meaningless reassurance. "I did not agree to Article 7," he was forced to explain in the Commons two years later, " . . . without having previously obtained from the President a definite assurance that we were no more committed to the abolition of Imperial Preference, than the American Government were committed to the abolition of their high protective tariffs."[64]

What, in the end, was Keynes's substantive role in the creation of the Lend-Lease Agreement? It is hard to imagine that anyone could have better identified and articulated the huge risks that Morgenthau, White, Hull, and Welles's demands posed for Britain's postwar solvency. But anyone who is married, as Keynes was, should know that facts and logic are not always helpful to one's cause. In Keynes's case, they certainly did not help it when, woven together with his supreme self-assuredness, they served to humiliate his harried, less informed, or less eloquent American interlocutors. And as Morgenthau's dialogue with Hopkins suggested, Keynes's lack of humility appears to have prodded Roosevelt's advisers to tighten their demands, lest they be caught out by clever arguments down the road.

Certainly Keynes was dealt an awful hand. But the least bad strategy might have been simply to feign cheerful ignorance of the stakes, and to hold out for divine intervention once the dealing was done. This was the Foreign Office approach to Lend-Lease consideration, an approach for which Keynes had nothing but principled disdain. "If there was no one left to appease," Keynes scoffed, echoing White's view of the State Department, "the FO would feel out of a job altogether."[65]

Remarkably, given Keynes's leading role on the front line of the financial side of Britain's war efforts, Churchill paid little heed to

Keynes's labors. His five-volume history of the war contains a single reference to the great economist.[66] The PM's strategy throughout the war was to focus on surviving it. Central to that strategy was to cultivate Roosevelt and his personal emissaries (such as Hopkins), whom he sought relentlessly to entrance with his Potemkin village of Anglo-America. All else was distraction.

Keynes, though he allowed his frustrations to bubble over in front of the Americans more often than did Churchill, nonetheless shared with the PM the tendency ultimately to ascribe kindly intentions to his negotiating counterparts, even when these were not manifest in their behavior. But things are sometimes exactly as they seem. Morgenthau and White were not making irrational demands; they were simply making unpalatable ones. "Now the advantage is ours here, and I personally think we should take it," Morgenthau would insist two years later at Bretton Woods. "If the advantage was theirs," White would add, "they would take it."[67]

CHAPTER 6

The Best-Laid Plans of White and Keynes

In spite of his instinctive fiscal conservatism, Henry Morgenthau was a committed New Dealer. Characteristically American, he also believed that what was good for his country was good for the world. The United States was a benign emerging superpower, and would use its power, unlike the European imperialists before it, to create a world based on economic cooperation and nondiscrimination. Central to this idea would be to boost the authority of governments over the rootless, selfish financiers who, partly through their hold over the national central banks, wreaked havoc in the currency markets, disrupted trade, and sowed political conflict. In the line he would make famous at Bretton Woods, he sought to "drive . . . the usurious money lenders from the temple of international finance."[1]

Morgenthau never pretended that he knew, practically and prudently, how to do this. He knew that it involved government control of monetary policy and central banking. He knew also that it involved creating some international body that would have the mission and the wherewithal to prevent competitive devaluations, without governments resorting to exchange controls. Naturally, he turned to Harry White to create the technical blueprint for this system.

On December 14, 1941, Morgenthau put flesh on the bones of White's new role as assistant secretary, directing him to prepare a memorandum on the establishment of an "inter-Allied stabilization fund," which would "provide the basis for postwar international monetary arrangements." However technocratic-sounding the assignment, Morgenthau's overarching motivation was supremely ambitious. Years later he explained to President Truman that his aim had been "to move the financial center of the world from London and Wall Street to the United States Treasury and to create a new concept between the nations of international finance."[2] This new concept involved, according to his biographer Blum, "making the American dollar the basic unit of exchange for the whole world after the war," an ambition planted in him by his trusted assistant.[3] For White, this was the opportunity that would make him famous.

White produced the first complete draft of what would become known as the "White Plan" in March of 1942. The scheme was naturally premised on world peace, which must have seemed grimly far off at the time. It was a mere few weeks after the fall of Singapore, one of the great Allied catastrophes of the war. One hundred thirty thousand British, Indian, and Australian troops had been taken prisoner of war in Malaya and Singapore. Disgrace had been heaped on disaster, as POWs outnumbered casualties by over forty times. Churchill, who called it the "largest capitulation" in British history, considered resigning. Together with the German "Channel dash," in which three enemy warships escaped from French ports to German waters through the supposedly blockaded English channel on February 12, the Asian debacle had "[shaken] the British Empire to its foundations," in the words of a British commander. "Nay, it would be fair to say they influenced opinion throughout the world. They produced the most unfortunate reverberations in the United States of America just at a time when harmony and understanding between the two nations was of paramount importance."[4] Churchill had not aided matters by appearing to lay blame for Far Eastern troubles on America's lack of a viable sea-power shield, which had been "dashed to the ground" by the Japanese at Pearl Harbor.[5]

White looked beyond the terrible tides of the war, seeing only the economic challenges that lay beyond them. He set out "three inescapable problems" that the United States would face in the immediate postwar world: first, "to prevent the disruption of foreign exchanges and the collapse of monetary and credit systems"; second, "to assure the restoration of foreign trade"; and third, "to supply the huge volume of capital that will be needed virtually throughout the world for reconstruction, for relief, and for economic recovery." He urged no delay in developing and implementing plans "for the creation of agencies with resources, powers and structure adequate to meet the three major post-war needs."[6] These were the ideas that led to the creation after the war of the three so-called Bretton Woods institutions: the International Monetary Fund (IMF), the World Trade Organization (WTO),[7] and the World Bank.

These matters should not wait until the end of hostilities, White insisted. Legislative action by all the participating nations, and the actual establishment of the critical agencies, would take time, and they needed to be up and running in short order. For Churchill, this type of airy edifice-building babble was galling, which accounted for his almost willful neglect of White's and Keynes's efforts. Worrying about "hypothetical post-war problems in the middle of a struggle" was a grave waste of time "when the same amount of thought concentrated on the question of types of aeroplane might have produced much more result." The director of military operations at the British War office, Major General John Kennedy, scoffed that "[t]he Atlantic Charter," with its grand political and economic vision of the future, "is not good enough an ideal up against the fanaticism of the Germans and the Japs."[8] But to White, the very act of pursuing visionary reconstruction proposals now would itself "be a factor in winning the war," as "the defeat of the Axis powers would be made easier if the victims of aggression, actual and potential, could have more assurance that a victory by the United Nations will not mean in the economic sphere, a mere return to the pre-war pattern of every-country-for-itself, of inevitable depression, of possible wide-spread economic chaos with the weaker nations succumbing first under the law-of-the-jungle that characterized international economic practices of the pre-war decade."

Furthermore, failure to act quickly would be catastrophic. The world would face "a period of chaotic competition, monetary disorders, depressions, political disruption, and finally . . . new wars within as well as among nations. . . . Just as the failure to develop an effective League of Nations has made possible two devastating wars within one generation, so the absence of a high degree of economic collaboration among the leading nations will, during the coming decade, inevitably result in economic warfare that will be but the prelude and instigator of military warfare on an even vaster scale."[9] As with his very first Treasury report eight years prior, White clearly suffered no lack of regard for the practical importance of his work.

White laid out a blueprint for two new agencies to carry out his plan: a "United and Associated Nations Stabilization Fund" and a "Bank for Reconstruction and Development of the United and Associated Nations." (He did not suggest a trade agency, which was consistent with his treating trade as a currency problem.) Confusingly, White's fund was to look much like a bank, and the bank much like a fund. But the names largely stuck: they would soon be incarnated as the International Monetary Fund and the International Bank for Reconstruction and Development, the latter now known as the World Bank. Although White expected his bank to play an important role in lending capital and guaranteeing private loans for the reconstruction of countries significantly damaged by the war (loan guarantees being a New Deal practice to hold down interest rates), the fund emerged as clearly the more geopolitically significant of the two proposed institutions.

The main stated purpose of White's Stabilization Fund would be to reduce, dramatically and perpetually, barriers to international trade and the associated capital flows. The pre-1914 gold standard had achieved both of these aims to an historically unprecedented degree, without any complex, formal international agreement of the sort White was proposing. But the gold standard had been made the bogeyman for all the errors of monetary policy in the 1920s.

The most important of White's aims, however—the one that would obsess him in the coming years—was very deliberately left unstated: to elevate the status of the dollar to that of the world's sole surrogate for gold, such that cross-border gold movements would no longer have the power to dictate changes in U.S. monetary policy. This would be set entirely at the discretion of American experts, and would be transmitted to the rest of the world by way of fixed exchange rates.

These were the sorts of ideas that worried the British establishment. C. R. King, an official in the American Department at the Foreign Office, observed that there was great conviction in the United States "that America will emerge, after total victory, militarily and economically supreme." Arthur Salter, the sharp-witted head of the British shipping mission to Washington, wrote that "it must be accepted that policy will increasingly be decided in Washington. To proceed as if it can be made in London and 'put over' in Washington, or as if British policy can in the main develop independently and be only 'co-ordinated' with America is merely to kick against the pricks."

But the Roosevelt administration would not wait for victory before pressing its world vision. While White was unveiling his economic blueprint, the president was laying out his political version, central to which was the dismantling of the European colonial empires. He infuriated his devoted pen pal the prime minister with an April 11 cable blasting "the unwillingness of the British Government to concede to the Indians the right of self-government."[10] Harry Hopkins is said to have described it as "wrathfully received."[11] Churchill saw it as hypocritical, meddlesome, and irresponsible, given the immediate importance to the Allied cause of a stable India. But American military successes in the Asian theater, such as the heavy damage inflicted on the Japanese in the May 4 Battle of the Coral Sea, contrasted embarrassingly with British defeats, and only served to bolster the American sense that the country had little need of sensitivity to British concerns and interests in mapping out the world's future.

Harry White, unlike American Treasury and Fed officials today, did not believe that the U.S. dollar could play the world role he ordained for it without the firm backing of gold. Fragments of a large unpublished manuscript in his archives titled "The Future of Gold," apparently written over the period between 1939 and 1942, provide fascinating insight into White's thinking about the nature of money and a well functioning international monetary system. This is one of a number of remarkably detailed, ruminative, and often politically provocative essays White managed to write while at the Treasury, and it is not at all clear how or whether he intended eventually to make them public.

White's assessment of gold's role in the international monetary system was vastly more favorable than Keynes's. "[G]old is the best medium of international exchange yet devised," he wrote. "[Gold's] superiority over any other means of settling balances . . . rests on the common experience of nations which has revealed time and again in many quarters of the globe that a country with adequate gold can engage more freely and effectively in international trade and finance than a country with little or none."[12]

Only dramatic global political developments could eliminate gold's vital monetary role—developments that he did not expect to materialize soon, if ever. White would have expected our modern system of fiat monies, revolving like small planets around a globally dominant fiat dollar, to be volatile and politically contentious. "There may possibly come a time when gold will no longer retain its superiority over other devices," White suggested, "but that can be only when national monetary systems and national monetary policies cease to exist and are replaced by an international authority which will decide the monetary, credit and trade policy that each nation is to pursue. A sort of monetary League of Nations which would control world economic policy."

"If and when that time arrives gold possibly will be no more needed to settle international balances than gold is now needed to settle balances among States within the country," White explained. Money and politics were inextricably linked.[13] Though he was probably not conscious of it, White was echoing in practical terms the more abstract ideas expressed by the German philosopher and sociologist Georg Simmel in a turn-of-the-century treatise titled *The Philosophy of Money*. "[E]xpanding economic relations eventually produce in the enlarged, and finally international, circle the same features that originally characterized only closed groups," Simmel observed of the rapidly globalizing world in which he lived. "To the extent that this happens, the pledge, that is the intrinsic value of the money," represented by gold, "can be reduced. . . . Even though we are still far from having a close and reliable relationship within or between nations, the trend is undoubtedly in that direction."[14]

"But until that millennium arrives," White clarified, bringing his argument back to contemporary political reality, "gold will continue to be sought by various governments because gold serves better than anything else as a combination war chest and protective cushion against the shocks of international change."[15] At another point in his essay, however, he characterized such a millennium as a distinctly dark one: "[W]ere all important countries to adopt a completely totalitarian form of government and barter their exports for imports so that there would be no balance due either of the trading countries, gold could be dispensed with," suggesting that the end of gold money meant the end of liberal democracy itself.[16] "When the day comes when one nation will have conquered all others (or all others except one or two) and will impose restrictions on the monetary behavior of the conquered countries—then gold is doomed. But when that catastrophe occurs many other institutions infinitely more valuable than monetary instruments will likewise be doomed."[17]

White asked whether the U.S. dollar could ever come to supplant gold as the international medium of exchange and store of value. His answer was that it could do so only to the extent the United States were ultimately willing and able to redeem those dollars for fixed measures of the cold, hard metal. "There are some who believe that a universally accepted currency not redeemable in gold . . . is compatible with the existence of national sovereignties," White observed, consciously or unconsciously encompassing Keynes. "A little thought should, however, reveal the impracticability of any such notion. Any foreign country is willing to accept dollars in payment of goods or services today because it is certain that it could convert those dollars in terms of gold at a fixed price."[18] It would be no different with a newly conjured international currency.

"One of the factors that contributes to the great confidence in the United States dollar which exists the world over," White concluded, "is undoubtedly our large gold holdings.[19] . . . [I]nternational agreement is not a substitute for gold."[20] Yet he was only shown to be correct a quarter century after Bretton Woods, when insufficient and rapidly declining U.S. gold stocks triggered a run on the dollar and the collapse of the monetary system that bore its name.

In preparing his plan, White must have taken heart from an *Economist* magazine article with the same title as his essay, "The Future of Gold." The article suggested that "The alternative to gold or to some international unit of account based on gold would be one or other of the existing currencies—inevitably the dollar, in the post-war economic set-up—as the standard of international values and payments." This was intellectual vindication for his postwar monetary plan.[21] White's Treasury colleague John Gunter sent him a memo on January 8, 1943, observing that White's "proposed international stabilization fund would seem to be the proper instrument for carrying out the economic objectives expressed in this editorial. Gold would be used as the foundation of an international currency system, and parities could be altered after international consideration in accordance with economic criteria."[22]

Yet there is a critical omission in White's essay, which helps explain why White's preferred monetary system collapsed in the 1920s, and again in the 1960s. There is no distinction in his essay between the use of gold as international money and the gold standard as such. There is no account of why the pre-1914 classical gold standard, with its *automatic* mechanisms for regulating the price of credit and the cross-border flows of gold, differed so fundamentally from the discretionary version, the gold-exchange standard, based on national hoarding and cross-border diplomatic haggling, which took hold in the 1920s. White rightly observes that "[g]overnments will take drastic action to prevent losses of gold, but there is no instance in modern history of a government taking drastic action to check an inflow of gold."[23] Yet he fails to connect the dots between this critical observation, on the one hand, and the monetary and trade chaos of the 1930s, on the other. It was the very fact that governments refrained from taking action to block foreigners from redeeming paper currencies for gold that made the pre-1914 gold standard so successful in promoting global economic integration.

White's plan involved no mechanism to ensure that the United States would operate a monetary policy consistent with maintaining adequate gold stocks. In fact, the system virtually ensured the opposite. Under a true gold standard, a dollar sent abroad entailed an automatic outflow of gold that would have to be counteracted by tighter monetary policy. Domestic credit would become more expensive, domestic prices would fall, exports would become more competitive, and any balance-of-payments deficit would tend to reverse in relatively short order. Under White's system, a dollar-based gold-exchange standard, in contrast, a dollar sent abroad could be immediately recycled in the United States in the form of a dollar bank deposit, which would then be used to create *more credit*, rather than credit tightening. Balance-of-payments deficits would tend to grow, rather than reverse. This is, therefore, a logical source of today's serial bubbles and chronic imbalances.

White's scheme contained a built-in tendency for more and more dollars to be forced into circulation around the globe. With proportionally less gold to back those dollars, there would be a rising likelihood of foreign holders of dollars panicking and demanding gold all at once.

White understood this risk, but chose to downplay it: "The steadily growing trend away from 'automatic' monetary systems toward a greater degree of 'management,'" of which White strongly approved, "can operate to greatly increase the length of time in which countries can have a favorable balance of payments, and other countries an unfavorable balance—provided the latter have plenty of gold to give up."[24] But there is the rub. A persistent balance-of-payments deficit means persistent falling gold reserves. The deficit country will inevitably run out of gold sooner or later.

Why did White choose to downplay this risk? He believed that the mechanical aspects of the gold standard, those which acted to reverse balance-of-payments deficits automatically, also unduly limited the scope for policy makers to regulate the behavior of the domestic economy. This was a standard Keynesian concern. His proposed Stabilization Fund could "be used to minimize the effects of inflowing or outflowing gold on the domestic economy."[25] It would do this by obliterating the signal that dangerous international imbalances were mounting.

"It is quite true," White pointed out, "that, insofar as stabilization funds act as insulators of domestic economies, they still further reduce the significance of the role of gold in the mechanism of adjustment." This was desirable, White argued, in that it would "thereby give the authorities in each country greater freedom in formulating and administering their respective domestic economic policies." His conclusion was that a stabilization fund was "a convenient instrument to countries which, while not wishing to resort to the drastic insulation of the domestic economy involved in exchange controls, nevertheless desire not to be deflected from the pursuit of given domestic economic objectives by changes in its international balances, which immediately reflect foreign disturbances and developments."[26] It was therefore a halfway house between state-controlled trading and inconvertible currencies, on the one hand, and free trade under a mechanical gold standard, on the other.

White's proposed global fund would set out to stabilize the international marketplace for currencies—that is, to make national currencies durably exchangeable for one another at a fixed price—while simultaneously allowing national governments far more room for discretion and intervention in managing their respective national economies than they had under the pre-1914 gold standard. This was a tall order. It raised critical questions of what the fund would do when its member governments chose to pursue domestic economic policies that were inconsistent with the maintenance of stable exchange rates.

The fund would operate under detailed and complex rules that would allow member governments to buy from it other members' currencies, provided such demand was limited, adequately collateralized by gold and other currencies, and needed strictly to meet legitimate, trade-related balance-of-payments difficulties—that is, not just to add to their stock of gold and stronger currencies. In return for these privileges, the member governments would pledge to abandon, within one year after joining the fund, all restrictions on foreign exchange transactions with other member countries; not to alter exchange rates without the fund's consent; not to engage in discriminatory bilateral clearing or exchange rate arrangements with other members; and gradually but continually to reduce import tariffs and other trade barriers. (The fund would be empowered only to opine on trade barriers, however, and would not have sanction powers.)

Critically, members would not be permitted "to adopt any monetary or general price measure or policy, the effect of which, in the opinion of a majority of member votes, would be to bring about sooner or later a serious disequilibrium in the balance of payments, if four-fifths of the member votes of the Fund submitted to the country in question their disapproval of the adoption of the measure."[27] In broad terms, discretion in national economic policy would be limited to what the large part of the other member governments believed to be necessary to maintaining the fixed-exchange-rate regime. Currency devaluations, which were to be rare, were to be offset by further contributions to the fund by the devaluing government.

An exception to the principle of liberal trade and currency transactions would be capital flows for investment—rather than trade—purposes. White's regime would allow members to block such flows, and indeed would require members receiving flows to cooperate in barring them when such requests were received from other members. White justified capital flow bans on the grounds that efforts by the rich to evade "new taxes or burdens of social legislation" had been "one of the chief causes of foreign exchange disturbances."[28] This was very much in keeping with his domestic New Deal thinking, yet contrasted with his generally liberal views on goods trade.

"High tariff policies in the main reflect adherence to the traditional, crude, mercantilist fallacies," he explained, and "So widely held are those fallacies, so persistently clung to by persons who should know better, so potent are they in shaping many aspects of domestic and foreign policy, and so unfortunate in their effects on world peace and prosperity, that one is tempted to list 'mercantilism' or its more expressive heir 'protectionism' as 'World Enemy No. 1', in the economic sphere." Yet despite White's swipe at protectionism, delivered with the characteristic martial bombast he adopted toward views he opposed, White curiously insisted in the next breath that import duties were fine and well when used for political and economic development objectives he deemed sensible. Many assumptions "essential to the belief that 'Free Trade' policy is ideal, are not valid," he explained. "They are unreal and unsound."[29] Lest such contextualization appear hopelessly to muddy his policy stance, he then confused it further by calling for a ban on commodity and service export subsidies without fund consent.

At base, White's fund would bring about a world congenial to American economic interests. The American export juggernaut would be protected by the commitment of other countries not to erect new trade barriers or to engage in competitive devaluation, as they had done in the 1930s, underpinned by the fund's ability to sanction them for such behavior. Conversely, the U.S. government would have virtually unlimited discretion in its own economic policies, as its dominant currency, backed by control of two-thirds of the world's monetary gold, would ensure that it never had to borrow from the fund, and its effective veto power, afforded by White's voting formula, would ensure it could never itself be censured. Other countries would sign up to the scheme in order to get vital emergency access to dollars, which would be backed by gold at a fixed price. (This assumed that the United States could and would always meet the gold conversion commitment—a commitment on which it would formally renege three decades later.)

To modern eyes, it may seem curious that the United States would invest such great political effort to establish a global regime in which all currencies were fixed to the dollar, when today the United States routinely demands that other large trading partners—China in particular—*unfix* their currencies from the dollar. But in the 1930s and '40s the United States was running large trade surpluses, and there was downward market pressure on other currencies, whereas today the United States is running large trade deficits, and the pressure is frequently the other way. In the '30s and '40s the United States aimed to counteract upward market pressure on the dollar through fixing exchange rates, whereas today the United States aims to accommodate downward market pressure on the dollar through floating rates. The United States was broadly unconcerned with "global imbalances" when it was a surplus country in the '40s, but is very concerned with such imbalances now that it is a chronic deficit country. The common denominator between the two eras is support for a weaker dollar to help U.S. exporters and protect domestic producers against foreign competition.

Most intriguing in a lengthy document proposing a new system to foster global economic exchange is White's passionate call for eliciting the counsel and consent of the world's foremost anticapitalist, nonmarket-based country. "There are certain to be some persons or governments, who either out of fear, or prejudice, or dislike would wish to exclude countries with socialist economies from participation," White observed. "Yet to exclude a country such as Russia would be an egregious error."[30]

A document that condemns high tariff policies as a leading enemy of peace and prosperity while simultaneously pressing for Soviet participation in the creation of a body that would reflect such views is clearly a curious one. White was surely correct that socialist economies needed to trade, but, given the Russian state's absolute control over imports, it had no logical role in a fund that provided temporary balance-of-payments deficit assistance in return for pledges not to restrict trade. But White's agenda was always vastly larger than his official brief, and he did not shy away from apparent contradiction in pursuing it. His platonic affection for liberal trade policies may well have been genuine, but his private views recorded post–Bretton Woods on the inevitable global spread of Soviet-style planning suggest he was far more interested in locking the United States and Russia into political alliance than in the creation of a system to revive trade among private enterprises.

"Molotov seems right to have perceived in the Americans' behaviour a fundamental condescension, of the same kind that underlay their attitude towards Britain," Max Hastings observed of the Soviet foreign minister's encounters with Roosevelt. The president, Molotov recounted late in life, saw Russia as "a poor country with no industry, no grain," which would necessarily "come and beg."[31] White, in contrast, saw in Russia the wave of the future. Around the world "in every case the change will be in the direction of increased govt. control over industry, and increased restrictions on the operations of competition and free enterprise," he would write a few years later in a never-published essay. "Russia is the first instance of a socialist economy in action. And it works!" he concluded.[32] In his fund and bank plan, therefore, White was appealing at least as much to his own government as to those of the other Allies in insisting that "[t]o deny [Russia] the privileges of joining in this cooperative effort to improve world economic relations would be to repeat the tragic errors of the last generation, and introduce a very discordant note in the new era millions everywhere are hoping for."[33] The passion is striking, given the largely technical nature of the document.

Providentially, Maynard Keynes, entirely on his own initiative, had begun germinating his own ideas for a new international monetary system in August 1941, just a few months before White began formally developing his. The façades of the two schemes would emerge looking remarkably similar. But the structural supports suggested very different engineering concepts, reflecting clashing national interests.

Keynes had been thinking about how to fix the international monetary system for over twenty years. He had analyzed it intensively in his 1923 *Tract on Monetary Reform*, and even proposed a world bank to create a supranational money, whose function would be to help countries manage temporary balance-of-payments problems without deflation, in his 1930 *Treatise on Money*. But the shock of the American Article VII bombshell prodded him to begin crafting a detailed blueprint for a new global system—one that would offer Britain a measure of protection against American monetary and trade diktat.

Like White, Keynes wanted a system that would support liberalized trade while keeping global payments imbalances from emerging— and, when they did emerge, allow them to be corrected with minimal economic pain. Keynes was repelled by the notion of any sort of renewed gold standard—the "barbarous relic," he labeled it. This jibe, in Skidelsky's words, "conceal[ed] a crucial lack of clarity on the question of whether the gold standard was inherently deflationary, or whether its deflationary consequences on Britain were the result of the policy mistake of overvaluing the pound [in 1925]."[34] In fact, Keynes blamed much on the gold standard that he might just as well have blamed on the weather.

Keynes argued, for example, that under the gold standard "The process of adjustment is *compulsory* for the debtor and *voluntary* for the creditor. . . . For whilst a country's reserve cannot fall below zero, there is no ceiling which sets an upper limit."[35] But this is true under our current fiat money system, just as it was under the gold standard. China today—the world's largest creditor, with an astonishing $3.2 trillion in foreign exchange reserves—illustrates this starkly.

Keynes further argued that debtors could often neither successfully deflate nor devalue their way out of debt, because of so-called negative terms of trade: that is, debtors become worse off if price-cutting fails to yield a sufficient offsetting rise in foreign demand. This was, not coincidentally, a problem that Keynes believed particularly to afflict Britain. "We always stand to lose through depreciation from the fact that a large part of our invisible [services] exports is fixed in terms of sterling," he observed. "To sell 10 per cent more textiles at a price 10 per cent less is simply giving the stuff away without a ha'porth of advantage."[36] Yet once again, this problem had nothing to do with the gold standard. For many nations and many of their products, it is very much an issue today.

Finally, Keynes argued that speculative capital would, without controls, periodically wreak havoc by flying from deficit to safe-haven surplus countries. Yet speculative capital does this precisely because of the lack of a credible anchor for the exchange rate, such as gold provided during the late nineteenth century. Back then, short-term capital flows tended to be stabilizing, rather than destabilizing, because investors believed that capital flight created an opportunity to profit from the eventual restoration of a currency's official gold price.[37] Furthermore, surplus countries are not necessarily safe havens: as the United States today illustrates, even the world's largest debtor nation can be a beneficiary, rather than victim, of hot money flows in a crisis. The key is that it happens to issue the world's dominant reserve currency.

Keynes acknowledged the success of the prewar gold standard, but maintained that it was an anomaly. He pointed out that when London was the chief global creditor center, a favorable UK payments balance produced the proper expansionary domestic pressures, whereas these had fallen away after the baton was passed to New York. He painted the failure of the postwar gold-exchange standard as the norm to which a gold-based international monetary system naturally tended. But this is like arguing that a bicycle is defective because it falls over when you stop pedaling. Unlike the Bank of England in the late nineteenth century, the U.S. Federal Reserve of the 1920s simply did not follow the cardinal rule of the gold standard—that is, to expand credit conditions when gold flowed in, and contract them when gold flowed out. It frequently did the opposite. It is no wonder that the results were as awful as they were.

Keynes's views on exchange rates were as volatile as today's currency markets, and often maddeningly opaque. In a 1936 interview he marked himself as "in general . . . in favour of independent national systems with fluctuating exchange rates"; yet there being "no reason why the exchange rate should in practice be constantly fluctuating" and "certain advantages in stability," he was "in favour of practical measures towards de facto stability so long as there are no fundamental grounds for a different policy." As regards "the practicability of stability," this would "depend (i) upon measures to control capital movements and (ii) the existence of a tendency for broad wage movements to be similar in the different countries concerned." As to what, practically, he was actually advising, he would "go as far . . . as to give some additional assurance as to the magnitude of the fluctuations which would normally be allowed, [and] provided there was no actual pledge," he believed that "in most ordinary circumstances a margin of 10 per cent should prove sufficient."[38] One can imagine the look of bewilderment on the interviewer's face.

Why was Keynes so difficult to pin down on so critical an issue? Keynes came of age intellectually during the First World War, when much that was taken for granted in terms of the world's political and economic foundations came crashing down. In particular, the gold standard—and with it, indelibly fixed exchange rates—seemed as natural to people then as it seems strange to them now. The issue of replacing the gold standard with something else was as difficult and fraught as the issue of replacing the dollar globally today. Even a thinker as radical and creative as Keynes never made a total break with it. The extreme of purely floating exchange rates, such as the world has known since 1971, was considered by few economists in the '30s (Lionel Robbins being a notable exception) to be a "system" as such, helping to restore equilibrium. Today associated with laissez-faire economics, floating exchange rates were then frowned upon by economists of the right as well as the left as both symptom and cause of disorder in monetary affairs; disorder that triggered others to initiate mutually destructive competitive responses. Keynes thought of freely floating rates as a sort of blind groping necessitated by the collapse of the gold standard, and certainly not as a viable alternative model for underpinning trade relations among nations.

By the time Keynes had begun drafting his postwar monetary plan in 1941, he was actually taking a firm stance against fluctuating exchange rates. "The method of depreciation is a bad method which one is driven to adopt failing something better," he wrote to the Foreign Office in April 1941.[39] In January 1942, he memoed: "[T]he atmosphere of settled exchange rates seems to me to be an important ingredient in achieving postwar stability. If money wage rates in a particular country have got thoroughly out of gear, there is nothing to be done but to alter the exchanges. In other contingencies the possible benefit to be gained is, I am sure, greatly exaggerated, and it would be exceedingly easy to do more harm than good. This is the lesson of nearly all the depreciations which took place after the last war." As for Britain, he observed that "even such advantage as used to exist in depreciating the exchange has been greatly diminished by the growing practice of linking money wage rates to the cost of living. If money wages in this country always go up when the cost of imported food stuffs rises, the power of exchange depreciation to help us begins to evaporate."[40]

Keynes was more an internationalist Englishman than an English internationalist. Therefore it was not surprising that "Keynes's advice," in the words of his great contemporary Joseph Schumpeter, "was in the first instance always English advice, born of English problems."[41]

These problems were mutating rapidly with global economic and political forces during the 1920s and '30s. In the '20s, memories were still fresh of Great Britain, the nineteenth century's imperial creditor nation, in Keynes's words "conduct[ing] the international orchestra," whereas by the '30s a grim acceptance had set in that Britain had a chronic payments deficit problem that could not be cured within the strictures of any idealist, "automatic" global system—particularly one whose terms would now be set by the United States.

Keynes's solidifying views against exchange rate fluctuations would have been welcomed by Morgenthau and White. But what he favored in its stead would have been anathema to Hull and Welles, in particular: capital export restrictions and import controls erected against countries with which Britain had an unfavorable trade balance. This would "Unquestionably . . . involve a discrimination against the United States if she persisted in maintaining an unbalanced creditor position."[42]

"I have assumed," Keynes wrote to a Treasury colleague in November 1941, "that we will continue our existing exchange controls after the war, and that we do not propose to return to *laissez-faire* currency arrangements on pre-war lines by which goods were freely bought and sold internationally in terms of gold or its equivalent. Since we ourselves have very little gold left and will owe great quantities of sterling to overseas creditors, this seems only commonsense. . . . The virtue of free trade depends on international trade being carried on by means of what is, in effect, *barter*. After the last war *laissez-faire* in foreign exchange led to chaos."[43]

Keynes's was, characteristically, a middle-ground British position. Treasury sparring partner Hubert Henderson, who labeled Keynes "an opportunist and eclectic to the end,"[44] thought it utopian to imagine the United States would ever take voluntary action, like lowering tariffs, to reduce its creditor position, or that any sort of postwar currency system could itself rectify Britain's chronic deficit payments position. For Henderson, as with the formidable German economic architect Hjalmar Schacht, managed trade and bilateral barter agreements were the wave of the future—not just a wartime exigency.[45]

Keynes was deeply troubled by the seeming impossibility of reconciling Britain's need for what he called a "Schachtian device" to manage its postwar trade and American demands for nondiscrimination. His correspondence during 1941 reflects a gyration between despair over American bullheadedness and optimism that the Americans would ultimately be compelled to adapt their ambitions to the facts on the ground, and the facts on the ground to their ambitions. He presciently suggested, for example, that the United States would be compelled to try to "mitigate her task [of reducing global imbalances] by making large presents for the reconstruction of Europe,"[46] which ultimately came in the form of the Marshall Plan.

Like White, Keynes insisted on a system that left vastly more autonomy and discretion to national economic policy makers. He saw deflation and unemployment as wholly unnecessary evils that were only perpetuated by human attachment to outworn or patently false economic doctrines. In the interests of preventing deflationary pressures, capital outflows, which were central to the automatic adjustment mechanism of the gold standard, needed to be subject to tight national controls (a position he began advocating as early as 1924). Governments needed to keep interest rates low enough to maintain full employment (a position he first articulated in his 1930 *Treatise on Money*), and not allow them to rise beyond this by dint of impersonal forces such as gold sales.

Keynes set out to spend several days starting Wednesday, September 3, cloistered in Tilton drafting, as he explained to his mother, "a heavy memorandum on post-war international currency plans." This was interrupted by a summons to London to meet with Bank of England governor Montagu Norman on Friday the fifth, at which he was asked to join the bank's board of directors. Unwilling to give up his role as an unpaid adviser to the chancellor and the Treasury, he agreed only after receiving dispensation to continue. He went back to his drafting over the weekend, and completed his work on Tuesday the ninth in the form of two papers: "Post War Currency Policy" and "Proposals for an International Currency Union" (later termed a "Clearing Union").[47]

Like White, Keynes chose to treat the problem of re-creating and sustaining a multilateral trading system, and eliminating discriminatory and trade-depressing bilateral agreements, as a currency problem, rather than a trade problem, which had the advantage of being of necessity technical and abstract, and therefore less likely to trigger parliamentary or congressional apoplexy. Nonetheless, he had one eye firmly trained on the trade-obsessed Hull, in proposing that countries participating in his scheme would pledge limits on tariffs, trade preferences, and export subsidies, and an outright ban on import quotas or barter agreements.

The basic mechanics of what became known as the "Keynes Plan" were more complex, and certainly more ambitious, than those of the White Plan. International transactions would be settled through a new International Clearing Bank (ICB). Neither the national central banks nor the ICB would actually hold foreign currency. The national central banks would buy and sell their own currencies among themselves by means of credits and debits, denominated in newly created "bank money," to their ICB "clearing accounts." Keynes would later call this bank money *bancor* (literally "bank gold" in French). Bancor was to have a fixed exchange rate with all members' currencies and gold. In addition to acquiring bancor through trade, national central banks could add bancor credits to their clearing account by paying in gold. But they would not be allowed to redeem bancor for gold; bancor could only be used for transfers into other national central bank clearing accounts. This unusual asymmetry was a reflection of Keynes's central idea that the ICB should be a tool for encouraging the growth of money in circulation globally, and for putting up barriers against monetary contraction.

Each item a member country exported would add bancors to its ICB account, and each item it imported would subtract bancors. Limits would be imposed on the amount of bancor a country could accumulate by selling more abroad than it bought, and on the amount of bancor debt it could rack up by buying more than it sold. This was to stop countries from building up excessive surpluses or deficits. Each country's limits would be proportional to its share of world trade. This method of establishing bancor quotas was, not incidentally, convivial to British interests, as Britain had little gold but needed to conduct lots of trade.

Once initial limits had been breached, deficit countries would be allowed to depreciate, and surplus countries to appreciate, their currencies. This would make deficit country goods cheaper, and surplus country goods more expensive, with the aim of stimulating a rebalancing of trade. Further bancor debit or credit position breaches would trigger mandatory action. For chronic debtors, this would include obligatory currency depreciation, rising interest payments to the ICB Reserve Fund, forced gold sales, and capital export restrictions. For chronic creditors, it would include currency appreciation and payment of a minimum of 5 percent interest on excess credits, rising to 10 percent on larger excess credits, to the ICB's Reserve Fund.

Keynes never believed that creditors would actually pay what in effect were fines; rather, he believed they would take the necessary actions—particularly expanding imports or appreciating their currencies—to avoid them. This was the idea behind the 2010 proposal of then–U.S. Treasury Secretary Tim Geithner for countries to commit to a cap on current account surpluses—an idea that White rejected out of hand when America was a surplus power in 1944. The view that creditor nations, rather than debtor nations, could be primarily culpable for imbalances was a radical position in White and Keynes's day.

The creation of a new international currency, bancor, was clearly the boldest aspect of Keynes's proposal. Keynes believed it would solve many of the problems that afflicted Britain and the global economy in the 1920s and '30s.

First, he argued, bancor would have international acceptability, and therefore render unnecessary major irritants such as blocked balances (inconvertible holdings of foreign currency) and bilateral clearing agreements (import discrimination to balance trade between pairs of countries). Second, bancor would facilitate an orderly mechanism for controlling the relative exchange values of different national currencies, and therefore dissuade countries from undertaking beggar-thy-neighbor competitive devaluations. Third, bancor would be a much less capricious global money than gold. The monetary gold supply was determined by unhelpful factors such as changes in mining technology and the vagaries of national gold reserve policies, whereas bancor supply would be governed by the actual needs of global commerce as well as technocratic decisions to expand or contract it to offset deflationary or inflationary tendencies in effective global demand. Fourth, creditors as well as debtors would be pressured to take corrective action to reduce imbalances. The mechanism of fining creditors was one of the many novel features of the plan, the idea being to encourage surplus countries to import more so as reduce their bancor balance—it was a matter of "use it or lose it." Fifth, the creation of bancor provided a mechanism for starting each country off after the war with a stock of reserves appropriate to its contribution to world commerce, without which many countries would be unwilling to liberalize policy for fear of imminent payments crisis. Finally, the creation of the institution of the ICB would take the destructive politics out of "the planning and regulation of the world's economic life."[48]

Keynes likened his ICB to a national banking system. Mr. X deposits the funds he does not currently wish to spend with his bank, which lends the money out to Miss Y, who needs it to expand her business. "No depositor in a local bank suffers because the balances, which he leaves idle, are employed to finance the business of someone else." The flaw in this statement is obvious. It assumes, of course, that the borrower is always willing and able to repay the funds. Keynes did not discuss this part. Instead, he emphasized that his scheme was a secure, closed credit system, in which at all times the sum of claims against it equals the sum of its claims against members. This could not, however, be logically reconciled with his principle that members could at any time purchase bancor credits with gold, in which case credits could exceed debits.

Keynes's overarching concern was the "deflationary and contractionist pressure" that an economy suffers without such credit arrangements, and he argued that parallel arrangements were necessary at the international level to avoid such pressure globally (as witnessed during the Great Depression). Creditor nations like the United States should not leave gold and other monetary resources idle: if they did not wish to spend them on imports, they should make them available to others that "find a difficulty in paying for their imports, and will need time and resources before they can establish a re-adjustment."[49] The net result, he believed, would be more trade and more economic growth for all nations.

Capital controls, Keynes argued, would also have to be made "a permanent feature of the post-war system,—at least so far as we [the British] are concerned."[50] His conceptual logic was that "the whole management of the domestic economy depends upon being free to have the appropriate rate of interest without reference to the rates prevailing elsewhere in the world. Capital control is a corollary to this."

This thinking has today become orthodox Keynesianism, advocated by globalization critics such as Joseph Stiglitz and opposed by global currency union advocates such as Robert Mundell. Writing to Roy Harrod in 1942, however, Keynes's concern had overwhelmingly to do with Britain's immediate situation. "[W]e shall end the war with somewhere approaching £m2,000 of overseas liquid funds in London to which we cannot possibly afford to allow immediate freedom of movement," he asserted. "This is a subject about which we must speak as little as possible at the present stage for fear of increasing the tendency, which is already showing itself, towards an unwillingness to hold sterling balances. But for us some system for the control of capital movements is absolutely indispensable the moment the war is over."[51] The ICB, he believed, would "make such control easier."[52]

Keynes saw his bank as a joint Anglo-American creation, with other countries brought in on established terms. This would "settle the charter and the main details of the new body without being subjected to the delays and confused counsels of an international conference."[53] Clearly, a massive Bretton Woods gathering was not what Keynes had in mind: he wanted only "a meeting of Ministers to o.k. the results" at the end.[54] As for the bank's subsequent operations, "I conceive of the management and the effective voting power as being permanently Anglo-American," Keynes wrote.[55] "The Head Office in London under an English Chairman would deal with the business of banks situated in the British Commonwealth (apart from Canada), Europe and the Middle East. The Head Office in New York under an American Chairman would deal with the business of banks situated in North and South America and the Far East."[56] This had all the naive charm of, say, British Marks and Spencer touting a global alliance of equals with American behemoth Wal-Mart.

Former Texas Agriculture Commissioner Jim Hightower once famously remarked that there was "nothing in the middle of the road but yellow lines and dead armadillos." Keynes consistently belied this. Few minds have ever been able to stake out a middle ground with such consistent bravado. His International Currency Union plan was no exception. It was not Schacht, it was not Hull; it eclectically blended managed trade with free trade. Creditor nations would be forced to adjust policy, yet debtors would not escape market discipline.

Members would be able borrow from the bank, and buy from others on this credit, yet all would be obliged to clear their accounts in good time or face an automatic adjustment. The bank would take gold as an input into the system—a grudging concession to history. Yet the bank was to be a black hole that would never let the gold out. This odd feature Keynes called "one-way convertibility"; it was a mark of his determination to strip gold of its historic monetary role.

In the end, the plans that emerged from Washington and Whitehall were either timeous twins or clashing cousins, depending on whether one viewed them at 35,000 feet or at ground level.

Both the White and Keynes plans were built around a new global monetary institution. White's International Stabilization Fund would allow member states to borrow against the collateral of their national currency ("an I.O.U. engraved on superior notepaper," quipped Keynes[57]) and gold. Keynes's International Clearing Bank was a more liberal lender, allowing completely unsecured overdrafts while also demanding fewer behavior constraints in return. Such overdrafts were a common element in British banking that were foreign to the American version, which almost certainly influenced the conceptual model developed by the respective authors. But Keynes also consciously designed his new bank to expand the freedoms of debtors, particularly Britain, and contract those of creditors, notably the United States; whereas White was looking to offer debtors only the bare inducements necessary not to resort to competitive devaluation or trade discrimination against creditors—particularly, of course, the United States. Throughout the long process of reconciling the two plans, the British were concerned that White's institution "looked too much like a charitable fund." They consistently referred to their own institution as "passive," just a "spare wheel on the financial coach" until it was needed.[58]

Both plans involved a new international currency unit. Keynes's bancor was intended to become more important over time, contributing to both the demonetization of gold and a lesser global dependence on the dollar. White's proposed "unitas," in contrast, was intended to appeal to those attracted to the idea of an international currency, even though it would actually make the world more, rather than less, dollar-centric.

White wanted to make the U.S. dollar, and only the U.S. dollar, synonymous with gold, which would give the U.S. government a virtual free hand to set interest rates and other monetary conditions at will—not just for the United States, but for the world. Keynes wanted to wean the world off gold, and dollars, by creating a new supranational currency, issuance of which would follow principles consistent with an "expansionist" policy.

White shared Keynes's belief that government had to be aggressive in countering "contractionist" tendencies in the economy, using both monetary and fiscal tools. His opposition to Keynes's ICB was grounded in the fact that the United States, whose currency had already risen to the global role that Keynes wanted to bestow on bancor, had no incentive to yield its power to expand or contract the supply of global money to a supranational structure. Whatever an "expansionist" bancor could do, the dollar could do as well—provided the U.S. government willed it. Yet White steered clear of this impolitic fact in his draft plans. "[I]f an attempt were made to recommend the use of the dollar as the international unit of account," he wrote in April 1942, "there would unquestionably be some opposition on the part of those countries who, out of reasons of national prestige or anticipated monetary loss, would prefer not to promote a broader use in international use of a currency of some other country."

White was scathing about the idea of a new international currency actually circulating in parallel with national currencies—an idea that Morgenthau had asked him to consider, apparently with the president's support. "A 'trade dollar' or 'Demos' or 'Victor' or 'what-have-you' unit of currency supplementing the United States dollar, whether of the same or different value," White wrote in the same memo, "would no more help foreign trade than would the adoption of a new flag. . . . The specific nature of the new currency is never described, nor are the gains that are presumed to result from such a currency ever stated in meaningful language."[59] At that time, the United States had not yet been formally presented with the Keynes Plan, although it is certainly possible that White had gotten wind of the bancor concept and was attacking it preemptively. The names "Demos" and "Victor," however, had been suggested by FDR himself.[60] Cleverly, White's memo laid the groundwork for his meaningless unit of account, unitas, which would merely be a Stabilization Fund gold-deposit receipt that looked and smelled like Keynes's bancor without having any substance or consequence. Fixed in value at $10, it was ten U.S. dollars by another name.

Keynes later observed that "unitas seems to serve no purpose,"[61] but its purpose was precisely to neutralize calls for a real international currency. The British pressed the Americans relentlessly to give more substance to the unitas—to bancorize it—but the opposite occurred: the Americans abandoned their proposed phantom money entirely once the bancor threat was eliminated through negotiations.

Had sterling not been supplanted globally by the dollar it is difficult to imagine that Keynes—an enlightened nationalist, but a nationalist all the same—would ever have propounded such an idea as bancor. And if he had, it would surely have been rejected peremptorily by his government. In short, where White and Keynes stood on the question of the postwar global monetary structure was determined by where they sat—Washington and London, respectively.

Both the White and Keynes plans envisioned gold having a continued monetary role, though vastly less than under the classical gold standard. White believed a role for gold was essential to maintaining public confidence, and would remain so indefinitely, whereas Keynes was openly committed to reducing that role as quickly and completely as possible. White's plan required that at least half of the "cash" component of each member's initial subscription to the fund's capital stock be in the form of gold.[62] Once it became clear that the Americans would not relent on the fund having a gold capital stock, the British fought relentlessly to reduce it. Under White's plan, member states would be free to determine how gold would or would not fit into their own national monetary standards. White's only concern in this regard was to ensure that the paucity of monetary gold held outside the United States did not operate as an undue drag on the ability of the United States to export. Under Keynes's plan, the Currency Union would hold no gold except that which members chose to sell to it for bancor. Bancor would not be redeemable for gold, however, but only for the currencies of countries with debit balances. (Why countries would willingly buy for gold what they could only sell for the system's weakest currencies was never specified.) Keynes's plan, like White's, left countries free to choose their own monetary standard, but Keynes could not resist remarking that he saw no sense in countries maintaining two-way convertibility between their currencies and gold.

Both plans aimed at stability in exchange rates. However, Keynes's plan set up a mechanistic approach for determining when and by how much a member state could, or would have to, devalue or revalue, whereas White's plan was less accommodative of exchange rate changes, requiring member states to secure fund approval for any change in its parities. White's harder line on fixed exchange rates reflected an American preoccupation with stopping others from devaluing against the dollar. On the flip side, Keynes's softer line reflected a British preoccupation with avoiding further bouts of a persistently overvalued pound.

Both plans envisioned a reduction in foreign exchange restrictions and controls. However, Keynes's plan left the method and degree of such controls to the discretion of each member state, whereas White's plan committed members to eliminating them within a year of the fund's creation.

Both plans reflected the view that capital flows could be destabilizing and could undermine the ability of governments to enforce their domestic taxation regimes. Keynes's plan left the method and degree of capital flow control to each member state, and he had no doubt that Britain would impose such controls. White's plan went even further, requiring member states to cooperate with each other by not accepting foreign deposits or investments without the permission of the sender's government.

Both plans contained measures to keep members' balance of payments in line. Keynes's plan provided for penalties when deficit or surplus positions became excessive, but only allowed the ICB Board to recommend, and not dictate, curative measures. White's plan was more intrusive, allowing the fund to bar monetary or price policies that it deemed likely to encourage imbalances.

Both plans aimed unambiguously at establishing robust multilateral clearing arrangements, so that countries would forswear discriminatory, trade-depressing, bilateral barter practices. Keynes's plan more directly encouraged "triangular trade" (that is, trade among three, or more, partners), as the borrowing country would borrow not from a particular nation but from all creditor nations as a whole.[63] Keynes's plan, however, also carved out a legitimate space for clearing within political blocs, such as the sterling area. White's plan, in contrast, treated exceptions to multilateral clearing as matters that would require fund scrutiny and approval.

Both plans aimed at providing temporary assistance to countries running balance-of-payments deficits, so that trade would not be impeded by short-term imbalances. Both plans also aimed at constraining the growth of such deficits. But Keynes's plan differed from White's in also imposing constraints on growing surplus positions. White, given America's position as the dominant international creditor, was, not surprisingly, much less concerned with constraining surpluses. His plan would have allowed the fund to oblige a country to change a policy that promoted excessive surpluses, as well as deficits, but it also gave the United States the voting power to block such action.

Both plans were concerned with the immediate postwar challenges of rebalancing the global economy as well as stabilizing it thereafter. Only White's plan included a specific scheme for allowing blocked (mostly sterling) balances to be sold to the fund and eliminated over time, although Keynes readily embraced the idea. Jacob Viner presciently warned that there were dangers in the plans, as they were merged through the political process, conflating short-term and longer-term needs. "The expectation that the U.S. will be alone or almost alone as a creditor is plausible for the first period," Viner wrote to Keynes in July 1943, but "Over the long pull . . . I think the U.S. is as likely to be short as to be long of foreign short-term funds," meaning that the United States was as likely to be a debtor as a creditor. "I put no stock in a 'chronic scarcity of dollars.'"[64]

Both plans involved precautions against their respective central institutions generating losses, which their members would have to cover. Keynes's plan, however, allowed countries far greater borrowing power. This was consistent with Keynes's conviction that unemployment and insufficient demand were the root cause of global imbalances, and needed to be countered by easy credit terms. But his plan put the United States, as the world's dominant creditor, at much greater risk of loss. Under White's plan, the United States was only on the hook for the $2 billion it paid in as subscribed capital (out of total fund capital of $5 billion). Under Keynes's plan, this figure rose to $23 billion, the total of all members' combined quotas, as calculated by Keynes's proposed formula. White's plan went so far as to lay down an explicit prohibition on member-state foreign debt defaults, unless they secured the (unlikely) consent of the American-dominated fund. Keynes's plan was silent on the default issue. These features of the two plans were, naturally, consistent with Britain being bankrupt, and America being determined not to suffer another bout of major foreign loan losses.

Both plans aimed at broad membership. However, Keynes's plan limited membership to countries conforming to certain general principles and standards of international economic conduct, whereas White's plan explicitly forswore membership restrictions based on the particular economic structure of a country. This was intended specifically to remove any political obstacles to Soviet participation. Keynes, in stark contrast to White, had no strong feelings about this, other than that it might help bring others along. As he wrote to Harrod in May 1942, "[I]t is a question whether it would be wise to present the rest of the world with what looked like an Anglo-American bloc. If there is anyone more unpopular than ourselves it is the United States; and if there is anyone more unpopular than the United States, it is Russia; and if there anyone more unpopular than Russia, it is ourselves."[65] The quip may have violated the logical principle of transitivity, but, rhetorically, it was all the more effective for it.

Both plans envisioned the voting power of members being heavily weighted in favor of the more economically powerful states. White, however, proposed that quotas and voting power be allocated in accordance with the amount of cash, gold, and securities a member subscribed to the fund, whereas Keynes proposed that they be allocated in accordance with past contribution to world trade volume; his plan involved no subscription of capital. White's formula gave the United States effective veto power without calling it such. Keynes proposed that the founder states—which he suggested might be limited to the United States and United Kingdom—be given explicit veto power during the first five years.

Both plans envisioned their new central institution operating in close cooperation with national governments. Consistent with Keynes's vision of the ICB as a global central bank, his plan had the ICB operating hand in glove with the central banks of the member nations. Consistent with White's (and Morgenthau's) view that the central banks were tools of venal private bankers, not having the national interest at heart, his plan granted the Stabilization Fund the authority to deal only with the member government treasuries.

Finally, both plans envisioned a reduction of tariffs and trade barriers. However, White's plan went much further in requiring specific commitments from member states. Keynes suggested only that members forswear adopting certain particularly egregious barriers or discriminatory policies. Both plans further aimed at eliminating export subsidies. White's plan banned them outright, in the absence of explicit fund consent. Keynes's plan carved out a license for domestic producer subsidies when goods were intended for domestic consumption, with the requirement that a countervailing levy would be imposed when such goods were exported.

The stage was now set for the two plans to confront each other. On the battlefield of intellectual flair, the Keynes Plan would surely triumph. But they would engage on terrain decidedly more favorable to White, as it was his nation that held the gold, and the only reliable vouchers for gold: U.S. dollars. Ultimately, this was what the rest of the world would need after the war, and Keynes, for all his brilliance, was not King Midas.

The British had only one element of leverage at their disposal, and that was the power to disengage. There could be no international conference and no new global monetary architecture without the participation of the British Empire. Yet in order for Britain credibly to walk away, it would have to find another source of significant financial assistance, not only for the remainder of the war but for the immediate postwar transition period.

Tantalizingly, this would come two years later, right before the announcement of an imminent major conference at Bretton Woods, in the form of a rearguard action by New York bankers against the Roosevelt Treasury. The bankers would dangle before the British a large loan in return for abandonment of the proposed financial architecture schemes, which threatened to undermine their international lending business. Relaying the offer to Keynes, Treasury Under-Secretary Sir David Waley would pose the conundrum: "[O]ur real trouble is that we do not know whether in 1945 co-operation with Mr. Morgenthau and Dr. White or co-operation with the New York bankers will be most likely to produce the practical results we wish."[66] Keynes would emphatically cast his lot with Morgenthau and White, who represented the only possible salvation for his vision of a new world monetary order. He would not turn back.

CHAPTER 7

Whitewash

For Harry White, the war represented a unique opportunity to entrench the dollar as the world's money. He would press for American and Allied soldiers to use the dollar, exclusively, as an invasion currency, and to overvalue local money so as to ensure that the populations gave the dollar an eager reception. In the case of each enemy Axis country, he wanted the dollar to operate as the only valid currency until a permanent economic settlement was reached between that country and the Allies.[1]

His monetary plan was the next step—the strategy for the postwar. The first full draft was completed in March of 1942, though he polished until May 8 before finally presenting it to the Treasury Secretary. In his cover letter, he laid stress not on the specifics of the plan itself but on whether and when an international conference should be called to take the major ideas forward. For White, the conference was the thing. He needed a world stage on which to make policy, and there would be plenty of time to tinker with the script before the players arrived.

The first step, White said, was to deal with "points of preliminary 'tactics,'" such as whether the Secretary should approach the president before, concurrently with, or after engaging the rival State Department. "[I]f the Treasury doesn't initiate a conference on the subject it almost certainly will be initiated elsewhere," he wrote, clearly anxious to secure his status as the conference's driving force, "and it should be preeminently Treasury responsibility."[2]

White's plan was the main item of discussion at Morgenthau's May 12 staff meeting. "It is a masterly job," the Secretary exuded. As for tactics, he wanted to approach Hull before going to Roosevelt, fearing that "without his support this thing would be torpedoed." The president would surely ask, "Well, what does Hull think?" Morgenthau gave White twenty-four hours to ruminate on tactics, after which White came back with the Solomonic proposal "to hit them both at the same time."[3]

Morgenthau ultimately changed course and sent the plan to the president first, telling him in a cover letter that "the time is ripe to dramatize our international economic objectives in terms of action which people everywhere will recognize as practical, powerful, and inspiring. In the flush of success our enemies always dwelt upon their 'New Orders' for Europe and for Asia. There could be no more solid demonstration of our confidence that the tide is turning than the announcement of the formulation in concrete terms, and the prepara-tion of specific instrumentalities for what really would be a New Deal in international economics." As expected, the president directed him to get "the opinions of the Secretary of State and the Under Secretary of State," but also to set the ball rolling by working with State, the Board of Economic Warfare, and the Federal Reserve Board "with a view to your calling a conference to be held in Washington of Finance Ministers of the United and Associated Nations."[4]

Morgenthau sent Hull a copy of the plan on May 20, telling him of his correspondence with the president and asking Hull to send a State Department representative to a planning meeting. Hull sent Leo Pas-volsky and Herbert Feis to a meeting with Morgenthau and White on May 25, where quibbles began off the bat about protocol and proce-dures, which Morgenthau interpreted as State trying to block Treasury from moving ahead. So the Secretary called another meeting at which he stacked the deck by inviting friends of White from other agencies and departments.

One such was White House economist Lauchlin Currie, who, like White, had come up as part of Jacob Viner's "freshman brain trust" at the Treasury. "Want to get in on a fight?" Morgenthau asked Currie. "There's dirty work at the crossroads."

"Oh, really?" replied Currie. "Well, I'm always prepared to gang up with the Treasury against State."

Morgenthau laughed. "What a good nose you have. Harry and I need you . . . [State's] idea is to kill it you see. Because we've got an idea and State hasn't, and they don't want anybody else to have any ideas."[5]

Morgenthau wanted to get letters out to Allied finance ministers, asking them to send financial experts to Washington to discuss proposals and prepare a conference agenda. White was also anxious to get "a clear indication of the degree of agreement existing among the technical advisers of the various governments," which would "give important guidance to our own plans for the postwar period in the field of international finance and monetary problems."[6] He was also determined to avoid having to confront Keynes until support for his plan could be solidified.

But State saw it differently. At a July 2 meeting, Acheson, ever sensitive to British concerns, said that State wanted private bilateral discussions with the key powers, particularly the British, before convening a large gathering. Morgenthau was annoyed and suspicious. "What has Mr. Hull got in mind?" he demanded bluntly of Acheson.

Morgenthau and White still viewed Acheson as one of their own. "The reason Dean Acheson is over in the State Department is merely that he preferred that building to ours," White would say at Bretton Woods a few years later, "but he turns his hat around and he is a Treasury man."[7]

Morgenthau pressed on: "Does [Hull] want us to go ahead with this thing? Does he want us to kind of let the thing peter out, or just what has he got in mind?" And who did Hull want representing the United States with the British? Acheson said he did not know, suspecting only that it would be "a committee of experts."

Morgenthau soon thought better of prosecuting a potentially protracted war with Hull over the issue of convening Allied financial experts. "I haven't got energy enough . . . to get into an interdepartmental fight," he conceded.[8] Treasury and State ultimately agreed that no international meeting would be called for the time being, and informal consultations would instead be organized with the British, the Russians, the Chinese, and other key nations.

Over the coming month the British struggled to divine who was in charge of negotiations on the American side. Acheson tried to tamp down any expectation of quick progress by informing the Treasury representative at the British Embassy, Sir Frederick Phillips, that sending people to London was difficult, as recommendations by the State Department would automatically be "hotly opposed by

Departments or individuals who resent having been left out." Phillips cabled London that divining when formal discussions would begin was impossible, as "it depends on the outcome of the struggle for power within the administration." He proposed giving Morgenthau and Acheson, simultaneously, an advance outline of Keynes's Clearing Union scheme (earlier called the International Currency Union) as a means to "seize the opportunity to influence Americans before their ideas have passed out of the formative stage."[9] The reaction in London was at first negative, given fears that the United States would, if the scheme were not presented as part of a wider discussion, attack it because of America's creditor status, which necessarily made it the Clearing Union's ultimate financier.[10] But the chancellor, Sir Kingsley Wood, concluded that it gave the British government the best chance to get the process on track, and authorized Phillips to brief Acheson and Morgenthau.

"Morgenthau was greatly interested," Phillips cabled back, "and asked me to explain the plan to him at length next week." White pressed Phillips for a written version. On August 4, Keynes circulated a new draft that he considered "suitable to be passed on to the Americans."[11] Keynes briefed Richard Law (later Lord Coleraine), parliamentary undersecretary of state at the Foreign Office, who then went to Washington late in the month armed with several copies for the State Department and Treasury. Only after receiving the Keynes Plan did White tell Adolf Berle and Leo Pasvolsky at State that he had earlier "unofficially" given a copy to Phillips.[12] So the British actually had a head start on peeling through their competitor's scheme.

The process of reconciling White and Keynes, or at least their plans, took two years. It began on July 8, 1942, when Phillips sent Sir Richard Hopkins at the Treasury in London a draft of a paper on postwar financial arrangements prepared in the American Treasury—the White Plan. Phillips had received it "indirectly," and instructed Hopkins that it should be shared only with Keynes, and that no one was to know that they had seen it or that the British even knew of its existence.

Despite the skull-and-bones secrecy of the transmission, the British government's chief economic adviser, Sir Frederick Leith-Ross, also sent London a copy, which he noted as having been received from its author, Harry White, the very next day. Keynes responded to Hopkins on August 3, calling White's scheme "a tremendous labour to read and digest," and one that "obviously won't work." That same day, he also sent a letter to Phillips, remarking that White's "actual technical solution strikes me as quite hopeless. He has not seen how to get round the gold standard difficulties and has forgotten all about the useful concept of bank money." This was Keynes's notion that the Clearing Union could create new international money out of thin air, just as a bank creates money by lending out its depositors' funds.

"But," Keynes then offered, "is there any reason why, when once the advantages of bank money have been pointed out to him, he should not collect and re-arrange his other ideas round this technique?" This was classic Keynes thinking: these Americans are in a lamentable muddle, yet once things are explained to them all will be well. "The general attitude of mind," Keynes graciously conceded, "seems to me most helpful and also enlightening," however incompetent the exposition.[13] Of course, White would not dream of making such a concession. There would be no international money; no new competitor to the dollar. But optimism born of intellectual hubris accompanied the Cambridge don throughout his long negotiations with the Americans.

Included with Keynes's letter to Phillips was a detailed memorandum on the White Plan, which started out in characteristic blistering fashion. The American paper was "difficult to understand and almost impossible to read. There are several points of detail which I have not found it possible to make consistent sense. . . . It would seem to be quite unworkable in practice and involves many difficulties, with which there is no attempt to deal and which are not even mentioned. . . . [O]ne sees how inadequate it is to solve the real problem," which for Keynes was being able to expand the volume of international money without shackles being imposed by gold or Americans.

White's Stabilization Fund, Keynes wrote, "might seem, at first sight, to have a closer resemblance to the Clearing Union than is the case. In fact the principles underlying it are fundamentally different." He dismissed White's creation as "not much more than a version of the gold standard."[14] Yet nine months later, confident that a compromise was in the offing, he wrote that "[c]riticisms in the press seem greatly to exaggerate the distinction between the two schemes in their treatment of gold."[15]

His memo having begun by shredding White's creation, Keynes then characteristically raised hopes for his competitor's redemption. "[I]t is striking and encouraging that the general objects are the same as those we have been pursuing," he suggested. Keynes highlighted three aspects of White's paper that were congenial to British interests. First, the material dealing with blocked sterling balances was "exceedingly generous." It raised Keynes's hopes that the Americans would help Britain through its immediate postwar liquidity problems, rather than exploit them. Second, the requirement that countries on the receiving end of capital flows cooperate with those trying to block the outflows was helpful. Keynes was only too happy to support ideas that would make capital flow restrictions more effective. Third, "the line taken towards Hullism is extremely moderate": there was no kowtowing to the sort of extreme free-trade principles, beloved of the State Department, that would bar imperial trade preferences outright. Keynes quoted extensively and approvingly from White's discourse blasting "hangovers from a Nineteenth Century economic creed"—in particular, the misguided notion "that interference with trade and with capital and gold movements, etc., are harmful."[16]

The British and American treasuries undertook detailed comparisons of each successive draft of the two proposals. White's and Keynes's respective archives contain charts meticulously laying out the corresponding provisions side by side.

On October 6, Berle presented Phillips with a list of questions related to the Clearing Union, focusing on the implications of Keynes's proposed bancor. Berle began their meeting by observing that "there were only two ways as yet worked out of settling [adverse trade] balances—gold, if gold is acceptable, and otherwise goods. Lord Keynes's proposals," he then observed, "really came to giving to the proposed Clearing Union a method of creating money which could be used in settling these balances. In practice this would probably mean that we would acquire considerable amounts of this new money." What would be its usefulness? Since the United States was being asked, in effect, to deliver goods on credit to other countries, "notably Britain," the terms on which it would provide such credit ultimately turned on this question.

Berle was saying politely that bancor, which was not to be redeemable for gold, would never be a credible store of value for a creditor country like the United States. There appeared to be an inflationary bias built into it. Keynes had indicated that the amount of bancor in circulation could be expanded or contracted to stimulate or reduce "effective world demand," but where was the mechanism to bring about a contraction? And given that there were likely to be few large creditor countries in the system, wouldn't the debtors have a voting majority and control the Clearing Union's policies? The Americans further "indicate[d] some fear that the Union would have Bank of Issue functions which would have an adverse reaction on the position of the dollar," according to Phillips.

The British had no good answers. Reviewing the long list of American concerns in London, Robert Brand, who would be Phillips' successor in Washington, concurred that the Clearing Union's governing board would clearly have "enormous powers, equivalent to creating as much gold as it likes without trouble or expense." It also, he noted wryly, "offers a wonderful possibility of its board coming to the assistance of weaker countries, so to speak, on the back of the stronger countries without the latter knowing it, or at any rate without Congresses or Parliaments knowing what was happening."[17]

The real negotiations started quite unexpectedly, when, on a trip to England in October to inspect military facilities and prepare currency arrangements for the impending North Africa landings, Morgenthau, who was accompanied by White, was persuaded by Ambassador Winant to bring White and Keynes together for a private discussion on the twenty-third. But Keynes had a meeting scheduled that afternoon, while White had to leave that evening. "When I mentioned Keynes's engagement in the afternoon," Winant's economic adviser, E. F. Penrose observed, "Dr. White, who was as much of a prima donna in his way as Keynes, said abruptly, 'I don't want to talk with anyone except Keynes.'" Keynes's engagement was canceled, and the meeting was arranged at the embassy.

The meeting was a classic Keynes-White tête-à-tête. "It was lively and at times somewhat acrimonious," Penrose recalled. "Keynes thought the fund proposed by White would not be large enough. White considered it would be impossible to get more, if as much, out of Congress for the U.S. share. This led to some controversy over the question whether the capital should be subscribed or created as a new issue, as Keynes proposed."

White's scheme had member nations putting capital into the fund, whereas Keynes's scheme had the fund creating the capital de novo in the form of bancors. "Keynes vigorously attacked the idea of subscribed capital but White held to it as the only approach that Congress would accept"—congressional obstruction being a standard card for White and Morgenthau to play when pressed by foreigners to do things they found objectionable.

> [White] also attacked as politically impossible the proposal of Keynes to use the Clearing Union to finance relief and reconstruction or any part of it. Keynes made it clear that the proposal that a four-fifths majority vote should be required before a change in a country's exchange rate could be made would not be acceptable to London. Britain, because of its precarious financial position, must retain considerable freedom to act unilaterally in such matters if necessary, he maintained. Differences arose on the voting system and other points. Finally, Keynes argued for direct negotiations between the U.S. and U.K. alone or possibly with the Dominions and the Soviet Union added, while White maintained that this would create suspicion of an Anglo-Saxon financial 'gang-up.' Keynes heatedly argued that, the subject matter being complicated, it was essential that the U.S. and U.K. should work out a plan themselves, invite the Russians, in order to allay suspicion, and perhaps the Dominions and the French, to join, and then set it up and invite the rest of the world to join.[18]

The two agreed to return to their respective colleagues with proposals to modify certain points.

From the American side, the meeting had been "unofficial," as the State Department had never actually given its blessing to begin negotiations on postwar economic planning. Such blessing was finally bestowed on November 13, at which point Phillips resumed discussions in Washington with Berle, Pasvolsky, and Feis. With the ball passing from Treasury to State, the emphasis on the American side also shifted from monetary relations to trade relations, reflecting Hull's stand on

Article VII. Navigating the ebb and flow of power on the American side was a constant source of frustration for the British. Keynes warned against trying to negotiate with what might be "merely a private tea-party of the State Department," worrying that the British government must "not open [itself] to subsequent attack by some other Department in Washington which was not represented and thinks it ought to have been"—namely, the Treasury.[19]

White began foreshadowing publication of his plan early in early 1943, with a January 7 speech before the American Economic Association titled "Postwar Currency Stabilization," in which he stated his belief that "the United Nations should establish an international stabilization fund and an international bank." The challenge Keynes faced in reconciling White's fund and his own bancor-based Clearing Union was made vividly clear in White's statement that "the dollar is the one great currency in whose strength there is universal confidence. It will probably become the cornerstone of the postwar structure of stable currencies," he predicted.[20]

Though White disappeared from the front lines of discussions for several months, the British were always acutely aware that he was the intellectual force behind the American proposal. Throughout, they therefore took great pains to stroke White's ego, recognizing that the merits of their own plan would never be sufficient to overcome the weakness of their bargaining position. "I think a wholesale recasting of his memorandum would not please him," Phillips said of White in a January 1943 letter to Keynes. "But if it were possible to produce a small number of amendments, or a number of short amendments, indicating closeness of study, he might be flattered. It is wonderful what can be done to alter the sense of a document sometimes by a few amendments."[21] The British pledged to work enthusiastically with White on developing those elements of his plan they found convivial, such as those dealing with blocked balances. But they also stressed that the International Clearing Union was central to their proposal, arguing that it was vital to accommodate gold-poor countries and to ensure a sufficient volume of "international currency" to avoid another depression.[22]

Frustration on the British side boiled over in January when the State Department informed Phillips that not only were Keynes's alternatives to the American plan unacceptable, but the administration planned to begin discussions with the Russians, Chinese, and others, without first reaching a common Anglo-American position. This was, Keynes wrote to Sir Wilfrid Eady at the UK Treasury, "a stupid, futile notion."[23] In a memo to the chancellor, Waley blasted "the preposterous procedure of the Americans."[24] When on February 1 the State Department sent a new draft of the White Plan to the British Embassy, informing them that copies were being simultaneously dispatched to the Russian, Chinese, and other ambassadors, the British were outraged. Keynes pressed for the British government to do the same with his plan. "[B]efore committing ourselves definitely to a major monkey-house," meaning a formal conference, "I should like to get the preliminary reactions of those monkeys who will be optional guests."[25]

On February 17, Phillips received a cable from London instructing him to inform Berle that "we are communicating Clearing Union draft to Russian and Chinese governments and intend shortly to communicate it informally to Allied financial experts in London. We will not do so however until we hear the result of your meeting" with the Americans.[26] The meeting went badly. Phillips responded that the Americans now intended to distribute copies of the White Plan to European and Latin American Allies as well as the dominions.

The British backed away from the idea of attempting a compromise statement at that point. Eady was fearful, given the radical differences in approach between the two plans and the vastly stronger financial position of the Americans, that "any premature suggestion that we think a compromise is possible would merely mean slight modifications of the Harry White paper."[27]

The State Department expressed no objection to the British distributing their plan internationally, provided it was presented, as was the American plan, as an expert draft and not a government pronouncement. The British quickly delivered copies to the Allies, including Russia and China. "It will, of course, be very unfortunate, if the impression is created that the rival plans are being put up for auction," Waley observed, "but there again we cannot help ourselves."[28]

The two sides waged a pitched campaign for months to publicize their respective plans. On March 4, Morgenthau sent copies of the White Plan to thirty-seven finance ministers, inviting them to send "one or more of your technical experts to Washington . . . to discuss with

our technical experts the feasibility of international monetary cooperation along the lines suggested therein or along any other lines you
may wish to discuss."[29] On the same day, the UK Treasury announced
that meetings were being held with Allied finance ministers to discuss
postwar currency and financial arrangements: representatives from
Russia, China, and the dominions had already participated.[30]

Keynes gave a pellucid sales pitch for his plan to the European
Allies on February 26, in which he laid out with great political polish
the central elements of his scheme. In particular, he argued, extending
the principles of domestic banking to the international monetary system was essential to promoting world trade while taming the scourge
of global imbalances, which tended to impose deflation and recession
on debtors. Keynes emphasized one particular "fundamental point" in
his speech; one that would, interestingly, have great resonance with
the United States today, in light of its large and persistent trade imbalance with China. "[W]here there is want of balance in trade dealings so
that the imports of some countries are much greater than their exports
and the exports of other countries much greater than their imports, . . .
the pressure of adjustment should not fall, as it has in the past, almost
wholly on the weaker country, the debtor. . . . We should like to have
a set-up which made it as much the duty of the creditor country as of
the debtor country to ensure a proper balance."[31] In 1943, however, the
United States naturally had no motivation to back creditor burdens.

The speech elicited a positive reaction from the Allies, most of
whom were attracted by the more genuinely international nature of
Keynes's plan. Still, national self-interest ruled supreme: "[South Afri-
can Prime Minister] Smuts," whose country was the preeminent gold-
mining nation, "will be mainly influenced by the consideration—which
plan seems to offer the more secure future for gold?" Phillips wrote to
Keynes on April 22.[32] And as Keynes himself noted, some such as Bank
of Greece governor Kyriakos Varvaressos were "very much scared of
crossing the Americans."[33]

Keynes encouraged supporting nations to "[let] the American
Treasury know quite definitely how much they prefer [the Clearing
Union]," but to "avoid controversy or advocacy at this stage, . . . probe
the White plan with questions rather than objections, and . . . urge that
it ought not to be too difficult to find a means of harmonising the plans

if a general conference of experts could be called together for this purpose."[34]

Leaks and rumors about the competing plans spread quickly through the British and American media. With questions bombarding the chancellor, Phillips was instructed to inform the Americans that the British government wished to publish its proposals as a parliamentary document known as a White Paper (no relation to the "White Plan"). Berle and Pasvolsky said they could find no grounds for objecting. White, who attended the meeting on March 15, reported the news to Morgenthau, who two days later sent the president a memo suggesting they, too, publish their proposals. FDR balked, and Morgenthau succeeded briefly in stalling British publication. "[T]he president is very emphatic—no publication of the American plan," Morgenthau told White. "He said, 'These things are too early. We haven't begun to win the war.'"[35]

But the president's hand was forced when the *Financial News* in London carried a detailed summary of the American plan on April 5. Whitehall was acutely embarrassed, and Phillips was immediately dispatched to assure Morgenthau that it had played no part in the leak. "Repeated rumors," Phillips said, suggest the source as "an alleged embassy in London."[36] Morgenthau accepted his assurances, and spent the remainder of the day in impromptu briefings before the press and the Senate on the plan and its leakage. Hurriedly, the White and Keynes plans were prepared for publication, and released in Washington and London respectively on April 7, neither making any reference to the existence of the other.

The press reaction was split along nationalistic lines. The American press largely took positions consistent with the interests of a creditor nation controlling much of the world's gold. The *New York Times*, sounding more like today's *Wall Street Journal*, responded to prepublication accounts of the plans mainly by blasting Keynes as "an antagonist of stability of foreign exchange rates and . . . a champion of currency devaluation and credit expansion. . . . The disintegration of the international division of labor and the excesses of economic nationalism were corollaries of some of the teachings of this eminent adviser to the British government." No new model is needed, the piece argued, as

> The gold standard was, without any international agreements, the most satisfactory international standard that has ever been devised. . . . It is

often said that the gold standard "failed." The truth is that governments sabotaged it deliberately, because it interfered with nationalistic "planning" that governments preferred to stability of exchange rates. . . . It is not necessary to invent elaborate technical devices to secure monetary stability. The nineteenth century developed them through the gold standard.[37]

The *New York World-Telegram* adopted a baseball analogy:

[T]he kid who owns the ball is usually captain and decides when and where the game will be played and who will be in the team. While international monetary stabilization is not baseball, it is a game. Gold is as necessary to that game as the ball and bat are to baseball. Since the U.S. now owns some twenty-two billions of the world's reported twenty-eight billions of gold, we think Uncle Sam is going to be the captain of the team or there will be no game . . . the idea of "supplanting gold as the governing factor" and apportioning the voting power on the basis of pre-war trade, which would give Britain about fifty per cent more voting power than the U.S., not only is not good baseball—it is not even cricket.[38]

The British press, for its part, was naturally favorable to the Keynes Plan, which was seen as a brilliant innovation to free Britain from the devastating tethers of gold, of which the country now had little, and tired laissez-faire dogmas. It was "a landmark on the path of progress towards a rational financial and economic system," according to *The Times* of London.[39] It was "enlightened, stimulating and admirable," according to the *Daily Herald*:

Here at last is something which breaks away from the doctrines of the past . . . an entirely new approach to the problem of international monetary arrangements. It will hardly commend itself to the Bank of England. For it departs from the rigid orthodoxy of that institution. The plan puts gold in its right place . . . [it] puts decisive control over vital external operations in the hands of the Government . . . [it] aims at setting up an international authority which is responsible to Governments instead of private banking interests. It provides the control through which alone we can avoid the disastrous recurrence of trade slumps and booms.[40]

Keynes was thrilled finally to have both plans out for public consumption. As was his wont, he adapted his views on what was best politically to the new hand reality had dealt him. Whereas he had previously considered it critical to forge a common position with the Americans privately, now he asserted that it was, in fact, much better to have competing plans out in the open. "If in fact we had managed to reach a compromise behind the scenes, isn't it about ten to one that Congress would have turned it down?" he wrote to Phillips on April 16. "The present tactics allow steam to be blown off at an early stage without injury to anyone. We must get over our teething troubles in public."[41]

Keynes was bombarded with correspondence on his plan. Among the flattering letters was one from Bank of England director Sir Edward Peacock, who declared the Keynes Plan "a great charter." Yet recognizing its revolutionary nature, he concluded pessimistically: "No doubt we shall be prevented from going so far, but one day we shall have it all and the document will stand as a witness of your foresight and knowledge and skill."[42] Sixty-six years later, the governor of the Bank of China would capture newspaper headlines globally with a statement lamenting the fact that Bretton Woods did not go so far.

Flush with confidence, Keynes asked Phillips in a letter dated April 16: "Should we not now aim at a general conference between all concerned to hammer things out and reach some compromise, say, in June? With the Europeans and the Dominions in sympathy with us, our position should be much stronger in a general than in a bilateral discussion," reversing his earlier preference for a joint U.S.-UK plan. "If only we could persuade the Americans that London is a better climate than Washington in summer! But I suppose that is hopeless."[43] Phillips, better able to take the American pulse from his position in Washington, tried to tamp down Keynes's buoyancy: "[A]ll that you say [about the superiority of the Clearing Union] is very true, but you do not meet the point of the simple-minded American citizen who has gathered vaguely that it is a question of issuing more international currency and who is shocked at the idea of a currency without any gold backing at all."[44]

Keynes, for all his imagination, optimism, and loathing of timidity, did at times reconcile himself with political reality. "I fully expect," he wrote to economist Roy Harrod on April 27, "that we shall do well to compromise with the American scheme and very likely accept their dress in the long run."[45]

Having been ennobled the previous spring, Keynes devoted his May 18 maiden speech to the House of Lords to explaining the logic of his monetary plan and contrasting it, ever so gently, with the American version, which he knew had the overwhelming force of gold and dollars behind it. Adopting a tone of unbridled humility, which he would find impossible to sustain over the coming year of domestic debate, Keynes sought to allay fears that the schemes would impose new golden shackles on Britain's ability to sustain a cheap money policy, while allowing the United States to expand its massive global creditor position.

As for the differences between the schemes, "I have not the slightest doubt in my own mind that a synthesis of the two schemes should be possible," he stated, praising Morgenthau and White for "putting forward proposals of great novelty and far-reaching importance" that had an "identical purpose" to his own.[46] This was in stark contrast to his privately expressed observation that "the principles underlying [the White Plan] are fundamentally different."[47] As for why the schemes had been released separately, rather than having been reconciled and released as one, "It seems to me to be far better," Keynes claimed, "that our own Treasury and the Treasury of the United States should have decided to seek wider counsels before concentrating on the preparation of an actual plan—much better that they should take this course than that, without open consultation with their Legislatures or with the other United Nations, they should have attempted to reach finality. The economic structure of the post-war world cannot be built in secret."[48] Yet when the Americans had stated as much several months earlier, Keynes blasted the idea of "bring[ing] in Russian and Chinese representatives at this early stage, before the British and Americans have cleared their own ideas between themselves." It was a "stupid, futile notion."[49] Though he now claimed to wish to take the counsel of interested non-Anglo-Saxon parties, he had repeatedly in the past dismissed them, as he would in the future, as "monkeys."

"When the facts change, I change my mind. What do you do, sir?" Keynes once famously retorted in response to the charge that he had changed his views on monetary policy. Yet in the case of his first speech in the Lords chamber, it is difficult to defend his candor on such grounds. The facts had not changed. The Americans had simply rejected his views on every major matter, and he did not dare say so.

Phillips reported from Washington that, with publication of the White Plan, Treasury had now been designated to "carry the ball" on postwar monetary arrangements. "The State Department are lying very low," he wrote to Keynes. "I think, therefore, I shall go to Morgenthau in future and not to Berle."[50] Indeed, Morgenthau shortly after informed Phillips that Stabilization Fund issues were Treasury matters, and that Hull was aware that Treasury was handling them. Berle continued to argue to White that "the development of the currency stabilization projects [should be considered] as part of the whole post-war program," of which State was in charge.[51] But the die was now cast. Treasury was running the show on monetary reform.

This was a huge bureaucratic and personal victory for White. He quickly convened bilateral meetings in Washington with other countries' experts, which began in late April. In dismay, Phillips cabled London that "[w]hatever they said in London," the "Dutch and Belgians arrived here with no intention of supporting Clearing Union."[52] Theoretical attractions of the Keynes Plan notwithstanding, the European Allies recognized that the Americans held all the cards, and that it would be politically reckless to oppose them. White picked them off one by one.

The Canadians were, after the Americans and the British, the most engaged in seeking to shape the technical details of the scheme. They in fact produced a plan of their own for an "International Exchange Union," although it was similar enough to the American plan that the British dubbed it "off-White."[53]

Not all the invited governments were particularly concerned with the technicalities of monetary arrangements. The Chinese, for example, were mainly anxious to ensure that they were treated no less favorably than the Russians, whom they felt were being given privileged status beyond what their financial and economic strength merited. As for the Russians, they did no more than express interest in the project: they never sent representatives.

White put the British off until the second half of June, much to their annoyance, when he began meetings with their experts, among whom Lionel Robbins and Dennis Robertson, as well as Phillips and embassy economic adviser Redvers Opie. For the British, the most important technical issue was that of creditor obligations. They emphasized that any multilateral settlement system needed creditors, as well as debtors, to take responsibility for keeping their balances within limits. This was a clear statement that the Americans needed to reduce their creditor balance.

White had appeared to make an important concession on this front back in February, in the ninth draft of his plan forwarded from Phillips to Keynes. This had so shocked Keynes that he treated it as a political own-goal the Americans would try to erase in due course: a "scarce currency" clause that would effectively allow countries to limit imports from a persistent creditor country. (A creditor country's currency could become "scarce" under White's Plan owing to exchange rates being fixed: that is, demand exceeds supply at the fixed price.) In a letter to Keynes dated March 3, Harrod could hardly contain his glee, and scolded Keynes for not recognizing its significance: "The cardinal point is that the Americans offer us in this what we could never have asked of them in the negotiations especially after signing Article VII, namely that we (and other countries) should be allowed to discriminate against American goods if dollars are running short."[54]

"I agree that, read literally, the interpretation you give to this is the only one which makes any sense," Keynes wrote back the next day, but "I should expect that the moment emphatic attention was drawn to this alternative, it would be withdrawn.[55]

Even the British press was incredulous. D. D. Braham, a *Times* of London leader writer, wrote to Keynes in April, after publication of the American plan, that "from one passage it looks as if [the Americans] actually proposed in certain cases to limit and ration American exports. Surely they can hardly mean this, for it would provoke a storm of protest by American manufacturers and even from American Labour."[56]

White indeed began backing away from the scarce currency provision in April, when the Canadians pressed him to clarify what action a country whose currency had become scarce would take to prevent its currency from appreciating. White reportedly responded that the burden of action lay entirely with the other countries, and that the proposal would be amended to clarify this. But when the Canadians asked whether "appropriate action" by other countries might include trade discrimination against the creditor country in question, this suggestion was "received with dismay."[57] And in a meeting in June with the British, White opined that it was more difficult for creditors than for debtors to reduce their balances, thus implying that the burden of adjustment was on the debtors.[58] Keynes, who was being briefed on the discussions back in London, was exasperated. "The greatest objection to [White's Plan] in its revised version is that a creditor country can go on absorbing great quantities of gold as heretofore." He insisted that numerous changes were necessary "unless we are to lose face altogether and appear to capitulate completely to dollar diplomacy."[59] Indeed, the American scheme was becoming more dollar-centric, reflecting White's growing hegemony in the American drafting process. The new proposed quota framework, for example, drew no distinction between dollars and gold. "It is derogatory to sterling to count dollars only as equivalent to gold," Ambassador Halifax cabled London from Washington.[60] But White was giving no ground. "[T]he British formula, so far as we are concerned," he said publicly on August 19, "is out."[61]

By the summer of 1943, the war had demonstrably turned the Allies' way. In February, the Russians had completed their destruction of the German Sixth Army, which was retreating after its brutal but unsuccessful siege of Stalingrad. Soviet forces liberated one city after another, chasing the fleeing German forces westward across the Ukraine. A German victory on the eastern front was now out of the question. The decisive American defeat of Japanese naval forces in the Battle of Midway in June 1942 paved the way for victories at Guadalcanal and in the long Solomon Islands campaign, allowing the Allies to pivot to the offensive for the remainder of the Pacific War. British and American forces captured Tunis in May, ending the war in North Africa. Palermo fell to the Allies on July 22; Mussolini was overthrown two days later. "The massed, angered forces of common humanity are on the march," Roosevelt told the American people in his Fireside Chat broadcast of July 28. "They are going forward—on the Russian front, in the vast Pacific area, and into Europe—converging upon their ultimate objectives, Berlin and Tokyo."[62]

Against this backdrop, the efforts of the American and British treasuries to forge a common position on the postwar international financial structure took on much greater meaning. If the two could agree, the other Allies would have little leverage and quickly fall into line. After the war, the defeated countries would be compelled to sign on. Yet agreement was painfully slow in coming.

White and Keynes corresponded on the plans between July and September 1943; White focusing more on the politics and Keynes on the substance of the plans. White's tone was businesslike; Keynes's warm, at times playful ("I call your special attention to the hidden and unostentatious beauties of the provision").[63] The sense of an unbridgeable personality gap is unmistakable.

Keynes headed back to Washington for intensive meetings with the U.S. Treasury in September and October. The areas of disagreement were the perennial ones. Keynes wanted to downgrade gold and the dollar and to elevate unitas to the status of genuine money, something resembling his bancor. White wanted gold to equal power and the dollar to equal gold. Unitas would be a mere bookkeeping device. Keynes wanted member states to have substantial leeway to alter exchange rates. White wanted such leeway to be strictly limited, with larger changes subject to Stabilization Fund approval. Keynes wanted the fund to be a passive transfer agent, with member states being able to draw liberally on its resources. White insisted that U.S. liability be strictly limited to a level Congress could tolerate.

Tensions naturally bubbled over once again. Roy Harrod nicely captured the atmosphere:

> Their modes of debate were diametrically opposed. White was full of vigour and manful thrust. He could be wrathful and rude. His earnestness carried him forward in a torrent of words, which sometimes outstripped his grammatical powers. Keynes, we know, was different; he detected any inconsistency in the opposition, even in the most abstruse matter, with lightning celerity, and pointed it out with seeming gentleness in barbed and sometimes offensive sentences. . . . His rudeness was sometimes carried to an indefensible length and feelings were ruffled; there might even be hot resentment. It was the old story; he was too ready to assume that his adversaries in debate would take all as fair. . . . "Do not let that clever fellow [Keynes] throw dust in your eyes," White used to tell his American associates, hinting that he, White was quite capable of seeing through it.[64]

Bernstein observed that White would so stress over impending sessions with Keynes, at which he would need to parry effectively in front of both delegations, that it would affect his health.[65]

Keynes recorded his own take on the encounters. "[I] got White round to see me," he wrote to Eady on October 3. "I started off by telling him frankly and crudely exactly what I thought about him. . . . Any reserves we may have about him are a pale reflection of what his colleagues feel. He is over-bearing, a bad colleague, always trying to bounce you, with harsh rasping voice, aesthetically oppressive in mind and manner; he has not the faintest conception how to behave or observe the rules of civilised intercourse."

Then, applying one of his standard rhetorical techniques, Keynes shifted gears abruptly:

> At the same time, I have a very great respect and even liking for him. In many respects he is the best man here. A very able and devoted public servant, carrying an immense burden of responsibility and initiative, of high integrity and of clear sighted idealist international purpose, genu-inely intending to do his best for the world. Moreover, his over-powering will combined with the fact that he has constructive ideas mean that he does get things done, which few else here do. He is not open to flattery in any crude sense.

Yet true to character, Keynes ultimately closes the circle. "The way to reach him is to respect his purpose, arouse his intellectual interest . . . and to tell him off very frankly and firmly without finesse when he has gone off the rails of relevant argument or appropriate behavior."[66] As for the quality of White's work, Keynes termed his Reconstruction Bank scheme "the work of a lunatic, or . . . some sort of bad joke. . . . It is, of course exactly analogous to the mixed bag of currencies in the mone-tary scheme," which Keynes was trying to sweep away with his bancor.[67]

Relations between the two men went from bad to worse. After an October 4 meeting on monetary matters, a British participant summed up the scene:

> What absolute Bedlam these discussions are! Keynes and White sit next [to] each other, each flanked by a long row of his own supporters. With-out any agenda or any prepared idea of what is going to be discussed they go for each other in a strident duet of discord, which after a crescendo of abuse on either side leads up to a chaotic adjournment.[68]

Keynes was fond of making Jewish quips about White and his dep-uty Edward Bernstein, referring to Bernstein as "a regular little rabbi, a reader out of the Talmud, to Harry's grand political rabbidom. . . .

The chap [Bernstein] knows every rat run in his local ghetto, but it is difficult to persuade him to come out for a walk with us on the high ways of the world."[69] This continued after a two-day marathon of compromise drafting, October 8 and 9, which were "full of explosions." Keynes threw White's draft record of their discussions on the floor.

"Keynes has been storming and raging," one British participant reported: "'This is intolerable. It is yet another Talmud. We had better simply break off negotiations.'" White, ever mindful of the gulf between his own background and that of his ennobled interlocutor, fired back: "We will try to produce something which Your Highness can understand."

Negotiations broke off, but a new American draft, more convivial to the British, came back in the afternoon, and "the scene ended with love, kisses and compliments all round."[70] Keynes, supremely satisfied with his performance, wrote to Eady of his diplomatic coup:

> [Bernstein] made a last minute effort to win back the ground he had lost, by persuading White, at the end of our meeting on Saturday morning, to produce a document for us to sign on the dotted line as a supplementary agreement . . . which brought about half of [the Stabilization Fund] right back again [in] the exact words which the Talmudist wrote many months ago. . . . [I] reacted rather violently, saying it was really intolerable at the eleventh hour to have all these matters re-opened in exactly the same terms that we had started with before the discussions began. The other members of my Group thought I had overdone it, but after we had left the meeting a telephone message came along half an hour later that the paper was withdrawn, so that peace and progress were restored. It was one example, in my judgment, of how important it is in this country to react strenuously.

He ended on a magnanimous note with regard to the grand rabbi, White: "[I] hold to the opinion which I have already expressed, that taking everything into account Harry White is probably just about the best man here, and the most serviceable to all concerned."[71]

The end product was a "Joint Statement by Experts of United and Associated Nations on the Establishment of an International Stabilization Fund," outlining principles both parties' technical experts were prepared to recommend to their respective governments, subject to agreement being reached on matters still under dispute. This was, however, just the beginning of an arduous and acrimonious process of securing such agreement. The British had insisted on inserting text stating a fundamental objection to the basic form of the fund outlined in the draft. Additionally, just as Keynes had refused to sign White's earlier draft, White refused to initial the revised, distributed version.

Now back in London, Keynes received an amended version from White with an accompanying letter calling for quick British agreement, joint publication and distribution to the Allies, and organization of an international conference. Keynes dampened his expectations by sending back a letter detailing a long succession of official procedures that would have to navigated in Whitehall and Westminster before the British government could sign off on a document. He also enclosed two new drafts, one based on unitas and one based on national currencies, urging White to accept the unitas version. His case was argued in Washington by Opie, who had succeeded Phillips after the latter's death on August 30. White rejected the unitas version, as "it would be regarded as involving a surrender of sovereignty and it would be thought that business would no longer be done in dollars, pounds, etc., but in a new-fangled international currency."[72] It would be seen in the United States as "tying up the dollar to a phoney international unit."[73] Congress would never accept this. Unitas was now dead. But Keynes made one suggestion that ultimately passed muster in Washington and at Bretton Woods. After White rejected the idea of calling the Stabilization Fund the "International Monetary Union," arguing that Congress would hate the word "Union," Keynes offered "International Monetary Fund" in its stead. It stuck.

White was bursting with frustration over the endless discussions on what he considered minor details. He insisted that the conference had to be held in March or April in order for the final product to be submitted to Congress in May, before the American election campaign would begin in earnest. Treasury's aim was to get its plan through the conference, make it part of the Democratic election platform, and brand Republicans rejecting the plan as isolationists who opposed vital international cooperation. White and Morgenthau could not comprehend the British process for approving a Joint Statement that could be taken to the conference, which required parliamentary approval. This was the opposite of the U.S. process, in which Congress would only have its say after the conference. White wanted to distribute the current statement text to the Russians and others immediately, but partially retreated after Keynes objected that it would lead to damaging leaks and rumors—White gave the statement to the Russians only.

As discussions plodded on into 1944, the U.S. press and banking community were becoming increasingly hostile toward what they believed to be Treasury's aims. Congressman Frederick C. Smith (R-OH), a member of the House Committee on Banking and Currency, decried the "Keynes-Morgenthau plan" as a "British plot to seize control of United States gold." America would be forced "to pour our gold into the European bottomless pit of debt."[74] The British, of course, saw it very differently. Keynes continued to fear, rightly, that with his own plan sidelined, the White Plan would erect a new international monetary edifice based entirely on the dollar. He pressed White to clarify the cryptic term "gold-convertible exchange." On February 3, White wrote to him suggesting that they "leave the definition of 'gold and gold-convertible exchange' for determination at the formal conference if one is held. There would appear to be no need to provide for this in the Joint Statement."[75] White would in the coming months repeatedly use this tactic of deferring matters on which his mind was set, and on which Keynes was set against him, until the conference, where he planned to isolate Keynes from the critical discussions.

In early 1944, though, Keynes's most pressing challenge was bringing his own government on board. The British government was itself divided on the merits of pursuing the Joint Statement. Some of the most influential figures in the country raised powerful arguments against it—and indeed even against Keynes's Clearing Union, which to the world was supposed to be the British plan.

One of these figures was economist and Treasury adviser Hubert Henderson, who argued that the Clearing Union was even worse than the gold standard (by which was meant the gold-exchange standard), which destroyed the British economy in the 1920s. Under the gold standard, countries could withdraw or suspend their obligation to exchange their currency for gold at a fixed price. But the Clearing Union involved an undefined British commitment to other nations, possibly in the nature of a treaty obligation, to maintain a fixed parity, perhaps at the cost of having to liquidate all its gold and monetary reserves. This was intolerable. Moreover, devaluation was scarcely a better means than deflation for curing a persistent balance-of-payments deficit, he argued, because it simply forced the country to sell more cheaply and buy more dearly. What was needed was full freedom to apply import restrictions, exchange controls, and bilateral clearing arrangements— expedients that were anathema to the U.S. Treasury and State Department. But bowing to the Americans by forswearing "discrimination" would involve the unacceptable risk that Britain would ultimately be forced "to go cap in hands for further credits to the United States, or to the Fund. We should have placed ourselves in a position in which we should be pursuing courses which had been stigmatized as undesirable, pleading financial difficulties as an excuse, and having to accept gratefully assistance doled out along with admonitions to conduct ourselves better in future."[76]

In this judgment, Henderson was backed by Waley. Though an early supporter of Keynes's Clearing Union, Waley ultimately concluded, presciently, that the obligation for multilateral clearing as proposed in the Joint Statement was fatal. "[T]his means an obligation to convert sterling on demand into whatever currency the holder of sterling might need. Clearly this is something beyond our powers in the immediate post-war period. . . . In the end, we shall find ourselves requiring substantial assistance from America for which she may impose conditions, including, possibly, adherence to the Monetary Scheme proposed, and some qualification of the exercise of our freedom under the Transitional Period Clause contemplated."[77]

Other major figures opposing not just the Joint Statement but Keynes's Clearing Union were Lord Beaverbrook, a member of the war cabinet, and Leo Amery, secretary of state for India, who articulated the imperialist opposition. "I am entirely in agreement with the Bank [of England]," wrote Beaverbrook to the cabinet. "I look with horror on the alternative Plan because it destroys the Sterling Area. This is all to be done at the compulsion of a Fund in Washington."[78]

"It is only by the fullest use of the bargaining power of our splendid consumers' market, whether within the Empire or with foreign countries, in order to secure special terms for ourselves, as well as by the firm control of our imports, that we can possibly hope to survive," Amery wrote. "We must be free to take whatever measures we think necessary to the safeguard of our own production, to develop Imperial Preference, to use our bargaining power with foreign countries, and to strengthen that wonderful monetary instrument the sterling system. We must enter into no international commitments which in any way limit that freedom."[79]

Perhaps the strongest proponent of the Joint Statement in the cabinet was Richard Law, who argued not that it was good but that it did not make things worse. "The new draft explicitly accepts the principle that the value of individual currencies should be changed to suit changing circumstances," he proffered meekly. "It also lays down explicitly that the Fund is not entitled to interfere in any way in the domestic, social or political policies of member countries."[80]

Given that the Joint Statement had such powerful, passionate, and articulate detractors, while its most influential supporters could at best muster the argument that it didn't seriously hamper British prerogatives, how is it that a majority of a cabinet committee reporting on February 18 recommended that discussions on the Joint Statement continue, and that the war cabinet on February 24 backed the majority report?

To be sure, the committee formally expressed misgivings regarding the position of the sterling area and arrangements regarding the crucial immediate postwar transitional period. It also recommended that British negotiators not concede any prospect of ending imperial preference, but should consider the matter only in the context of general tariff cuts and allowance for state purchasing and subsidies in the agricultural sector. Still, it is curious on the face of it that the Joint Statement survived.

The reason is Lend-Lease. Britain could not sustain its war effort without it, and the American Treasury viewed a British commitment to postwar currency stability and nondiscriminatory trade as vital consideration for it. At the same time White and Morgenthau were prodding the British to sign on to the Joint Statement, they were also pushing for the elimination of nonmilitary American Lend-Lease aid.[81] The aim was to keep British balances below $1 billion, which would tie Britain into a position of extended dependence. This infuriated Churchill, as well as the U.S. State Department. "Sometimes it appears to us (perhaps unjustly)," Keynes observed sharply, "that the United States Treasury would prefer us to end the war with exiguous gold and dollar reserves so that they will be in a position to force [solutions] on us."[82] But it played well with American public opinion. The British embassy was painfully aware of this. In the American imagination, "Lend-Lease is stripping America to supply the British who have not even paid their [first world] war debts," according to an embassy report to the Foreign Office.[83] For Britain to snub the United States and reject the Joint Statement was, therefore, to place nonmilitary American aid in dangerous jeopardy.

Still, British opposition to the Joint Statement did not melt away. Beaverbrook produced a dissenting report, with fierce supporters from the Bank of England, opposing the scheme as a gold standard in disguise that would depress the British economy, reduce sterling's international role, destroy imperial preference, and decimate British agriculture.

Keynes directed his fire at both the bank and Beaverbrook. In a letter to the chancellor dated February 23, Keynes blasted the bank for "not facing any of the realities. . . . We shall end the war owing to all our friends and close associates far more money than we can pay. We are in no position, therefore, to set up as international bankers . . . unless we can secure a general settlement on the basis of temporary American assistance followed by an international scheme." British freedom to engineer new postwar social and economic policies is "impossible without further American assistance . . . the Americans are strong enough to offer inducements to many or most of our friends to walk out on us, if we ostentatiously set out to start up an independent shop."[84]

As for Beaverbrook, Keynes wrote to him in frustration on March 8. "Surely it is not possible to cast *me* for the role of a defender of the gold standard and the Bank for the role of pointing out what a shocking affair it is. You cannot have forgotten back history so much as to think that that makes sense!" Beaverbrook had been deceived by the bank, Keynes insisted. The economic foundations of the empire, such as the sterling area, were doomed if Britain did not cooperate with the Americans. "There is not the slightest chance of the countries of the sterling area agreeing to continue it unless we enter into an obligation of convertibility . . . it is only under the aegis of an international scheme that we can hope to preserve the sterling area." To ask the dominions "to enter into a currency bloc with us on the basis of no obligation of convertibility with the outside world is to ask the impossible . . . South Africa and India would walk out forthwith." The Bank of England, Keynes thundered, was "engaged in a desperate gamble in the interests of the old arrangements and old-fashioned ideas, which there is no possibility of sustaining. . . . The whole thing is sheer rubbish from beginning to end. For God's sake have nothing to do with it![85]

"You bring such charm to the discussion of economics," Beaverbrook responded, "that I am almost reconciled to disagreeing with you. For I can hardly suppose that you would trouble to preach with such eloquence to the converted." He then went on to lay out his own views, which even in his day would have had more than a whiff of musty nostalgia.

"I am at variance with the underlying doctrine because it is essentially international and free-trade, and because my beliefs are neither the one nor the other," Beaverbrook explained. "I put a value upon imperial preference and on the protection of domestic agriculture which is higher than anything assigned to them under the Plan," he continued. "And I would not be prepared to support a proposition which destroyed the preference and sacrificed agriculture on account of compensations which appear to be both dubious and inadequate." He rejected the notion that economic growth required demolishing trade barriers. "I believe that it is possible to secure expansion within the Imperial ambit," he asserted. "Indeed, we shall build on a firmer foundation if we do so."

Regarding the diplomatic challenge the British were up against, however, it was Beaverbrook, rather than Keynes, whose views were better adapted to the times. The notion that Britain could bind the United States into a system that would further Britain's economic and imperial interests was "a perilous illusion. The days when we could control the Americans have passed away and there is no prospect of their return."[86]

Back in Washington, Morgenthau had lost all patience. Having tried and failed to pressure the chancellor, through Winant, to expedite British government approval of the Joint Statement, he vented to Winant by cable on April 10: "[T]he U.K. representatives have placed us in a most embarrassing position by their delay," which has "made it impossible for us to keep the Congress, our public and other governments informed, has given rise to harmful rumors, and has increased the difficulty of carrying through our program." Unless the British agreed to publication of the Joint Statement next week it would be impossible, he believed, to hold a conference this year.[87]

But the British government was now also under pressure from the dominions, which were insisting on larger quotas, as well as assurances on matters related to, though not touched on, in the scheme. India, for example, was demanding to know how Britain would pay for Indian war supplies, for which India was accumulating massive inconvertible sterling balances in London.

White had his own problems with foreigners: the Chinese, he told Opie, were haranguing him for a copy of the Joint Statement, and he could not put off the Latin Americans for much longer. Furthermore, Opie reported to Keynes on April 13, the New York bankers were converging on Washington to kill the drive for an international fund by supporting the Dewey bill to underwrite bilateral U.S. reconstruction and stabilization grants and loans in its stead. "White repeated that the delaying tactics are being used because they think the temper of Congress will be such after November that no broad-minded international schemes will stand a chance. The Administration take this as a serious threat."[88]

The war cabinet in London was feeling the heat from Washington but continued to attach caveats, related to matters such as quotas and the need for a parallel international investment organization, to its blessing of the Joint Statement. White, supremely annoyed, rebuffed them. He would not discuss quotas until the conference, and would not allow the monetary scheme to be tied to an investment agreement.

White and Morgenthau briefly turned their attention to getting other nations on board. This they treated largely as a formality, even cabling the American ambassador in China to tell him that "the statement will be released here irrespective of whether it is released in Chungking."[89] The only real concern was with Russia. White prepared a cable for the Secretary telling Ambassador Averell Harriman in Moscow to call on the people's commissar of finance, informing him that the British chancellor had signed off on the Joint Statement, which he had not, and requesting publication in Moscow simultaneous with that in Washington and London. The commissar responded that he had not yet received the response of his experts, and so could not agree to endorse the text. But after some frantic further exchanges, Foreign Minister Molotov told Harriman, just a few hours before the statement was released to the press in Washington, that whereas major differences existed among the Russian experts "if it is necessary . . . to the Government of the United States of America to have the concurrence of the Government of the Soviet Republic to secure due effect in the rest of the world, the Soviet Government is willing to instruct its experts to associate themselves with Mr Morgenthau's project."[90] The Soviets would use the same diplomatic tactic at Bretton Woods.

Back in London, Keynes could read the writing on the wall. "Dr. White is a man with a memory," he wrote to the chancellor on April 16. "We may find ourselves in a position where we are forced to accept his general conditions without any of the admirable and far-reaching safeguards which we have worked, with such immense labour and forethoughtfulness, into the present document."

The cabinet reluctantly dropped its conditions. The Joint Statement, the essential prelude to a conference, could finally go forward. Still, even as the chancellor, Sir John Anderson, was finalizing arrangements with Morgenthau for publication on April 21 of the Joint Statement in Washington and London, Keynes was frantically cabling Opie suggesting alterations to the text. Though these were ignored in Washington, Keynes did persuade the chancellor to allow him to prepare explanatory notes detailing how and why the Joint Statement differed from the Clearing Union plan, which were released in London together with the statement. Keynes asked the chancellor to send a copy to White in advance, "but he should not be asked or expected to agree with it. He has not earned such a privilege," Keynes added, clearly piqued over White's repeated snubs. "And, in the circumstances, we should be acting as whipt curs to offer it."[91]

At his press conference in Washington, Morgenthau was beaming over his triumph in getting both the Russians and the British on board. When asked about smaller nations, he quipped "We'll ask their advice and then fix it for them," provoking surprised laughter from the journalists. When pressed over details of the plan, "Morgenthau seemed if anything slightly more muddled over the recommendations than his questioners."[92] White consistently intervened to answer for or correct his boss.

Political wrangling in London did not end with publication of the Joint Statement, since the statement was formally only an agreement on principles among technical experts, and not one approved by national governments. The chancellor resisted Morgenthau's entreaties to agree immediately to head the UK delegation to the conference, which the Secretary now wanted to be held on or about May 26. Winant explained to Morgenthau that the imperative of getting parliamentary approval combined with sea-travel security challenges made such an early trip impossible. In Washington, White boiled over with Opie yet again regarding the delay, arguing that many in the administration believed that nationalists in Britain were seeking to constitute an exclusive empire bloc for the purposes of buttressing Britain as a European power. (Unstated was the fact that White himself was clearly among those who believed this.) These British nationalists were playing into the hands of American "imperialist-isolationists"—the "world's worst enemies," White called them, according to Opie.[93]

Keynes briefed the chancellor before the House of Commons debate on May 10, tutoring him particularly on how to crush any suggestion that the Joint Statement represented a return to the gold standard. Of course, Keynes himself had suggested precisely this before he and the British government had been obliged to capitulate to the White Plan. But now he could do no more than try to push back the battle against gold and the dollar to the conference itself. Though Keynes "spent seven hours in the accursed [Commons] Gallery, lacerated in mind and body" listening to "incredible stupidity" on the monetary plan, the motion to back the Joint Statement was ultimately agreed.[94]

It was now on to the House of Lords, where there were calls to defer debate until specific nonmonetary matters of international cooperation had been considered. Keynes pressed for expeditious consideration of the statement in the Lords, arguing that "there is a logical reason for dealing with monetary proposals first. It is extraordinarily difficult to frame any proposals about tariffs if countries are free to alter the value of their currencies without agreement and at short notice. Tariffs and currency depreciations are in many cases alternatives. . . . It is very difficult while you have monetary chaos to have order of any kind in other directions."[95]

Keynes parried skeptics with alacrity, wherever they turned up. He responded to a critical letter in *The Times* of London on the same day: "No country has more to gain from it than ourselves. For it is characteristic of our trade that our important sources of supply are not always our best customers." But if Britain were to reject an international scheme, and to insist on "having many different kinds of sterling, each subject to different conditions of use, [then] farewell to London as an international centre. Farewell, also, to the sterling area and all it stands for, . . . [W]ho, except in conditions of war and out of a readiness to help us finance it, would bank in London if the funds deposited there were not freely available?"[96]

The debate was finally engaged in the House of Lords on May 23. Reacting to the concern that the Joint Statement differed considerably from the Keynes Plan, Keynes first tried to make light of losing the single most critical element of his plan: a new international currency. "There were, it is true, certain features of elegance, clarity and logic in the Clearing Union plan which have disappeared," he lamented. "And this, by me at least, is to be much regretted." The result, he claimed, was that "there is no longer any need for a new-fangled international monetary unit." Keynes would never have tarred his beloved bancor with the term "new-fangled" had he not accepted that the game was up.

He turned to allegorical humor to downplay the significance of this concession. "Your Lordships will remember how little any of us liked the names proposed—bancor, unitas, dolphin, bezant, daric and heaven knows what. Some of your Lordships were good enough to join in the search for something better":

I recall a story of a country parish in the last century where they were accustomed to give their children Biblical names—Amos, Ezekiel, Obadiah and so forth. Needing a name for a dog, after a long and vain search of the Scriptures they called the dog "Moreover". We hit on no such happy solution, with the result that it has been the dog that died. The loss of the dog we need not too much regret, though I still think that it was a more thoroughbred animal than what has now come out from a mixed marriage of ideas. Yet, perhaps, as sometimes occurs, this dog of mixed origin is a sturdier and more serviceable animal and will prove not less loyal and faithful to the purposes for which it has been bred.[97]

Having reduced the essence of his plan to that of a dead dog—a plan for which he and the British government had argued relentlessly with the Americans over a course of years—he then went on to blast his compatriot naysayers for supporting the techniques of "little England-ism." For "to suppose that a system of bilateral and barter agreements, with no one who owns sterling knowing just what he can do with it—to suppose that this is the best way of encouraging the Dominions to cen-tre their financial systems on London, seems to me pretty near frenzy." Reality dictated that "with our own resources so greatly impaired and encumbered, it is only if sterling is firmly placed in an international setting that the necessary confidence in it can be sustained." Going it alone would be the height of economic irresponsibility. "Do the critics think it preferable, if the winds of the trade cycle blow, to diminish our demand for imports by increasing unemployment at home, rather than meet the emergency out of this Fund which will be expressly provided for such temporary purposes?"

As with his maiden House of Lords speech a year prior, there were moments in his peroration in which Keynes, clearly seeking to exploit any and all arguments that might win favor, appeared deliberately to steer his fellow lordships away from what he either knew or believed to be the truth. Some such statements were innocuous, as far as politics go, such as his observation that the discussions with the United States had been without "expense of temper," which clearly could not have included some critical sessions with White. Other statements were less innocuous, perhaps materially misleading, such as his claim that he was "certain that the people of this country are of the same mind as Hull," the U.S. secretary of state whose ideas on trade Keynes had previously blasted as lunatic, but who was now apparently implement-ing excellent ideas with "disinterestedness and generosity."[98] It would seem that, in reconciling himself to inevitable American hegemony in setting the terms of the postwar monetary apparatus, Keynes was at least as concerned with maintaining his standing in the process as he was with molding the actual terms. Having previously dismissed the American plan privately as "not much more than a version of the gold standard,"[99] he now told the House of Lords: "If I have any authority to pronounce on what is and what is not the essence and meaning of a gold standard, I should say that this plan is the exact opposite of it." Yet in ultimately asking rhetorically, "What alternative is open to us which gives comparable aid, or better, more hopeful opportunities for the future?" Keynes was accurately, if not candidly, capturing the dire nature of Britain's financial situation.[100]

Keynes, in arguing in favor of a new multilateral currency system while insisting that preferences in imperial trade could be maintained, struck many of his colleagues, such as Lord Balfour and Dennis Robertson, as contradicting himself. Could countries legitimately be free to spend the proceeds of their exports to one country on the imports of any other, as implied by currency multilateralism, if a larger country (say, Britain) were free to tell a smaller one that it would only buy its products if the latter agreed to purchase the larger country's products in return?

"[I] think you are in danger of digging in on a distinction by *content*—a distinction between the monetary and the commercial—" Robertson wrote to Keynes on May 22, "which has only a superficial validity, and may prove an intellectual quicksand."[101] Keynes responded testily that he "remain[ed] more (or worse) than unrepentant," but he appeared to be at pains to clothe in logic what was only defensible in terms of political necessity.[102] For at that moment he was trying to tug London toward Washington.

The motion in the Lords chamber was in the end agreed, owing above all to Keynes's reassurances. But these naturally produced a backlash in the American press, particularly his claims that if the United States kept "obstinately" exporting more than it imported the Joint Statement provisions freed "countries from any obligation to take its exports, or, if taken, to pay for them."[103] The German press, which followed the monetary discussions closely, focused cuttingly on the American-British power play. The *Deutsche Bergwerks Zeitung* observed that Keynes had initially taken the lead in the "monetary duel" by shrewdly protecting

British interests under the pretext of saving the world economy, but that the Americans were ultimately able to impose their dollar imperialism because of superior political might.[104] The *Kölnische Zeitung* accused Keynes of speaking not as an economist but as a man who was dressing up inevitable British concessions for political reasons.[105]

Keynes wrote in soothing tones to White that the "misrepresentation" and "rush of imperial sentiment" in the British press, which White would certainly have been following, was not to "be taken too seriously; it is essentially a superficial and a passing phase." Yet the Americans were angered not merely by British press coverage, but by Keynes's seeming duplicity in asserting British postwar monetary and commercial prerogatives in London. "When I said to him that his speech in the House of Lords had caused us considerable trouble here," Pasvolsky recorded, "he replied that the situation was so bad that he felt it absolutely necessary to say the things he had said."[106]

Morgenthau had been compelled by the drawn-out British political theater to push back his conference date target, yet again, from May to early July. (Each delay had been held to mean the end of the world.) As always, the timetable was dictated by the American election cycle: Morgenthau would now sandwich the conference between the Republican convention in late June and the Democratic convention a few weeks later. This would enable him to inject his postwar monetary ambitions directly into the campaign.

Meanwhile Opie, having spent time in New York trying to persuade the bankers to back the monetary plan, found them open, as an alternative, to offering Britain a large loan, provided that an agreement could be reached to stabilize the sterling-dollar rate. After reading Opie's account, Waley wrote to Keynes asking whether it might not be at least as important to pursue the loan as it was to pursue the monetary plan. "Taking a short view it is of much more immediate importance to us that we should be given the option of borrowing up to 3 billion dollars from the United States for the transition period than it is that the Monetary Plan should be accepted for the post-transition period."[107] Keynes, seemingly horrified at the idea that his far-reaching ambitions could be squashed by the mere dangling of a bankers' loan, fired back that "the wise and prudent course is to run with the U.S. Treasury rather than with its disgruntled critics." The bankers "do not know their own mind and have no power whatever to implement their promises."[108] The unkind feelings were apparently mutual: Opie had reported to the Foreign Office that Randolph Burgess, an officer of the Federal Reserve Bank of New York and one of the New York bankers' leading voices, had told him that "it would have a bad effect in banking and business circles here, and also in Congress if Lord Keynes were a member of the United Kingdom delegation" to the conference.[109] His was "the philosophy of deficit spending over again—the use of credit as a cure-all."[110]

Now himself anxious to get an international conference under way before the political tides turned firmly against it, Keynes wrote nervously to White on May 24 that "we are wondering when the invitation is going to come from Mr Morgenthau." He also pleaded, only a dab in jest, "For God's sake do not take us to Washington in July, which would surely be a most unfriendly act."[111] That very day, White called a meeting with British and Russian representatives announcing that the conference would start in the first week of July, though the exact timing and locale, he claimed, had not yet been fixed. An international drafting committee would need to be convened about three weeks prior. White and Opie each suggested countries that might be invited to send experts to the drafting sessions. The Russians, as was their standard practice, made no comment, other than to indicate that they would refer the matter to Moscow. The following day, May 25, Hull formally issued conference invitations to forty-four nations, revealing the starting date as July 1 and the locale as Bretton Woods, New Hampshire. Morgenthau issued a press release announcing the details the day after.

Keynes was unnerved by White's game plan. There were to be three stages: the preconference drafting committee meetings in mid-June, to be held in Atlantic City; an enormous multiweek conference starting July 1 at Bretton Woods; and a postconference ratification process in all participating countries' legislatures. This was hardly the model that Keynes envisioned, which was to be a tightly controlled Anglo-American staging. "Dr. White's conception of all this seems to get 'curiouser and curiouser,'" he wrote to Waley on May 30; "42 nations, making 43 in all, have been invited for July 1." Twenty-one of these, including Iran, Iraq, Venezuela, and Colombia, would "clearly have nothing to contribute and . . . merely encumber the ground." It was "the most monstrous monkey-house assembled for years." The American press, he noted, had "indicated that 'the Conference beginning on July 1 may last several weeks.' Unless this is a misprint for several days, it is not easy to see how the main monkey-house is going to occupy itself," given White's plans for preconference drafting. "It would seem probable that acute alcoholic poisoning would set in before the end."[112]

For his part, White had no intention of allowing the drafting committee to draft anything of substance. The Cuban delegates, for example, "would be silent members [whose] main function would be to bring cigars," he quipped at the May 24 meeting.[113] The committee exercise was to be a conference dry-run and American intelligence-gathering event, created by White specifically to ensure that the main event at Bretton Woods would be as close as possible to choreographed Kabuki theater.

For all of Keynes's self-deception and political dissembling to keep the embers of his Clearing Union scheme glowing, in the face of American determination to stomp them out, he remained throughout the many years of Lend-Lease and Bretton Woods negotiations his country's most perspicacious assayer of its financial challenges. None of his writings illustrates this more powerfully than a ten-thousand-word memo titled, simply, "The Problem of our External Finance in the Transition," which he distributed to ministers and various departments on June 12, just before his departure for Atlantic City.

"Nearly the whole of our 1914–1918 external debt was canalised into the American debt—and that we shuffled out of," Keynes wrote. "On the assumption that this time we intend to pay, the fact that we owe money all over the place . . . means that the effort required to emerge without loss of honour, dignity and credit will be immensely greater." His analysis demonstrated that Britain was clearly living on borrowed time and money. The numbers were stark. He calculated that in the first three years after the war Britain would face a balance-of-payments deficit between £1.5 billion and £2.25 billion ($6 billion–$9 billion), which had somehow to be financed. He outlined a detailed scheme to close the gap, which included making repayments countercyclical, toughening export payment terms with the Allies, further restricting dominion access to sterling-area dollar reserves, boosting exports, and gaining release from the restrictions on dollar reserve buildups written into Lend-Lease.

The first hurdle Britain had to overcome was denial. Here is where Keynes shows his true genius as a practical economist—he analyzes the national psyche at least as incisively as he analyzes the numbers:

> All our reflex actions are those of a rich man, so we promise others too much. Our longings for relaxation from the war are so intense that we promise ourselves too much. As a proud and great Power, we disdain to chaffer with others smaller and more exorbitant than ourselves. Having been so recently in dire extremity, our financial policy is rooted in appeasement. Above all, the financial problems of the war have been surmounted so easily and so silently that the average man sees no reason to suppose that the financial problems of the peace will be any more difficult. The Supply Departments have demanded of the Treasury that money should be no object. And the Treasury has so contrived that it has been no object. This success is the greatest obstacle of all to getting the problems of this memorandum taken seriously.

Beyond this, it was vital for Britain to wean itself off obligations to the United States as quickly and completely as possible, which would require further great national sacrifice. "[T]he *terms* and the consequences of losing our financial independence . . . should deeply concern us. . . . We must reduce our requirements for American aid to the least possible—say, to $2 to $3 billion . . . and even be prepared, if the worst befalls, to do without it altogether." In one sentence, he reveals that, whatever he might have said to the British Parliament and press in order to keep the Joint Statement alive, he understood fully the dangers of the game Britain was playing with its ambitious and much more powerful former colony: "Recent discussion in the United States and evidence given before Congress make it quite clear that there are quarters in the United States intending to use the grant of post-war credits to us as an opportunity for imposing (entirely, of course, for our good) the American conception of the international economic system."[114] This clearly included the abolition of imperial preference, the abolition of exchange controls preventing the use of sterling-area balances to buy American exports, and the enthronement of the dollar atop the international monetary system. Harry White was at the forefront of such quarters. But Keynes, who set sail for New York on June 16, continued to impute goodwill to him. No doubt, he had convinced himself that, in furtherance of his country's vital interests, he had no choice but to proceed on that assumption.

Yet the fact remains that Waley had communicated to Keynes a tantalizingly simple Plan B: stand up to the U.S. Treasury, and borrow dollars privately instead. These would have come with fewer geopolitical strings. There must have been some small part of him that rejected this option not because it was futile, but because it would have meant conceding the death of his brainchild—the Clearing Union.

On the voyage over, Keynes and the British team, which included Eady, Robbins, and several Bank of England and Foreign Office officials, produced two "boat drafts" dealing with the fund and the bank. Keynes also found time for some leisure reading, which included Friedrich Hayek's newly published *The Road to Serfdom*. Keynes penned a response to Hayek, in which he, surely to the chagrin of many of his disciples, called it "a grand book. . . . Morally and philosophically I find myself in agreement with virtually the whole of it; and not only in agreement, but in a deeply moved agreement." Keeping to form, however, Keynes then launched a critique, devoting several paragraphs to defending his "middle course" against Hayek's argument that substituting government planning for markets inevitably led to the loss of individual freedom, as well as declining prosperity. The intellectual duel between the two still largely defines the boundaries of economic policy debate.[115]

The British delegation arrived in New York on June 23, quickly boarding a train for Atlantic City, where they checked into the Claridge Hotel—home for the previous and coming week to the pre–Bretton Woods drafting sessions. Keynes wasted no time getting down to business, heading to a private meeting with White at which he presented him with the "boat drafts." White's reaction was not recorded, but can be easily imagined.

The British and American delegations began their formal negotiating sessions the following day, June 24. The initial encounter was devoted to issues related to the bank, which proved smooth sailing. The meetings "went very well indeed," Lionel Robbins wrote in his diary. "Keynes was in his most lucid and persuasive mood; and the effect was irresistible . . . . The Americans sat entranced as the God-like visitor sang and the golden light played around them. . . . [S]o far as the Bank is concerned, I am clear that we are off with a fly-ing start."[116] It was no surprise that White would subsequently place Keynes in charge of managing the bank negotiations a week later at Bretton Woods, since the entrancer showed he could do no harm to American interests on this issue.

June 25 was devoted to fund issues, and it was here that fundamen-tal splits were laid bare. The British delegation stressed the importance of countries being able to change their exchange rates, while the Amer-ican delegation emphasized the importance of exchange rate stability. The British stressed the rights of countries with respect to the fund, while the Americans emphasized the importance of the fund's powers as against the individual countries. The British wanted a larger fund and the Americans a much smaller one. The British wanted a long tran-sitional period in which they would retain freedom of action on the trade and monetary fronts, while the Americans wanted such a period to be as short as possible. The British were unhappy with the American quota formula, but the Americans refused to discuss the issue, leading Keynes to conclude, reluctantly, that they would be obliged to take that formula as the starting point for discussions at Bretton Woods.

Keynes nonetheless convinced himself that he and White had an understanding that the Americans and British would maneuver a com-mon position through conference. His letter to Sir Richard Hopkins on June 25 reveals the illusory ground on which this confidence rested:

> White is anxious that not too many doubts and choices between alterna-tives should be finally settled here at Atlantic City, since it is important for him there should be no appearance of asking the members of the American Delegation who are not here and the other powers not repre-sented here to rubber-stamp something already substantially finished. At the same time he agrees that we and the Americans should reach as high a degree of agreement behind the scenes as to which of the alternatives we are ready to drop and which we agree in pressing. Thus to the largest

extent possible White and I will have an agreed text, but on the surface a good many matters may be presented in alternative versions.[117]

As with Churchill's letters to Roosevelt, pathos suffuses Keynes's missive—a sense that its writer simply cannot bring himself to acknowledge his powerlessness. Keynes paints himself and White as secret collaborators in a Bretton Woods fix-up, suggesting conspiratorially that the conference debate, "consist[ing] of about 60 persons in a room where those at the back can hear nothing," would essentially be for show. "The staging of the vast monkey-house at Bretton Woods is, of course, in order that the President can say that 44 nations have agreed on the Fund and the Bank."[118] In reality, Keynes was himself just another member of the monkey house White had to keep occupied and distracted in order to implement the White Plan.

British minutes of a meeting with the U.S. delegation the next day, June 26, show White resolutely resistant to Keynes's redrafted Article IV of the statement of principles, asserting member states' "ultimate rights" over their exchange rates. White was insistent that the cardinal mission of the fund was to uphold exchange rate stability. Keynes's fund, White argued, would look to the American people to be just a giant credit scheme—which is to a large extent what the fund has become today.

"[White] thought, therefore, that Lord Keynes's criticisms and proposals went right to the root of the plan, and that if [Keynes] insisted on them it would be impossible to reach agreement," according to the British minutes.[119] Keynes argued that the lesson of the 1930s was that international obligations to sustain a fixed exchange rate, come what may, were politically unsupportable; White argued that the lesson of the 1930s was that exchange rate instability was politically disastrous.

Keynes's suggested compromise was that countries would not be allowed to access the facilities of the fund while at the same time exercising their rights to devalue. White responded, according to American minutes of the meeting, that it was "very grave" for the British to suggest "that the consequence of failure to comply with the exchange provision shall be merely deprivation of resources, [as] a country may at that time have used up its credits at the Fund and not have any further interest in these facilities." He dismissed Keynes's suggestion as "a direct violation of our understanding."[120]

The two men clashed as well over the length of the postwar transition period during which countries could maintain trade controls. White wanted three years, after which fund approval would be necessary. Keynes wanted each country to be its own judge. White responded incredulously by asking whether this meant that even ten years was not sufficient, to which Keynes replied that after a certain period a country could be subject to expulsion from the fund if the fund felt it had a bad case. Keynes declared his position final, and threatened to break off negotiations. White simply changed the subject, choosing to bide his time until the conference, where he could isolate Keynes and resolve the matter on his own.[121]

On June 28 the two butted heads once again, this time over the meaning of the critical but inscrutable terms "gold-convertible currency" and "convertible exchange," which appeared several times in the statement of principles. The issuer of a currency considered as good as gold would potentially reap enormous benefits. Other countries would naturally want to hold vast reserves of such a currency in order to settle international payments and to act as a buffer against unforeseen financial difficulties. The issuer would, in contrast, need minimal foreign exchange reserves. It would earn "seigniorage" profits from the interest on the assets it received in return for its non-interest-bearing currency. It could, within limits, persistently buy more from abroad than it sold by simply printing money. Its firms would not suffer foreign exchange risk on the vast bulk of its trade. And finally there would be the non-quantifiable prestige associated with minting global money.

Keynes understood the economic and political risks to Britain of "gold-convertible currency" coming to mean U.S. dollars, and not sterling. He proposed replacing the term with the words "monetary reserves." The Americans countered by suggesting "gold and dollars" as an alternative, thereby baring their true ambitions. Keynes objected that the dollar should not be given any special position, arguing that other currencies would also be gold-convertible in the future. As with the contentious issue of the transition period, White simply chose to disengage, deferring the issue until the conference. Keynes was unaware that it was central to White's vision of a new world order to have the dollar crowned as the new gold at Bretton Woods. White and his staff had already submitted a memo to Morgenthau in which all references to "gold-convertible exchange" and "holdings of convertible exchange" had been replaced by "dollars."[122] But he submitted no amendment to the statement of principles, knowing that many delegations would object. He was instead determined to achieve the switch on the sly at Bretton Woods.

Keynes continued to paint a picture at odds with this record of discord on critical issues. "[A]ll has really gone very well indeed. There has not been a single moment of heat or serious dispute, and amiability has prevailed," he wrote to Hopkins on June 30, this despite the fact that Keynes himself had threatened to walk out at one point. "White has proved an altogether admirable chairman," he continued. "His kindness to me personally has been extreme. And behind the scenes he has always been out to find a way of agreement except when his own political difficulties stood in the way." Again, Keynes insisted that the lack of any tangible progress with the Americans was not a sign of failure, but cleverness: "The technique has been not to reach formal agreement on any matters, since White is much concerned not to present Bretton Woods with anything like a *fait accompli* or dotted line." On the critical issue of exchange rates, "we have not got [agreement] from them in so many words," yet this was due to a mere American attachment to legalism. "White and Bernstein have been brought over to our point of view, but they are having the usual trouble which always occurs in this country and is one of the causes of preventing anything sensible being done; that is that they have to consult their lawyers, who are proving difficult."[123] So what in the official British record was noted as clear disagreement with the Americans was, by Keynes's spin, simply an intentional lack of "formal agreement" designed to create the appearance of an open process, or a mere matter of bringing 'round the lawyers.

White himself sharply contradicted Keynes's account of the secret harmony they had achieved. There were "troublesome differences between the British and ourselves," he reported to Morgenthau on June 25, "which the American delegation will have to contend with at the conference." He laid out a laundry list of items, chief among which the fact that "[t]he British want to increase the flexibility and ease of alterations of exchange rates. We think we should not budge one bit."[124] No mention was made of obstructive lawyers.

Whereas Keynes and the British delegation were White's biggest nuisance at Atlantic City, other delegations naturally pushed for their own national interests to be taken on board. White instructed his team of technical advisers to engage with the foreign delegates as much as possible, but to "stick to the party line" and never mention the possibility of U.S. compromise.[125] The issue that raised the most concerns was that of national quotas. White forbade discussion of the subject outside the American group, and the quota formula and table prepared by the Treasury was kept secret. Delegates were told only that the aggregate quotas would be between $8 billion and $8.5 billion. Countries therefore understood that any increase in their quota meant a cut in someone else's. This was meant to keep them from fighting the U.S. delegation by making clear to them that they would also have to fight each other.[126]

The remaining delegation White had to manage was his own. This he set out to do by keeping them in the dark. Not inviting them to Atlantic City, he instead brought his own private army of technical assistants and secretaries, whom he began training on June 15, four days before the first foreign delegations began arriving. They were to play an essential role in channeling the energy, aims, ambitions, and vanities of the mass of delegates into meaningless debate.

White would structure the conference with himself at the head of a commission dealing with the fund. Keynes would be shunted to off to head a commission dealing with the bank, which by this time had become peripheral to White's postwar agenda. Within the commissions would be multiple committees dealing with specific issues of substance. All the committees would have foreign chairmen and reporting delegates. These would essentially be the "monkey-houses" foreseen by Keynes. To ensure that the monkey houses did not get out of hand, all the secretaries and assistants would be White's closest Treasury associates and handpicked others from the Federal Reserve, the State Department, and other U.S. government agencies. It was they, and not the foreigners, or even the American delegates, who would select the subjects for discussion, count the votes, and—critically— write the minutes of the meetings and the final act. White instructed his team not to interfere in the committee discussions, but warned them that they were not under any circumstance to deviate from the official American position.

Prior to the arrival of the fifteen foreign delegations at Atlantic City, White's team was broken into four groups, each of which worked intensively for five days on a group of issues for which the U.S. Treasury and foreign delegations were seeking amendments to the Joint Statement of Principles.[127] The issues included member country obligations, quotas and voting power, levies, withdrawal and suspension of members, and changes in exchange rate parities. Each day, the groups came together at a general meeting run by White, in which changes to the Joint Statement were suggested and discussed. White permitted only his closest assistants to see the full draft of the amended Joint Statement, refusing requests from others to review it. One complained that he and his colleagues "had been pressing for a complete document, mostly because difficulties arose in trying to discuss one little section of the document not knowing how the other sections would read." When they were finally allowed to see the draft of the amended statement, "copies were numbered and taken back from us after the meeting."[128] White even forbade anyone from recording written minutes of the meetings.[129]

The extreme secrecy White imposed not only annoyed members of his team in Atlantic City, but angered the Treasury Secretary in Washington. "[I don't] know what's going on other than I hear when you're short of bath towels," Morgenthau barked into the phone on June 22, the eighth day of the meetings.

"[I've been working] day and night with the American group to agree our positions," White explained. "We're going over the various points, seeing where we're going to have disagreements or run into trouble, but it's all . . . just an exchange of view and discussion basis." His aim, he explained, was to get a complete draft into shape that he could present to the British. White had told his team that the discussions with foreigners were not to be "serious" until the British arrived on June 23.

"Yeah, but look; Harry, you're leaving me completely high and dry, and all the rest of the American delegates and then you expect us to come up there and sign on the dotted line, and it won't work. It just won't," Morgenthau shot back.

"Well, I was going to suggest that. . . ."

"I mean it just won't work," Morgenthau continued, cutting White off. "It's very nice. I mean, I know you are working your head off, but you're leaving . . . all the rest of us completely high and dry."

White tried to placate the Secretary by suggesting that a few of the American delegates might come and join the meetings. Or he could brief them on the American position before Bretton Woods.

"Yeah, but supposing I don't like at all what's been agreed to," Morgenthau posited, sounding as if he knew he wouldn't understand enough of the technicalities to agree or disagree. "The point is, if you'd send me the stuff and kept me posted as you went along, I would know," he clarified, meekly. "If I don't read it, it's my own fault, but if I don't have anything from you, then it's your fault."[130]

White quickly fired off an after-the-fact memo to Morgenthau defending his management of the Atlantic City event, emphasizing the importance of the time spent enlarging and revising the drafts on the fund and the bank, exposing the American experts to the views of the foreign delegations, and training the experts to play their critical role supporting the American delegates at Bretton Woods. But Morgenthau knew that White was a man with an agenda, and so he instructed Bernstein to keep him informed of developments at Atlantic City. What he learned was that there was no shortage of controversy on what the fund should be or do, either between various American interests or among participating governments.[131] Harry was throwing up smoke.

It was too late, however, for Morgenthau to grab the reins. On June 30, the delegates were shepherded onto a chartered train bound for Bretton Woods. Their departure marked a successful conclusion to White's staging of the conference overture. He had kept the British constructively occupied while giving away nothing of substance. He had acquired actionable intelligence on the issues that would animate the other delegations. He had kept Morgenthau and the American delegates at bay. And he had trained a private militia that would be instrumental in controlling the outcome of the main drama to come.

U.S. delegation head and conference president Henry Morgenthau, Jr., addressing a session of the Bretton Woods conference, July 1944. (Courtesy National Archives, photo no. 208-N-29536)

CHAPTER 8

History Is Made

June 1944 was a momentous month. American troops reached the center of Rome on June 4. The following evening, British infantrymen landed by gliders in France, six miles north of Caen; by midnight June 6, 155,000 American, British, and Canadian troops were ashore in Normandy. By June 10 that total would reach 325,000; by June 20, half a million. The legendary Allied "Operation Overlord," which had very nearly been grounded by relentless stormy weather, was in full swing.

Despite setbacks—Churchill had feared much worse, and had unsuccessfully lobbied FDR for an alternative southern European front—the Allies were grinding back the well-fortified German defenders. Resistance would have been much worse had it not been for a massive and sustained Anglo-American deception operation, the likes of which had never been seen in all of military history. By June 25, with American forces advancing through the suburbs of Cherbourg, German Field Marshal von Rundstedt still suspected that Normandy was a mere diversion; thousands of German soldiers lay in wait in the Pas-de-Calais area for an invasion by the phantom First United States Army Group. On the eastern front, the Red Army was making sweeping advances toward Minsk, killing 130,000 German troops and taking 66,000 prisoners in the month's final week. Yet there was no letup in the horror of Nazi atrocities; 444 miles from Minsk, railway cars carrying 1,795 Greek Jews rolled into the concentration camps of Auschwitz on June 30. Half of them were dead. The other half were in a coma; they were quickly murdered.[1]

That same day, a world away in the majestic White Mountains of New Hampshire, workers were feverishly preparing the grounds for the most important international gathering since the Paris Peace Conference of 1919—one that would look beyond the carnage of war to establish a new world order founded on commerce and cooperation. Two sons of European Jewish immigrants, the American Treasury Secretary and his deputy, were huddled on-site with an American advance team, scripting the logistics of Henry Morgenthau's election to the conference presidency the following afternoon.

Harry White was worried that the Secretary's acceptance speech would get lost in what Morgenthau called the folderol. "How about the press?" White asked. "Will the Secretary's speech get a good play?"

"Oh, yes," Treasury's Fred Smith assured him, "because they have the Sunday papers. That's the basic reason" for moving the speech forward to Saturday, earlier than originally planned.[2]

Central to the Treasury blueprint for winning over the more pliable skeptics in Congress was cultivating the press with a degree of access and openness unprecedented for a major international political event. The administration was determined not to repeat its searing experience with hostile media men at last year's United Nations Food and Agriculture conference in Hot Springs, Virginia. "Officials here have already made it obvious that Bretton Woods is to be no 'Hot Springs' in respect to treatment of the press," wrote the *Christian Science Monitor* approvingly. "Conferences between newspapermen and officials are slated daily."[3]

The speech details settled, the other critical item was handling the ever-prickly British delegation head. Many in Congress were convinced that the conference plan was the work of the wily and profligate British, led by a slick-tongued, aristocratic bamboozler—Lord Keynes. Morgenthau and White agreed that they could not let the man near the podium on the opening day. "[T]ell him . . . if he speaks the middle of next week sometime, singly, he will get all the play in the press," Morgenthau instructed White; "[otherwise he] will be drowned under by the President and the rest of us."[4] In fact, Morgenthau and White hoped to drown Keynes under as deeply as possible.

As usual, White was well ahead of his boss. A day earlier Keynes had penned a letter to London reporting "White's idea that I should make a full dress oration" at a yet-to-be-arranged plenary meeting after "sufficient progress" had been made on the International Monetary Fund.[5]

British delegate Lionel Robbins described the actual conference opening as a "long series of banal or inaudible speeches." For him, the main event of the day was a private dinner party hosted by Keynes in his drawing room, commemorating a somewhat unrelated event: the five hundredth anniversary of the "Concordat" between King's College, Cambridge, and New College, Oxford.[6] King's also having a more recent concordat link with Yale, among Keynes's guests were Dean Acheson, the patrician Yalie who would five years later become secretary of state, and his fellow alum H. H. "Daddy" Kung, head of the Chinese delegation.

The larger-than-life Kung served as China's vice premier and finance minister, chairman of the board of the Bank of China, and president of the boards of Yenching University, Cheeloo University, Oberlin in China, the Chinese Industrial Cooperatives, the Confucius Society, and the Public Finance Association. A seventy-fifth-generation descendant of Confucius, Kung made his fortune in chain stores, banks, cotton mills, and mining. Skillfully playing the Chinese game of family politics, Kung became finance minister in Chiang Kai-shek's Nationalist government in 1933, at the age of fifty-one.[7]

Bretton Woods being an unrivaled opportunity for impromptu diplomacy, Acheson did not pass up the opportunity. "With the delicate skill of a great corporation lawyer," Robbins recorded, Acheson tried "to draw the weather-beaten Kung into some admission of the divided nature of the present Chinese policy. As might have been expected, the old pirate was much too adroit to fall into this trap, . . . deviat[ing] into a long historical excursus on the nature of his relations with President Roosevelt and Neville Chamberlain. . . . The dual broke off with honours even."[8]

As for Harry White, in spite of being the architect of the conference he could never fully escape from under Keynes's imposing presence. The *Christian Science Monitor* reported criticism in Washington over the absence of "the nation's leading economists" from the U.S. delegation—certainly no one to match the minds of Keynes, Robbins, and Dennis Robertson on the British side—and questioned whether the deliberations would therefore show "a Keynesian slant."[9] The more colorful and nationalist *Chicago Tribune* captioned Keynes's photo with the words "The Englishman Who Rules America,"[10] and groaned that he "overshadow[ed] all other figures" at the conference. Harry White the paper mocked as being among Keynes's "ardent admirers and disciples." For his part, White bristled at the suggestion that he was a mere American echo chamber for Keynes's newfangled ideas, conceding to the press only that "[a]ny economist who is not acquainted with his work is a dodo."[11]

As for the proposed new International Monetary Fund, the American people would be "crazy . . . to go into this scheme," the *Tribune* said:

> [I]ts author, John Maynard Keynes . . . is an ardent inflationist. He was never able to get his government before the war to accept his theories, because it was a creditor nation, and it would have been idiocy to water the pound to let the other nations pay their British debts in depreciated money.
>
> Now England is a debtor nation. As Keynes put it in his speech in the house of lords in May, "We have burdened ourselves with a weight of deferred indebtedness to other countries beneath which we shall stagger." Keynes proposes to ease the burden by the fantastic scheme now under consideration. The American people will want to help the busted British nation to rehabilitate itself, but no American except a White, a Morgenthau, or a Roosevelt, completely dominated by the British, will approve of giving this help at the expense of our own solvency.[12]

The *Wall Street Journal* was similarly scathing in mocking the idea of "an elaborate conference in a salubrious corner of the United States," putatively intended to stabilize currencies, when the real motivation was bailing out Britain.[13] *Time* magazine painted the rival British and American interests by evoking the Independence Day backdrop:

> [Most] of the preliminary skirmishing between the British and the Americans in the Battle of the Blueprints has taken place under cover. The first open blow was struck last spring by John Maynard Keynes, First Baron Tilton, with a proposal that in effect would give the British dominance in world currency arrangements. The second was a counterproposal by Harry D. White for the U.S. Treasury, giving the U.S. the upper hand through its vast hoard of gold. To the white-pillared Mount Washington

Hotel, the chosen battlefield, Lord Keynes led a British delegation of 15 which included two of England's best economic brains: Lionel C. Robbins and Dennis H. Robertson.[14]

The next morning, July 1, just a few hours before the arrival of the forty-three foreign delegations, the American delegation and advisers assembled for their first official strategy session. Morgenthau chaired the American group as well as being president of the conference as a whole—a bit like being the team coach as well as the tournament umpire. He played this dual role with aplomb, not least because, having no pride of authorship in the details of the American positions, he had no emotional attachment to them. When foreign delegates howled, he could tell them with a straight face, a clean conscience, and an uncluttered mind that something could be worked out. The working out would be the job of Harry White and his technicians.

Judge Fred Vinson, deputy chief of the Office of Economic Stabilization, as well as a former baseball player and Kentucky congressman, was the delegation's vice chairman. Vinson's home state being host to the famous Kentucky Derby, he was fond of horse-racing analogies, and took to alerting foreign delegation heads when the conference was "coming down the home stretch," and warning that the United Nations "horse" might "fall down and break a leg" before reaching "the wire."[15]

Harry White had no special title within the American delegation, but he was as essential to Morgenthau at Bretton Woods as General Marshall was to FDR in Europe. By virtue of his self-appointment as chairman of Commission One, covering the International Monetary Fund and the new global currency regime, White had arrogated to himself vast power over the drafting of the conference's critical provisions. Morgenthau had no clue about the organizational dynamics White had scripted to give himself control of the conference, but the Secretary was determined to keep White from hogging the limelight. He designated Treasury economist Edward ("Eddie") Bernstein and lawyer Ansel Luxford to run the daily press conferences, anonymously. "It's just another example of the petty rivalry between White and Morgenthau, based on who's going to be getting credit," Bernstein explained many years later. He was "amazed at how deep this will to get credit can go. Keynes had it too. He wanted it to be his plan."[16]

Also from the administration were Acheson, representing the State Department, and Leo Crowley, head of the Foreign Economic Administration. Marriner Eccles spoke for the Federal Reserve.

Congress had four representatives in the delegation. Morgenthau chose one Senate and one House of Representatives figure from each party. New York Senator Robert Wagner and Kentucky Congressman Brent Spence represented the Democrats. Wagner, chairman of the Senate Committee on Banking and Currency, was a prominent New Deal, pro-labor progressive and a member of FDR's brain trust, having served in the New York state legislature with him before the First World War. Spence, chairman of the corresponding House committee, was likewise an earnest advocate of liberal domestic economic legislation and foreign policy initiatives, such as Philippine independence. A city solicitor who made his name by reputedly defending the city of Newport successfully against every lawsuit filed against it from 1916 to 1924, he first won election to Congress in 1930. A quiet figure and an undistinguished speaker, he earned a reputation for integrity among his colleagues, untypically never amending his speeches on the House floor before they appeared in the *Congressional Record*.[17]

Host-state New Hampshire Senator Charles Tobey and Michigan Congressman Jesse Wolcott represented the Republicans. Tobey, an independent, sharp-tongued, one-time isolationist, and a member of Wagner's committee, was a controversial choice, having been plucked by Morgenthau and Senate Majority Leader Alben Barkley over the head of Ohio Senator Robert Taft, chairman of the Republican Senate Steering Committee and a fellow member of Wagner's committee, who had already pronounced that membership in the fund would be "like pouring money down a sewer."[18] Wolcott, a member of Spence's committee, was a World War I veteran (serving as a second lieutenant in a machine gun company) who went on to become a public prosecutor before entering Congress with Spence in 1930. He would in 1958 become a director and later chairman of the Federal Deposit Insurance Corporation. Having a penchant for societies of all sorts, he was a member of the American Legion, Veterans of Foreign

Wars, Freemasons, Elks, Knights of Pythias, Lions, Moose, and Odd Fellows.[19]

Two delegates came from outside government. Edward E. Brown, president of the First National Bank of Chicago, was selected for being prominent among "the tractable element of the banking community."[20] The *Chicago Tribune* described its local boy as an "outstanding exception" among the U.S. delegates, who were otherwise "New Deal hacks"[21] and "of the order of mediocrities."[22] *Time* magazine painted a somewhat less flattering picture of Brown, reporting that he "went about for days [at the conference] in the same rumpled blue serge suit with cigar ashes accumulated on its front, his eyes bleary from lack of sleep."[23] Keynes took a blended view, describing Brown as "an enormous man of 20 stone [280 pounds] who lives exclusively on beef . . . and nods his head like a bull in a stall. But . . . his mental grasp and force of character are altogether unusual. It is a long time since I met a more competent or distinguished banker."[24]

Vassar economics professor Mabel Newcomer was the sole woman in the group. Starting in the mid-1920s, she was repeatedly appointed to state commissions on fiscal matters related to subjects as diverse as taxation, school finance, home ownership, and rural life.[25] Taciturn, she left virtually no footprint in the Bretton Woods proceedings. The *New York Times* did, however, take a keen interest in her; a July 4 headline noted that the conference kept her "Too Busy for Her Mountain-Climbing Hobby." Asked "How . . . does a woman ever get to be an economics professor and qualify as an expert on international finance and foreign exchange?" Newcomer explained to the reporter that it "just happened."[26]

The twelve-strong delegation was assisted by an equal number of technical advisers from the Treasury, Federal Reserve, State Department, Foreign Economic Administration, Securities and Exchange Commission, and Department of Commerce, as well as four legal advisers, seven technical secretaries, four assistants to the chairman, and one delegation secretary-general.

Morgenthau implored the assembled to abjure partisanship; they had to "work as a team and present a united front." This conference is "bigger than either the Republican or the Democratic party." Differences within the group needed to be settled "over the bar in the room here."

This called forth a point of order from Senator Wagner: "Where is the bar?"[27]

White, who rarely indulged the congressmen's banter, laid out at length the key American and foreign delegation positions. Other nations, he said, believed that in the coming years "the United States will be . . . putting pressure on the monetary systems of the rest of the world . . . by virtue of the fact that the United States will be cornering a larger proportion of the world markets and will be in a position to develop what we call an export surplus." They will want the United States "to be subject to some pressure through the Fund . . . to adopt a policy which will put less pressure on their exchange and enable them to sell more goods here." But the United States would not tolerate interference from the fund on its surplus position.

"We have been perfectly adamant on that point," White insisted, sounding as if he were a Chinese official today. "We have taken the position of absolutely no, on that."[28]

Keynes and others even wanted "to charge us interest, as a lender," he continued. But the U.S. position was "the opposite of that . . . we want to charge them." The reason was that the "Fund is designed for a special purpose, and that purpose is to prevent competitive depreciation of currencies."[29]

Gold in Fort Knox, White went on, was "why the United States is in an enviable position . . . why we are in a powerful position at this Conference . . . why we dominate practically the financial world, because we have the where-with-all to buy any currency we want. If only England was in that position, or any of the other countries, it would be a very different story."[30]

Creditors, White believed, set the terms. Desperate debtors, even those with emissaries as eloquent as Lord Keynes, could only bring words to bear—words like "adamant" and "tranche," which amused Morgenthau no end. "We are learning a lot of new English words, aren't we?" the Secretary commented after reading a characteristic complaint from the arch-prolific Keynes.[31] By this late stage in the Anglo-American financial drama, the British delegation head had largely been reduced to the status of an articulate annoyance, and Morgenthau could joke about his impassioned missives. As Stalin might have put it, how many divisions did King's College have?

Still, the very fact that the U.S. position was so strong was precisely what led American opponents of the conference to question its purpose. "[T]he average American doesn't need to be told that most of the world's monetary gold is buried safely away in Kentucky," observed the *Christian Science Monitor*, so "when experts from other lands come to talk about money and loans and trade and repayments it gives the uninitiated the uncomfortable feeling that there may be thieves in the pantry."[32]

Such views failed to reckon with the fact that whereas the United States held virtually all the cards at Bretton Woods, the rest of the world had a familiar, if unpalatable, fallback position: barter. "Lord Keynes, with considerable tact but very evident intention," observed the *Washington Post*, "took time out to drive that point home":

> In a press interview he pointed out that Great Britain might be forced to resort to some very unacceptable means of pushing her foreign trade, should the monetary plan be rejected. A return to the barter system was, he said, the only alternative in sight, and it might have to be tried as a "last expedient." That is a possibility that the United States certainly does not wish to see realized. The British, as two of their cabinet ministers recently asserted, may be "broke" (since they lack the wherewithal to meet their external obligations), but they are not without facilities for pushing their goods into foreign markets by means of bilateral trade agreements.[33]

Germany had been operating this way for years, compelling foreign holders of marks to redeem them for German goods. Britain could do the same with the massive blocked sterling balances of the empire and the neutral nations, making the once lustrous pound convertible into nothing more than whatever wares Britain chose to make available to them. The hapless always have at least one credible card to play: that their circumstances cannot get much worse. "To Senator Taft it is probably unthinkable the creditor should not be in a position to call the tune on the debtors," observed Walter Lippmann, the renowned political columnist whom White admired enormously,

> But in fact this is more nearly the true position of affairs than the American experts have cared to disclose or than foreign governments have wished

to say bluntly. For in a world where there is only one great power capable of extending large international credits, the creditor-borrower relationship of normal private affairs does not prevail. The other great powers are in a position to have a very great deal to say about the terms on which they will accept credit. That is the fact which we have soberly to comprehend . . . if the great creditor does not offer terms which fit their internal needs and their sense of national dignity, they have an alternative to the system of general international trading which this country desires. The alternative is government controlled trading on a bilateral or barter basis.

It is not a good alternative, and the world will be a poorer and more troubled place if it is adopted. But let us have no illusions whatever: the other great financial powers will surely think this poor alternative the lesser of two evils if they cannot get credit to restore general trade except on terms which they regard as dictation of their domestic policy by the United States, and as humiliating.

This may be deplorable. But it is one of the facts of life, and the sooner we face it the better.[34]

The *Times* of London made the same point: "Defeat of the fund and the bank would oblige the United States either to undertake the duties and accept the risks of both institutions, or to watch the progressive decline of its export trade in a world turning more and more to Government controls and barter arrangements."[35] The Americans would therefore have to play ball, as their expression went.

Over in Europe, Soviet forces dramatically reconquered Minsk, the capital city of White Russia, on July 3, taking more than 150,000 German soldiers prisoner and capturing two thousand tanks.[36] Meanwhile, back at Bretton Woods, White outlined his carefully designed committee process at a late-night American delegation meeting.

The committees would each be chaired by non-Americans—on fund matters, by delegates from China, the Soviet Union, Brazil, and Peru. Members of each committee would be issued a working document, the pre-prepared Joint Statement of Principles—a product of White's Treasury team, tweaked at the margins to mollify Keynes and the British. Alternative text wordings submitted by the various delegations represented at Atlantic City were noted as "A," "B," "C," et cetera. "A" was always the American alternative. "A" text had in principle been cleared in advance with the British, and would appear in the official conference record as being jointly proposed by the United States and the United Kingdom. White assured Vinson and Wolcott, who would be representing the United States on different committees, but who had little grasp of the whys and wherefores of his scheme, that "the boys," meaning the technicians, "will be with you" and would "indicate whether they think something ought to be said."

Vinson struggled to deduce any sort of procedural rules from White's tutorial. How would you know when something was "passed"? The committees sounded like "catch as catch can," he observed.

There should be just "one general rule," Fed research director Emanuel Goldenweiser suggested, "that anybody can talk as long as he pleases provided he doesn't say anything! Separate the business of the Committee from the talk."

This was "facetiousness," he clarified. Yet it was also precisely what White had in mind.

Treasury's Emilio Collado—who would after the war become the first U.S. executive director of the World Bank—weighed in. The committee chairmen have "got to go through the motions, at least of asking whether there are any alternatives, because, after all . . . there were thirty countries not represented" at Atlantic City.[37]

Coordinating meaningful debate on floor motions, however, would prove nearly impossible. "There were a great many . . . varieties of unintelligible English spoken," the Russian-born Goldenweiser observed. The Russians, for example, "didn't speak English; neither did their translators . . . they were struggling between the firing squad on the one hand and the English language on the other."[38]

In any case, there was, in White's mind, never a risk of committee debates actually shaping the fund. The secretaries were all American, appointed by White, and it was they who wrote the official minutes. Moreover, the fund committees reported up to Commission One, which was chaired by White himself.

When at one point Acheson suggested that there might be "a raising of hands vote" if there were "any objection to the ruling of the chair," White quickly smacked him down. It was best, he insisted, for the chairman just "to ascertain the sense of the meeting. It is much safer [that] way," he explained, "if it is legal."[39]

"Who presides at Commission One this afternoon?" Morgenthau asked naively. The Secretary had chastised White for keeping him in the dark during the Atlantic City proceedings, yet he remained strikingly ignorant of what his deputy was orchestrating at Bretton Woods or how.

"An American," White replied evasively.

"Who is it?"

"I presume that will be my job," White offered, as if the thought had only just occurred to him, "because that is all technical discussion."

"You reluctantly accept!" said Morgenthau, cottoning on.

"I accept reluctantly and inevitably!" White affirmed, dabbling at levity. "The importance why we need somebody to chairman this, who knows the complete matter," he continued clunkily, "is that he should prevent coming to a vote on matters which he doesn't wish to come to a vote on, and in general arranging the discussion in such a way that we are never caught with an agreement among the Commission on something we don't want, because then it is too late."

Morgenthau was satisfied: "I don't know anybody more competent."[40]

Important issues related to the future of the dollar and gold came up in several guises over the first two weeks. One item of great concern within the American delegation was the scarce-currency provisions. White had been struggling to contain the political damage from the scarce-currency concept since he first articulated it a year and half ago. This was potentially a vehicle for other nations to gang up on the United States over its persistent trade surpluses, to erect discriminatory barriers against U.S. exports, and to demand changes in U.S. economic policies. "You take Keynes's speech in the House of Lords," Eccles said. "He was very anxious to point out the wrong policy that America was pursuing . . . and I think that to accept . . . the right of the Fund to criticize us for our policy . . . would be something that we couldn't possibly accept."

"[T]he tendency of the foreign countries is always to assume that the fault is all ours," added White.

Acheson wanted to "leave the scarce currency provisions alone." A two-thirds majority of the votes, effectively five-sixths of the member states, would be required to direct a report at the United States. This "killed off crackpot criticisms."

"That practically gives us a veto," White conceded.

Still, the politics of the provision were worrying. "Bob Taft will [insist] you are giving up sovereignty here," legal adviser Oscar Cox put back.

Taft, in fact, continued his attacks throughout the conference. "It will not be long before all our assets are gone and the fund is entirely made up of weak or worthless currencies," he declared. "The whole of the elaborate machinery seems to be designed to cover up the fact that our money is, in effect, to be loaned away by a board in which we have only a minority interest." He predicted that the fund and bank would be rejected by Congress.[41]

"I think all of us here in Congress realize the possibilities of a flag-waving speech," said Wolcott. "[I]f I was talking to the House against this Fund, I wouldn't bother about the gold points [or] rates of exchange. Nobody understands that in the House. I would wave the flag on this here."[42]

The more colorful media continued to prod them to do just that. "We're chin deep in foreigners trying to arrange a polygamous marriage between Miss America, aged 168 last Tuesday, and the united nations, assorted ages," wrote an on-site correspondent from the *Chicago Tribune*. "Can't say they're really in love with the lady but she's got quite a dowry, and business is business. No telling what the outcome will be—or the *outgo*, for that matter. Some folks remember a ceremony, some years back, when a lot of these gents wearing morning coats and striped pants promised to love, honor, and repay."[43]

Still, the prospect of precipitating a major conference row by rejecting any fund powers to issue a report on currency scarcity—even a report with no powers of compulsion—was unappealing. There were bigger fish to fry. In the end, the group deemed the clause requiring that "a representative of the member whose currency is involved shall participate in the preparation of the report" to provide sufficient political cover to let the provision go forward.

Another irritant was the silver interests. Twenty-five western senators had written a letter to President Roosevelt on June 21 urging the remonetization of silver; the conference plans, they argued, suffered from a "basic, organic defect" in failing to assign a role for the metal in the monetary base.[44] They had allies in the Mexican delegation, which demanded "extra credit facilities" for silver-producing countries.[45] The idea was, not surprisingly, treated with disdain by countries without major silver-mining industries. An Indian representative stated bluntly at a press conference that his country had "no interest whatever" in a monetary role for silver.[46] The British deemed it "totally unacceptable." Of the Americans, Robbins observed that they were reluctant to fuel a domestic political problem by opposing the silver interests publicly, "preferring to handle the matter," as they did others, "by obscure deals in the *couloirs* of the Conference." The Mexicans eventually climbed down after being offered what some termed the "Coconut Clause—a face-saving phrase which permits the Fund . . . to accept various commodities, including possibly silver, as collateral."[47]

A "minor sensation" was caused by the discovery that a publicity representative of the American Smelting and Refining company, which had extensive silver-mining properties in the United States and Mexico, had somehow gained admission to the Mount Washington without accreditation. Robbins reported that the man appeared to have "borrowed a pass from one of the lesser delegates and had been going round the Conference for two days organising the silver bloc."[48] Questioned at a press conference on the man's presence and agenda, a baffled Morgenthau deflected inquiries to a State Department press officer. Obliged to depart the conference, Smelting's poor Mr. David Hinshaw told reporters that he had "never been so humiliated."[49]

While some fought to make silver a monetary complement to gold, White's personal obsession was making the dollar as good as gold. To the extent that could be done by decree, he intended to use the IMF as his vehicle. Keynes, however, had fiercely resisted White's earlier attempts to give the dollar any form of special status. So it would have to be done out of his sight. White's committee process was perfect for this.

As with Operation Overlord in Normandy, White's dollar strategy relied on deception and enemy errors. He accomplished the first critical maneuver on July 6, at a meeting of the Fund Commission's Committee 2. The Joint Statement working document indicated that the par value of a member country's currency, which would be agreed with the fund when the country was admitted, would "be expressed in terms of gold." The Americans submitted "Alternative A" text, which said that the par value would instead "be expressed in terms of gold, *as a common denominator, or in terms of a gold-convertible currency unit of the weight and fineness in effect on July 1, 1944.*" The text had never, however, been approved by the British; Keynes had never even seen it.

Bernstein explained that the suggested revision was "insignificant," but "so worded to show no obligation to sell gold was implied." It was obvious that "there will exist a gold-convertible currency by definition within the terms of the agreement," he said. Keynes had prior to the conference repeatedly insisted that the term "gold-convertible currency" could have no fixed meaning, and was therefore unacceptable. Yet no one in the committee meeting raised an issue with this, and the revised text successfully went up to the Fund Commission.[50]

"The Commission meeting this afternoon is extremely important," White told Morgenthau at a July 13 morning strategy session. "That is where we either fish or cut bait on most of these things."[51] What "things" he left unclear. White never raised the issue of the dollar's role in any American delegation meeting, despite it being the most important one to him; he was determined to handle it below the radar, through his carefully chosen operatives.

At the 2:30 p.m. commission meeting the matter of the inscrutable "gold-convertible currency" naturally came up.[52] The Indian delegate wanted to know what exactly it was: "I think it is high time," he interjected during a lengthy technical discussion in which White had invoked the term, "that the USA delegation give us a definition of gold and gold convertible exchange." At that point, Dennis Robertson, the British delegate on the committee, apparently imagining that the issue was one of mere bookkeeping, suggested that "payment of official gold subscription should be expressed as official holdings of gold and United States dollars." This change would, he remarked incautiously, require wording changes elsewhere in the agreement. Bernstein concurred with Robertson that "gold convertible exchange" was hard to define, and that getting a definition "which would be satisfactory to everyone here . . . would involve a long discussion." But as a "practical" matter, he explained, since national monetary authorities could freely purchase gold for dollars in the United States, and international holdings of currencies that might be used to purchase dollars were small, "it would be easier for this purpose to regard the United States dollar as what was intended when we speak of gold convertible exchange."

White must have had difficulty concealing his flush of excitement. With Keynes preoccupied managing the World Bank proceedings, Robertson had walked straight into White's trap. He now made his second critical maneuver, peremptorily ending the commission's discussion of the matter. "Unless there are any objections," he said, "this question will be referred to the Special Committee." No objections being raised, he quickly passed on to another issue.[53]

The next morning, 9:30 a.m. on July 14, Morgenthau began a meeting of the full American team by reporting cheerily that White had "worked up until three o'clock this morning with the Drafting Committee on the Fund and he feels [the text] is in excellent shape."[54] Morgenthau had no idea what exactly that meant, and likely no interest. But among the achievements of the committee, composed entirely of White's technicians, was strategically replacing "gold" with "gold and U.S. dollars" throughout the 96-page Final Act. White never submitted the changes for consideration in Commission One, yet they would become an important part of the IMF Articles of Agreement. Keynes would only discover them after his departure from Bretton Woods.

"Britain is 'Broke,'" the *New York Times* blared on July 7. "It is no use to beat about the bush," said Minister of Labour Ernest Bevin. "We have spent everything in this struggle and I am glad we have." British bombers were that day dropping 2,500 bombs on Caen, France, in preparation for its recapture over the next two days, while the Americans were liberating Saipan Island in the Pacific, with nearly 4,300 Japanese dying in a final "banzai" charge on U.S. troops.[55] The *Times* article said that "pessimistic reports . . . from Bretton Woods about the future of the Monetary Conference were noted [in London] as discouraging auguries for . . . the difficult task" of boosting Britain's export opportunities.[56]

Keynes, however, was of a cheerier disposition. In a July 4 letter to Bank of England Governor Lord Catto, he resumed his Atlantic City narrative: that the British delegation was building a common position with the Americans "behind the scenes," and that all was going swimmingly with White. "Harry White is fighting various battles in his own camp and in his own Press and is most disinclined to take on any issue with us if he can possibly help it—which, of course, makes it very much more easy for us to obtain satisfaction." Regarding the area of greatest concern to Catto, sovereignty over the exchange rate (what Keynes called the "Catto clause"), Keynes reported near-victory. Despite "American lawyers making it much more difficult than it need be," Keynes had "persuaded White of the wisdom of trying to find a way of conceding the substance of this to us:

> that is to say, a country is entitled in the last resort to alter its exchange rate without a breach of obligation and without having to leave the Fund, provided it is prepared to be cut off from the privileges of the Fund and in the case of a prolonged dispute, being called upon to withdraw. . . . The trouble was not really between us and White, but between White and the rest of his Delegation. . . . He has really been fighting manfully to keep faith with us. . . . [Harry] has been all smiles, kindness and geniality. The position definitely is that we are allies and the common foe is from without.[57]

Keynes continued to attack the idea of Britain taking a private loan from American bankers as an alternative to signing on to a deal at Bretton Woods. The *New York Times* quoted "the British financial expert and advocate of deficit financing and cheap money" as saying that the program being advocated by banking opponents of the conference, which would involve lending Britain $5 billion, was "too good to be true."[58] White himself hit back at banker critics, telling the press that the only losers from a Bretton Woods deal would be the "buzzards" in the foreign exchange markets.[59]

In contrast to Keynes's account of Anglo-American harmony, tensions within the British "family," as the *New York Times* sarcastically referred to the empire, were embarrassingly put on display. Robbins on July 2 recorded "a special confabulation between Keynes and the Indian representatives on the sterling balance question which . . . threaten[ed] to be a sore point throughout the Conference."[60] India, the *Times* reported, later "created a 'scene'" in front of the other delegations by demanding that the fund provide some means of turning Britain's huge sterling debt to India into dollars. At nearly $12 billion, Britain's Indian debt alone was 50 percent greater than the entire proposed fund capitalization. Egypt joined India in insisting "on some international magic to give their pounds the ability to purchase something that is wanted"; pounds being worthless as long as Britain's industrial capacity was focused on war production rather than supplying creditors with useful exports.[61] Robbins called it "not particularly pleasant having to stand up before the assembled nations and defend a position in which we are unable to pay our debts on terms acceptable to our creditors."[62]

Telegrams between the British delegation and the Foreign Office show an escalating concern that London's status as "the financial centre of the world" was crumbling.[63] The government was fighting for provisions in the IMF agreement that would maximize its freedom to control capital outflows, yet actions taken to stop the dwindling of its dollar reserves by limiting sterling convertibility would, the delegation wrote on July 10, "be used as a strong political argument by India e.g. against keeping reserves in London." Meanwhile the "Canadians, Dutch and Belgians all tell us that if London wants to remain in business even our present proposal goes dangerously far."[64] In spite of the empire fraying in front of their eyes, the mandarins in Whitehall still managed to maintain their imperial self-image. "The Chancellor approves your acquiescing in the quota proposals," begins one draft telegram, but "It would of course be very welcome to us if something could be done to mitigate the disappointment of the smaller people, particularly the Dominions other than Australia and the European Allies."[65] The second sentence was stricken before the message was sent.

In spite of Keynes's own upbeat prose, Robbins reported that "Keynes is showing obvious signs of exhaustion" after the first week, "and we are all very concerned about him. He is not the easiest of men to control, and the eagerness of his mind is such that it is intolerable to him to go slow."[66] The Americans felt a mix of deep regard for Keynes's brilliance and frustration with his inability to conform to the bureau-cratic role assigned him. Goldenweiser called Keynes "the outstanding personality at Bretton Woods. . . . He shone in two respects":

> in the fact that he is, of course, one of the brightest lights of mankind in both thinking and expression and in his ability to influence people, and he shone also by being the world's worst chairman. He presided over meet-ings of the Bank in a way that was entirely intolerable because he had his own documents all fixed up so that he could go through in a hurry. . . . He spoke while he was sitting down in a meeting and it was difficult to hear him. He spoke indistinctly when presiding and was impatient of any difference of opinion. . . . His function at Bretton Woods was primarily performed in a suite of rooms on the second floor to which everybody went for inspiration and guidance and compromise.[67]

Acheson, the chief American delegate to Keynes's Commission Two, told Morgenthau that "the Commission meetings on the Bank, which are conducted by Keynes, are being rushed in a perfectly impossible and outrageous way."

> Now that comes from the fact that Keynes is under great pressure. He knows this thing inside out so that when anybody says Section 15-C he knows what it is. Nobody else in the room knows. So before you have an opportunity to turn to Section 15-C and see what he is talking about, he says, "I hear no objections to that," and it is passed.

> Well, everybody is trying to find Section 15-C. He then says, we are now talking about Section 26-D. Then they begin fiddling around with their papers, and before you find that, it is passed.[68]

"[I'll] go and call on him and in a very nice way tell him that at least half a dozen people have come to me perfectly livid and I think he is making a mistake," Morgenthau responded, "and I am going to ask him very respectfully if he wouldn't do the thing at half speed." Acheson assented, telling Morgenthau to assure Keynes, who had been deter-mined to leave on the nineteenth, it would still be "possible for him to finish by Wednesday when the train leaves." This was not to be the case.

White had little sympathy: "Just because Keynes is an autocrat doesn't mean that you have to take it. You stand up and you say you don't like the way things are running." White offered to attend the next Commission Two meeting and do just that. "[People] are either too scared to talk to him or too nice to talk to him, but I am sure that if he is called to task strongly, and you have the crowd behind you, he will modify his procedure."

"Could you do it privately rather than publicly?" Morgenthau pleaded, clearly disturbed by the image of a public clash of the Titans.

"Maybe," conceded White.

White had Commission One under martial law, but he hadn't felt any need to bother with Commission Two. He was happy to let Keynes lord over a monkey house. So even the American team under Acheson was in disarray. No one knew the official position.

"I know nothing about the Bank," Acheson insisted. "I am playing this by ear." Americans on different committees were agreeing to opposing provisions. One was calling another a liar. "I was almost going nuts," Acheson explained.

White assured Acheson he would get all the expert help he needed, but only after he, White, had concluded the fund business.

Acheson wasn't satisfied. He insisted White had gotten the Bank Commission and committees into "the most chaotic mess in the world. . . . We appointed *ad hoc* committees, section committees, drafting committees and all kinds of committees. A draft comes in from somewhere and nobody reads it, so it gets referred to somebody else; the delegates are going crazy."

"There is no confusion as far as the Fund is concerned," White assured him. "All the important problems have been settled."

"I am sure they have been settled," shot back a sarcastic Acheson, "but I don't think the delegates know that."

"The procedure is very simple, Dean." Acheson just didn't know how to play the game. "When there was disagreement [in Commission One], instead of referring it back to the committees or instead of discussing it at any length in the committees, we let a few people discuss it, and immediately referred it to the ad hoc committees, created especially for that purpose, to refer back to the Fund Commission," where he, White, was in control, "and not to the committees. . . . I don't see how anything could be simpler or more effective."[69]

The British view of White's conference organization was, quite naturally, at one with Acheson's. "With all their virtues as technicians—and these are very great—the Americans are not good organisers of international conferences," Robbins wrote. "The administration here is quite incredibly bad. . . . [T]he different committees waste a great deal of time arguing whether questions . . . are or are not being dealt with in some other part of the conference. . . . [I]f there is to be a Peace Conference. . . . it will be very considerably worse than Versailles."[70] What Robbins did not grasp is that it was White's clear intention for the committees to waste time; he had already made the key decisions he intended to shepherd into the final text.

The British having prior to the conference resolved themselves to losing nearly all the substantive debates, the greatest area of tension with the Americans over the fund and the bank came not over the content of their character, but the siting of their buildings. The British still hoped to have the fund offices in London, while the Americans were adamant that both the fund and the bank be in the United States (specifically Washington, rather than New York, but they did not say so publicly). The British were determined at least to save face, and to avoid immediate confrontation with a hostile home press, by postponing the decision until after the conference. Keynes pleaded his case to White in a letter marked "personal" and "private," which White disdainfully read out to the American delegation on July 10. His take on the question was uncompromising.

"[I]f you don't get this settled in the Conference, [the likelihood of the United States getting both the Fund and the Bank] is reduced, and that is why they want to postpone," White told the group:

> Maybe they hope to get some arrangement whereby they will get some and we will get others. I think it is important enough for us to push the issue here in the Conference where I am sure we will get a favorable vote. . . . I think we are strategically in an invulnerable position to get it now. . . . [T]hey can't back out on the basis that they don't like where the head office is. Their public won't stand for it and the world won't stand

for it. So the thing to do is to put it through on a vote here. If they don't like it, it is too bad. . . . We are putting in twice as much money as anybody else, three times as much . . . it is preposterous that the head office should be any place else. We can vote it anyplace we want . . . that is why they don't want it to come to a vote.

White concluded: "I don't see why we should put ourselves in a position to be subject to political manipulation," by which he meant having the matter taken outside American control.[71]

The American delegation was steadfast behind him—few of them were tutored in the technicalities of monetary architecture, but they knew Congress would insist on the physical edifice being within walking distance. "We have several questions involving Great Britain which are very embarrassing to Congress," said Wolcott. "[W]hat is going to happen to her outposts in the Western hemisphere[?] . . . and there has always been a certain jealousy that the financial center of the world is London. . . . We think that Congress will take the attitude that . . . we should have the Fund and the Bank."

"Then the answer is that we have got to fight it out here and now," Morgenthau summed up. "[A]nd if there is no business, we will adjourn."

"Go out and get drunk," declared Senator Wagner.[72]

On critical political issues like the location of the fund and bank, White and Morgenthau used private meetings with the various foreign delegations to, in effect, trade quota allocations for votes.

"You don't think it [will] get back to the British?" White asked of the stratagem.

"Sure, it probably will," Acheson responded.

"Don't forget Liberia," Morgenthau interjected helpfully; "they are instructed to vote with us."

"Liberia, the Philippines, and Ethiopia," Luxford clarified.

"Have you talked with them about their quotas?" asked Acheson.

White and Acheson went down the list. "I talked to Luxembourg and left it indecisive, because they want ten billion," White said. "They can give only five, and I want to see how much there is left over. But I made sure that Liberia and Ethiopia were seen."

Luxford explained the importance of the horse-trading: "The reason [we need] this is because you can argue and argue, and we haven't good arguments for some of the things we have to push through."[73]

Keynes continued pressing his case for keeping the fund and bank location off the conference agenda in a "long-winded letter" to Morgenthau dated July 13. "[H]e repeats himself about five times," the Secretary grumbled to his team the following morning. As a matter of political protocol, Keynes argued, the location of the fund was a matter of "high policy" and beyond the remit of conference delegates.

"I am unalterably opposed to [Keynes's position] and I am not going to change," Spence said; everyone chimed in behind him. "I think you ought to talk to him as plainly as diplomacy will allow. . . . Profanity wouldn't hurt."[74]

Keynes ultimately brought the matter to a private meeting with Morgenthau in which he was "very combative"; he repeatedly stressed that if the Americans pressed for a vote on the issue he would be compelled by Whitehall to "withdraw" from the conference. Morgenthau was unmoved: "that is the way our delegation—particularly the congressional delegation, feels."

"Well, the trouble with you people is, all the time you are thinking about the Presidential election—everything is Congress. You keep throwing it at us all the time," Keynes shot back.

"We have had considerable discussion over a long period of time about how we should handle Congress this time so we shouldn't make the same mistake Woodrow Wilson made," Morgenthau responded calmly. It had nothing to do with the presidential election: "President Roosevelt is going to win, hands down." It was about avoiding another reversal like the disastrous defeat of Wilson's League of Nations in Congress. "You know that Senator Lodge's papers show that if Wilson had ever sent for him and talked to him, he, Lodge, would have gotten the thing through the Senate."

After putting up a brief indignant defense, Keynes left the meeting in what Morgenthau described "an excellent humor."[75] Keynes knew that it was time once again to ratify political reality. He cabled the chancellor, Sir John Anderson, on July 14: "I believe that we are on a losing wicket here and hope that I may be instructed on lines either (1) or (3)"—that is, either to acquiesce or to argue for show only.[76]

White wanted an immediate vote on the matter, but Robbins pleaded that the Americans not raise the matter publicly until Keynes heard back from London in a few days. "We know we will be beaten and we hope to avoid being humiliated," Vinson reported Robbins saying.

"We can wait," White conceded graciously.[77]

The chancellor told Keynes on the seventeenth to write back to Morgenthau stating that he, Keynes, had actually understated the chancellor's political difficulties on the location issue, but that the British government would nonetheless withdraw its objections to a conference vote. Britain still reserved the right to condition its ultimate acceptance of the fund on designation of a home "decided to be in the best interests of the Fund."[78] Keynes told Morgenthau that he intended to make a public statement laying out the British position before the vote on the fund location.

The next day, July 18, the conference voted to base the fund and the bank in the nation with the largest quota—code words for the United States. The *New York Times* trumpeted the result the following day: "British Give Up Fight to Retain London as World Fund Center."[79]

Morgenthau reviewed Keynes's press release with White and Acheson. Acheson sympathized with Keynes's line of reasoning—that the location of the fund was a matter among governments. White was exasperated. "The governments are represented by the delegates," he insisted. "After they decide it, like any other point, any government can accept or reject it."

Morgenthau broke up the fight. "Are you through?" he asked. "Now, to me it boils down to this—and I will be willing to face this thing—these groups—once and for all—that the financial center of the world is going to be New York and we don't want to postpone this thing until another day where we may not be in as advantageous a position and maybe have them to get in a horse-trading position and maybe end up by having it in London." Two days later, Morgenthau virtually accused Acheson of treason, telling White, Luxford, and Vinson that "[w]ord for word, the speech that Acheson made to me when he was trying to stop us from bringing the matter up as to the location of the Bank—it doesn't seem to me as if it was an accident. Either he gave it to the English or the English gave it to him."[80]

Sometimes White and Morgenthau found it difficult to know which side Acheson was on. They would not have been surprised to have read Robbins writing on July 2 that British relations with "our intimate friends on the State Department side . . . are as friendly as ever."[81] Acheson, according to Robbins, was "very apologetic" about U.S. bullheadedness on the headquarters. "I know our attitude is perfectly illogical, and I can well believe that sometimes you think that you are dealing with a set of people who are perfectly crazy," Robbins quoted Acheson saying over drinks on July 13. "You fellows will have to give way on this matter if there is to be any hope of the fund getting through [Congress]. . . . I am simply telling you what the situation is."

Robbins was equally ill at ease in being unable to allay Acheson's concerns over lack of British movement on Lend-Lease Article VII—specifically, a British commitment to dismantling imperial preference and allowing currency convertibility after the war. The issue remained a political minefield in London, but Robbins was under no illusion that the British could continue to duck it. "[H]owever much we resent it, . . . in the American mind, Article VII and lend-lease are intimately associated; and it would be a fatal thing for us to proceed to formulate our policy in regard to long-term commercial arrangements without knowing how the Americans will react to our proposals for dealing with the short-term financial situation. We need the cash and we shan't get it if we go back on our written obligations."[82]

Regarding White, Acheson's feelings were by this point positively hostile. Reflecting on Bretton Woods a quarter century later, Acheson would reveal that he had "often been so outraged by Harry White's capacity for rudeness . . . that the charges made against him" of "Communist sympathies . . . would have seemed mild compared to expressions I have used."[83]

In the end, settling the question of where the Bretton Woods institutions would be located wouldn't be done by conference protocol or legal niceties. This was a question of opportunity and power. The United States had been blessed by a unique confluence of events with a momentary window in which it could, in return for its now-vital financing services, not only put an end to competitive devaluation and trade protectionism—the scourge of the 1930s, from the administration's perspective—but permanently eliminate the old European powers as rivals and obstacles on the global stage. "Now the advantage is ours here," the Secretary declared, calling for an end to the dithering and hand-wringing, "and I personally think we should take it."

"If the advantage was theirs," White added, "they would take it."[84]

Despite the amicable British climbdown on the location issue, Keynes erupted the very next day. Curiously, the matter was an obscure one: the future of the Bank for International Settlements (BIS)—a discrete, little-known central bankers league nestled in the small Alpine city of Basel, Switzerland.

The Norwegians, supported by other European delegations, had early on in the conference proposed the immediate liquidation of the BIS, owing to its cooperation with the Nazi regime that now controlled the member states Germany had invaded. Robbins described the Norwegian delegation leader, central bank director Wilhelm Keilhau, as "a queer, Peer Gyntish figure, with an explosive voice and absurd habits of gesticulation."[85] The Dutch, whose delegation head, J. W. Beyen, had as BIS president in 1939 controversially authorized a transfer of Czech gold to Germany following the Nazi overrun of Czechoslovakia, opposed the resolution. They were joined by the British, represented by Nigel Ronald of the Foreign Office and George Bolton of the Bank of England, who objected to the Norwegian resolution on the grounds that it bore no connection with either the IMF or the World Bank. Acheson and the State Department supported the British position, much to White's annoyance. Brown, the banker, joined Acheson; Brown's bank having helped establish the BIS at the request of the State and Treasury departments in 1929, he privately supported dissolution, but did not want to suffer the embarrassment of having the institution shuttered by action taken at Bretton Woods.

A comedy of confusions began on the afternoon of July 19, when Luxford and his American colleagues tried to head off an expected British point of order on the resolution by rewording it such that it made membership in the IMF and the BIS incompatible. This would provide the necessary link between BIS and the fund, and thereby neutralize the British objection. Robbins called the American initiative "political intrigue behind the scenes."[86] At this point there was as yet no official version of the resolution, but what filtered up to Keynes from his colleagues at 7:20 p.m. was that a BIS resolution had been approved by a committee operating within Commission Three, over British and Dutch objections; that the press had been briefed on its approval; and that it was about to be ratified by the commission imminently. Keynes was apoplectic, descending on Morgenthau in his suite in advance of their dinner date to vent. "[T]he man was livid over this BIS thing, and said that if this thing went through at nine o'clock he was going to get up and leave the Conference . . . the inference was that he had been double-crossed," Morgenthau told White, Vinson, and Luxford just after 9:30 that night. Morgenthau's wife Elinor, who was present at the explosion, described Keynes as "so excited about it" he was "quivering."[87] Acheson, according to Robbins, went "out of his way to repudiate all responsibility for what was happening."[88]

What makes the clash particularly curious is that White and Keynes both objected to the Luxford formulation, albeit for different reasons. White was opposed on the grounds that it would bolster the BIS by suggesting that it was a living, viable alternative to his IMF. "[I]t makes it more difficult for us in the Fund," White explained to the American team, "because [opponents] can say, 'Why don't you give the BIS more powers?'"[89] Keynes, for his part, insisted that his government actually supported BIS dissolution—a position that White found implausible, given Ronald's and Bolton's clear rejection of the Norwegian proposal. In any case, Keynes later that night presented Morgenthau with a one-page memo citing only a narrow technical objection to the Luxford formulation, related to the possibility of Britain having clashing legal commitments to both the BIS and the fund. Morgenthau was flummoxed by the arcana, but genuinely moved by the emotional sincerity of Keynes's outburst. "[Bernard] Baruch has fed me full of this stuff that you can't believe Keynes, and Keynes double-crossed him at Versailles, and so forth and so on, and I have been looking for it, but I have seen no evidence of it," the Secretary told his team.[90] Characteristically, he had little interest in the technicalities of what to do with the BIS, but he insisted on holding a powwow with the British the following morning to resolve the matter and to soothe ruffled feathers.

The fact that the biggest rupture at the conference between Keynes and the American delegation should emerge over a side issue about which there was no substantive disagreement is explicable only in terms of Keynes's rapidly deteriorating health and accompanying hair-trigger sensitivity. "It was impossible to be as excited about it as he was on technical ground," Luxford observed.[91] Word quickly spread through the conference, including the reporters in the bar, that Keynes had had a heart attack that evening, the most dire accounts appearing in the German press in the form of adulatory obituaries.[92] "[W]e have all felt that as regards Keynes's health we were on the edge of a precipice," Robbins wrote after the incident. "[I] now feel that it is a race between the exhaustion of his powers and the termination of the Conference."[93] Catto cabled Keynes more reserved sentiments: "Very concerned at report in papers here that you have had a heart attack. Hope you are all right but please rest. Love to you both."[94]

On the morning of the twentieth, Luxford read Morgenthau a revised resolution, one much more to White's liking, calling only for the BIS to be "liquidated at the earliest possible moment."

"God, that is short and sweet," Morgenthau observed happily.[95]

After a briefing from his team, Morgenthau invited Keynes, Ronald, and Bolton into the room, handing them copies of the terse new American formulation. Keynes, in a much improved condition and clearly desirous of a rapprochement, immediately assented, despite Ronald and Bolton having the day prior opposed any resolution not explicitly connected to the IMF or the World Bank. Bolton protested mildly that he didn't "quite know what the earliest possible moment" meant. "Not very early!" Keynes predicted.[96] He was right. Despite the resolution becoming part of the Bretton Woods agreements, the BIS remains, nearly seventy years on, very much in business. Ironically, this is Keynes's most tangible legacy from the conference.

As for the other nations present, not even the likes of Russia, France, China, or India had hopes of materially changing the structure of the fund or the bank; none of them individually was central enough to the global economy to stop White's blueprint from going forward. Their delegations came, therefore, with few aims beyond maximizing their status and borrowing capacity within the new institutions, while minimizing their liabilities toward them. This they could only hope to accomplish by petitioning the American delegation, as the United States was the sole nation able to bring to bear sufficient gold reserves to make the schemes credible.

Other than the United States, United Kingdom, and Canada, few delegations came equipped to make intellectual contributions to the architecture of the fund or the bank. Most of the delegates, Robbins put it coldly, "just sit listlessly about and only come to life when it is a question of easier terms for the drawing of quotas or special concessions for the liberated areas." The Europeans, he noted, "hated the US and lose no opportunity . . . to express these feelings on the assumption that we [fellow Europeans], as men of superior quality, must adopt the same point of view, even if, for political reasons, we have to pretend the contrary." However, he admonished, "any disposition to get into a corner with precious European cliques of no great administrative or political ability and preen ourselves on our cultural superiority to the New World would be almost the greatest folly we could commit."[97]

The one issue on which almost all delegations took an impassioned interest was national quotas in the fund. Quotas represented borrowing capacity. Yet quotas were also deeply political. They not only translated into voting power within the two institutions, but governments saw them as publicly conspicuous quantitative measures of each country's importance in the global economic hierarchy. Being accorded a higher quota than one's rivals was widely taken as a mark of superior status in the eyes of the international community. For a delegation to go home with a lower quota than that achieved by a rival delegation, or group of delegations, could be seen as a shameful capitulation. The great diplomatic challenge for White and Morgenthau, therefore, was to generate a constellation of quota allocations that allowed each delegation to return home with a victory narrative, while at the same time limiting the total American capital contribution to a level Congress could accept.

The British wanted to show strength with the empire by negotiating higher quotas for its constituents than whatever the Americans proposed. The Americans were always conscious of the cumulative voting strength of the empire, and made clear to the press that the latter would never be allowed to outvote them.[98] Russia wanted a quota at least as great as Britain's. India needed to be on par with China. China demanded to be number four, ahead of France. France insisted on besting the three Benelux countries combined, so that France would be ensured the last seat on the fund's executive committee even if Benelux became a full political union. Over in the New World, Colombia and Bolivia demanded parity with Chile, which in turn sought equality with Cuba—by lowering Cuba's quota, if necessary. And on it went. Each delegation argued that quotas should be determined by metrics favorable to their own country. Whereas national income, trade volume, gold holdings, and gold production were the main economic indicators put forward, the Chinese and Indians naturally preferred population. Russia demanded war damage as a consideration, which remained a sticking point for much of the conference.

Unlike their preferences with the fund, delegations preferred lower quotas with the World Bank.[99] A larger bank quota did not entitle a country to borrow more—that was based on an evaluation of the need. "[I]n the Fund [countries] looked at themselves as prospective borrowers," whereas "in the Bank, they were guarantors of loans."[100] And, consistent with Keynes's assertion that it would have been "worse than a mistake to attempt the invidious task of discriminating between members and assessing their credit-worthiness," bank quotas were merely liabilities for underpriced lending.[101] The Latin Americans were particularly anxious to distance themselves from the war reconstruction function of the bank, as they had acquired large sums of dollars during the war, which they had no desire to put to use subsidizing the rebuilding of competitor exporting nations in Europe.[102]

Each country would be required to put up a gold contribution equivalent to the lesser of 25 percent of its quota or 10 percent of its holdings. "For the rest," snipped the *New York Times*, "it can throw in its own paper money, valued at an arbitrary figure, whether or not it is convertible into gold or represents anything but the product of the printing press. On the basis of this quota, it can 'buy' currencies of real value—meaning in the main American dollars—to twice the amount of its quota."[103] The *Chicago Tribune* was characteristically more colorful:

The mythical country of Bargravia, with nothing but a printing press, would put up its share in currency, which is nothing more than due-bills spendable in that picturesque land. . . . The people of that proud country, replacing the buildings destroyed during the war, would be eager to buy American products . . . [and] seek to convert considerable sums into American dollars to buy American goods. . . . While Bargravians were turning their money into dollars [through the fund], the people of 42 other countries would be doing the same thing. In no time the international currency fund would run out of dollars, and its assets would consist of bargas, belgas, drachmas, pesetas, francs, pounds, and other currencies.[104]

What the plan amounts to, then, is a scheme by which our good neighbors in Europe and Asia will obtain our goods and pay for them with our money, taken from the international stabilization fund. Out of the fund will go the gold that everybody wants and into the fund will go the paper moneys that nobody wants. Before long, there will be no more dollars and no more gold in the fund, and we shall be pressed to ante up again, and so on, ad infinitum, or at least until we are as busted as the rest.[105]

The conference had an official Quota Committee, which was a matter of proper form only. The substance of quota allocations was controlled entirely by the Americans. White and the Americans hammered out successive drafts of quota tables behind closed doors, raising some allocations and lowering others as the need or compulsion arose. The initial allocations had been done in advance of the conference by secret formula, although on-site refinements took on progressively more subjective elements.

"When you think of the fight Jugoslavia has put up . . . it seems to me that is one country we ought to stretch ourselves on," White offered at a July 9 meeting with his colleagues. And on Greece: "Keynes says Varvaressos is such a lovely chap, he would like to do something for him."

Morgenthau generally took little interest in how the numbers were determined. But he did want to get his marching orders straight. "Just one minute," he interrupted White. "Now, is Poland to stay at a hundred or not to stay at a hundred. What is your pleasure, please?"

Once armed with the figures and parameters on his negotiating wiggle room, Morgenthau would be sent off to close the deal with each country, generally at fifteen-minute intervals. "Now we have the Iranians at four [o'clock]. Whom did we say we would see at four-fifteen?"

"The Netherlands—the Czechoslovakians at four-thirty," said his assistant and diarist, Mrs. Klotz.

"The Chileans, I think, are next in line," said Collado. "They are the ones who are giving us a little trouble."

"The Chileans at four-forty-five," Morgenthau affirmed.

The one area of intense political debate within the U.S. delegation was how to deal with the European colonial powers. Did they have a right to bigger quotas because of their large, far-flung colonies? Senator Wagner couldn't abide it. "[A]t Tehran it was decided that these countries shall have their freedom if they want it. . . . Now, are we doing something in here to say to them, 'We are holding you down?'"

"I think the Queen of the Netherlands would be very disturbed if you did anything," White suggested, in reference to the Dutch East Indies.

"The Queen?" Wagner shot back. "She is a Queen, but she is not my Queen. I am for America."

"It sounds like a song," observed Morgenthau.

Luxford suggested a provision providing for a quota adjustment in the case of a country being "divided into two separate sovereignties." White thought that would be "a very excellent thing." Acheson, hewing firmly to conservative State Department tradition, pronounced it "a terrible thing." It "would just raise hell." How would you handle the "Russian business . . . dividing these sixteen republics"?

"The Russian thing isn't involved," White said curtly. "They are not going to have that problem."

White would not long after the conference pen an essay—most surely not meant to be seen while he was in government, if ever—blasting U.S. and Western hypocrisy toward the Soviet Union.[106] White was, of course, wrong about the sustainability of "the Russian thing," but it would take nearly five decades before that would be settled.

The sparring within the delegation continued until Morgenthau suggested a formula whereby Hull would be consulted if the Quota Committee opted to consider Luxford's sovereignty-change clause. The group agreed that the clause would be dropped if Hull objected—which Acheson considered a certainty.[107] As in the Paris peace settlement twenty-five years earlier, the high principle of national self-determination in the postwar world was much easier to state than to implement.

Installed godfather-like in his suite, Morgenthau received each delegation head to hear his pleas and protestations. Granted an audience at 9:00 p.m. on July 15, an emotional Pierre Mendès-France, who had flown in from Algiers to head the French delegation, complained that the Americans had "taken key positions . . . which are in fact against us . . . these questions are always settled against our interest." White had told him in June that the French quota would be $500 million; now it was down to $425 million. France was being sacrificed to placate the Chinese, who insisted on claiming the number four spot on the quota ranking, ahead of France. The Americans were also backtracking on the Russian proposal to reduce contributions for countries suffering war devastation, which the Americans had told France would amount to 25 percent in its case.

"How [will] it look when I come back to my people," Mendès-France asked, "and explain to them, 'I went some months ago to Bretton Woods, and explained our position. I told them we want to ask this, this, and this, and in all these questions I have to tell you I come with zero'?"

Morgenthau suggested that France might be guaranteed a quota high enough for it to claim a fifth directorship, up from a previously planned three, within the fund and bank. That did the trick; Mendès-France thanked him. "I told you," Morgenthau said, "I would not go to bed until I tried to correct [the] impression" that the American delegation was "unfriendly to France." Now, he concluded, "I can go to bed."[108]

Russia was a far tougher nut to crack. Led by M. S. Stepanov, the deputy commissar of foreign trade, the Russian delegation could not give an inch on any matter, however small, without cabling Moscow and waiting many days for a response. "They sit silent at all committees," Robbins noted, "taking voluminous notes, and if occasion arises to present one of their own amendments, calling for exceptions to suit their own convenience, they just rise and put the motion with the minimum explanation possible."[109] In negotiations, they "refrained from extensive debate and counter-argumentation," according to American technical adviser Raymond Mikesell. They "countered every contrary argument by a simple restatement of their original position . . . they counted not on logic and persuasion for winning their point but upon sheer doggedness and the fact that they knew that the United States delegation would make every effort to satisfy them because of the political importance of Soviet membership."[110] The Americans had been prepared for this. Back in 1943, Russian Ambassador Gromyko had told his underlings, in front of White and Bernstein, "Remember! You are observers. You are not to give any opinion of any kind."[111]

"There is," Robbins observed of the Russians, "something morally impressive about such monumental selfishness. But I cannot think," he concluded presciently, that "it augurs well for the future of the world."[112] White was blind to this; for him, it was reactionary forces in the United States and western Europe that were stoking frictions with the Russians and preventing economic and political cooperation.

Russia's main objective was simple. As a major gold producer, Russia wanted the rest of the world to need as much of the metal as possible for monetary purposes. The Russians therefore had an interest in some form of a revived gold-exchange standard. This fact was not lost on the Nazi government in Germany, whose economy minister and central bank head, Walther Funk, blasted the Bretton Woods monetary plans as a sop to the Soviets.[113]

Russia's primary initial demand was a quota on par with the United Kingdom's, though Stepanov indicated that his government would ultimately be satisfied with something just below that. Since the United Kingdom was slotted to get $1.3 billion, White translated this into a demand for $1.2 billion, which Stepanov later confirmed. This was much more than the $800 billion the American technicians had penciled in, and well beyond what could be justified by Russia's contribution to world trade. But other Russian demands were politically even more difficult to accommodate.

The Russians wanted a 50 percent deduction on their gold contribution, on the grounds that they had suffered massive physical damage from enemy occupation. White explained to the American delegation that his technicians had suggested to the Russians prior to the conference that a 25 percent deduction might be feasible, but the British strongly objected to this—they insisted that such a concession would require an equivalent accommodation for them. Other delegations, such as the French, pressed the same demand.[114]

The Russians also stated that only half of their gold contribution could be physically held in Washington, and about a quarter of the remainder would have to be held in Moscow itself.[115] A related Russian proposal was that the fund itself should hold gold in each of the four countries with the highest quota, the amount of which would be equivalent to the host country's own gold subscription. This would effectively have blocked the fund from ever making use of Russia's gold contribution without the Kremlin's approval.[116]

The Russians further wanted the freedom to change the par value of their currency provided it "did not affect international transactions." This proved a brainteaser for the American delegation and technicians. How could such a change not affect international transactions? And if it couldn't, why make it? But from the Russian perspective, the fact that the ruble was not used in foreign trade, and that the official ruble exchange rate bore no relation to internal Russian prices and costs, meant that the country deserved a blanket exemption from fund rules on maintaining exchange rate parities.

Russia being a major gold-mining country, Moscow also wanted an exemption of up to ten years from requirements for larger gold contributions from countries that acquire new gold. Finally, and most difficultly, the Russians were the only delegation that refused to accept the principle that each country's fund and bank quota be the same—they insisted on putting $300 million less into the bank than the fund.

White suggested that the Russians could be persuaded "to withdraw those provisions," or most of them, "in exchange for a substantial, larger quota" in the fund. This set off a tense standoff with Eccles, who was angered by the Russian demands. "It looks to me . . . that until they are willing to change their whole approach to this thing that the chance of getting together is not very bright. Now they have entirely a different interest in this matter than capitalistic countries. Their interest openly is to get this credit."

White fired back, "What is China's interest and Poland's interest and Greek interest?" Russia was playing the same game everyone else was.

Many countries were in this for the right reason, Eccles insisted—stabilizing exchange rates. But "Russia and China want to get all the money they can get."[117] Echoing Eccles, Treasury's Mikesell wrote seven years after the fact that the Russians were "not interested in the solution of the fundamental problems with which the Fund was designed to deal, namely, stable exchange rates." They were concerned mainly with "what it would cost them to join [and] how much could they get out of it in the way of credits."[118]

Eccles observed that this "of course has been the criticism of the program, that it is a lending fund and not a stabilization fund."[119] The newspapers were indeed making this point. "[T]he fear," explained the *Christian Science Monitor*, "is that countries 'temporarily' short of foreign exchange might make a habit of using the fund, selling it their own exchange and buying it out of export countries' currencies until the fund became loaded up with questionable currencies like a commercial bank which might become so loaded up with the notes, repeatedly renewed, of over-adventurous borrowers, that finally it would be insolvent."[120]

"[I]t seems to me," Eccles concluded, "that if we make the concession that Russia wants, why, you destroy any possible chance of getting the Fund through in this country."

Brown agreed. The Russians were demanding too much special treatment. "[A]ll the banking discussion and newspaper discussions on this has been that the United States puts in good currency, puts in gold . . . they put in a lot of currencies."

"Which currency would you say isn't valuable?" asked a growingly agitated White.

"The Greeks, and so forth. . . . Isn't there one thing on this Russian attitude we might bring in, that this is a Stabilization Fund and as I see it, it is [becoming] a grab-bag."

This angered White, setting him off on a long, heated lecture. "No. I don't think that is an appropriate supposition. . . . [The] USSR has advantages which no other country has. She has large gold production, she has tremendous productive capacity, and last and most important, she herself can determine how much she is going to sell. No capitalistic country can do that, because they have got to sell at a profit."

White's long-standing fascination with Soviet state planning was suddenly on full display. "Now, then, when USSR says, very frankly,

"We are going to use this Fund to buy things because this is a time of need and this is what a stabilization fund is for and we will pay you back after five, six or seven years," I say that is a stabilization operation and no different than what happens in any other country . . . there is a tendency completely to distort the analysis and to point a finger at USSR, because they are doing frankly what the other countries are going to do anyway. What do you think Poland and the Netherlands or France or Belgium or China are going to do? If they didn't do it, in my judgment, their financial ministers would be stupid. . . .

From the point of view of the ability to repurchase foreign exchange which she buys from the Fund, I put USSR on the top of the list and instead of giving her one billion dollars you could give her two billion and the Fund would operate still better and your exports would do a lot more business. That is quite a speech, but I think it is necessary in the light of the misunderstanding which is prevalent not only here but outside on what the nature of the Stabilization Fund is. I have heard it from Keynes. I had to argue the same point."

Eccles was unmoved: "Your speech hasn't changed my point of view a particle."

"[T]his conference is absolutely stalled by these Russian demands," Brown concluded. "I think the time has come when unless it is resolved that the Conference will fail just because it can't complete its task within the two weeks, that it is necessary for us at this time to show our teeth."

"Not unless they are good teeth," White corrected him.

"[I] think the question of negotiations is over," Eccles insisted. "I think you have reached the point where you say . . . this is the position and that is final. Let's adopt their tactics."

Luxford was nervous. Could the conference afford to lose Russia? "[T]he question before us right now is the biggest question that this Delegation will decide in this Conference. Are we going to get Russia in here or aren't we? This is so much more important than the rest of the quotas put together."

Bernstein added that Russia had shown itself to be a good credit "through the dark days of the thirties." So "if they want the prestige of a large quota, let them have the prestige of a large quota and let us have a fund which in principle will work universally. . . . And that means wiping out all exceptions" of the sort Russia was demanding.[121]

A consensus painfully emerged to split the difference within the group: the Russians could have a larger quota or a smaller gold contribution. But not both.

The press followed the deliberations energetically, naturally relying on leaks from the negotiators. The *New York Times* reported unnamed American officials remarking that Russian demands for "more use of the assets of the proposed world monetary fund in return for a smaller contribution of gold . . . typif[ied] the unabashed self-interest of their demands in such conferences." The paper observed that "[t]he Americans, oddly enough, seem to like that about the Russians."[122] Indeed, the American team tended to get on swimmingly with the Russians; the two sides could occasionally be found "singing the Red Army songs" in the basement nightclub. And when "stimulated by considerable quantities of vodka, [the Russians] joined in singing familiar American songs."[123]

The *Chicago Tribune* blasted Russia for "trying to avoid making a contribution of gold to the fund proportionate to her means." Like its hometown hero, Brown, the paper believed the Russians "[weren't] seriously seeking a plan to stabilize currencies. They are seeking a way of getting good out of the United States without giving anything of equal value in return. They can't be blamed too severely for trying to put this over, but our representatives can be blamed most severely for giving them encouragement." The fund, the paper concluded, "is designed to enrich other countries at our expense and make inflation in America inevitable.[124]

Morgenthau, who had been back in Washington during his delegation's debate on Russia, followed White's instructions to offer the Russians the choice between a $1.2 billion quota and no further concessions or a $900 million quota with a 25 percent reduction in the Russian gold contribution. But the Russians still insisted on having both. Morgenthau was angry. He had little political wiggle room, and the Russians were not budging.

"Now, frankly, after having the most friendly relations with your people, I am quite shocked that two great nations should begin what we call 'to horse trade,'" Morgenthau told Stepanov on July 11. "This isn't the spirit which my Government has approached this problem with." Rep. Wolcott, Morgenthau explained, had assured him that what the Russians were demanding was "just impossible . . . the whole thing would be defeated in Congress."

Stepanov's tone, certainly his translator's rendition of it, was unfailingly gracious. He expressed his "deep appreciation and admiration for [Morgenthau's] attitude and that of the [American] delegation." That said, he wanted Morgenthau to understand that he faced insuperable political difficulties back home on the issue of Russia's gold contribution, as Moscow believed that the two countries' technical experts had already agreed on the reduction. As to the quota, there had been a mutual "misunderstanding concerning the calculation." White's proposed formula had produced the $800 million figure; using different data, the Russians arrived at $1.2 billion.

Morgenthau tried to clear the air of politics. "I am not a diplomat, I am not a lawyer, I am just a farmer," he assured Stepanov.

"Mr. Stepanov says that he is no diplomat, himself," the translator responded, "no lawyer, no financier, just a businessman." This must have been an awkward profession coming from a Communist.

Russia's request for a quota a bit under the United Kingdom's was "quite new," Morgenthau continued. The experts had never discussed it. But the United States had acceded to it, Morgenthau explained, "largely due to the magnificent fight that [Russia was] making." This was "against [what] most of the rest of the Delegations" supported. On this basis, Morgenthau asked again that Stepanov's government "accept one or the other of these proposals."

Stepanov insisted that $800 million was "much less than the sum [Russia is] entitled to get according to the American formula . . . we don't request anything which we are not entitled to." But Russia had not "furnished any data" to back its much larger figure, Morgenthau put back to him. Other delegations were saying that Russia had $4 billion in gold, and was dedicating 700,000 men to mining much more. "This is gossip I am repeating."

"Well, you can't stop the gossiping," Stepanov replied.

Morgenthau asked whether Stepanov would object to his cabling Ambassador Harriman in Moscow and asking him to discuss the American proposal with Molotov. Stepanov said he was expecting a direct answer from Moscow, but that he had no objections to the Secretary informing his ambassador of the discussions—in fact, "it would be even helpful." The two parted with mutual pledges of goodwill and hopes for future economic cooperation.[125]

Three days later, an eternity in conference time, the Russian delegation had yet to get a response from Moscow; Harriman had been told the delegation had received instructions, but Stepanov explained that his instructions were unchanged.

Morgenthau tried to turn up the pressure. "With all courtesy," he told Stepanov, "the whole Conference is being held up . . . there is [a quota] meeting at two o'clock today, so we will have to publicly take a position."

Stepanov was unfazed. The two sides, he said, could agree to disagree on the 25 percent reduction in Russia's gold contribution until new instructions arrived from Moscow. Morgenthau persisted: the United States would back a $1.2 billion quota for Russia and also accept the Russian position on newly mined gold, but the 25 percent discount for war devastation would cause "a lot trouble with the other countries." Stepanov remained cordial but immovable.[126]

Further Russian demands continued to pop up without warning in committee meetings. After hours of monkish silence in a late-night drafting meeting, a Soviet adviser startled his counterparts by blurting out laboriously: "The Union (pause) of Soviet (pause) Socialist (pause) Republics (long pause) eenseest on Alternative E"—an out-of-order call for war-ravaged economies to be granted special World Bank credit facilities.[127]

At Stepanov's request, he and Morgenthau reconvened the next morning, July 15, with White, Soviet delegate N. F. Chechulin, and others from the two sides. "Mr. Stepanov has come to talk about questions on which he finds some difficulties," his translator began. "[I]n his opinion they are not difficult." Stepanov then proceeded to lay out a lengthy series of concerns relating to gold contributions to the fund and Russian sovereignty in currency par value changes.

"Has he finished?" Morgenthau asked the translator after some time. He had not. Stepanov had "a few points" to raise on the bank as well.

"May I say this to Mr. Stepanov," Morgenthau said, clearly fed up. "He has brought up enough questions to take us ten hours to discuss, and Mr. White has a Commission at ten o'clock."

He wouldn't make it. Deferring the bank questions until the afternoon, White tried in vain to get Stepanov to accept alternative language on par values that would not give the public impression that Russia was rendering the fund toothless. Stepanov raised hopes by saying he needed "to consider it," and then immediately dashed them by saying it would require "having another agreement of [the Soviet] Government. Therefore we should like to insist on the wording that we proposed at the start of the conversation, if there is no difference in substance."

Morgenthau thought he was losing his mind. "Mr. Stepanov has said two different things," he shot back. "First he said he would like time to consider the language . . . then in the next breath he has changed his mind and has gone back to his own language."

"It isn't he has changed his mind . . . Mr. Stepanov is willing to consider it, but still he will have to get the agreement of the Government."

"You mean you have to cable?" asked Morgenthau in disbelief.

"Cable."

"What is the use?" White asked resignedly.

Morgenthau was beaten: "we will accept your language."

"Thank you very much."

"You tell Mr. Stepanov I am afraid it is the last time he is going to say thank you at this Conference!"

Laugher briefly lightened the mood. Then the difficult negotiations resumed, now over where Moscow's gold contribution would be physically held. Two notes came up from a committee stating that they were waiting for the American and Russian delegates; Morgenthau and White agreed to support the Russian position, and Luxford left to join the committee meeting together with P. A. Maletin, the Soviet deputy people's commissar of finance. Morgenthau finally returned to the vexing issue of the 25 percent reduction in the Russian gold contribution. This was where he made his stand.

"The American delegation cannot go along with any proposal that the devastated areas make a deduction of their gold contribution. We are very sorry."

"Not only will you not support it, but you are against it?" asked a disbelieving Stepanov.

"We will try not to oppose it," White replied. "There are plenty of countries who may, but if there are not, then we will have to oppose it."[128]

That afternoon, the draft fund quota list was presented to the full conference. "Judge Vinson opened for the US with a great blast of eloquence designed to cast a halo of respectability over the horsedealing of the last fortnight," Robbins recorded. China, France, India, New Zealand, and others made formal protests. Robbins spoke last, urging the delegates to accept the list as the best that was likely to be forthcoming. "I must confess," he reflected later that day, "that I have never felt greater distaste for anything I have had to do in Government service."[129] But the list was accepted without further debate; a significant conference milestone had been passed, but much remained to be done.

On Monday, July 17, Morgenthau called a meeting of key American personnel and major delegation heads to settle on a do-or-die end date for the conference. Many of the American and British experts and support staff were nearing exhaustion; stenographers were collapsing. Work was routinely proceeding through half the night, with White and others subsisting on a few hours sleep. It had become clear that a final text could not be achieved by the July 19 deadline. "We may have to get the President to get out an order to seize the hotel as of Wednesday night, and put troops in here to run it," Morgenthau said. "[W]e may have to carry the manager of the hotel out with two soldiers! If that is necessary, Judge Vinson will give the orders."

Acheson suggested that Saturday the twenty-second was the earliest they could finish. White agreed that was feasible; the trains could depart on Sunday. Luxford was the only one to voice doubts, thereby incurring the full brunt of the Secretary's annoyance. "What are you going to do, Luxford—stay here until Christmas? . . . Everybody here is talking about Saturday or Sunday. Why . . . did it suddenly dawn on you that you couldn't do it?"

Keynes and the other delegation heads made it official: they would be out by Sunday night.[130] The *New York Times* blared the news on the front page the following morning, July 18: "CONFERENCE ADDS 3 DAYS TO TALKS; SNARLED ON BANK."[131] Over the next week, White and his team worked flat out assembling the Final Act from the various committee and commission texts, as well as critical text prepared by his own special committee, beyond the reach of the foreigners.

"SOVIETS DEADLOCK MONETARY PARLEY," announced the *New York Times* on July 20.[132] Despite their relentless demands for special treatment, the Russians were ultimately willing to be voted down on the war-damage concessions. The concessions offered by the Americans on newly mined gold were worth far more. Still, the Russians dug in on one major issue, the only issue standing in the way of a historic agreement: Moscow would only make a $900 million subscription to the bank, $300 million less than the quota they demanded from the fund. Every other delegation accepted an identical bank and fund quota. "It is a disgrace," the Belgian delegation head Georges Theunis shouted at Robbins after leaving a Bank Commission meeting. "The Americans give way to the Russians every time. And you too, you British, are just as bad. You are on your knees to them. You wait. You'll see what a harvest you'll reap at the peace conference."[133]

The matter finally came to a head on July 21, the penultimate day of the conference, at a 10:15 a.m. meeting of delegation heads, chaired by Vinson, on the quota issue. The Indian representative, Sir Jeremy Raisman, threw down the gauntlet: "If there is a reduction in the subscription of any important country, I don't think I could get my country to agree to a subscription equal to its quota, . . . it would certainly put me in grave difficulties if there were a serious departure from that principle." Poland offered to go up $25 million to help fill the Russian shortfall; China pledged $50 million. Stepanov sat silent.

Keynes intervened. "Mr. Secretary, the Soviet Delegate has not yet spoken. Before he does so, I should like to make an appeal to him." Keynes argued that the willingness of Poland and China to up their bank subscriptions, and his own country to take a large stake, showed that the Russians were overestimating the financial risks. "I do urge, most sincerely," he concluded forcefully, "that it is scarcely consistent with the honor and dignity of a great country to remain so uncompromising at this stage."

Stepanov, whose modus operandi was to speak only as necessary, and even then mainly just to highlight "the stand which the Russians were making against Hitler's hordes in their homeland,"[134] was obliged to break his silence. He was, he said, "deeply moved by the willingness of the other delegations to reach the goal which was mentioned." But he could not agree with India's effort "to connect their own quota with the quota of the USSR," which had "suffered so greatly in this war." In any case, he had "no authorization to mention any other figure"; Moscow had authorized $900 million, no more.[135]

The Canadian representative then suggested that he might get Ottawa to agree to bump up its subscription to 10 percent of the American figure (which it did, adding $25 million). Morgenthau asked to confer with Vinson and the Russians in private. The group of delegation heads reconvened at 3:15 p.m., at which time Vinson announced, to no surprise, that the Russian delegation had received "no further communications from their Government." But the U.S. and Latin American delegations added to pledges from Canada, Poland, and China, and the $300 million hole was finally filled. Stepanov said nothing.

The group hurriedly agreed to send the final quota table up to Keynes's Commission Two at 6:00 p.m., after which Morgenthau would chair a final executive plenary session at 6:30 p.m.[136] "The Russians by stonewalling tactics have got everything they wanted," Keynes wrote to Catto the next day. "It has been the concern of the American policy to appease the Russians and get them in. For my own part," Keynes concluded, "I think this was wise."[137]

Morgenthau assembled the American team for the final time the next morning, July 22. Russian headaches notwithstanding, the Secretary had reason to be supremely satisfied. Bernstein later reflected that "to those who had experience of getting international cooperation after World War I, the Bretton Woods Conference seemed like a miracle."[138] It had succeeded primarily "because everything of importance had been discussed and settled in the two years" prior.[139] Yet in herding forty-four national delegations into the enormously complex scheme for global monetary cooperation, Morgenthau had, critically, also kept his own delegation from splintering on partisan lines. This was no mean feat with an election looming and hoards of press roaming the isolated retreat. Morgenthau, Wolcott, Tobey, and Spence exchanged genuine sentiments of mutual praise. "[T]his has been a most successful experiment in democracy," Morgenthau said proudly.

"As one who has played around with psychological warfare," added State Department Press Division head Michael McDermott, " . . . I wouldn't be at all surprised if this Conference didn't contribute a good deal" to ending the war. The Germans "couldn't but say, 'My God, what are we up against?' and quit."

Tragically, this was not to be the case; the Germans would fight on another eight and a half months. Furthermore, Morgenthau's own soon-to-be publicized ideas for deindustrializing postwar Germany would arguably serve to buttress rather than weaken German war morale, and thereby extend the war and its attendant carnage.

Brown pledged to "do what I can to sell [the agreement] to the bankers of the country." Morgenthau was grateful, "because they seem to be the only people who right now are vociferous [against] this thing."

"And Bob Taft," corrected Senator Tobey.

"I will leave Taft to you!" put back Morgenthau. "He is your personal meat." Taft and the bankers would indeed put up a formidable resistance.

As for the Russians, who had put up the greatest obstacles to securing an agreement at Bretton Woods, there were no hard feelings: "The Russian Delegation is on the golf tee, wherever that is, waiting for us," Morgenthau announced, ending the meeting.[140]

"The broadcasting companies . . . made arrangements for a broadcast at the end of the Bretton Woods Conference, with White explaining what we had accomplished," Bernstein recalled many years later, but "Morgenthau did not let White make that broadcast." The Secretary told Bernstein to step in—once again anonymously. "Mr. Morgenthau had always had an ambivalent attitude toward Harry White, and he was jealous at Bretton Woods because more attention was paid to White than to him."[141]

That evening, the massive, elegant dining hall played host to the conference's closing banquet and ratification ceremony. "Tired, pale as a sheet,"[142] Keynes entered the packed hall, slightly late, and ambled slowly toward his empty seat. As he did, the assemblage stood up nearly as one, in a silent tribute to the figure who, in Skidelsky's words, "gave the Bretton Woods Agreement its distinction not its substance."[143] As arguably the world's greatest public intellectual, Keynes had elevated the gathering to something beyond a major political event. Even if the final lawyer-laden text held only scattered traces of his thinking, and fewer of his prose ("Cherokee," Keynes called the American legalese), Bretton Woods, largely because of his presence, would always represent a vision of how global cooperation might be fashioned from the mind up.

It is certainly doubtful anyone could have delivered a more sprightly, eloquent, and gracious dinner address than did Keynes. Full of easy humor, clever allusions, and generosity of spirit, it had to have made all present in the hall—at least those whose command of English would allow—conscious of the fact that they had been participants in an historic enterprise. Keynes paid tribute to Morgenthau's "wise and kindly guidance," and to White's "indomitable will and energy, always governed by good temper and humor." He praised Acheson, Cox, Luxford, Collado, and the other American lawyers—lawyers having been a traditional target of his waspish wit—for having "turned our jargon into prose and our prose into poetry." Alluding to the ever-present press, he even pronounced himself "greatly encouraged . . . by the critical, skeptical, and even carping spirit in which our proceedings have been watched," as he was convinced that it was "better [to] *begin* in disillusion than . . . [to] *end* in it." Subtly, he closed by positing that what the forty-four nations had "accomplished here in Bretton Woods [was] something more significant than what is embodied in this Final Act." Indeed, since so little of the Final Act encapsulated his grander vision of a global Clearing Union, this was an article of faith in which he placed great hopes. He departed the hall to a hearty round of "For He's a Jolly Good Fellow" from his fellow delegates. Though seemingly a spontaneous serenade, Bernstein later said he had told the orchestra to play it.[144]

In his closing address, Morgenthau situated the conference's achievements firmly within the wider palette of the war and its causes. He condemned "the planless, senseless rivalry" and "the outright economic aggression" that had led the world "down the steep, disastrous road to war. That sort of extreme nationalism," he proclaimed, "belongs to an era that is dead. Today the only enlightened form of national self-interest lies in international accord. At Bretton Woods," he said, the Allied nations had "taken practical steps toward putting this lesson into practice in the monetary and economic field." He stretched the event's immediate significance just a bit by according it "some small part" in prodding Count von Stauffenberg and his German military collaborators to attempt an assassination of Hitler—very nearly successful—at his Rastenburg headquarters two days earlier.[145] Morgenthau received a somewhat less personalized parting musical tribute than did Keynes—the band played "The Star-Spangled Banner."

In addition to the pomp and ceremony, the evening featured one happy unexpected development that Morgenthau took great pleasure in relaying to the delegates at the start of the speech making. "[T]he Conference jumped to its feet and cheered to the echo" on hearing the news, Robbins recorded. "So in the end everything has ended in a blaze of optimism and friendly feeling."[146]

Like a runaway bride who returns after the church lights are out and the door is being locked, the Russians had made a startling reappearance twenty-four hours after the conference's formal business had concluded. At 7:00 p.m., thirty minutes before the dinner, Stepanov went to see Morgenthau. His translator reported triumphantly that "Mr. Stepanov . . . has the answer from Mr. Molotov, and that answer is that he is happy to agree to your proposition."

Morgenthau was not certain he understood. Stepanov clarified: "Mr. Molotov says that we will agree to increase our quota" in the bank.

"To how much?" asked an incredulous Morgenthau.

"To $1,200,000,000," the same as in the fund.

"Mr. Molotov agrees to that?"

"He says that he agrees with Mr. Morgenthau."

"Well, you tell Mr. Molotov that I want to thank him from the bottom of my heart."[147]

Back in April, Molotov had told Harriman just hours before the Joint Statement was to be released to the press, without Russian support, that the Soviet government was, in the end, "willing to instruct its experts to associate themselves with Mr Morgenthau's project."[148] And here once again, at Bretton Woods, Moscow chose to personalize its characteristically tardy gesture, which now anomalously left the bank with $300 million more capital than the fund. "Mr. Molotov says that he agrees to the size of the quota," Stepanov explained, "because Mr. Morgenthau asked the Soviet Delegation to do it."

"I want you to say this to Mr. Molotov. This confirms the long time respect and confidence that I have in the Union of Soviet and Socialist Republics," proclaimed the ebullient Treasury Secretary.

Stepanov pounded home the message: "Mr. Molotov wanted to raise the quota because you asked them to and because of his high regard for you."[149]

Russian regard for Americans at Bretton Woods was not limited to Morgenthau, however. I. D. Zlobin, chief of the Monetary Division of the People's Commissariat of Finance, published a curious account of his time at Bretton Woods after his return home, as part of an article titled "Meetings in America" in a Moscow journal called *The War and the Working Class*. The story focused on Zlobin's friendly relations with Harry White. White, he said, had invited Zlobin and Chechulin to his country cottage outside Washington when the two were in the capital:[150] White would later tell a grand jury that both before and after the conference he had entertained the entire Russian delegation at his house.[151] At Bretton Woods, Zlobin continued, they played volleyball with White and other members of the Russian and American groups. (Mikesell noted that the Russians took the games "very seriously.")[152] "Later on," Zlobin wrote, "whenever there was an occasion that we had to put through some decisions of interest to us, White would always jokingly say, 'All I can place at your disposal are our own votes and the votes of the 22 Latin American Republics.'"[153] The joke was lost on the FBI, which would add the article to the file it had been building on White since 1942.

Ohio Republican Senator Robert Taft testifying before the Senate Banking and Currency Committee against the Bretton Woods agreements, July 1945. (Thomas D. McAvoy/Time & Life Pictures/Getty Images)

CHAPTER 9

Begging Like Fala

No sooner had the delegations departed Bretton Woods than controversy erupted between the British and the Americans over the meaning of what had been signed. "We, all of us, had to sign, of course, before we had had a chance of reading through a clean and consecutive copy of the document," Keynes offered by way of explanation five months later. "All we had seen of it was the dotted line. Our only excuse," he added, lifting some prose from Shakespeare, "is the knowledge that our hosts had made final arrangements to throw us out of the hotel, unhousseled, disappointed, unaneled, within a few hours."[1]

Dennis Robertson, and not Keynes, had represented Britain in the fund discussions, but even he had not participated in the final formulation of the Articles of Agreement. White's team had drafted the fund text behind the scenes, and Keynes and the other delegation heads saw it for the first time just as they were being "unhousseled." Still, the fact that Keynes would aver to having "never seen the final text of the clauses now under discussion at the time I signed the paper" was astonishing, given the vital importance he and his government had attached to its creation over a period of nearly three years.[2] No doubt, Harry White was only too pleased to have secured the signatures under the strain of a checkout deadline, as the previous two years of negotiations had failed to yield the gains he had engineered in just the final few days of the conference.

In particular, the designation of the U.S. dollar as the only "gold-convertible currency" had at a stroke remade the old gold-exchange standard into a dollar standard—one that would endure to the present day, surviving even the shedding of the gold anchor in 1971. Had Keynes managed to read the text before initialing it he doubtlessly would have fought this. Yet, curiously, there is no record of his having drawn attention to it even after the event. He resumed his tussles with White only over matters of theoretical shorter-term consequence. It may be that Keynes was simply too embarrassed by the discovery of an oversight this momentous to shine attention on it, understanding, as he must have, that White would not yield an inch of conquered diplomatic territory this valuable.

The clauses that sent Keynes into a tizzy related to member-government obligations to support convertibility of their currencies at a fixed rate. These were ambiguous and in places contradictory, having been written in haste under heavy lawyering, leading to the potential for widely different interpretations. Keynes and Robertson could agree neither on what the implied obligations were nor on which one of the two was primarily to blame for the confusion. Keynes faulted Robertson for not spotting the offending text; Robertson countered that Keynes had authorized it, but ultimately shouldered responsibility for the "blunder."[3]

The substance of Keynes's concern was that Britain might be forced to intervene in the currency markets in some way, or barred from intervening in another, such that it would ultimately be unable to control outflows of gold or dollars. This could lead to the "financial Dunkirk" he feared above all else. He wrote a long letter to White on October 6 pleading for changes to the text. The missive was trademark Keynes: a dizzying swirl of logic, passion, angst, and humor. White never responded. But Keynes took advantage of a November trip to Washington to wangle a meeting with him on the eighteenth. Where White agreed with Keynes's interpretation, he offered to support it down the road; where not, he insisted on letting any ambiguity lie unresolved. In no case would he let Congress get wind of a dispute: the text could not be amended.

Keynes would not relent. "We cannot be expected to sign an instrument which is either self-contradictory or hopelessly obscure," he wrote to the chancellor on December 29, in a sterile show of principle.[4] Contradiction and obscurity are the stuff of diplomacy, and Keynes lacked the seasoned diplomat's cynicism to see that what couldn't be, wouldn't be. He therefore tended to pick the wrong fights. In this case, he scared the chancellor into pressing the matter with Morgenthau, which succeeded only in triggering a diplomatic incident. The Secretary passed the letter on to White, who not only refused to budge but demanded that the chancellor take it back, change its date, or expunge references to faulty drafting so as to hide the dispute from congressional prying. (The chancellor took option three.) In the end, it was a tempest in a teacup, as the fledgling fund would be in no position to impose White's antidevaluation agenda on a hapless war-torn world.

Transatlantic tussles over Bretton Woods were mild at this point compared to the political knockabouts on the American and British home fronts. However much public disagreement over the wisdom of the White and Keynes plans existed before July 1944, opposition, particularly from the big banks, was still relatively muted, owing to the hope that an unwieldy international conference would itself bring down the elaborate edifice. But a White-Lite plan had emerged intact, and was suddenly on the verge of becoming the law of the lands. Those who opposed it now had to make their stand.

With the coming battle in mind, Morgenthau asked Roosevelt in late December to recommend White's promotion to assistant secretary of the Treasury. "He will have to carry the brunt of the fight of the Bretton Woods legislation and the additional prestige of being Assistant Secretary will be most useful. He has earned his reward many times over. . . . White has been more than a match for people like Lord Keynes."[5] This was meant, of course, as the highest form of praise. The president assented, and White finally received his first truly prestigious government title on January 23, 1945.

A few weeks earlier, on January 4, Randolph Burgess and a group of influential bankers had met with Morgenthau and his staff to probe for common ground. Burgess came armed with a report prepared by the American Bankers Association and the Reserve City Bankers Association largely accepting the bank plan (as the bank would guarantee their foreign investments), but rejecting the fund as unsound. The fund, the report said, was too big and too complicated. Its remit was too broad and too vague, and it was empowered to lend too freely to uncreditworthy governments. Morgenthau acknowledged that the blueprint was not perfect. But he stressed that the project was vital and urgent, that the best experts in the world had collaborated in its creation, and that it had been blessed by forty-four countries. If one country tried to change it now, all would do similarly, and the public would naturally suspect the bankers for wrecking the agreement. "If it were this or nothing," Burgess said, "he would take this."[6] The Secretary insisted it was this or nothing.

Thinking he had a deal, Morgenthau was enraged when the American Bankers Association issued its report in February, rejecting the fund. So did the U.S. Chamber of Commerce. The private National Economic Council also attacked the fund, in spicier prose. "The 'Stabilization' Fund has nothing to do with stabilization. It is a machine for turning worthless foreign paper currency into dollars. Both 'schemes' [the Fund and the Bank] are mixed up with the fantastic debt theories of Lord Keynes."[7] The battle lines had been drawn.

Huddling with his staff on February 5, Morgenthau told them that this was a fight between bankers and government, one that government had to win. "It is this or nothing, and this is the first thing . . . that is going to go before the world [after the war in Europe], not just before the American people, to looking forward to a better world in business. . . . It is up to the Government to take the risk on the interest rates and not up to the individuals," he said. This was his way of saying that government would set monetary conditions, not banks—and certainly not that bankers' hive in Britain. Will we "have five banks in New York dictate foreign exchange rates . . . having London lead us around by the nose, which they have done in the last hundred years?" he asked rhetorically. The New York bankers were even "against the Federal Reserve System," Luxford pointed out. They were extremists. "We might distort it," White suggested, "and say the speculators are against it."[8]

The key problem Treasury faced in influencing public opinion was that the Bretton Woods agreements were simply too abstruse and complicated to engage it. "There is virtually no public opinion about the Bretton Woods conference," concluded a report submitted by the Office of War Information to the Treasury. "There is no general discussion of it because there is no interest; and there is no interest because there is no comprehension of the issues involved and the plans proposed, or their importance."[9] Congressmen did not get it either. As Luxford related to Morgenthau, "one sympathetic Congressman (Voorhis) had told me that 'Congress had no opinion on subject because Congress did not understand it.'"[10] Even Fed board chairman Marriner Eccles, a delegate at Bretton Woods, found it all a haze. "Harry, your plan is so darned complicated," he complained to White. "I asked our people to put [it] down briefly in layman's language so I could understand the darned thing, just what it means."[11]

On March 1, White told his staff that Treasury would launch a new initiative to explain Bretton Woods to the public and shape the political debate. The department had hired a public relations firm. Randolph Feltus, an outsider, would organize the campaign. Its key elements were clear. Treasury would heel to the right; the left was already on board, and the key was to impress moderates and bring around influential conservatives. The department's New Deal instincts were to attack the banks, but this tack had to be changed. The enemy would hereafter be the "isolationists." Details and numbers would be avoided; the story would be economic and political security. Bretton Woods was to be "hitched to the star of Yalta," the Crimea Conference of Allied leaders in February. Treasury itself would keep a distance from the campaign, as in the public's mind "The Treasury is suspect. The Treasury is New Deal looney."[12] For White, this must have stung.

Outreach was key; outreach to businessmen, journalists, economists, and all manner of private and community groups. "Clergymen of four big Protestant denominations were welcomed to Washington this week . . . for off-the-record 'educational' sessions," reported the *Wall Street Journal* on April 13. "Some of the ministers left this city full of enthusiasm and determined to preach the gospel of Bretton Woods in their churches."[13] But ultimately the target was a higher authority, Congress.

FDR had sent a formal message to Congress on February 12 urging immediate adoption of the Bretton Woods agreements. Hearings began on March 7. Morgenthau led off before the House Committee on Banking and Currency, hewing carefully to the PR strategy, which came naturally to him given his lack of affinity for numbers and specifics. "[E]conomic security in the midst of political chaos is impossible," he said. "But political security in the midst of economic chaos is equally impossible." Bretton Woods was essential to achieving both. From the perspective of the American national interest, the IMF was vital to ensuring there was no repeat of the 1930s, when U.S. trade collapsed owing to nations "set[ting] up monetary barriers against us." Currency values needed to be stabilized. But the war had shown "the futility of trying to attempt stabilization of currency working with only three countries or six countries," as the United States had done with the Tripartite Agreement. The stabilization system had to be global.

Defending the details of Bretton Woods was, of course, left to Harry White, who began his testimony on Friday, March 9, carrying on the following week through Thursday the fifteenth, and then returning over a month later, on April 19. He began by emphasizing that the Bretton Woods agreements had been a compromise among forty-four nations, but that "the United States delegation was there for one purpose: to protect its interests." He then went on to define these interests in terms of recent history. After the First World War, countries had sought to reestablish the gold standard. This, White said, had been good for the U.S. economy, but other countries, notably Britain, had a different experience. Britain could not attain "what she regarded as an adequate share of world markets, without which she could not have relatively full employment at home." A growing number of Britons blamed their troubles on the country's resumption of the pre–World War I exchange parity. The political pressure eventually became overwhelming, and Britain abandoned the parity in 1931. As sterling depreciated, country after country followed, determined not to allow others to get an export advantage. Currency war led to trade war, as governments, led by Germany in 1932, began making special bilateral clearing agreements with each other in order to control ever more tightly what countries that exported to them could purchase from them in return. World trade collapsed. The depression worsened.

A Bretton Woods agreement to stabilize exchange rates at that time "would definitely have made a considerable contribution to checking the war and possibly it might even have prevented it," White said. The United States now had the most to gain from adoption of the proposals, not because it would need assistance from the fund or the bank but because it would "get assurance that other countries will be enabled to pursue monetary credit and trade policies that we regard as essential for a high level of world trade."

Floating exchange rates during White's time at the Treasury were anathema to powerful U.S. commercial interests—large exporters and domestic producers—owing to upward pressure on the dollar. Foreign currencies falling against the dollar tended to depress U.S. exports and fuel imports competitive with American-made goods. But Britain, the world's largest international debtor nation, was deeply concerned with being compelled by the United States to stabilize the pound at what might be an overvalued exchange rate. The British "have surrounded the word 'stabilization' there with an unpleasant aura of rigidity," White remarked during his testimony. "[T]hey shudder a bit at the word 'stabilization.'" This is why the United States "agreed to substitute the word 'monetary' for 'stabilization'" in naming the fund and describing its functions, he explained.

White then went on to give a lengthy and lucid tutorial on the functions and organization of the fund and bank, one that remains the clearest overview of the original American blueprint yet recorded. This included a careful rebuttal of British Conservative MP Robert Boothby's hostile critique of the ambiguities in the Bretton Woods agreements, published in the form of a letter to the *New York Times*, excerpts of which were read out by a committee member.

Where White faltered, however, is precisely where the United States stumbled in its stewardship of the Bretton Woods monetary system in the 1960s. Was the system to be based on cold, hard, scarce gold, or on dollars that could be produced at will by the U.S. government? White insisted that it was both, though he was at constant pains to explain how this could be.

Does "the scheme not involve a return to the gold standard?" Boothby had asked. "It depends," White offered in reply, "entirely upon what is meant by 'the gold standard.'" If it meant that countries had to keep their exchange rates stable within 1 percent of the parity, then the answer was yes. If it meant that countries were restricted in their ability to issue more currency without having a specific level of gold reserves, then the answer was no. White thought this freedom a virtue.

When pressed by committee members on what Article IV, Section 1 of the fund agreement meant when it said that each member state's currency would be expressed in gold "or in terms of the United States dollar of the weight and fineness in effect on July 1, 1944," White insisted that the two were the same. "[T]o us, and to the world," he explained, "the United States dollar and gold are synonymous. . . . It is a mere matter of convenience of expression rather than significance other than reiteration of the fact that dollars and gold are virtually synonymous."

But what about other currencies? Could the fund not adopt, Ohio Republican Frederick Smith asked, "bancor" or "unitas" in the place of gold and dollars?

"What is a 'bancor' or 'unitas'?" White responded in badly feigned innocence. "There is no such currency."

"Well, you ought to know," Smith shot back. "You had that in your. . . ."

"I had a suggestion that something of that kind might be adopted as an international unit of account," White interrupted, "but, as you know, before the Bretton Woods Conference, that was dropped. . . ."

"You would have to have a name for that unit of account, would you not?" Smith put back to him.

"It is because we had to have a name that we used the alternative 'U.S. dollar.' We think that is a pretty good name," White ventured. "We were glad the other countries accepted the phrase, 'gold or dollars.'"

This was, of course, a great stretching of the truth. White had substituted dollars for "gold-convertible currency" behind the backs of the other conference delegates precisely because he knew many would have fought it, as Keynes had in the years leading to the conference.

Smith pressed on. "[D]ollars would be the same as gold?"

"[T]here is no likelihood," White insisted, "that . . . the United States will, at any time, be faced with the difficulty of buying and selling gold at a fixed price freely."

He would, in due course, be proven wrong. When the United States printed money without regard to its plummeting gold stock during the Vietnam War and Great Society program buildups of the 1960s, it triggered a run on American gold, a fall in the dollar, and an end to fixed exchange rates. Dollars were not synonymous with gold, as White had contended; only gold was gold. But the fiction that they were one and the same was central to White's task of convincing Congress that the United States had complete freedom of action, while convincing the world that it did not—that the United States could be compelled to disgorge gold if it emitted more dollars than the world wanted to hold.

In the Senate, where White testified before the Committee on Banking and Currency for several days between June 14 and 28, he faced a very different adversary from Smith. In debate, Smith, a medical doctor, was meticulous and pointed. In contrast, fellow Ohioan Robert Taft, a man of grand principles rather than detail, was given to bombast and sweeping judgments. For Taft, the issues were simple. The fund was an outlandish scheme to funnel American gold to foreign debtors. Whereas Smith had brought out White's prickly, defensive sarcasm, Taft actually had a calming influence on White, whose confidence was clearly buoyed by his superior command of the details and economic logic behind the fund and the bank.

Smith and Taft both, however, recognized that there was no more politically effective way to undermine White's assurances than to quote his formidable British counterpart, Lord Keynes, particularly with regard to the so-called scarce-currency provisions. Keynes had characterized these as an instrument by which fund members might block imports from countries with excessive creditor positions, namely, the United States. Randolph Burgess had told the Senate these provisions were "an abomination of the wicked." White, after paying due homage to Keynes's "integrity and ability and understanding of the subject," rubbished his interpretation by insisting that the agreement provided only for the fund to "make a report" to the American representative. Once the report made its way to Senator Taft's committee, he could, "after giving it the consideration it deserves . . . throw it in the basket."

In the end, the fact that the Bretton Woods Agreements Act passed comfortably through both committees, in spite of considerable critical testimony from prominent bankers and economists, owed little to technical arguments and much to the Roosevelt and Truman administrations' successful framing of the debate. Bretton Woods was a matter of war and peace. "I think history will look back," White said grandiloquently to Smith at one point, "and indict those who fail to vote the approval of the Bretton Woods proposals in the same way that we now look back and indict certain groups in 1921 who prevented our adherence to an international organization designed for the purpose of preventing wars." This was a time of optimism. America had triumphed in Europe and the Pacific. Fear of being branded an isolationist split the Republican Party, and ultimately gave the act an overwhelming majority of 345 to 18 in the House on June 7. The Charter of the United Nations was signed by representatives of fifty countries in San Francisco, with White in attendance as a technical adviser, on June 26. And on July 19, Bretton Woods passed the Senate by a vote of 61 to 16. Vindicating Roosevelt's calculation that putting the monetary conference in Bretton Woods would win over at least one likely opponent, New Hampshire Senator Tobey told his colleagues in the rotunda that it was "unthinkable that we should permit economic war to engulf the world, or that we should withdraw within ourselves." He voted in favor. President Truman signed Bretton Woods into law on July 31.

The British debate was largely a mirror image of the American one. The Federation of British Industries and the London Chamber of Commerce lined up against the agreement, with the chamber arguing that the system favored creditor nations, and would thereby foster conflict rather than promote stability. "[A]ny financial system which permits [surplus countries] to profit by this unwillingness [to increase imports] and to use the proceeds of their sales to depress the exchange rate and threaten the internal stability of the country to which they have sold, or alternatively, to invest the proceeds in that country, thereby gradually acquiring control of its fixed assets, must in the long run lead not to cooperation but to chaos."[14] This was a timeless debtor-country argument.

Just as the "isolationists" led the congressional attack on Bretton Woods in the United States, the "imperialists" led the parliamentary attack in Britain. Keynes and the chancellor were worried that inflamed political sparring in Westminster would threaten ratification of the agreements in Washington, and therefore every effort was made to delay parliamentary debate until the Americans had passed their legislation. The *Economist* reflected the center of gravity in British opinion on Bretton Woods: the economics of the agreement were bad, but so were those of angering their banker, the United States. "How much economic hazard is a reasonable price for continued American generosity and friendship—or at least for the avoidance of American disappointment and resentment?"[15] Uncharacteristically, the *Economist* had no answer.

1. Treasury Secretary Henry Morgenthau, Jr., 1940s. (© CORBIS)

2. Secretary of State Cordell Hull (*left*) and Secretary of War Henry L. Stimson (*right*) testifying before the House Foreign Affairs Committee in support of the FDR administration's bill to aid Britain's war effort, January 15 and 16, 1941. (Hulton Archive/ Getty Images)

3A. Lend-Lease administrator Edward R. Stettinius, Jr., and President Roosevelt discussing a report to be presented to Congress evaluating Lend-Lease aid, December 1942. (Library of Congress)

3B. Federal Reserve Chairman Marriner Eccles speaking at a press conference following the Fed's announcement of an increase in bank reserve requirements, January 30, 1937. (Library of Congress)

4. President Roosevelt and Treasury Secretary Henry Morgenthau, Jr., on the campaign trail in Poughkeepsie, N.Y., November 6, 1944. (© Bettmann/CORBIS)

5. Members of the U.S. delegation to the Bretton Woods conference, July 1944. *From left to right, standing*: H. D. White, Frederick Vinson, Dean Acheson, Edward E. Brown, Marriner Eccles, Jesse Wolcott; *seated*: Robert Wagner, Brent Spence, Henry Morgenthau, Jr., Charles Tobey (not present: Leo Crowley, Mabel Newcomer). (Alfred Eisenstaedt/ Time & Life Pictures/Getty Images)

6A. The Mount Washington Hotel, location of the Bretton Woods conference, July 1944. (Alfred Eisenstaedt/Time & Life Pictures/Getty Images)

6B. Delegates at the Bretton Woods conference, July 1944. (Alfred Eisenstaedt/ Time & Life Pictures/Getty Images)

7A. Undersecretary of State Dean Acheson, September 1945. (George Skadding/
Time & Life Pictures/Getty Images)

7B. U.S. delegation members Frederick Vinson and Edward E. Brown in
conversation at the Bretton Woods conference, July 1944. (Alfred Eisenstaedt/
Time & Life Pictures/Getty Images)

8A. J. M. Keynes, flanked by Soviet delegation head M. S. Stepanov (*left*) and U.S. delegation head Henry Morgenthau, Jr. (*right*), addressing delegates at the Bretton Woods conference, July 1944. (© Bettmann/CORBIS)

8B. H. D. White (*center*), flanked by British economists and delegation members Lionel Robbins (*left*) and Dennis H. Robertson (*right*), at the Bretton Woods conference, July 1944. (Courtesy of the International Monetary Fund)

9. J. M. Keynes (*center*), flanked by Soviet delegation head M. S. Stepanov (*left*) and Yugoslav delegation head Vladimir Rybar (*right*), at the Bretton Woods conference, July 1944. (Hulton Archive/Getty Images)

10. U.S. delegation head and conference chairman Henry Morgenthau, Jr., and J. M. Keynes in conversation at the Bretton Woods conference, July 1944. (Alfred Eisenstaedt/ Time & Life Pictures/Getty Images)

11. British Prime Minister Winston Churchill and President Roosevelt meeting at Wolfe's Cove railroad station prior to the Quebec Conference, September 1944. (U.S. Army, courtesy of Harry S. Truman Library)

12. J. M. Keynes, British Ambassador Lord Halifax, U.S. Secretary of State James F. Byrnes, and Treasury Secretary Frederick Vinson seated at the signing of the $4.4 billion Anglo-American Financial Agreement in Washington, D.C., December 6, 1945. Standing behind Byrnes are Undersecretary of State Dean Acheson and (to the right) Assistant Secretary of State for Economic Affairs Will Clayton. (AP Photo)

13. H. D. White and J. M. Keynes at the inaugural meeting of the IMF board of governors in Savannah, Ga., March 8, 1946. (Courtesy of the International Monetary Fund)

14. Assistant Secretary of State for Economic Affairs Will Clayton, Treasury Secretary Frederick Vinson, and H. D. White at the inaugural meeting of the IMF board of governors in Savannah, Ga., March 1946. (Thomas D. McAvoy/Time & Life Pictures/Getty Images)

15. Three prominent figures who accused H. D. White of being a Soviet agent. *Clockwise from top left*: American journalist and confessed Soviet spy Whittaker Chambers, 1948; confessed Soviet spy Elizabeth Bentley, 1948; FBI Director J. Edgar Hoover, undated. (Top images: Library of Congress; bottom image: Federal Bureau of Investigation)

16. H. D. White testifying before the House Un-American Activities Committee, Washington, D.C., August 13, 1948. (AP Photo/Harvey Georges)

Where Bretton Woods was, Lend-Lease was never far behind. In September 1944, a month before his meeting in Washington with White, Keynes arrived aboard the *Île de France* in Halifax, Nova Scotia, for so-called Stage II Lend-Lease negotiations ("Phase II" in American parlance)—covering the period between victory in Europe and victory in the Pacific. With the Allies now anticipating Germany's defeat as early as December, these discussions took on an air of urgency. Britain was so destitute by this point that its commitment to fighting on against Japan took on a mercenary tinge. Lend-Lease would expire once Britain was out of the war, and the UK Treasury saw fighting in the Pacific theater as an opportunity to scale down war production while using any excess in Lend-Lease supplies to boost exports and reserves.[16] Morgenthau suspected such motivation, and said that he would "sort of put them on the witness stand [as to] what they would contribute in the Pacific."[17]

Morgenthau, who remained the closest thing to a British advocate in the cabinet, nonetheless continued to play the Scrooge role demanded of him in Washington. On the sidelines of the Quebec military conference between Roosevelt and Churchill in September, code-named "Octagon," Morgenthau and the PM's adviser, Lord Cherwell, hammered out Stage II aid parameters on the sidelines. The Treasury Secretary responded sharply to Cherwell's claim that the empire would require $2–3 billion in nonmunitions aid by insisting that Britain was merely eager to reestablish its position in world trade. He demanded hard data to back Cherwell's case: "I want it all," he said. "Not just information on food and munitions, but the whole British economic program."[18]

Morgenthau, though determined to ensure that the British had sufficient resources to prosecute the war without suffering extreme privations at home, was not averse to using Lend-Lease to reshape the postwar world in America's image. In particular, he applied U.S. financial leverage in support of decolonization. In an October meeting with Keynes, he suggested British and American troop cuts in India and other British colonies as a way of pushing the process. Keynes bristled, insisting that British expenditures for imperial troops abroad were a matter for Britain alone. Morgenthau backed off, but shortage of funds would in any case cause the imperial sun to set in short order.

On Lend-Lease, Morgenthau remained a pushover next to his deputy. Whereas the Secretary insisted that Britain be treated as a "friend who is broke," and that the United States should "make it possible for her to stage a comeback and gradually meet her obligations," White protested that the administration should not take responsibility for putting Britain back on its feet. Any commitment to restoring British prosperity threatened the financial and political position of the United States in the postwar world.[19] He mischievously advised Keynes, "completely off the record," that Britain should consider running its gold and dollar reserves down to a bare minimum in Stage II as a mechanism to secure more generous assistance from the United States in Stage III—the period following victory in the Pacific.[20] Keynes was not foolish enough to take this suggestion seriously.

For his part, Roosevelt had only the foggiest grasp of macroeconomics, and certainly never saw it as a geopolitical weapon the way White did. The president astonished Keynes at a November press conference by saying "he had no idea what was meant by Stage II."[21] His own top advisers were concerned by his performance in Quebec. Morgenthau told Hull and Stimson that the president had been "casual about Lend-Lease." Hull, in failing health and unable to go to Quebec, blasted the president for "giv[ing] away the bait" by failing to win British commercial concessions and diluting the requirement that Britain export nothing obtained under, or even similar to that obtained under, Lend-Lease.[22] He would inform the president of his desire to resign two weeks later, and would be replaced by Undersecretary of State Edward Stettinius on December 1.

Roosevelt was nonetheless wholly receptive to the possibilities of putting British penury to American advantage. "I had no idea that England was broke," he remarked to Morgenthau after a briefing on British finances in August. "I will go over there and make a couple of talks and take over the British Empire." The quip reflected his genuine loathing of Britain's attachment to the old, discredited ways of doing business abroad. Churchill's increasingly overt support for the outworn ruling families of southern Europe, crowned by his freelancing efforts to carve out spheres of European influence with Stalin in Moscow in October, infuriated Roosevelt. The prime minister's ham-fisted efforts to prop up the increasingly unpopular Greek monarchy with British troops, even over the objections of his own top ministers, provoked a storm of protest in the United States, where it was widely seen as a ruthless British assertion of imperial self-interest. The president complained that the PM was growing "mid Victorian" and suffering from "imperialist obsessions."[23]

By November, having had to suffer through Churchill's provocations in the midst of an election campaign, Roosevelt, by Morgenthau's account, began acting "as though he had never heard [of the Quebec Agreement]."[24] Knowing that he would face bruising opposition to further British aid on Capitol Hill, the president was no longer in any mood to take a generous view of Britain's Lend-Lease obligations. This would only subject him to the charge that he was aiding British exports at the expense of American firms. Even prominent American friends of the prime minister like Bernard Baruch were painting the administration as a crazed Lady Bountiful. "Winston Churchill said that he did not accept a portfolio to liquidate the British Empire," Baruch observed in a letter to Morgenthau, "[but] simple Americans like myself will wonder if this action is of such a nature as to tend to liquidate the American standards of living." The British, he said, had "been crying poor mouth" for too long.[25]

The president reinstated the reexport restrictions and lopped $600 million, or 10 percent, off his Stage II commitment to Churchill. But far more significantly, he made it nonbinding. When Morgenthau suggested that this would violate "the spirit of Quebec," Roosevelt brushed him aside. There would be no more commitments. The British would hereon in have to rely on "American good will."

When the American terms were delivered to the British, Keynes put forth that the absence of a formal commitment was not critical. The American government's word was "as good as if not better than their bond." Of course, to say otherwise at that point would have been to acknowledge his own failure in negotiations. Churchill, for his part, was certain that if the program proved insufficient Roosevelt would come to the rescue with another "brain wave."[26] But the chronically ill president would, just a few months later, have not a brain wave but a brain hemorrhage. He died on April 12, 1945, a few weeks after Congress had imposed further restrictions on Lend-Lease. Now, Churchill would have to deal with the largely unknown figure of Harry S. Truman in the White House.

On May 2, Soviet Marshal Georgy Zhukov accepted the surrender of Berlin. On May 3 the Austrian cities of Innsbruck and Salzburg surrendered to the Americans, who took two thousand prisoners in Hitler's former mountain retreat of Berchtesgaden. The next day U.S. forces overran the Flossenbürg concentration camp; among those liberated was former French Prime Minister Léon Blum.[27] German resistance continued to fall away, until on May 8, the day Soviet forces captured Prague, the Allies accepted Germany's unconditional surrender. Though isolated fighting would continue, the war in Europe was formally over.

The United States, at this point having shipped only about a sixth of the military supplies programmed for 1945, now repossessed most of the equipment destined for British use in Europe. Stage II of Lend-Lease had officially begun, but such hostility to British aid had set in that the Quebec framework, in which Churchill had invested such great hopes, was effectively dead. "De facto and de jure," a British official reported home from Washington, "we are where we were before the Keynes discussions."[28]

Churchill pleaded with Truman, "When I met President Roosevelt in Quebec . . . we both initialed an agreement about Lend-Lease after the defeat of Germany. . . . I hope that your people can be told that the principles your predecessor and I agreed at Quebec will stand." Truman, for his part, under stern pressure from a Congress and top military brass resolutely hostile to what they saw as wholly unjustified British demands, parted ways with Churchill and Morgenthau on Quebec. "I don't want to give them everything they ask for," Truman scolded the Secretary on May 23. "I never have," Morgenthau responded testily; "in fact, they have complained about it."

Morgenthau had risen to great heights of national and global influence over the previous twelve years, arrogating powers long in the preserve of the State Department, on the back of his long friendship with FDR. White, who had toiled for years at the Treasury as the bureaucratic equivalent of a day laborer, had in turn made himself indispensable to the Secretary by giving him the intellectual wherewithal to sustain and expand these powers. But with Roosevelt's passing, both men suddenly found themselves flotsam in the political seas. "[T]his is wrong and that is wrong," the Secretary said, angrily mimicking those in Washington and London who now blamed him for all that was dysfunctional in the Anglo-American military alliance. "Churchill gets on the floor in Parliament and thanks Lord Keynes for the wonderful job he did, and I never get a line. I'm not going to take it. I was willing to take it from Roosevelt because I was his friend, but I want a little more now."[29]

He would not get it. Truman unmoored the White House from FDR's Treasury, and the State and War departments quickly moved in to change the new president's course. Truman, like his predecessor, also turned to a close friend and confidante to manage international financial issues: Judge Fred Vinson, now head of the Office of War Mobilization and Reconversion. Vinson's surrogates drafted a hard-line letter on Lend-Lease for Truman to send to Churchill, stating that new strategic and supply considerations since Quebec dictated a reexamination of U.S. Lend-Lease assistance to Britain. The letter further called attention to the fact that "British gold and foreign exchange holdings are now considerably higher than was anticipated," and that this suggested that the British government should "relax its position with respect to permitting dollar payments on certain items."

White, who had long backed a tougher line with the British, urged Morgenthau to initial the letter, which drove a thick wedge between the two men. Morgenthau instead ordered Frank Coe, a successor of White's as director of the Treasury's Division of Monetary Research, to write an alternative draft pledging fidelity to the Quebec Agreement. Vinson dithered over which version to send to the president (ultimately choosing the hard-line version). Meanwhile, the State Department advocated providing Britain with Stage III financial assistance in the form of a thirty-year, 2.5 percent interest loan instead of a grant, and further requiring it to be conditional on Britain dismantling imperial preference, making sterling freely convertible, and cooperating with the United States on the establishment of a global free-trade system. America and Britain were now farther apart than they had been since the war began, and Morgenthau was floating helplessly in the political gulf between them.

In June 1945, "fed up" with banging his head against the wall on British questions, Morgenthau turned his attention to Germany, where he believed he might still hold some sway. But neither the president nor the key men now around him would associate themselves with his ideas. Morgenthau had convinced himself that "[the president] and

I saw pretty much eye to eye on Germany," but the truth was very different. Morgenthau "couldn't keep from meddling" in German questions, Truman griped to Stimson.[30] Such meddling would subsequently become the least honorable part of the Treasury Secretary's legacy.

Morgenthau's biographer John Morton Blum understatedly referred to the Secretary's involvement in postwar planning for Germany, which began in the summer of 1944, as "the most controversial and agonizing episode" of his career—an episode in which White's role was at least equally controversial. Morgenthau, Blum noted, had prior to the end of the Bretton Woods conference "given little thought to German questions. Still, he had distrusted the Germans since the time of the First World War, which he attributed to their aggression, and he never forgot the cruelty that he had personally observed on the Turkish front. . . . The Germans, Morgenthau believed, would cultivate dreams of world domination even in defeat."[31]

On August 6, 1944, during a flight to London to review Lend-Lease and British dollar balances, White presented the Secretary with a State Department memorandum on postwar policy toward Germany, written mainly by Pasvolsky and Acheson. It called for short-term reparations in kind and for eliminating Germany's economic domination of Europe, but longer term it envisioned full integration of a healthy, industrialized Germany into the global economy—a "stern peace with reconciliation."

Morgenthau was repulsed. This was flabby, he thought, and recklessly naive. White shared Morgenthau's view that such a policy would leave Germany in a position to pursue catastrophic armed aggression yet again—a temptation to which a violent and troublesome nation would inevitably succumb. In a radio broadcast from London, the Secretary told British listeners: "It is not enough for us to say, 'we will disarm Germany and Japan and *hope* that they will learn to behave themselves as decent people.'" He radically split both his British and American government interlocutors by arguing that Germany needed to be partitioned into two independent, deindustrialized states. The economy was to be remade around tiny agricultural provinces. Further, the Saar, Ruhr, and Upper Silesia regions were to be internationalized, and other areas hived off to neighboring countries.

Angered that the State Department was proceeding against what he discovered to be the agreement among Roosevelt, Churchill, and Stalin to dismember Germany, made at the Tehran conference in November 1943, Morgenthau, on his return home from Europe, petitioned the president for his intervention. FDR agreed that the State Department was off script. "We either have to castrate the German people," Morgenthau recorded the president saying, "or you have got to treat them in such manner so they can't just go on reproducing people who want to continue the way they have in the past."[32] The Secretary took that as his cue to initiate Treasury's own analysis—an analysis that he would shape, and for which White, as usual, would provide most of the substance.

It was a mark of his desire for Keynes's approbation that White offered as support for his work the claim that "Keynes seems to be wholly in our corner" on German partition.[33] This was at best an exaggeration, as Keynes was sympathetic only to a temporary partition and rejected entirely the idea of deindustrializing the country.[34] For his part, Morgenthau cared little what Keynes thought, and focused his energies on gaining the support of Stimson, Hull, and others in the administration who mattered.

In this exercise, Morgenthau could not have resembled Keynes less, relying on unrefined instinct and emotion rather than facts and reason, at times straying into the realm of the bizarre. "Don't you think the thing to do is to take a leaf from Hitler's book," he asked Stimson, "and completely remove [German] children from their parents and make them wards of the state, and have ex-US Army officers, English Army officers and Russian Army officers run these schools and have these children learn the true spirit of democracy? . . . I also gave [Stimson] my idea of the possibility of removing all industry from Germany and simply reducing them to an agricultural population of small landowners." Stimson objected that this would require moving millions out of the country. "Well, that is not nearly as bad as sending them to gas chambers," the Secretary pointed out. Stimson said Morgenthau was advocating "our taking mass vengeance . . . in the shape of clumsy economic action," which would "produce a very dangerous reaction in Germany and probably a new war."[35] But Morgenthau would not waver, confident that he had the president's support.

Completed on September 4, 1944, the Treasury report titled "Program to Prevent Germany from Starting a World War III" would quickly become known as the Morgenthau Plan. E. F. Penrose, Ambassador Winant's economic adviser, paid White the backhanded compliment of having come "as nearly as possible to clothing [Morgenthau's] bad thesis with an appearance of intellectual respectability."[36] Not infrequently, later commentators would suggest that the Morgenthau Plan was in reality "the White Plan." This is accurate insofar as White penned and believed in much of it, arguing that peace required Germany being reduced to the status of "fifth-rate power,"[37] but misleading in the sense that Morgenthau both instigated the work and forced White's pen in a more extreme direction than White would have taken it on his own. Former U.S. Defense Intelligence Agency official John Dietrich quotes Morgenthau's son to the effect that the "so-called Morgenthau Plan seems to have been conceived in the mind of Harry Dexter White."[38] Yet the son goes on to say that "Morgenthau's response to White went far beyond anything that White himself had hoped for. In no time Morgenthau was proceeding with a driving fury, confounding even his most ardent and loyal supporters."[39]

Winant's political adviser Philip Moseley suggested that the plan would replace a German hegemony on the Continent by a Russian one, and there can be little doubt that White was aware and supportive of such a shift.[40] Yet White still pushed back against Morgenthau's idea to deindustrialize the Rhine, arguing that it would put fifteen million people in extreme hardship. "I am not going to be budged," Morgenthau nevertheless insisted. "I can be overruled by the President, but nobody else is going to overrule me."[41] White fell into line.

On September 12, Roosevelt summoned Morgenthau to come to Quebec immediately for the Octagon meetings with the British—the Secretary's first invitation to an Anglo-American leaders conference. Though Roosevelt said nothing about the purpose of his summons, Morgenthau suspected that "he had tried out [my plan for Germany] on Churchill and got nowhere." This was almost certainly right, although Churchill had also petitioned Roosevelt to bring Morgenthau up to discuss Stage II of Lend-Lease. The two matters were to become damagingly intertwined.

At a state dinner on the thirteenth, the president asked Morgenthau to outline his German plan for the prime minister. As the Secretary concluded, Churchill "turned loose on me the full flood of his rhetoric, sarcasm and violence," Morgenthau recorded. "He looked on the

Treasury Plan, he said, as he would chaining himself to a dead German." The ideas were positively "un-Christian," Churchill insisted. The president hardly spoke, choosing instead to "let the Prime Minister wear himself out attacking me."[42]

Morgenthau had a sleepless night, but talks on the German issue took a sharp right turn the next day. Churchill's position had improbably changed. He explained: "At first I was violently opposed to [Morgenthau's] idea. But the President with Mr. Morgenthau—from whom we had much to ask—were so insistent that in the end we agreed to consider it."[43] But what did he mean by having "much to ask"?

At a noon meeting on the fourteenth between Roosevelt and Churchill—attended by Morgenthau, Cherwell, Foreign Secretary Anthony Eden, and Foreign Office Permanent Under-Secretary Sir Alexander Cadogan—the first item of business was Stage II Lend-Lease aid to Britain. Six and a half billion dollars was at stake. The president toyed with the prime minister, telling stories to avoid initialing the memorandum. "What do you want me to do," Churchill bawled at one point, "stand up and beg like Fala?" the president's dog. According to White, Roosevelt then asked for the PM's oral consent to the Morgenthau Plan. There was, it seemed, a quid pro quo.

Churchill had asked—or, more accurately, begged—for Stage II Lend-Lease aid on the fourteenth. Roosevelt dawdled to first get a commitment from Churchill on Germany. Churchill apparently gave it, but nothing was yet recorded. So at a noon meeting with Roosevelt, Morgenthau, Eden, and Cherwell on the fifteenth, Churchill exploited the fact that there was no official written understanding on Germany, and proceeded to dictate his own. Having earlier been persuaded by Cherwell that there were valuable export opportunities for Britain implicit in the Morgenthau Plan, Churchill reduced the plan to six sentences focused on the necessity of shutting down "the metallurgical, chemical and electrical industries" of the Ruhr and the Saar and allowing "injured countries . . . to remove the machinery they require to repair the losses they have suffered." Germany would be converted into "a country primarily agricultural and pastoral in its character."

Eden was livid, and he exchanged heated words with Churchill after the meeting. How would Germany pay for imports, Eden insisted, if it could not manufacture? Churchill warned Eden not to oppose the plan before the war cabinet. "[T]he future of my people is at stake," he intoned, "and when I have to choose between my people and the German people, I am going to choose my people."[44]

When the PM referred to his people's future being "at stake," it was Lend-Lease, rather than German pastoralization, he had primarily in mind. Cherwell himself had told Robert Brand, the British Treasury representative in Washington, that Britain was "very much more likely to get the loan if he got Winston to sign the document."[45] Cherwell and Churchill were in effect making the best for Britain out of a bad plan for Germany. FDR initialed Churchill's dictated text, following which he also initialed the American Stage II Lend-Lease commitment. Once again, just as they had at Bretton Woods, the British acceded to an American geopolitical scheme, slightly watered down, in return for vitally needed dollars.

Morgenthau, who wanted the world to believe that Churchill had come to back his German plan wholly on its merits, said White's memory was wrong—there had been no quid pro quo. At a September 20 meeting of the Cabinet Committee on Germany in Washington, Stimson grilled Morgenthau on the connection between the agreements on Germany and Lend-Lease. Morgenthau pointed to White's own Quebec minutes, which supported the Secretary's disingenuous claim that Churchill had "agreed to the policy on Germany prior to the final drafting" of the Lend-Lease memo.[46] Hull did not believe a word. Even White, the loyal deputy, virtually called the Secretary a liar. "You put special stress on when they signed the document," White said, "but if I may remind you, what Churchill said to the President when he was trying to get the President to agree on the [Lend-Lease] document . . . 'What do you want me to do, stand up and beg like Fala?' And the document was signed on Lend-Lease after, but there was practically an oral commitment before. . . . But in any case the more significant thing in my mind is that you tied them both up together."[47]

The rift in the cabinet was now irreparable. Morgenthau called "the thing up in Quebec . . . the high spot of my whole career in government. I got more personal satisfaction out of those forty-eight hours than with anything I have ever been connected with."[48] On the other side, Hull, who believed that the plan was "blind vengeance" that could wipe out 40 percent of the German population, wrote that the "whole development at Quebec . . . angered me as much as anything that had happened during my career as Secretary of State. If the Morgenthau plan leaked out, as it inevitably would—and shortly did—it might well mean a bitter-end German resistance that could cause the loss of thousands of American lives."[49]

Despite the cabinet split, the president's support for Morgenthau's approach ensured that it would win out. On September 22, the first draft of the now-infamous Joint Chiefs of Staff directive 1067 (JCS 1067) for postwar occupied Germany was approved by the cabinet committee, notwithstanding the bitterness among its members. Among other harsh provisions, this secret document directed Supreme Allied Commander Dwight Eisenhower to "take no steps looking toward the economic rehabilitation of Germany nor designed to strengthen the German economy." He was only to seek outside supplies for the German population "necessary to prevent starvation or widespread disease or such civil unrest as would endanger the occupying forces."

As Hull anticipated, details of the Morgenthau Plan and the cabinet turmoil it generated began spilling out in the *Washington Post*, the *New York Times*, the *Wall Street Journal*, and publications around the world. In Germany, the Nazi regime exploited it to the fullest in order to boost German resistance. Propaganda Minister Joseph Goebbels publicly declared it proof that the Anglo-Saxons, like the Bolsheviks, were determined to "get rid of thirty to forty million Germans." Minister of Armaments and War Production Albert Speer later reflected that "the Morgenthau Plan was made to order for Hitler and the Party, insofar as they could point to it for proof that defeat would finally seal the fate of all Germans."[50] Hitler himself said the plan would result in "the uprooting of 15 or 20 million Germans and transport abroad, the enslavement of the rest of our people, the ruination of our German youth, but above all, the starvation of our masses."[51]

The revelations naturally caused a political firestorm in the United States. Republican presidential candidate Thomas Dewey called news of the plan "as good as ten fresh German divisions." Roosevelt's own son-in-law, Lieutenant Colonel John Boettiger, estimated it was "worth thirty divisions to the Germans." Lieutenant Colonel Marshall Knappen wrote after the war that "weary men returning from the field reported that the Germans fought with twice their previous determination after the announcement of the Morgenthau policy." General Omar Bradley reflected that "in early September most men in the Allied high command believed that victory over Germany was imminent. The near-miraculous revitalization of the German Army in October had come as a shock, dissipating some of the optimism." Eisenhower himself reported "a noticeable and fanatical zeal" among German soldiers. "The Germans are convinced they are fighting for their very existence."[52] The Morgenthau Plan clearly raised the potency of Nazi war propaganda, and may well have extended the war and inflated Allied casualties.

Hull had earlier warned Roosevelt that his association with the plan would damage him politically, and now the president was running for cover. On September 26, he dissolved the Cabinet Committee on Germany. On October 3, he told Stimson, incredibly, that "he had no idea how he could have initialed" the Quebec memorandum dictated by Churchill. He was "frankly staggered" by what it said. He told a press conference that "every story that came out [about the cabinet split] was essentially untrue in its basic facts." Over in London, Churchill turned tail as well, and his six-sentence version of the Morgenthau Plan died without ever officially reaching the cabinet. Long after the war, in July 1949, the former prime minister would even apologize for the memorandum. It had "undoubtedly proposed treatment of Germany that was a harsh treatment. . . . I am sorry that I put my initials to it."[53]

JCS 1067 would eventually be replaced by the more enlightened, and vastly less punitive, JCS 1779, but this was not until July 1947, over two years after the war in Europe had ended. In the meantime, its intellectual forebear, the Morgenthau Plan, served as valuable propaganda not just for the Nazis during the war but for the Soviet regime after the war. Foreign Minister Molotov took a swipe at it in a Council of Foreign Ministers speech in Paris in July 1946, declaring that "it would be incorrect to adopt the course of Germany's annihilation as a state or that of its agrarianization, including the annihilation of its main industrial centers." However disingenuous was the Soviet show of concern for the German people, there can be little doubt that the Morgenthau policy of dismantling German industry not only pushed Germany into an economic tailspin after the war, but severely impeded European economic recovery, contributing enormously to the cost of the subsequent U.S. reconstruction effort.

Despite the significant economic and geopolitical costs of the Morgenthau Plan to the United States and western Europe, it is difficult to identify virtually anything on the plus side of the ledger. Unless one believes, as Morgenthau and White did, that without a radical deindustrialization program Germany would have launched another war in short order, it is fair to conclude that the plan was an unmitigated U.S. foreign policy disaster. For the British, it was yet a further cost of doing business with a determined and occasionally undisciplined monopoly creditor. For the world, it was an example of dollar diplomacy at its worst.

Morgenthau and White—particularly White—were also the lead players in another aspect of the postwar German occupation that was to prove misguided, costly, and conducive only to Soviet interests. In early 1944, planning began in earnest for producing an occupation currency for Germany. White, who a year earlier had been informed in writing by the Secretary that he was "to take supervision over and assume full responsibility for Treasury's participation in all economic and financial matters . . . in connection with the operations of the Army and Navy and the civilian affairs in the foreign areas in which our armed forces are operating," took charge.[54] The British agreed that the currency should be printed in the United States, but the Russians demanded the right to print their own notes, using a duplicate set of American plates. This would, of course, allow them to print as much German money as they wished. Morgenthau was resistant, but irresolute. White, in contrast, was wholly supportive, as well as resolute. "[T]he United States had not been doing enough for the Soviet Union," White insisted, and "if the Soviets profited as a result of this transaction we should be happy to give them this token of our appreciation of their efforts."[55]

The director of the Bureau of Engraving and Printing, Alvin Hall, was staunchly opposed to giving the Russians the plates, which elicited a fierce reaction from White. The Russians, he insisted, "must be trusted to the same degree and to the same extent as the other allies."[56] This was inexcusably naive, at best. According to the account of Elizabeth Bentley, the spy who went public in 1948, it may have been criminal. White, she claimed, was acting on the request of Nathan Gregory Silvermaster's underground to secure duplicate plates for the Soviets. These claims are uncorroborated, yet there can be no doubt from White's words and subsequent behavior that he was pushing his authority to and beyond its limits in order to accommodate Soviet interests.[57]

On April 14, White received a letter from Army Chief of Staff George Marshall stating that "if the United States Treasury and the State Department, in conjunction with the Foreign Office and the British Treasury, decide to furnish duplicate plates to the Soviet Government, it appears that this action could be taken any time after May 1, 1944, without interference with General Eisenhower's requirements for Allied military mark currency." White exploited an authority vacuum on the issue and immediately told Hall that "the Combined Chiefs of Staff *had directed* that glass positives [of the Allied mark plates] be turned over to the Russian government" (italics added). This was a gross misrepresentation of Marshall's letter, which White never showed to Hall. Hall then went to Morgenthau for authorization, and the Secretary, who acknowledged that he had been less than fully informed on the matter, gave it.[58]

The predictable upshot of White's decision to give the currency plates to the Russians was that they printed a lot of it. The western Allies put into circulation a total of about 10.5 billion Allied marks, almost precisely what White had told the Soviets they would do, beginning in September 1944, when Eisenhower's troops first crossed the German border in the Eifel region. The Soviets likely issued something north of 78 billion marks.[59] Much of this wound up being redeemed by the U.S. government at the fixed exchange rate advocated by White, resulting in the Soviets effectively raiding the American Treasury for $300–$500 million, or over twelve times that in current dollars. (The British Treasury was looted for another $300 million or so).[60] White had wanted to give the Soviets a "token of our appreciation of their efforts," and this was no doubt a generous one. The generosity ceased in July 1945, however, when the United States declared the Russian marks, fortunately distinguishable by a dash in front of the serial number, invalid in western Germany.

On July 5, 1945, Henry Morgenthau—wounded, unrepentant, and politically isolated—confronted President Truman bluntly. "[T]here is all this gossip . . . about my being through. . . . Well, Mr. President, if you have any doubts in your mind after my record of twelve years here, and after several months with you and when I have given you my loyal support, you ought to know your mind now, and if you don't know it, I want to get out now." Truman was noncommittal. Morgenthau said he would write a resignation letter, offering to "break in Vinson as my successor" while the president was away at the Potsdam conference of victorious leaders. "Oh," Truman responded, "Vinson is going with me on account of Lend-Lease," adding to the sting. Later that day, Morgenthau submitted his resignation and received back the president's signed acceptance, which Morgenthau had drafted for him. Truman announced his intention to appoint Vinson the next day. The Secretary called Vinson to congratulate him, and learned that he was staying in Washington—contrary to Truman's statement.

Morgenthau, not wanting to carry on right under Vinson's shadow in Washington, was now determined to leave immediately. A presidential intermediary, Judge Samuel Rosenman, called on Morgenthau that same day, indicating that Truman would second that emotion. Rosenman suggested a bargain of sorts. "Do you want to stay in public life because if you do I think it would put Truman definitely under obligation to yourself if you would resign. . . . Then if you had any idea of doing something with Bretton Woods he would be under obligation to you."

"Well, I have no such ideas," Morgenthau responded, "but people around me are talking about my being Governor of both the Bank and the Fund or possibly President of the Bank. . . . But I haven't really thought about it."

"Well, I can't promise you anything, but if you did resign he would be under obligation to you."

Morgenthau drafted a new resignation letter, which he gave to Rosenman on July 13, asking the president to relieve him of his duties immediately, now that the issue of his successor was settled. He also gave Rosenman a second and third letter—alternative draft replies from the president. The third letter had the president asking him to accept appointment as governor of the fund and the bank. Rosenman sent the letters to Truman.

"I have received your dispatch," the president cabled back to Rosenman on the fourteenth. "I concur only in the exchange of the first two cables. . . . Do not . . . release the third cable." This was shorthand for saying he would not appoint Morgenthau to the fund or the bank.

Despite claiming he did not actually want an appointment either at the fund or the bank, Morgenthau was bitter at the way Truman handled his resignation.[61] His public career was suddenly over.

For White, however, things would only get more interesting.

The Anglo-American alliance under Roosevelt and Churchill had been wobbly at times, but ultimately secure. Yet with Roosevelt's passing in April 1945, one of its load-bearing pillars had faltered, and in July the second pillar took a blow as well: Churchill's Conservative Party was defeated in the British general elections. Clement Attlee took the helm. His Labour Party had ridden to victory on the back of its economic program, which called for greater state intervention and social protection. This was at odds with the Bretton Woods program of rigid and convertible currencies, which required more, not less, elastic policies on the home front.

At the same time, the new American administration was making it more difficult for a bankrupt Britain to weather the transition to Bretton Woods. On August 6, the United States dropped an atomic bomb on Hiroshima, and on August 9 dropped a second one on Nagasaki. The Japanese government surrendered less than a week later, on August 14—or roughly nine months earlier than the British had anticipated. This meant that Phase II of Lend-Lease, on which the British had been banking to tide them over into 1946, had come to an abrupt end. President Truman wasted no time in defining Phase III, ordering an immediate termination of all British Lend-Lease aid just three days later, on August 17. For Britain, this was a crippling body blow. Keynes was anticipating a balance-of-payments deficit of about $5.6 billion, which had to be financed somehow.

In 1944, Keynes had laid out three policy alternatives for his government to address the crisis, which he labeled Austerity, Temptation, and Justice. Austerity, a concept that has certainly never been associated with Keynsianism, Keynes rejected as an invitation to "serious political and social disruption," as well as Britain's "withdrawal, for the time being, from the position of first-class Power." Temptation he defined as succumbing to the lure of a large, low-interest American loan, at the price of having to swallow the Article VII principles of convertible currencies and trade multilateralism. This too had to be rejected, as it would lead to debt bondage as well as the moral outrage of Britain exiting the war owing over $20 billion in sterling and dollar debts—roughly what the Allies were seeking in German reparations. Justice, naturally, as its name implied, was the only acceptable option. This would involve the United States paying Britain $3–4 billion toward its war bills, defined largely as a "reimbursement" of British pre-Lend-Lease expenditure in the United States, as well as levies on the dominions in the form of debt cancellation and retrospective war cost contributions. All these countries had, according to Keynes, either incurred moral debts to Britain, or, like gold-rich South Africa, had extracted "windfall profits" from the war.[62]

Naturally, this treatise was seductively uplifting in Whitehall; so much so that when Keynes departed for Washington in September 1945 on a mission to save Britain from financial catastrophe, yet again, he did so under orders to fly the banner of Justice. For his countrymen, Keynes interwove national interest with universal righteousness so flawlessly and effortlessly as to make the two appear interchangeable. Yet to the Americans, the idea that they owed Britain a moral debt for her war efforts was an affront to their generosity and sacrifice in saving Europe from itself for the second time in a quarter century. The British Embassy in Washington warned against London taking such a tack. "What we cannot put to the American people," Brand wrote to Keynes, "is that it is justice that they should give us a free grant on the ground that they should have entered the war before they did and therefore owe us the $3 billion we spent here."[63] A Gallup poll that month found 60 percent of the American public against even a loan to Britain;[64] a $3 billion "reimbursement" was inconceivable. Yet so enchanted was Whitehall by Justice that it circulated a document comparing Britain's war efforts favorably to America's, which found its way to the *New York Times* and triggered a wholly unwelcome American press blowback.[65]

Negotiations began on September 13. Harry White's leading role on British financial matters had been taken over by Vinson and Assistant

Secretary of State for Economic Affairs Will Clayton—a striking, articulate six-foot-six former Texas cotton merchant who followed closely in the footsteps of Hull and Acheson in championing global free trade. White had been set adrift in the political wilderness following Morgenthau's resignation, and rather than being pushed into the cage with Keynes again was reduced to greeting his esteemed nemesis and coaching him "not to lose his temper except at the right moments."[66] White was by this time anticipating a new life at the fund or the bank, but his old life was about to come back and haunt him.

Keynes was joined by Halifax to lead the British side. Now sixty-two, white-haired and visibly frail, Keynes was still at the height of his wasp-tongued eloquence. His rendition of the noble Symphonia Britannica, Britain's heroic and profligate sacrifice to bring victory to the Anglo-American common cause, had the usual effect on his listeners: wowing his compatriots while irritating the natives he had been sent to impress. As American banker Russell Leffingwell observed, "There is nothing more disturbing, I think, than the sending of Lord Keynes here. Brilliant man that he is, he is too brilliant to be persuasive with us Americans . . . rightly or wrongly, how many trust him? How many will accept his sales talk? No one."[67]

The American side immediately began stabbing through the fog of Keynes's wispy words. Clayton said that the American people would not understand why Britain had been getting war supplies from the United States for free while it was building up debts within the empire for the same sort of goods. Marriner Eccles compared Britain to a foundering company whose creditors had to take a haircut to set it aright. Henry Wallace suggested that the British offer India independence in return for debt forgiveness. Vinson, following a characteristic and badly aimed quip by Keynes about lawyers, exploded: "That is just the kind of statement you would make."

After two weeks of such diplomacy, Justice was dead. The Americans had skinned it alive. For Clayton, it was time for the British to live up to their Article VII commitments: to end trade discrimination and the monetary-control paraphernalia that went with it. That was what they had signed up for with Lend-Lease. That they should now come back to Washington amnesic, hat in hand, led by the silver-tongued spokesman for deficit spending was galling.

Lionel Robbins, who arrived on September 27 as part of a negotiations reinforcement team, much to Keynes's annoyance, observed despondently that Keynes now bore the burden of "dehypnotising London. . . . [H]aving himself made the magic passes that now hold the King's Treasurers entranced in rapturous contemplation of ideal 'justice', it will be up to him . . . to reverse the process."[68] Britain would now have to retreat to Temptation—securing an American commercial loan—in order to avoid Keynes's most hated option, Austerity.

Keynes asked London for permission to reverse the course he himself had so fervently charted, and to begin seeking a no-interest American loan. The reaction from the Labour ministerial team of Hugh Dalton (chancellor), Ernest Bevin (foreign secretary), and Richard Cripps (president of the Board of Trade) was sheer disbelief. How had Keynes, who had been negotiating with the Americans for years, so misread them and so misled London? It was, after all, Keynes himself who had insisted in the most passionate terms that Britain hold fast against any more American loans.

Positions in London began to harden. At no point in the previous three years had Britain come closer to rejecting American postwar economic demands, of which Bretton Woods was the centerpiece, and turning its back on desperately needed financial assistance. Brutal austerity and a deep rupture in Anglo-American relations were beginning to seem possible, perhaps even inevitable. Still, Dalton slowly and painfully began giving Keynes wiggle room. On October 8, nearly a month after negotiations in Washington had started, he told Halifax that a fifty-year $5 billion interest-free loan might now be acceptable, with caveats such as London's "undisputed right to restrict Britain's total imports."[69] But Dalton still expected Keynes to push for $2 billion to come in the form of a repayment of pre-Lend-Lease British purchases in the United States

The stress was taking its toll on Keynes, who appears to have suffered a mild heart attack on October 7.[70] At an October 9 negotiation session, Clayton drew the line at a fifty-year, $5 billion, 2 percent interest loan, with interest waiver provisions for years of outright British penury. This is the best offer Britain would get, but Keynes did not grasp it. Instead, he became tragically entranced by a bizarre offstage siren song from, of all characters, Harry Dexter White, whom Keynes now called "our most ardent advocate behind the scenes in favour of the no-interest principle."[71]

Despite his marginalization within the administration at that point, White had set up a technical committee to advise Vinson on the British financial position, from which he excluded Bernstein and Luxford, who were known to be sympathetic to the British case. He devised a technically complex, and politically implausible, scheme for the United States to buy at a discount a large portion of Britain's sterling-area debt, thereby transforming this debt into a smaller obligation to the United States. A critical implication was that Britain would therefore allegedly need only a $3 billion American loan to cover its current account needs, rather than a $5 billion loan. White clearly recognized—as did Keynes, however sheepishly—that the arrangement threatened the survival of the sterling area.[72]

The upshot of White's intervention, and Keynes's indulgence of it, was terrible for Britain. Rather than try to persuade Dalton to hit Vinson's bid, Keynes tried to get further negotiating authority to water down Dalton's waiver conditions and to incorporate White's scheme to "canalize" Britain's sterling debts into a single, smaller dollar debt. Dalton, a PhD economist who had written a book on the principles of public finance, rejected the terms outright, not only on technical grounds but on the basis that it lacked "the sweet breath of justice."[73] The reference to "justice," tossed back in Keynes's face, must have cut Keynes to the core. Worse, Vinson himself rejected White's scheme as "too fancy." What he took away from it was only that Britain must be exaggerating its needs, and that the loan could be cut. White's precise intentions were shrouded in the haze of his technocratic contraption, but there can be no doubt that the result of his intervention was Keynes's worst diplomatic failure.

White warned Keynes that a "nasty surprise" was coming, never suggesting that he, White, might be responsible for it. The surprise came on October 18, when Vinson told Keynes, Halifax, and Brand that the best he could now offer was $3.5 billion at 2 percent interest, repayable over fifty years, and about $500 million to "clean up" Lend-Lease at $2\frac{3}{8}$ percent, repayable over thirty years. This triggered a predictable Keynes "explosion" and a threat to break off negotiations. Yet Keynes remained painfully aware of the sheer awfulness of departing empty handed. It would mean the collapse of Bretton Woods, which the signatories were obliged to ratify by the end of the year. There was the unbearable prospect of the socialist state-traders and reactionary imperialists obliterating the vital center ground in British politics. And there was looming "Starvation Corner," as he called it, for Britain.

So Keynes plowed on, for weeks, painstakingly trying to eke out a bit more on the loan and better terms on the waiver conditions. But Clayton and Vinson never bought into the underlying British pessimism about postwar imbalances. Clayton even argued that American "over-seas expenditure [would soon] overtake her exports," and Keynes wasn't sure he was wrong.[74] And so the Americans, too, pushed for concessions, on November 10 trying to eat into British transitional rights under Bretton Woods. Sounding much like Churchill at Quebec in 1944 crying "What do you want me to do, stand up and beg like Fala?" Keynes, who had just that morning been prepared to settle the deal on previous American terms, now demanded "Why do you persecute us like this?"[75]

When the two sides met again on November 15, Halifax began with a somber and resigned assessment of the state of discussions. An impasse had been reached. Perhaps a year hence, there might be some basis on which to resume. But as it stood, there was no question of Britain ratifying the Bretton Woods agreements. Vinson urged that they continue talking through the problem areas. Unfortunately, this was a cue for Keynes to resume an exasperated tour of the offending clauses in the American proposal.

An American participant interjected that much hinged on future British gold reserves. "You might find a great deal of gold hidden in a cave," he said. Keynes lit up. "Gold in a cave!" he enthused sarcastically to his colleague Frank Lee. "Frank, put that down in the Agreement. We accept that."[76] Vinson was furious.

Eccles wanted more assurances that the United States would be repaid. If the United States were going to finance a bankrupt concern, it had the right to priority over earlier creditors. Now Keynes was livid. "You cannot treat a great nation as if it were a bankrupt company." Privately Keynes said of Eccles that it was "No wonder that man is a Mormon. No single woman could stand him." The day after the meeting, UK Treasury official Freddie Harmer described Keynes as "almost uncontrollable . . . [his] health cannot stand the strain."

The two sides were playing chicken. The British warned that Bretton Woods would fall if they didn't get financial assistance on reasonable terms. The Americans warned that financial assistance was conditional on Britain ratifying Bretton Woods. Both sides had to reckon with powerful domestic political forces that were relentlessly hostile to the concessions their team was making, sometimes without authorization. Keynes described the endless parrying to Richard Kahn as "the most harassing and exhausting negotiation you can imagine."

Having persuaded his government so effectively of the need to take every precaution against accepting American terms that would strip Britain of its financial independence, Keynes was now buffeted by a ferocious blowback from London. He had conceded to the Americans on highly sensitive areas ranging from Bretton Woods transitional rights to sterling convertibility to trade preferences to creditor priorities. Exhausted and surely conscious of his personal legacy as a diplomat and a coauthor of Bretton Woods, he was now determined to leave Washington with an agreement—any agreement—in short order. "If I can turn up back home in time for the Annual Congregation [at King's College on December 8]," he wrote to Richard Kahn longingly, "it will be a great happiness."

Attlee and Dalton, however, likely stirred up by an alarmed Eady in London, rejected Keynes's pledges on convertibility. Events in 1947 would show their concerns to be justified. Keynes's pleas to sign the deal were not only dismissed, but Treasury permanent Secretary Edward Bridges was sent to Washington effectively to supersede Keynes as the operational head of negotiations. Keynes threatened to resign, but quickly backed down. At a climactic all-day negotiating session with the Americans on December 2, a Sunday, Vinson, reading the situation, lavished praise on Keynes's conduct of the discussions, possibly anxious to keep his wounded and staggering adversary in the ring. The end result was "exactly as anticipated," Robbins recorded: "humiliation."

The Americans accepted only some minor modifications on creditor priority and the deadline for convertibility of current sterling-area earnings—the British now had a year from the date of congressional and presidential ratification, which would give them roughly until the spring of 1947 (instead of Keynes's promised end of 1946). The headline loan amount, technically a line of credit, was to be set at $3.75 billion, with an interest rate of 2 percent. This was substantially less than Clayton's original offer of $5 billion, but $650 million was added on for Lend-Lease "clean-up" in return for the British concessions, bringing the total loan figure to $4.4 billion. Given that total American Lend-Lease aid to Britain, net of the $5 billion of so-called Reverse Lend-Lease assistance from Britain, had amounted to $22 billion, this was, from the administration's perspective, an act of extraordinary American magnanimity.

Before the agreement was initialed, there were several further days of tense cabling with London, and a final smackdown from a semi-sober Vinson, who had to be extracted from a Willard Hotel nightclub. The British finally capitulated. Halifax and Vinson signed the Anglo-American Financial Agreement at the State Department at 10:30 a.m. on December 6, the official photograph of which reveals a "detached and lifeless" Keynes. After a brief trip to New York, Lydia and Maynard Keynes set sail for home aboard the *Queen Elizabeth* on December 11—three days after the King's College Congregation. Robbins recalled Keynes sitting in his cabin, "grey with anxiety . . . receiving, with growing anger and contempt, the misrepresentations, as they came from the wireless operators, of *his* efforts and *his* loan, and polishing the periods of the defence which he was gathering all his remaining forces to make."[77]

The debate in the House of Commons began and ended on December 13, while Keynes was still at sea. Attlee and Dalton, up against a December 31 deadline to ratify Bretton Woods, and the loan terms that went with it, were determined to ram through the vote at breakneck speed, before any opposition could gather momentum. The debate was short, sharp, and passionate. "Now we have a pistol pointed at our heads, and are told that we have to pass the whole thing in three days," protested an enraged Robert Boothby, but to no avail.

Conservative MP Lieutenant-Colonel Sir Thomas Moore quoted his housekeeper in speaking against the bill. "Tell those gentlemen in the House of Commons to stand up for Britain and not trail after the Americans and their spam," she had said to him. Sir Thomas "had the impression, not being an economist, that currency had to be tied to or based on something; whether it was gold, or marbles, or shrimps, did not seem to matter very much, except that as marbles are easy to make, and shrimps are easy to catch, gold for many reasons possessed a more stable quality." The British pound, in a sharp break with the past, now had "no such basis of gold," but that was no reason to surrender "the British integrity area . . . for the doubtful and unknown blessings of the World Monetary Fund." Britain should stand up and show "that we are not crawling to get this loan."

Labour MP Jennie Lee insisted that "whether we want a trade war with America or not, we have got it. . . . There is nothing in the terms of this loan which gives us any reason to suppose that an administration which could offer a niggardly, barbaric, antediluvian settlement such as this, can solve the unemployment problem in their own country much less help the world." Conservative MP David Eccles described Britain as a small nation "standing between the revised imperialism of Russia and the commercial aggression of America." He called the terms of the agreement "harsh, and . . . unworthy of two allies who have just saved the world by their exertions." But the dollar credit was, in the end, indispensable, and he would therefore reluctantly vote in favor.

Churchill, now leader of the opposition, objected to the melding of the loan, the commercial commitments, and Bretton Woods. But he drew a firm line between the invaluable and "unsordid" wartime American Lend-Lease aid, which his government had negotiated, and the terrible terms that Attlee was bringing before the House. Making sterling convertible within fifteen months was "too bad to be true." The new Labour government was clearly at fault, having alarmed the Americans with the "dazzling expectations" they raised within the British electorate, "not only of a far higher standard of life, but of a far easier life, than any that has existed in Britain before." He called on his fellow Conservatives neither to approve nor reject the convoluted agreement that had been put before the House with "indecent haste," but to abstain.

Bevin, speaking for the government, blasted Churchill for suggesting that he could have achieved better terms. This was "a libel on the Administration of the United States." The opposition might abstain, "But do not let us have any cowards on this side," he implored his fellow Labour members. "The country," he thundered, "is up against an economic position very much like it was militarily in 1940," at Dunkirk and after. "[N]ow is the time for us to put our shoulders to the wheel and help this old country through as we did on that occasion."[78] The bill passed by a vote of 345 to 98.[79]

Keynes arrived in England on December 17, immediately heading from Southampton to London, where debate on Bretton Woods and the loan in the House of Lords had already started. Exhausted, he sat through five hours of debate that day. War stories and analogies poured forth. "We fought at Dunkirk," Lord Woolton noted, "but to-day we are surrendering what I conceive to be our just rights. We are surrendering them to the power of the dollar, because those responsible for the affairs of this country do not dare to retreat on the economic fastnesses of the Empire." The war had left Britain the largest debtor nation in history, while America "had become rich beyond her dreams." He called on the United States, as Keynes had earlier, "for rightful restitution of the dollars we paid in advance of what became a common cause." The Americans were now demanding British ratification of Bretton Woods before the end of the year as a condition for a loan, but "[t]hat is not the way that I like to think of this country being treated."

Lord Kenilworth recalled that the Americans "with whom [the government] were negotiating are the sort of people who, in the early difficult days, took over the Courtauld interest in America for a sum of money that was so ridiculous . . . that it cost the British taxpayer nearly £30,000,000." The terms now attached to Bretton Woods and the loan "were bound to cause a weakening of the bonds of Empire."

As he had done in May 1944, shortly before departing for Bretton Woods, Keynes now set out to persuade the House of Lords to support a new international monetary architecture, one largely written by an ambitious American technocrat. In so doing, Keynes would need to apply all the earnest conviction he could muster to sell publicly what he had failed in years of negotiations to change privately. He had prepared a speech on the boat over from New York, but having been knocked sideways by the caustic tone of the Lords debate carefully recalibrated. What emerged as he led off the second day of deliberation, despite the great physical strain under which he now labored, showed the full force of his rhetorical powers. Adorning his language in the humble garb he reserved for the Lords chamber, Keynes portrayed his months of grueling and contentious negotiations in Washington as a slow and necessarily imperfect melding of two distinct national narratives, each coherent only on its own terms. He set out to persuade the hall of noble wounded prides not that they were wrong in believing that the deal offered less than Britain deserved, but that it was the best that could be achieved given the benign peculiarities of the American political culture.

Far from being the cruel quid pro quo that some in Parliament were portraying the plan to be, "Each part is complementary to the rest," Keynes explained. "Whether it be well or ill-conceived," it needed to be considered "in the rounded whole which your Lordships have before you." The "long-term organisation of world commerce and foreign exchanges on a multilateral and non-discriminatory basis" was logically coupled with "short-term proposals for the early reconversion of the sterling area in the same direction; and an offer of financial aid from the United States to enable this country to overcome the immediate difficulties of transition." Each part "has been subjected to reasonable criticism." Yet he wondered "if this first great attempt at organising international order out of the chaos of the war in a way which will not interfere with the diversity of national policy yet which will minimize the causes of friction and ill will between nations, is being viewed in its right perspective." The soothing, deferential prose could not have been more different from the relentless logical bludgeoning to which he had frequently subjected his American negotiating counterparts in the months prior.

Perhaps Keynes's greatest challenge was to persuade his colleagues of what he called the "intense good will" of the American people toward Britain. This was hardly evident to them, but the question of American intentions was essential, given the risks Britain was being asked to undertake. Yes, Keynes argued, Britain had made great sacrifices in the past, which had not been fully appreciated. Yet it was not "becoming in us to respond by showing our medals. . . . The Americans—and are they wrong?—find a post-mortem on relative services and sacrifices amongst the leading Allies extremely distasteful and dissatisfying." The American outlook was, as always, practical and focused on the future.

In the end, Keynes insisted, the financial assistance offered Britain "should make a great and indispensable contribution to the strength of this country, abroad as well as at home." Yet he could not disguise his own bitterness over the terms of the assistance. "I shall never so long as I live cease to regret that this is not an interest-free loan." For this, he laid much of the blame on Congress, taking a well-worn page from the U.S. Treasury's diplomatic playbook.

As the questions and interruptions in the chamber began, Keynes took on a more defensive and aggressive posture. "I have heard the suggestion made that we should have recourse to a commercial loan without strings," he threw out defiantly. "I wonder if those who put this forward have any knowledge of the facts." Any such loan, he insisted, would have been on less favorable terms. But his passion truly bubbled over when he came to Bretton Woods. "It is not easy to have patience with those who pretend that some of us who were very early in the field to attack and denounce the false premises and false conclusions of unrestricted *laissez-faire* and its particular manifestations in the former gold standard . . . are now spending their later years in the service of the State to walk backwards and resurrect and re-erect the idols which they had played some part in throwing out of the market place."

Keynes was clearly determined to cement his legacy as a revolutionary of biblical proportions, one who had broken with the dogmas of the past and set the world on "a great step forward towards the goal of international economic order amidst national diversities of policies." He could not abide being painted as a reactionary who had merely signed up for a reconstituted gold standard. Such critics were naive utopians who failed to appreciate that Britain could not dictate to powers as diverse as the United States and Soviet Russia. "The work of destruction has been accomplished," he proclaimed, "and the site has been cleared for a new structure."

Five more hours of debate ensued, whereafter the vote was taken. In a mark of disgruntled resignation, half the peers abstained. The resolution to approve the financial agreement was carried by a margin of 90 to 8. The British debt to the United States was ultimately repaid with a final installment of $83.25 million in December 2006, under the government of Prime Minister Tony Blair.

With the parliamentary drama complete, Keynes now lashed out privately at the British opponents of the IMF and the American loan terms with the same vitriol he would have mustered for anyone who had *supported* them, had he himself not in the end been in a position to claim paternity of the historic Bretton Woods plan. "A section of the Socialists," he wrote to Halifax on New Year's Day 1946, "thought they detected too definite a smell of *laissez-faire*, at any rate anti-planning, in the American conception of international affairs. This is only half-true; but the doctrine of non-discrimination does commit us to abjure Schachtian methods, which their Jewish economic advisers (who, like so many Jews, are either Nazi or Communist at heart and have no notion of how the British Commonwealth was founded or is sustained) were hankering after."

As for "[a] section of the Conservatives, led by Max [Beaverbrook] and supported by others too near Winston [Churchill], [they] were convinced, with some reason, that the proposed commercial policy ruled out [Imperial] Preference as a serious, substantial policy for the future. . . . It annoyed them, of course, to have me pointing out the Empire in question would not include Canada (or probably South Africa) and would have to be built on the British loyalty and goodwill of India, Palestine, Egypt and Eire."[80]

As for the sterling convertibility conditions, which had been widely condemned on the left and the right, Keynes insisted the American loan could never have been secured without accepting them. But it was Keynes himself who had, prior to departing for the United States, convinced the British government that the loan terms he would end up endorsing in Washington amounted to debt bondage and a moral affront—"an outrageous crown and conclusion of all that has happened."[81]

One does not have to sympathize with all of the content or color of Keynes's self-defense to ask reasonably whether he, or any other British representative, could actually have achieved a better result for Britain. Of course, we cannot know for certain what precisely was feasible, or what the consequences of various alternatives would ultimately have been. But immediate postwar history, as we will see shortly, showed that Britain got nothing out of Bretton Woods that it could not have gotten on better terms many years later. What Britain actually needed in 1945 was short-term financing at reasonable cost with few geopolitical strings attached, and possibly a lower exchange rate. Keynes had willfully pursued neither.

Regarding the exchange rate, Keynes rejected devaluation repeatedly, most notably at a Washington press conference on September 12, 1945. "We can sell anything we can produce [at the current exchange rate]," he claimed. "Our problem is to reconvert our industry quick enough [so as] to have the exports, and in those circumstances you can't imagine anything more foolish than to be trying to sell those exports at quite unnecessarily low prices." James Meade, a future Nobel Prize winner, argued compellingly, as did many other British economists, that Keynes was logically and empirically wrong. White himself had told the Senate Banking Committee just before Keynes's Washington mission that he expected Britain to devalue, and that this undercut its case for large-scale transitional assistance.[82]

Regarding financing, American bankers had dangled just this prospect before the British in May of 1944, and Keynes dismissed it with characteristic disdain. That he chose to push on with Bretton Woods, and then the American loan, in spite of what he had said privately many times were misguided economic principles and wretched terms for Britain, suggests more than a touch of personal pride and concern for his place in history. A career diplomat, or indeed anyone less invested in having his name attached to a new monetary system, would likely have sought out crisis financing on more conventional terms than those imposed by the Americans through Bretton Woods. Indeed, British Treasury official Sir Richard ("Otto") Clarke reflected years later that "The simplest plan, which had much to commend it . . . but for which nobody could have persuaded Keynes, was to abandon the concept of a 'Grand Design'" and negotiate smaller loans from the Export-Import Bank, Canada, and elsewhere. "We could easily have said [to the Americans] 'We are willing to sign the Bretton Woods Agreement . . . but we are not willing to accept any prior commitments at all until we see how the new world develops. . . . In fact events by 1947 showed that the multilateral theologians' concepts of the course of events had been utterly wrong. . . . [Therefore] postponing the 'Grand Design' negotiation, and borrowing relatively small amounts if necessary expensively, would have been well justified by events."[83]

Once Britain had agreed to the American loan terms, the ground was clear for representatives of thirty countries to sign the IMF Articles of Agreement between December 27 and 31. Among the fourteen countries present at the conference that failed to ratify the agreement was the Soviet Union. Stating that its officials had not had adequate time to study the proposals, the Soviet government did subsequently send a low-ranking observer to the inaugural meeting of the fund and bank board of governors in March 1946, but never joined either institution.[84]

In reality, the Soviets had studied the proposals very seriously. Just a few days before the Washington signing, the Soviet Foreign and Trade ministries had drawn up memoranda highlighting the advantages of membership—in particular, Soviet influence over the allocation of international credits, the ability to monitor the fund and the bank from the inside, access to cheap credits from the fund and possibly the bank, facilitation of gold sales, and access to U.S. credits as an inducement to Soviet participation. "It is known that the Americans made credits to Britain conditional on joining the Fund," one such memo stated. Harry White, who was the U.S. administration's most powerful advocate of Soviet participation, had in January 1945 actually proposed a $10 billion, 2 percent interest reconstruction credit for Russia—more than three times what he advocated in transitional assistance for Britain.

The fact that such a credit was not, in the end, offered turned out to be a key reason for the Soviet Foreign Ministry ultimately advising against ratifying Bretton Woods. "[A]s the government of the U.S.A. did not offer the U.S.S.R. a credit . . . our membership in these organizations could be read as our weakness, as a forced step taken under the pressure of the U.S.A. Our negative attitude toward membership in the Fund and the Bank would show our independent position in this matter." Stalin, of course, would certainly have had other reasons for rejecting Soviet commitments to American-dominated economic institutions.[85]

Legendary American diplomat George Kennan in his famed long telegram from Moscow on February 22, 1946, laid out some of those reasons. "In international economic matters," Kennan argued, "Soviet policy will really be dominated by pursuit of autarchy for the Soviet Union and Soviet-dominated adjacent areas taken together." One of the rationales behind this stance would be the belief that the "capitalist world is beset with internal conflicts inherent in the nature of capitalist society. These conflicts are insoluble by means of peaceful compromise. Greatest of them is that between England and U.S."[86] Though the Soviets clearly saw the clash of Anglo-American interests through a distorted ideological lens, they were right to see the wartime alliance between the two western powers as a temporary masking of diverging national interests. This would play itself out in the coming years.

Although White's efforts to secure generous postwar American financial assistance for Russia were unavailing, he was not ineffectual from Moscow's perspective. Soviet intelligence cables from San Francisco to Moscow in May and June 1945, intercepted and decoded by the U.S. Army's Signal Intelligence Service, refer repeatedly to revelations on the internal discussions of the U.S. delegation at the UN founding conference, provided by a source named "RICHARD." Richard, alternatively referred to as Jurist and Lawyer, was cited in eighteen Soviet cables between March 16, 1944, and January 8, 1946. It was only after 1995, however, when the U.S. National Security Agency began releasing what is known as the Venona decrypts, that the world became acquainted with the content of the cables and the identities of the various Russian and American figures. Based on the other names, dates, and places referenced in the cables, it is clear that Richard, Jurist, and Lawyer are cover names for Harry Dexter White.[87]

J. M. Keynes and H. D. White at the inaugural meeting of the IMF board of governors in Savannah, Ga., March 1946. (Thomas D. McAvoy/Time & Life Pictures/Getty Images)

CHAPTER 10

Out with the Old Order, In with the New

O n the evening of September 2, 1939, the day after Nazi armored columns rumbled into Poland, a nerve-ridden Whittaker Chambers downed a scotch and soda before spilling out names of U.S. officials involved in Soviet espionage to Roosevelt's internal security adviser, Adolf Berle. Now an ex-Communist and *Time* magazine writer, Chambers, fearful that the Nazi-Soviet Pact presaged German and Russian intelligence cooperation within and against the United States, had hoped to tell his tale to the president himself. But his interlocutor, anticommunist *Plain Talk* editor Isaac Don Levine, had been unable to arrange it. Berle would have to do.

Chambers named over a dozen individuals. Harry White was not one of them, he later insisted; he had hoped White would heed his warnings and break away from the movement.[1] Levine's notes from the meeting, though, bore White's name, as does the memorandum Berle subsequently prepared for the president, which is more than curious. Several scotches may have loosened Chambers' tongue while fogging his memory bank.

FDR apparently thought little of Berle's memo, and took no action. In March 1941, Berle went to the FBI and asked what it knew about Chambers; at that point, the bureau had only noted his past participation in radical activities. Yet after being approached by multiple sources claiming that Chambers had valuable information on Soviet espionage, the FBI only interviewed Chambers for the first time in May 1942. Chambers told them about his meeting with Berle, saying that he had neglected to tell Berle about White. The FBI waited over a year, until June 1943, before requesting and receiving a copy of Berle's 1939 memo to FDR.[2]

With the sudden breakdown of the February 1945 Yalta accords, U.S.-Soviet relations began deteriorating rapidly, and U.S. government interest in domestic Communist influence heated up. On March 20, State Department security officer Ray Murphy questioned Chambers for two hours, noting the latter's characterization of Harry White as "a member at large but rather timid" who had placed underground and party members such as Harold Glasser, Solomon ("Sol") Adler, and Frank Coe in Treasury positions.[3] The FBI resumed interviewing Chambers again in May 1945. Yet despite its reputation for over-zealousness in its pursuit of Communists, the FBI was anything but zealous at this point. Then along came Elizabeth Bentley.

Elizabeth Bentley walked into an FBI field office in New Haven, Connecticut, on August 23. Thirty-seven years old, five feet seven inches tall, 142 pounds, buxom, with big feet, a ruddy complexion, and poor taste in clothes, according to agents who spoke with her, Bentley told them a murky story about a self-claimed New York National Guard official approaching her for information about Russians transacting with her employer. Bentley's own very different published account of her motivations for going to the FBI, pangs of conscience over her treason, is only one of many reasons why elements of her testimony have been widely challenged over the years.[4]

Remarkably, given how central Bentley was to become to the FBI's investigations into Soviet espionage, they chose not to follow up with her. She returned on her own two months later, this time saying that she was "involved in Soviet espionage." She now had their attention. Called back for a third interview on November 7, Bentley was interrogated for eight hours, after which she signed a 31-page statement. Her confession continued on for weeks, leading to a 107-page FBI report that named more than eighty complicit individuals.

The FBI put great stock in Bentley's claims, as she had "reported with a high degree of accuracy [things] which were only known with the Government itself." These included confidential policy discussions on Lend-Lease, currency issues, and even the approximate D-Day landing schedule. Her claims in many cases corroborated and expanded on what they had been told by Whittaker Chambers back in May.[5]

By her account, Bentley had joined the American Communist Party in 1935, a year after returning from studies in Italy, where she had become revolted by fascism. In 1938 she was instructed to take orders from one individual only, "Timmy," and not to meet with other party members. She eventually discovered that Timmy was actually Jacob Golos, a Russian-born member of the American Communist Party's three-man Control Commission and an NKVD agent. She became his assistant and his lover.

Following the German invasion of Russia in June of 1941, Golos received orders to get trusted individuals placed in strategic U.S. government positions to funnel intelligence to Moscow. The following month, Golos told Bentley that she was to be the courier between himself and Ukrainian-born Nathan Gregory ("Greg") Silvermaster, an economist in the Farm Security Administration, who was putting together a network of like-minded individuals in key government positions. The group included Frank Coe, Solomon Adler, William Ludwig ("Lud") Ullmann, Lauchlin Currie, George Silverman, Sonia Gold, Irving Kaplan, and Harry Dexter White. Silvermaster and Ullmann photographed massive amounts of military and political intelligence, purloined by White and others, in Silvermaster's basement; Bentley then regularly transported the film in a large knitting bag from Washington to New York, where Golos would pass it on to the Russians. Following Golos's death in 1943, Bentley also took over Victor Perlo's network, which included onetime White assistant Harold Glasser. All these individuals worked in the Treasury at some point under FDR and Truman.

Neither Bentley nor Chambers nor Silvermaster ever knew whether Harry White was a party member or just a "fellow traveller." Silvermaster told her that he and White had become friendly around 1936, and that he had guessed White's Russian connections after visiting White's house with his wife one evening and spotting the telltale Bokhara rug. White subsequently told him about his past activities and offered to provide what help he could.

White was an enormously valuable resource because he had access to virtually all the Treasury Department's confidential material, as well as secret information the Treasury received from other departments. White was also willing and able to pull strings to help other agents in difficulty, such as Silvermaster himself when he was accused of "very probably" being a Soviet agent in 1942, and again in 1944. Undersecretary of Agriculture Paul Appleby wrote a memo to his subordinates on March 23, 1944, stating that White had asked him whether he could place Silvermaster, who had "been under attack by the Dies Committee [the House Special Committee on Un-American Activities, or HUAC]," in the department. White also gave recommendations for key individuals such as Ullmann, and placed new agents in the Treasury.[6]

Silvermaster described White, much as Chambers had, as timid and nervous. White was frequently agitated because "he doesn't want his right hand to know what the left is doing." White had been spooked by the rupture with Chambers, and had promised his wife, "who was not a Communist and disliked his revolutionary activities, that he would stay out of espionage in the future, and he lived in terror that she would find out he had broken his word." Silvermaster tried to calm White by telling him that his information was only going to one man in the American Communist Party's Central Committee, although White could surely not have doubted it was ultimately headed to Moscow.[7]

How credible, ultimately, is Elizabeth Bentley? There are clear errors and inconsistencies in her multiple recountings—comprising FBI statements, government testimony, and an autobiography—of her life in the Communist underground and the dozens of government officials she said had been part of it. These "appear to result mainly from her tendency to add details in order to add an air of verisimilitude to her story, [but] do not bulk large in the total context of her story [and] do not suggest that she is lying."[8] Yet they do highlight the need for corroboration—not least in the case of White, the most important of the figures she implicates.

Unlike Chambers, Bentley never claimed to have met White, and had no physical evidence supporting her allegations against him. Some of her assertions can be safely discounted, such as her own role in getting American-designed German currency to the Soviets in 1944 in advance of the Allied German occupation: the Soviets had tried and failed to reproduce it "until I was able through Harry Dexter White to arrange that the United States Treasury Department turn the actual printing plates over to the Russians!" she chirped in her memoir. Whether she did or did not get involved was immaterial to the outcome; White operated aboveground, and needed no prodding in that case. However, too many of Bentley's claims are corroborated for her account of White's role to be dismissed. Chambers and Bentley each fingered White to the FBI independently of the other. Victor Perlo's ex-wife also denounced White in an unsigned letter to President Roosevelt sent in April 1944; she acknowledged writing it after the FBI traced it to her.[9] And more was to emerge in later years.

On November 8, FBI director J. Edgar Hoover wrote to the White House's FBI liaison, Brigadier General Harry Vaughan, indicating that information from a "highly confidential source" suggested that a number of government employees were providing information to outsiders who were in turn transmitting it to "espionage agents of the Soviet Government." The employees named were, in order, Nathan Gregory Silvermaster, Harry White, George Silverman, Lauchlin Currie, and Victor Perlo. Hoover suggested that the president would want to have these "preliminary data" immediately.

On November 27, Hoover sent Vaughan a more detailed seventy-one-page memorandum, copies of which were also delivered to Secretary of State James Byrnes, Attorney General Tom Clark, and others. One of Clark's successors, General Herbert Brownell, would later testify before Congress that the memo summarized "[Harry] White's espionage activities in abbreviated form." Concise as that summary was, it "constituted adequate warning . . . of the extreme danger to the security of the country in appointing White," the most senior official mentioned in the memo, "to the International Monetary Fund or continuing him in Government in any capacity." The FBI put White under full surveillance. They would ultimately accumulate over thirteen thousand pages of material on him.

On January 23, 1946, President Truman nominated White for the post of American executive director at the IMF. Truman later revealed that it was also "planned that the United States would support Mr. White for election to the top managerial position in the International Monetary Fund—that of managing director—a more important post than that of a member of the board of executive directors."[10] But those plans were disrupted by Hoover.

When Hoover learned of the nomination, he had the bureau prepare a special report on White for the president, based on information provided by thirty sources, which was delivered to Vaughan on February 4. Hoover was determined to ensure that White's nomination go no further. He wrote an accompanying letter to Vaughan stressing White's role as "a valuable adjunct to an underground Soviet espionage organization." White was providing original documents as well as verbatim copies and notes, which were being photographed in Silvermaster's house and delivered through channels to Jacob Golos, a known Soviet agent. White was considered especially valuable because of his ability to place individuals of high regard to Soviet intelligence into the Treasury Department. The espionage activities of Treasury colleagues of White's such as Harold Glasser and Sonia Gold, a secretary who allegedly received her appointment through White, were detailed. Hoover's assessment was based on "numerous confidential sources whose reliability has been established." White continued to be in close personal contact with nearly all the individuals in the spy ring. A Canadian source, Hoover added, was aware of at least some of the allegations in the FBI memo, and was deeply anxious to ensure that White not be appointed to a position at either the IMF or World Bank, where he would have great influence over international financial arrangements. Revelation of facts related to White's improper activities could also jeopardize the successful operation of the fund and the bank, Hoover stressed.

Truman later stated that he was not aware of the accusations against White until early February 1946—around the time Hoover's report was received by Vaughan, and two weeks after he had nominated White for the IMF executive director post.[11] White's nomination was approved by the Senate Committee on Banking and Currency on February 5, the day that Byrnes received the report from Hoover and a day before Vinson received it from Truman. Byrnes later said he had been shocked by the report and advised the president to withdraw the nomination. Vinson, who loathed White, wanted him out of government service entirely. Truman, by Byrnes' account, called the secretary of the Senate to inquire about the status of White's nomination and was chagrined when told it had gone through. Byrnes and Truman discussed ways of reversing it, but the president was chary.

Vinson, Clark, and Hoover had a lengthy meeting on February 22 to discuss options for advising the president, among which were for the president to dismiss White with no statement or to ask White for his resignation. Truman, according to his later recounting, ultimately decided to proceed with White's appointment in order to protect the FBI investigation by not signaling its existence to the spy ring, and to move White out of Treasury and into a position less sensitive in terms of national security.

Further FBI reports began circulating through the government in the spring, detailing the alleged espionage activities of other of White's former colleagues named by Bentley, including Frank Coe, who would in 1958 move to China to work for Mao's government, and William Ludwig Ullmann.[12] White, who by this time may well have been aware that he was being watched and investigated, would begin his new duties at the IMF in early May.[13] Hoover would later say that the FBI's surveillance of White was subsequently "hampered" by the fund's extraterritorial privileges.

Keynes, who had been appointed British governor of both the IMF and the World Bank on February 19, met with Vinson in Washington on March 5. Vinson told him that the administration had decided not to put White's name forward for the IMF's top job, despite White being a "natural" for it. They had decided instead to back an American for the World Bank post in order to secure "the confidence of the American investment market." It would not be "proper," they had concluded with uncharacteristic fair-mindedness, "to have Americans as the heads of both bodies." Though Keynes had had his fair share of tussles with Harry White, he was disappointed; the IMF, he believed, would need a first-class head to be effective.

No doubt, American bankers would have preferred one of their own to run the World Bank. But the American Bankers Association had a year ago formally thrown its support behind the bank; if any institution lacked their confidence, it was the fund. In reality, the administration had likely concluded that installing an American at the fund above White would have raised too many awkward questions about why the "natural" candidate was being passed over.

Vinson had obviously been in no position to tell Keynes the truth about the FBI reports. These had quite simply changed the course of history. In their absence, the tradition of a European heading the IMF and an American heading the World Bank would surely have been reversed—assuming the Americans would not have laid claim to both.

The other news Keynes received was far more disturbing. The British had been assuming that the fund and bank would be based in New York, but Vinson told him that the administration would insist on Washington. Keynes, in his own words, reacted "vehemently," as he had at Bretton Woods when the Americans ruled out London, declaring that putting the fund and bank in Washington would make them a mere "appanage" of the U.S. administration. Vinson retorted that basing them in New York would place them "under the taint of 'international finance.'" This was code for the administration's loathing of bankers. The decision, he indicated politely, was final.[14]

Keynes and Lydia traveled by train 750 miles south to Wilmington Island, near Savannah, Georgia, for what Keynes expected to be a relaxing victory lap for Bretton Woods: another international conference, this time to inaugurate the fund and the bank and to decide on the few outstanding matters, such as their location and the role of the executive directors. Keynes was immediately enamored with the gracious charm of the southern town, calling it "a beautiful woman . . . whose face was concealed behind a veil of delicate lace."[15]

Three hundred delegates, observers, support staff, and media attended the event. Vinson, as conference chair, welcomed the guests on March 9, recalling what the delegates had composed together at Bretton Woods: no less than "an economic Magna Carta," he said. Paul Bareau of the UK Treasury's Washington delegation called the speech "long and turgid . . . full of emotional and fundamentally insincere expressions of hope."[16] For his part, Vinson was no less put off by Keynes's less cumbrous fare. With a recent dance performance of *The Sleeping Beauty* foremost in his mind, Keynes wove an extended metaphor of fairies, each of which he hoped would shower the new Bretton Woods creations with wisdom and good fortune. Let us hope, he concluded, "that there is no malicious fairy" who would turn them into "politicians," always pursuing dark, ulterior motives. For then "the best that could befall . . . would be for [them] to fall into an eternal slumber, never to waken or be heard of again in the courts of mankind."

Vinson seethed through the vigorous applause; he took the speech as a personal attack on him. "I don't mind being called malicious," he muttered, "but I *do* mind being called a fairy."[17]

Though the architecture of the IMF had been largely hammered out even before Bretton Woods, the two main issues that remained brought out the enduring divide between the American and British visions. For the Americans, the fund was to be a means of affording the U.S. government new powers to police international finance—both the behavior of other governments and that of private bankers. The British, in contrast, sought to make the fund a passive source of international credit, free from the wiles of dollar diplomacy.

The first issue was where the fund, and the bank, would be located. Keynes, seeing that other delegations supported him, ignored Vinson's warnings earlier in the month and took up the fight for placing them in New York, rather than Washington. This was, he insisted, necessary to ensure that they were legitimately international and independent of any single government. There were also technical advantages, he argued, in basing them in a major financial center with close proximity to the United Nations' Economic and Social Council. The Americans, Bareau wrote, "brushed [this] aside with complete brutality."[18] Will Clayton responded that the British were being inconsistent, since they were also insisting that the executive directors should represent the *national* interest, and spend much of their time at home. As intergovernmental institutions, he pointed out, the fund and the bank were better shielded from private financial and commercial interests in Washington.

Keynes would later claim he had the support of a majority of the delegates, as well as the New York Fed.[19] (The Fed board of governors in Washington was, naturally, full-square behind the administration.) Yet in the face of implacable American resistance to foreign interference in the choice of which of their own cities would prevail, the British, as well as the French and the Indians, dropped their objections to Washington. Vinson, Keynes wrote to Dalton, "rail-road[ed] this decision through the Conference, vocally supported (as became usual) by a pathetic procession of stooges, of which Ethiopia (represented by an American banker), Salvador, Guatemala, Mexico and China were prominent, with most of the rest discreetly silent."[20]

As important as the symbolism of location was, the more substantive issue to be resolved was the role of the directors, particularly those of the fund. Given their vision of an activist fund, working to correct national policies that were creating dangerous international financial imbalances, the Americans insisted that the directors be full-time and well remunerated, with a large battalion of specialist technical staff behind them. The British, who wanted a fund that was more like an automatic credit mechanism than a nosy new American-dominated bureaucracy with a mind of its own, countered that its directors should already have important day jobs in their own governments or central banks; their role in the fund should be only part-time, mainly ensuring that their respective countries' national interests were protected. Keynes thought that thirty technicians, rather than the three hundred the Americans envisioned, would be sufficient to handle the fund's tasks.

"The Americans have no idea how to make these institutions into operating international concerns," Keynes complained in a letter to Richard Kahn, "and in almost every direction their ideas are bad. Yet they plainly intend to force their own conceptions on the rest of us. The result is that the institutions look like becoming American concerns, run by gigantic American staffs, with the rest of us very much on the side-lines."[21]

Keynes in the end concentrated his attack on what he saw to be obscenely high tax-free salaries for directors *and* their alternates, both of which would struggle to find ways to occupy themselves in their full-time appointments. He was particularly repulsed by the fact that many of those deciding the salary issue in Savannah would be precisely the ones who would be receiving the appointments. Clayton offered one concession; only the director *or* his alternate need be continually available, not both. This was not enough for Keynes, who spoke out strongly but politely against the salaries before the board of governors.

White rose to confront Keynes for the final time. "The question of salaries which is before us, whether a few thousand dollars more or less, is not the real problem," he insisted. The real problem was what sort of fund this was to be. "It has been our belief from the very beginning that the Fund constitutes a very powerful instrument for the coordination of monetary policies, for the prevention of economic warfare and for an attempt to foster sound monetary policies throughout the world." But this was not the British view, he said.

"I believe that [Lord Keynes's] views and those of his Government stem from something that goes very far back," he continued, "from the very first conversation we had with our British friends several years ago, when early drafts were being considered. . . . Throughout the discussions at Atlantic City, throughout the Bretton Woods discussions their views have [been] the same." The British have always wanted an "International Clearing Union [in which] the greater emphasis should be upon the provision of short-term credit." The fund, they believed, should have "as little discretion as possible in [determining] whether or not the policies pursued by any member governments were or were not in accord with certain principles. . . . We submit," he concluded, "that the thesis that salaries shall be lower than are necessary to attract competent men . . . may become, I hope undesignedly, an instrument to divert the purposes and divert the general policy of the Fund so that it will become closer akin to the hearts of those who foresee in the Fund little else than a source of credit and an automatic source."[22]

This was harsh, but it did capture the core of the difference between the American and British visions for the fund. As Bareau observed from the British perspective, the Americans "visualized the Fund as a new revolutionary active intruder into the international monetary relations of its member countries. They were inheritors of the New Deal suspicion of the private commercial banker and were therefore intent on keeping not merely the control but the day-to-day organisation of the International Monetary Fund in the hands of government representatives." Yet the Americans had not actually sold the world on that vision. "We [the British] lost on every issue," Bareau concluded, "not by the process of rational argument in debate but by the solid massing of the cohorts which voted automatically with America"—particularly the Latin Americans, "whose representatives could be depended on to read sometimes with considerable difficulty the speeches prepared for them by the Secretariat of the United States delegation."

Keynes was powerless in the face of such a force. In the end, he alone voted against the salary provisions—the only negative vote recorded at the conference. "The lobbying for votes, the mobilisation of supporters, the politics of the lunch and the dinner table were not arts in which Keynes excelled," Bareau noted. "All the more reason for his bitter disappointment at the manner in which a trip he had anticipated as a pleasant interlude . . . should have turned out as it did. 'I went to Savannah to meet the world,' [Keynes] said, 'and all I met was a tyrant.'"[23]

Keynes, however, displayed his usual powers of emotional recovery. He records having left Savannah on March 18 in a fine mood; it was a "lovely middle March evening, with a full moon over the rivers and lakes of this delta, and the sea, with a temperature of about 70 at 10 o'clock in the evening." He was pleased that former Belgian Finance Minister Camille Gutt, an "old trusted friend . . . though no longer very young or very vigorous," had agreed to his suggestion to stand for the fund managing-director position; Gutt was formally elected on May 6. As for White, he "led a 'Bacchic rout of satyrs and Silenuses' from Latin America into the dining room" for the closing dinner, "with 'vine leaves'—or perhaps cocktail sticks—in his hair and loudly bellowing 'Onward Christian Soldiers.'"[24]

Though Keynes departed Savannah in good spirits, he had a perilous journey home. He collapsed on the train to Washington on the morning of the nineteenth, managing to recover a few hours later. He went on to New York before boarding the *Queen Mary* for Southampton, England, on the twenty-first. He came down with a stomach bug en route. British banker George Bolton later said that Keynes spent much of the voyage writing an article "condemning American policy with extraordinary ferocity and passionately recommending H. M. Government to refuse to ratify the Fund and Bank agreement," though Keynes biographer Donald Moggridge called this a muddled misrecollection. The feelings Bolton ascribed to Keynes were most surely there, yet it would have been wholly uncharacteristic of him to declare failure like this. In any case, the British government had already ratified Bretton Woods.

The cabinet paper that Keynes did in the end write, dated March 27, was much more in keeping with his practice throughout the Bretton Woods saga. While not covering up his disappointments, he put a sympathetic spin on American behavior, suggesting that Clayton's insistence on a powerful IMF executive should be seen more charitably as a way to protect administration prerogatives in foreign economic policy from arrogation by Congress.[25] "It may have been rather stupid of us not to tumble to all this sooner," he suggested. "Some of our criticism and opposition may have seemed churlish and a little off the point. But we were not handled in a way which made apprehension easy."[26]

A strange strain of optimism seemed to suffuse Keynes's economic thinking in late March and early April. Writings and conversations now pointed toward "the invisible hand" as a possible way out of Britain's huge financial problems[27]—an "invisible hand which I had tried to eject from economic thinking twenty years ago," Keynes noted. This was, observed former Bank of England economist Henry Clay in a letter to now-retired Montagu Norman, "an interesting confession for our arch-planner."

"I think he relied on intellect, which perhaps means that he ignored the 'invisible hand,'" Norman responded, "and I guess he was led astray by Harry White. But surely it is easy to arrange a loan if you ignore its repayment, and is there any hope of that, unless there is to be such an inflation across the Atlantic as will affect their claims and provide an easy way out?"[28]

In the last bit of correspondence between the two, White wrote to Keynes on March 27 that he agreed with Keynes's upbeat forthcoming article on the U.S. balance of payments. "Altogether the possibility of scarcity of dollars during the next five years seems to me, as it does to you, to be remote," White wrote, "barring of course untoward political developments."[29] There would, unfortunately, be many of these.

Keynes began an Easter respite at his home in Sussex on April 12. Over the next week he was in fine form, appearing to be on the mend yet again—even doing some long walking. Yet on April 21, Easter Sunday, he suffered another attack. This time, he would not recover. He died in his bed, age sixty-two.

"The British Empire seems to be running off almost as fast as the American Loan," Churchill thundered before the House of Commons on December 20, 1946. "The haste is appalling." As if secretly synchronized, the pillars of empire and sterling's international acceptability were crumbling in tandem. As well flagged as both had been, the trauma was no less for it.

Dollars hung over every question of how the empire would be dismantled. Keynes had asked all the apt but awkward questions about the emperor's clothes. "Take the case of Egypt," he said in February of 1946. "How do we propose to reply to the Egyptian demand that we should take our troops out of Egypt? Is it appreciated that we are paying the cost of keeping them there by *borrowing it from Egypt*?

What is the answer if Egypt tells us (as, of course, she will) that she is no longer prepared to provide us with the necessary funds?"[30] The answer was to evacuate them, but only to move them to Palestine. This, it was hoped, would buy time east of the Sinai until something—anything—could be worked out with the Arabs, the Zionists, and the Americans.

Newly minted Labour MP Richard Crossman, who would become a cabinet minister under Harold Wilson in the 1960s, served on an early-1946 Anglo-American committee of inquiry looking into the problems associated with Jewish resettlement in Palestine. Initially pro-Arab, he became a convert to the Zionist cause over the course of his travels and meetings. Never lost on him was the domestic political influence of Zionist supporters in the United States, many of whom were "passionately anti-British" and therefore in a position to scuttle the American loan. The pro-Jewish approach to the question of British-mandate Palestine had the distinct advantage, he noted, of being "[a]cceptable to American public opinion." The pro-Arab approach, on the other side, "is certain to intensify anti-British and isolationist influences and might even endanger the Loan."

"I appreciate that your country has been greatly weakened by the war," Jemal Husseini, cousin of the Mufti of Jerusalem, told Crossman sympathetically, "and that you will need American support to keep your Empire together."

Crossman would not deny it. "If Arab policy was so inept as to compel us to choose between American and Arab friendship," he warned, "I myself as a realist would have to choose American."[31]

Anglo-American friendship was by this point in short supply. A UK Mass-Observation poll in March of 1946 found that only 22 percent of Britons took a favorable view of the Americans, down from 58 percent in 1945. The end of Lend-Lease and the protracted loan negotiations came up frequently in verbal responses. A June State Department poll found only 38 percent of Americans approving of any sort of loan to Britain, with 48 percent against.[32] The loan would, in the words of one congressional opponent, "promote too damned much Socialism at home and too much damned Imperialism abroad."[33] Growing fear of the Soviet menace, however, turned the tide of the Washington debate. Churchill's famous "Iron Curtain" speech on March 5 in Fulton,

Missouri, did much, as did Stalin's denunciation of it, to rally skeptics such as Republican Senator Arthur Vandenberg, who had earlier accused Britain of "beginning to 'Shylock' us" following the December House of Lords loan debate. In the end, Congress approved the loan only by the narrow margins of 46–34 in the Senate, on May 14, and 219–155 in the House on July 13.

Back in February, a few weeks before his final American trip, Keynes had been full of foreboding about the way in which American lending was merely plugging the dike between the material aspirations of the war-weary British populace, both reflected in and encouraged by the famous Beveridge Plan for universal social insurance, and Whitehall's inertial devotion to "cut[ting] a dash in the world considerably above our means."[34] The country, he observed, was "sticky with self-pity and not prepared to accept peacefully and wisely the fact that her position and her resources are *not* what they once were." Keeping British forces in India would require $500 million a year; the Middle East, another $300 million. This was a quarter of the American loan. "Psycho-analysis would, I think, show that" the gap between aspiration and capacity "was the real background of the [cold British] reception of the American loan and the associated proposals."[35]

On July 22, the King David Hotel in Jerusalem was blown up by the Irgun Jewish underground under the leadership of Menachim Begin, once a British Army corporal and decades later an Israeli prime minister. Ninety-one died: British, Arabs, and Jews. "Almost any solution in which the United States will join us could be made to work," injected Churchill hopefully shortly after the disaster. Yet the Truman administration was on its own political navigating system. Unlike FDR, Truman had no overriding strategic purpose, like defeating the Nazis, for which he could profitably harness his government to British interests. On October 4, he undercut both the British and his own State Department's efforts to create a binational Palestine (the so-called Morrison-Grady Plan) with a statement that was widely read as an outright endorsement of partition and the creation of a Jewish state. Attlee reacted bitterly, remonstrating Truman for refusing to delay the statement. It was clear that the converse of Churchill's statement was closer to the truth: any solution to Britain's imperial quandaries that lacked U.S. support was now hopeless.[36]

The summer of 1946 also witnessed the collapse of British efforts to contain ethnic conflict in India. Jawaharlal Nehru, elected president of the Hindu-dominated Indian National Congress in July, failed to bring Mohammad Ali Jinnah (known as the *Quaid-i-Azam*, or "Great Leader") and his Muslim League into a constitutional arrangement for a united, independent India. Following Jinnah's announcement that the league would withdraw cooperation and pursue an independent Pakistan, thousands died as communal violence spread from Calcutta.

Meanwhile, things went from bad to worse in Greece. British forces were pinned down fighting Communist guerrillas in the north of the country. Precious borrowed dollars were evaporating in supporting the operations. Bevin, in the United States for six weeks in November and December, warned Byrnes that the British might have to withdraw for lack of cash, but with the antispending Republicans having just been swept into control of Congress Byrnes was in no position to offer American military support.

Attlee, meanwhile, was coming to the conclusion that not just Greece but Palestine and India needed to be painfully reappraised. He wrote a private letter to Bevin on December 1 laying out his thinking. "I am beginning to doubt whether the Greek game is worth the candle," he wrote bluntly. As for Palestine, "The Middle East position is only an outpost position." Britain's far-flung military commitments might simply be unsustainable without American support, which was not likely to be forthcoming. "There is a tendency in America to regard us as an outpost," he observed resignedly, "but an outpost that they will not have to defend."

A brutal winter, the worst in sixty years, strained the economic and political viability of Britain's far-flung commitments to the breaking point. Attlee signed an independence agreement with Burmese General Aung San on January 27, 1947. Over a dramatic seven days in February, one pillar after another of British imperial might came crashing down. On the fourteenth, Bevin announced that Britain's Palestine mandate would be handed back to the United Nations. On the eighteenth, the cabinet agreed to withdraw the troops from Greece. And on the twentieth, Attlee announced in the House that Britain would leave India.

"Scuttle!" came back the Conservative cry. Churchill would fling the word at the Labour government incessantly in the coming months. But the die had been cast.

What a difference a year had made. "I know that if the British Empire fell," Bevin told the Commons back in February 1946, " . . . it would mean that the [British] standard of living would fall considerably." Indeed, in 1946 it was still axiomatic for many in Britain's ruling circles that the empire was a source of economic strength. Now it was clear that it had become an unsustainable dollar drain. And with Britain massively indebted from the war, it had few economic levers it could pull to bring rebellious colonies such as India into line.

Washington was unprepared for the speed with which the old order was collapsing. "There are only two powers left," Acheson observed somberly in February 1947, referring to the United States and the Soviet Union. "The British are finished."[37] Acheson was now chief of staff to General George Marshall, newly installed as secretary of state in place of the ailing Byrnes. Though FDR had come close to burying Lend-Lease over British military actions in Greece, Marshall and Truman were now scrambling to hold back a Communist takeover of the country in the wake of a British retreat. On March 12, Truman made an historic speech before a joint session of Congress, laying out what came to be known as the "Truman Doctrine." The United States would pledge economic and military support to Greece, and Turkey, in order to prevent their coming under Soviet domination. This was the first in a domino-chain of geopolitical challenges the United States would face in the coming decades in filling the vacuum left by the implosion of the British Empire.

Truman's signing of the British loan legislation on July 15, 1946, launched the pound sterling on an agonizing yearlong death march—full sterling convertibility was thereafter ordained for July 15, 1947. The loan was meant precisely to buffer this shock, but dollars were draining away at an alarming pace. "[T]he speed at which we have been exhausting these Credits has been rapidly mounting, and the situation now shows every sign of going out of control," Dalton, the chancellor, wrote to his cabinet colleagues on March 21, 1947. The problem was being exacerbated by a rapid rise in American prices, which was driving up Britain's import bill beyond what had been anticipated. Dalton implored his colleagues that heroic efforts would be required in the coming months to cut dollar imports and boost exports while sustaining food rations.[38]

On May 28, Dalton spelled out the dire balance-of-payments problem. There was, he said, a burgeoning global dollar shortage that "threatens to create a world economic crisis." Keynes and White had been wrong with their optimistic forecasts the previous spring. Britain and France, for example, were each accumulating visible trade deficits with the United States that would reach nearly $1 billion for the full year. "[T]he crisis which is coming upon us" in Britain, Dalton stressed, "differs in kind from any other we have experienced. Currency depreciation or adjustment or repudiation of external indebtedness provides us no way out. Our overseas income is insufficient for our overseas needs." The problems had "been concealed successively by lend-lease, borrowing for sterling and the United States and Canadian credits," but this was all coming to an end. The country was now facing "dollar starvation." He noted that Britain might be able to draw on a maximum of $324 million a year in credits from the new IMF, though he warned that the fund board, and "particularly the United States, are bound to scrutinise carefully the situation of any Member which is drawing heavily."[39] Otto Clarke at Treasury warned too that "the righting of great trade disequilibria is not the fund's business."

Clarke worried that British "commitments under the Anglo-American Financial Agreement make the whole problem much worse." Without dollar earnings from the rest of the world, Britain would have to "cut down . . . imports from the American Continent to the bone." But given Britain's nondiscrimination commitments, this was impossible without cutting imports from elsewhere as well, which would produce a cascading collapse of world trade. Convertibility led to the same result, as other countries would try to accumulate convertible sterling by cutting imports from Britain, which would force Britain to cut imports in turn. In the end, he felt, the only hope appeared to be the dramatic proposal made in June by General Marshall.[40]

Marshall could not save the pound from convertibility, however. During the week of July 20, $106 million was drained from the British coffers. The outflow rose to $126 million the following week, and another $127 million the week after. It reached $183 million the week of August 16. Dalton tried to stabilize reserves at $2.5 billion by accelerating drafts on the American loan, but now only $850 million of it remained. With worsening global dollar scarcity and sterling alone convertible among the currencies of the European belligerents, there was simply no way to stanch the flow. On August 20, the British government suspended convertibility.[41] The dream of reestablishing sterling as a world currency was shattered.

At the time of Marshall's famed Harvard speech on June 5, 1947, American and British visions for Europe's economic organization could hardly have been more divergent. Attlee's government was busy nationalizing coal mines, railways, and electricity supply. Central planning was to be the bedrock of British economic security. Will Clayton, now America's first undersecretary of state for economic affairs, returned from a visit to Europe in May with a radically different blueprint. Britain was to be part of an economically integrated Europe, which was itself to be unashamedly capitalist and free-trading. Back in Washington, such ideas were filtered through the prism of George Kennan's long telegram from Moscow the previous year: those who didn't follow the American model, it was believed, were apt to end up following the Soviet one.

Clayton, having become a Democrat only because the Republicans had become protectionists, possessed in spades both Hull's dedication to free trade and White's commitment to stable currencies. As important to Marshall on foreign economic matters as White had been to Morgenthau, Clayton also had a bold, far-reaching, generous, and practical vision for reviving Europe's war-shattered economies along firmly free-market lines.

In France in particular, which he saw firsthand in May, Clayton was deeply disturbed by the failures of central planning. The government was combating an inflation crisis with price controls, to which farmers reacted by holding back produce and starving the cities.[42] Looting and hoarding were the rule; the economic bonds of civilized society were in tatters.[43] Clayton was under no illusion that the situation could be remedied without a radical change in policies, or that the policies could be changed on the basis of American lectures. The United States would have to offer massive financial aid—grants, and not loans, lines of credit, or lend-lease—in return for major market reforms. This was a world away from White's 1945 vision of American postwar aid, the centerpiece of which had been $10 billion in unconditional reconstruction credits to the now increasingly belligerent Soviet Union.

Though Marshall, on his return from a fruitless mission to Moscow in April, had told Americans by radio of Europe's dire economic crisis and the need for bold and immediate action, it was Clayton who laid the intellectual foundation for what became the Marshall Plan. Clayton characteristically declined to draw attention to himself, yet Acheson attributes over half the content, the part devoted to Europe's condition and its causes, to him. Indeed, a side-by-side comparison of Marshall's words with those of Clayton in a May 27 memo bears out the latter's critical role.[44]

The genius of the general's speech, a mere 1,442 words, lay not only in its vision but in its remarkably deft diplomatic touch. It threw a lifeline to America's European allies, who could not simultaneously fund immediate survival needs and the regeneration of vital business and trading links. In doing so, it put the onus on the Europeans themselves to craft a compelling plan for cooperation and recovery and to spell out for an ever-skeptical Congress and American public what assistance would be necessary to achieve it. Finally, in not excluding the Soviets it carefully avoided cleaving Europe, but it also did not solicit their agreement; the terms would be American, and the Soviets would have to exclude themselves at their own political cost.

Lest Marshall's message be lost on the Europeans, Acheson worked through friends in the British media to drive it home. Bevin was quick to seize on the opportunity, rallying French Foreign Minister Georges Bidault for a meeting with Molotov, which took place in Paris two weeks later. Clayton gave him prior assurance that Washington would not allow Soviet demands to stop Marshall's plan from going forward; there would, in essence, be no repeat of the Russian obstructionism at Bretton Woods. By Bevin's account, Molotov, after receiving a telegram from Moscow, threw up predictable objections relating to Russian sovereignty, thereby making matters "much more simple." The Russians were out. A joint Anglo-French communiqué on July 3 invited twenty-two other European countries to send representatives to Paris to craft a recovery plan.[45]

Bevin did not, however, so much welcome the American initiative as cling to it for dear life. Britain was, he protested meekly to Clayton and Ambassador Lew Douglas, being "lumped in," as if it were "merely another European country." Surely, Britain could not be treated like the Soviets were treating Yugoslavia. "Britain with an Empire is on a different basis."[46] Bevin saw Marshall's plan as an opportunity for his nation "to establish a new financial partnership" with the United States. But Clayton was emphatic: there would be "no piecemeal approach to the European problem"; the United States would not create any "special partner."[47] That Bevin, in appealing to British exceptionalism, could have expected a sympathetic American response seems remarkable today. Yet in 1947 reform of the imperial mind-set lagged well behind the frantic pace of global reordering.

Over the next three months, Clayton worked doggedly on three fronts of what he saw as the same battle: extracting a compelling Marshall Plan assistance request from the Paris delegates, achieving a breakthrough on global trade liberalization, and encouraging the formation of a "European federation" to coordinate Europe's economic efforts and implement a customs union.

On the Marshall Plan front, the eponymous author had rebuffed Clayton's repeated pleadings throughout the summer for interim assistance to the increasingly desperate and frustrated Europeans. In September Marshall relented; on the tenth he publicly pressed Congress for quick appropriations to mitigate "hunger and cold this winter." This had a profound effect on the Paris discussions, and on the twenty-second the Europeans finally submitted an "initial" report and assistance request that satisfied American expectations. Clayton immediately left Paris for London to press his case on trade liberalization, which he saw as an essential complement to American aid.

This proved a tougher nut to crack. Throughout the summer, Clayton had struggled simultaneously with London over the dismantling of imperial preference and with protectionists in his own capital determined to erect new wool import tariffs. He ultimately won Truman over in the wool wars, thereby salvaging troubled global trade talks in Geneva. The British resisted mightily in the face of Clayton's public upbraids on imperial preference. They had committed to dismantling it in return for Lend-Lease, and then again for the loan. Vinson's promises to Congress in 1946 that Britain would "*immediately* accept the principles of fair and non-discriminatory currency and trade practices" if given the loan had been shown to be hollow.[48] The British were now balking anew, despite the dangling Marshall carrot. But in late September they offered a reduction in, rather than elimination of, preference margins, while cutting their reciprocal demands for U.S. tariff reductions. Clayton had wanted to go much further (he always did), but backed the compromise in order to achieve his more cherished end: a successful conclusion of the General Agreement on Tariffs and Trade (GATT), predecessor to the World Trade Organization. His lofty aspirations now realized, Clayton wrote his sixth and final letter resigning from the State Department on October 7, bowing at last, at age sixty-eight, to his wife's demands that the couple leave Washington for good.[49]

"This vast project [the GATT], which makes all previous international economic accords look puny," wrote the *New York Times* on October 15, "is the realization of Mr. Clayton's dream: that a group of like-minded democratic nations could deliberately reverse the historical trend toward the strangulation of world trade. It is a big step that nobody but Mr. Clayton and a few of his colleagues thought would ever be taken."

Europeans had generally shown regard for Harry White's technical prowess and indefatigability in crafting the International Monetary Fund, but neither White nor his fund were ever objects of affection or inspiration. Clayton, in contrast, was widely seen as "both the symbol of and dynamic force behind the most constructive aspects of American international economic policy."[50] Tributes in the British and French press were effusive in spite of—in some cases because of—Clayton's relentless pressure on European governments to cooperate more and nationalize less. "A champion of liberalism," *Le Monde* called Clayton. "Our diplomats . . . will deplore the absence of one of the Americans who knew best European affairs."[51]

Clayton's efforts to break down Europe's old national (and imperial) economic silos, and to lay the foundation for a new, open, market-based free-trade area in their place, yielded little in 1947. Yet by 1957 he could rightfully add this to his legacy. His frenetic summer shuttle diplomacy faced formidable obstacles, thrown up first and foremost by a British government committed to more state control of industry and to preserving the economic remnants of an empire with which its trade was twice that with Europe. But Clayton's own increasingly irritated State Department colleagues also came to see his obsession with customs unions as a lofty long-run ambition that threw up barriers to achieving the short-run priority of boosting European industrial and agricultural production.[52] Though Clayton failed to get the firm commitments he wanted from the Europeans in September of '47, Marshall aid was in the end conditioned on European governments pursuing market- and investment-friendly policies—conditions that happened to jibe well with French interests in securing long-term access to German resources such as coal and coke. The integration of defeated Germany into the postwar European economy became an important pillar of the Marshall aid structure—in stark contrast to White's IMF and Morgenthau Plan blueprints.

Signed into law as the Economic Cooperation Act by President Truman on April 3, 1948, the Marshall Plan ultimately committed $13 billion ($122 billion in today's dollars) of economic and technical aid to sixteen European countries, including Germany, through the end of 1951. In addition to providing vital immediate assistance in the form of food, staples, fuel, and machinery, Marshall intervention played an important longer-term role in areas such as industrial and agricultural modernization, transport renewal, and trade revival, and provided a critical impetus to some of the watershed agreements along the road to European integration.[53] Clayton, Acheson noted admiringly, "was nearly a decade ahead of the [1957] Treaty of Rome," the European Union's founding document.[54] Britain, interestingly, did not finally dismantle imperial preference until joining the European Economic Community in 1973.

It is in the end little wonder that the Marshall Plan, and not Lend-Lease, is so often wrongly held to be the object of Churchill's designation "the most unsordid act." That American self-interest was well served by it should not detract from its merits as an act of enlightened internationalism unparalleled in modern history.

For the remainder of his life, Will Clayton would remain an outspoken advocate of European and transatlantic economic, monetary, and diplomatic integration. He not infrequently chided his own country for thinking too parochially about its role in the world. "If we don't stop the prostitution of national policy to serve the selfish ends of [economic interest groups]," he wrote to the *New York Times* in 1958, "we will lose the feeble hold we now have on the leadership of the free world."[55] On Clayton's death in 1966, Truman wrote that he "was one of those rare public servants who was not only dedicated to the public's interest but had a world outlook in which he saw the position of the United States in relation and harmony to all nations."[56] Few tributes achieve such a congruence of generosity and actuality.

The International Monetary Fund began operations on March 1, 1947. Immediately following, one country after another invoked the right to retain wartime exchange restrictions articulated in the fund's transitional-period provisions. On March 31, Harry White wrote a resignation letter to President Truman, saying that he had "for some time cherished the idea of returning to private enterprise." With "the work of the Fund . . . off to a good start [and with] the period of active operations . . . just beginning," it was "an opportunity" for his "successor to take over." Truman formally accepted his resignation in a letter dated April 7, remarking on White's "ceaseless efforts to make a real contribution to the stability of international trade through the International [World] Bank and the International Monetary Fund." The reference to White's "efforts" to contribute to stabilizing trade was an acknowledgement that such stabilization was still some way off.

In a rosy account of the IMF's first year of operations presented in April 1947, White wrote that although "no member country eligible to purchase foreign exchange has applied," it was "absurd" to suggest that this was "an indication of failure, or breakdown, or of something wrong." This was the result of unremarkable temporary factors that would soon change.[57]

In June 1947 the IMF executive directors took a hard-line stance on financial assistance requests, insisting publicly they would "look behind" them to ensure they were consistent with IMF articles; that is, that assistance was not to be used for reconstruction. Over the course of the next twelve months, however, the fund instead turned a blind eye, doling out $600 million as a stopgap measure until Marshall funding could take over in the spring of 1948.[58] The fund then went back into virtual hibernation.

In May of '48 White would pen an intensely gloomy draft statement to introduce amendments to the fund articles, which was never published or even presented publicly. The contrast to his cheery article a year prior was stark. Now he ventured that "a candid appraisal of the contributions which [the Fund and the Bank] have so far made toward the stated objectives would force us to the conclusion that achievement has been much less than anticipated." This "would be much less disturbing if there were any substantial hopes that in the next few years the situation would change. But there is no such hope." White now believed that the IMF needed to increase its monetary firepower dramatically. Remarkably, he now proposed "an international medium of exchange," something he had steadfastly opposed when Keynes had championed it, "to supplement IMF resources." The British loan had helped tremendously (though White had denied before the Senate Banking Committee in June 1945 that Britain even needed any special transitional assistance); the Marshall Plan had helped as well. "[B]ut these efforts are not enough to compensate for the losses sustained by the world because of the split of One World into at least two."[59]

White's hopes for a postwar Soviet-American alliance, outlined in an earlier sharply worded unpublished essay condemning American and Western hypocrisy toward Russia, were by this time in tatters.[60] "I doubt if any responsible official of the member governments [of the IMF] in the spring of 1944 believed that by 1948—only three years after the cessation of hostilities—the tensions between certain of the major powers would have been so pronounced and that the world, instead of drawing together during these years, would have moved so precipitously toward a split," he wrote.[61] Disillusioned with a "Democratic Party [that] can no longer fight for peace and a better America," he placed his hopes for a reversal of growing Soviet-American hostility in Henry Wallace, whom he passionately supported, as he had Bob La Follette in 1924, as the Progressive Party presidential candidate.[62] For his part, Wallace—whose campaign was, in his own words, "dedicated to the proposition that the Russians earnestly wanted peace"—intended to bring White back to political life as his Treasury Secretary.[63] Kennan later remarked scathingly, presumably with White in mind, that "nowhere in Washington had the hopes entertained for postwar collaboration with Russia been more elaborate, more naive, or more tenaciously (one might say almost ferociously) pursued than in the Treasury Department."[64]

In August 1947, White was interviewed by the FBI for two hours regarding his relationship with Greg and Helen Silvermaster, George Silverman, Lud Ullmann, William Taylor, Harold Glasser, Sol Adler, Sonya Gold, and Lauchlin Currie. In early September, he suffered a severe heart attack. While bedridden at his new home in New York in October, White received a grand jury summons from a federal marshal. His wife sent back a letter with a doctor's note indicating that White was too ill to attend. By his brother's account, White was confined to his bed until December.[65] He ultimately testified on March 24 and 25, 1948. White admitted that he had had a "general conversation" with Coe about Coe's own earlier grand jury testimony, and another with Silverman about his FBI interview and upcoming grand jury appearance. Unaware of Bentley's and Chambers' FBI statements and grand jury testimony about him, he would surely have been shocked to learn that the prosecutor knew that White had called Silverman and had asked to see him: it meant his phone was being tapped.[66] The tap was inadmissible in court, however, and could not have been used to prosecute him. Bentley's testimony also offered no material corroboration of her claims against White. The grand jury ultimately lacked the hard evidence to indict White.

Bentley made her dramatic first appearance before the House Un-American Activities Committee on July 31, and would testify four more times through August 11. On day one she was asked about the members and activities of the Silvermaster group. After naming Ullmann and Adler she was asked if there were others from the Treasury. "Yes," she replied: "Harry Dexter White." White was the most senior of the thirty former government officials she went on to name.[67]

Was White a Communist? she was asked. "I don't know whether Mr. White was a card-carrying Communist or not." What was the extent of his role with the group? "He gave information to Mr. Silvermaster which was relayed to me." Did White know where the information was going? "I know that both the Silvermasters and Ullmann knew exactly where it was going. From what they said, Mr. White knew where it was going but preferred not to mention the fact." Did others besides Lauchlin Currie try to place ring members in specific government positions? "Mr. White, of course, helped get people into place."

The media was now in a tizzy; White was pressed to respond. "This is the most fantastic thing I have ever heard of," he said by phone of Bentley's testimony. "I have never heard of the woman before. I am shocked." He would ask the committee for permission to testify and "refute these charges."[68]

Chambers went before the committee six times in August. On the first day, August 3, he was asked about his 1939 meeting with Berle in which he had named Communists in the government. Had he named Harry Dexter White? "No," Chambers responded, "because at that time I thought that I had broken Mr. White away, and it was about 4 years later that I first told the FBI about Mr. White." Did he tell the FBI because he had become convinced White had not broken away? "Yes." Was White a Communist? "I can't say positively that he was a registered member of the Communist Party, but he certainly was a fellow traveler so far within the fold that his not being a Communist would be a mistake on both sides."[69]

Chambers' testimony on White upped the ante on Bentley's insofar as he claimed to have known White personally. Chambers' claims regarding Alger Hiss were also explosive; the subsequent legal confrontation between the two would make both into household names. The president himself, now in the midst of a tough election campaign, famously reacted by dismissing the investigations as a Republican "red herring."

The stage was now set for White's own dramatic committee appearance. Though accomplished in the art of congressional testimony, White was used to parrying attacks against Treasury policy, and not against his integrity and patriotism. This was to be the most momentous confrontation of his life.

On the morning of August 13, White, his chichi swirled tie standing out against a gray three-piece pinstripe suit, entered the packed committee room with cameras flashing. Facing the committee in front of a bevy of microphones, he raised his right hand and took the required oath. In an opening statement, he set out to establish himself as a loyal American in the Progressive tradition:

> I have read in the newspapers charges that have been made against me by a Miss Elizabeth Bentley, and a Mr. Whittaker Chambers. I am coming

before you because I think it is important that the truth be made known to the committee and to the public. . . .

I should like to state at the start that I am not now and never have been a Communist, nor even close to becoming one; that I cannot recollect ever knowing either a Miss Bentley or a Mr. Whittaker Chambers. . . .

The press reported that the witnesses claim that I helped to obtain key posts for persons I knew were engaged in espionage work to help them in that work. That allegation is unqualifiedly false. . . .

The principles in which I believe, and by which I live, make it impossible for me to ever do a disloyal act or anything against the interests of our country. . . .

My creed is the American creed. I believe in freedom of religion, freedom of speech, freedom of thought, freedom of the press, freedom of criticism, and freedom of movement. I believe in the goal of equality of opportunity. . . .

I believe in the right and duty of every citizen to work for, to expect, and to obtain an increasing measure of political, economic, and emotional security for all. I am opposed to discrimination in any form. . . .

I believe in the freedom of choice of one's representatives in Government, untrammeled by machine guns, secret police, or a police state.

I am opposed to arbitrary and unwarranted use of power or authority from whatever source or against any individual or group.

I believe in a government of law, not of men, where law is above any man, and not any man above the law.

I consider these principles sacred. I regard them as the basic fabric of our American way of life, and I believe in them as living realities, and not as mere words or paper.

That is my creed, . . .

I am ready for any questions you may wish to ask.

The gallery broke into applause.

White was on friendly turf. The committee had by this time culti-vated a public reputation for unseemly grandstanding, and White played this to his advantage. Despite his well-earned reputation for prickliness, he studiously avoided confrontation with his accusers—for a time.

Did White know Whittaker Chambers? "To the best of my recollection I remember no such name," he responded. Did White ever go into Nathan Gregory Silvermaster's basement? Yes, they played Ping-Pong there.

The chairman pounced: hadn't White suffered a severe heart attack, and asked the committee for five or ten minutes rest after each hour of testimony? "For a person who had a severe heart condition," Parnell Thomas observed, "you certainly can play a lot of sports."

"The heart attack which I suffered was last year. I am speaking of playing ping-pong . . . many years prior to that," White corrected. "I hope that clears that up, Mr. Chairman."

More applause.

Had White noticed any photographic equipment in the basement? "I did not, but the fact that I did not notice, does not mean that it was not there . . . it was a pretty cluttered up cellar, as I remember." Was Silvermaster a Communist? He had assured White that he wasn't; White believed him. "[But] I can well understand and thoroughly sympathize with the view," he added, "that if there is any slightest question of a man's being a Communist, he ought not to . . . hold a position where there was any confidential information passed . . . a mere suspicion was enough." And later: "I would not have employed anybody I knew or suspected to be a Communist to [a high] government post."

In contrast to the committee chairman, the committee's youngest member spoke sparingly and "stuck soberly to the business at hand."[70] Thirty-five-year-old freshman Republican Congressman Richard Nixon set his sights narrowly on setting White up for a perjury charge, prodding him to state categorically that he had never met Chambers. White stuck carefully to his prepared phrasing, offering repeatedly that he did not "recollect" having met him.

The committee pressed on with other names—Coe, Glasser, Perlo. White was directed to a list of names with blue checks next to them: which ones had White worked with?

"Red checks would be more appropriate," White offered acerbically. "I added it from your point of view," he directed to Thomas. White was back in familiar form.

Was White the author of the famous Morgenthau plan? John McDowell asked.

"Did you also hear," White responded, that "I was the author of the famous White plan, by chance?" McDowell tried to shift gears, but White wanted to go on. "I thought you asked a question," White insisted. "You would not ask immaterial questions."

Thomas tried to stop the applause.

"Mr. Chairman," F. Edward Hébert said angrily, "I suggest you instruct the witness that it is obvious that he is a great wit, that he is a great entertainer . . . but I would ask you to instruct the witness to answer the questions."[71] White ceased the barbs, and the hearing wound down without further event. The *New York Times* the next day drew a "sharp contrast" between the "outspoken" White and earlier witnesses, many of whom had invoked their Fifth Amendment privileges and refused to answer "pertinent questions."[72] White had gone so far as to suggest that the hearings were akin to unconstitutional "star chamber proceedings," bringing forth rebukes from both Thomas and Nixon.[73]

White left Washington for New York by train immediately following his testimony. He saw his doctor in New York the following day, August 14, and then boarded another train bound for his summer home in Fitzwilliam, New Hampshire. En route, he suffered terrible chest pains—it was much like Keynes's journey from Savannah to Washington two years earlier. The next day, August 15, local doctors diagnosed a severe heart attack; nothing, they said, could be done. The following evening White was dead.

Conspiracy stories began to circulate almost immediately. White had been liquidated by Soviet intelligence. His death had been elaborately faked. He had fled to Uruguay. None of the tales had the slimmest reed of hard evidence to back them.

HUAC naturally came in for harsh media criticism in the wake of White's fatal coronary, as the strain of the hearings appeared to be the proximate cause. On the surface, at least, the White case itself was now dead. But more was to emerge.

On January 25, 1950, Alger Hiss was sentenced to five years in prison for perjury. Truman, who had publicly attacked the espionage investigations, now conceded in private that "the s.o.b. . . . is guilty as hell."[74] Key to the case had been papers Whittaker Chambers had squirreled away in early 1938 as a "life preserver" in preparation for his defection from the Soviet underground. Originally intended to dissuade potential attackers "should the party move against [his] life,"[75] the papers were surrendered to Hiss's lawyers during pretrial discovery in November 1948; Hiss in turn asked his lawyers to surrender the papers to the Department of Justice. These included sixty-five pages of copies of State Department documents, shown to have been typed on Hiss's typewriter, and four pages of summaries in Hiss's handwriting.

The next day, January 26, 1950, Richard Nixon revealed on the floor of the House that he had since December 1948 been holding "photostatic copies of eight pages of documents in the handwriting of Mr. White which Mr. Chambers turned over to the Justice Department on November 17, 1948."[76] Nixon proceeded to read from the pages.

The original documents comprised a four-page, double-sided memorandum, written in White's hand on yellow-lined paper, with material dated from January 10 to February 15, 1938, that had been part of Chambers' "life preserver."[77] Handwriting analysis by the FBI and the Veterans Administration confirmed White's authorship.[78]

The memo is a mixture of concise information and commentary on Treasury and State Department positions related to foreign policy and military matters. European economic and political developments are covered, including revelations from the U.S. ambassador to France (and former ambassador to the Soviet Union), William Bullitt, on his private discussions with French political leaders over their intentions toward Russia and Germany. Possible American actions against Japan, such as a trade embargo or an asset freeze, are outlined, and Japanese military protection of their oil storage facilities is described. Personal directives from the president to the Treasury Secretary are revealed. White makes clear that he is recording confidential information: he states explicitly that the Treasury economic warfare plan for Japan, called for by the president, "remains unknown outside of Treasury."

In August 1951, Bentley and Chambers went before the Senate Internal Security Subcommittee (the McCarran Committee), testifying against White once again. The following year, Chambers would publish his explosive autobiography, *Witness*, which provided a full narrative of his dealings with White. White's name would again become front-page news in November 1953, when Attorney General Brownell would raise it in a full frontal public attack on (now former president) Truman. "Harry Dexter White was a Russian spy," Brownell stated categorically. "He smuggled secret documents to Russian agents for transmission to Moscow. Harry Dexter White was known to be a Communist agent by the very people who appointed him to the most sensitive position he ever held in Government service," that of IMF executive director. Truman was blindsided. "As soon as we found White was disloyal, we fired him," he shot back. He later fudged this to the claim that "White was fired by resignation."

The enormous discord within the government over the White and Hiss cases stemmed at least partly from the fact that U.S. counter-intelligence officials actually knew much more about the systematic nature of Soviet espionage than they chose to share with the White House. Incredibly, their trove of striking evidence would remain unknown to the public until half a century after the end of the Second World War.

Following the outbreak of the war in 1939, the United States began collecting copies of all cables going into and out of the country—as was standard wartime practice around the world. The Soviet Embassy in Washington and the consulates in New York and San Francisco were fully aware that their cable traffic was being monitored, but raised no objections. The complex Russian cable cipher system, known as a one-time pad system, was theoretically unbreakable.

Colonel Carter Clarke was undeterred. As chief of the U.S. Army's Special Branch, he reacted to rumors in early 1943 of secret Nazi-Soviet peace negotiations by ordering the elite code breakers of the Signal Intelligence Service to study the cables for evidence of such talks. The name given to the top secret project was Venona.

The task was daunting. But after examining thousands of cables, the American code crackers were able to identify a procedural mistake in the ciphering that made it vulnerable to cracking. By the time they successfully decoded the first message, however, it was 1946 and the war was over. Yet what they found was still important and unexpected. The cables, rather than going between Soviet diplomats in the United States and their Foreign Affairs Commissariat in Moscow, went between U.S.-based Russian intelligence field officers and the head of the KGB's Foreign Intelligence Directorate. They contained no evidence of Nazi-Soviet peace overtures, but instead copious evidence of a systematic Soviet espionage operation within the United States.

One of the first cables deciphered was a 1944 message from New York to Moscow showing that the Soviets had infiltrated the United States' highly classified atomic bomb project. By 1948, U.S. military intelligence had learned that the Soviets had recruited and installed spies in every diplomatically and militarily important U.S. government department and agency. At this point the cable-cracking effort was still tightly held, and only a small number of FBI and CIA officials were in the loop; the CIA did not even begin to receive copies of the decoded messages until 1953. Whereas most of the critical decoding work took place between 1947 and 1952, the effort to crack all the susceptible cables actually continued on through 1980. After many more years of intense private and congressional efforts to open the files to public scrutiny, scholars finally got their first glimpse in 1995. Over the following two years, all the nearly three thousand Venona messages, more than five thousand pages of text, were released by the National Security Agency.[79] The first books analyzing the intelligence trove only began appearing in 1999.[80]

Truman, who was deeply mistrustful of Hoover, had been unaware that Soviet cable traffic was an important source behind the FBI's espionage reports. Precisely why is undocumented, although Army Chief of Staff Omar Bradley was known to have been concerned about White House press leaks, and may have decided on that basis to keep the existence of the Venona Project hidden from the president himself. Such powerful corroborating evidence for Bentley and Chambers' claims would presumably have led the president to act more aggressively.[81] How much a difference it might have made in White's case, however, is unclear, as the first internal FBI memo identifying White in a decrypted cable does not appear until October 16, 1950.[82]

The testimony of confessed Soviet agents like Chambers and Bentley is one thing, but a mass of intercepted coded Soviet communications is quite another; it is clearly more probative. Eight of the individuals named by Chambers to Berle in 1939 appear in the Venona cables.[83] (Five others are corroborated through other evidence.)[84] Eleven of the fourteen individuals identified by Bentley in 1945 as being part of the Silvermaster group—including Silvermaster, Ullmann, Silverman, Coe, Gold, Currie, Adler, and White—appear in the cables. Eighteen cables refer to White, by his various code names, all dated between March 16, 1944, and January 8, 1946.[85] White's Venona code names also appear independently in the notes of former KGB archivist Vasili Mitrokhin, who, incredibly, managed to smuggle six large cases of Soviet foreign intelligence out of its offices; he and the papers were exfiltrated from Russia to Britain by MI6 (British Military Intelligence) in 1992.[86]

Cables dated April 29, 1944, and January 18, 1945, report information from White on high-level administration discussions of a possible multibillion-dollar loan to the Soviet Union. The second cable in particular provides evidence of White coordinating with his handlers, in this case Silverman, his pursuit of Russian interests at the highest levels of the U.S. government. The Soviets had on January 3, 1945, formally requested a $6 billion loan at 2¼ percent interest repayable over thirty years; White successfully lobbied Morgenthau a week later to petition the president for more money at better terms: $10 billion at 2 percent interest repayable over thirty-five years.[87] "In RICHARD'S [White's] words," reports the January 18 cable to Moscow, "we could get a loan under more favorable conditions" than Moscow was seeking. FDR, however, never approved a loan.

Another cable on the same day provides corroborating evidence for the allegations that White used his position to secure appointments for other underground members. "According to ROBERT'S [Silvermaster's] report," the cable reads, "he may be presented with an opportunity of obtaining from RICHARD [White] ROUBLE'S [probably Harold Glasser's] appointment to RICHARD'S post, as the latter will soon be appointed assistant secretary."

Between White's House and Senate testimonies on Bretton Woods in the spring of 1945, White had been sent to San Francisco as a technical adviser to the U.S. delegation. State Department official Alger Hiss, who also appears as a source in the cables, was the conference's acting secretary-general. On April 6, a week after Stettinius invited White to join the delegation in San Francisco, Akhmerov received instructions from Moscow to "make arrangements with ROBERT [Silvermaster] about maintaining contact with RICHARD [White] and PILOT [White's assistant William Ludwig Ullmann] in BABYLON [San Francisco]."[88] A month later, cables began arriving in Moscow from San Francisco. "Truman and Stettinius," a May 5 message from KGB officer Vladimir Pravdin reports White stating, "want to achieve the success of the conference at any price." The United States, White told Pravdin, "will agree on the [Soviet] veto." Other deciphered fragments of cables sent between May 4 and June 8 reveal White discussing the views of other American delegation members, such as Leo Pasvolsky, Assistant Secretary of State Nelson Rockefeller, Senator Arthur Vandenberg, and Congressman Charles Eaton, and later evaluating Latin American delegates (one of which White appears to call "a fool"). Pravdin was in San Francisco working undercover as a TASS news agency journalist, and what White knew of Pravdin's primary occupation is unclear. But White was certainly aware that what he was telling Pravdin was not meant for the press.

Whittaker Chambers had provided hard evidence that White was writing down and distributing classified information. KGB files only first seen by Western scholars in the 1990s record Silvermaster telling Akhmerov in mid-1944 that "'J' [White] knows where his info. goes, which is precisely why he transmits it in the first place,"[89] and the Venona decrypts suggest that White was passing official documents. One cable dated August 4–5, 1944, has White telling a Russian agent code-named "KOL'TsOV," whom the FBI concluded was likely Nikolai Fedorovich Chechulin,[90] a State Bank deputy president and Bretton Woods delegate, that "attaining the document [is] extremely risky." Pravdin, according to KGB archives, wrote to Moscow on October 29, 1945, that White was "convinced that the question of his dismissal is a matter of weeks or months," and complained that White was no longer passing "information or documents." White was now only "giving advice on major political and economic matters." His Treasury colleague Coe was also "hiding from" Pravdin. "Nobody [in the Silvermaster group] . . . wanted to work" any longer.[91]

The Russians with whom White met, like Pravdin, all had cover identities, and the Silvermaster contacts, according to Bentley, had told White that his information was destined for the Communist Party USA (CPUSA), rather than the Soviet underground. White's handlers clearly sought to provide him with a degree of plausible deniability, yet the Venona decrypts leave little doubt that White was well aware of where his information was headed. A deciphered portion of the KOL'TsOV cable reports: "As regards the technique of further work with us [White] said his wife was . . . ready for any self-sacrifice." White "himself did not think about his personal security, but a compromise . . . would lead to a political scandal and . . . the discredit of all supporters of the new course, therefore he would have to be very cautious." The cable further suggests that White took steps to hide his meetings, as he did with Chambers. "[White] has no suitable apartment for a permanent meeting place[;] all his friends are family people," a term referring to followers of the "new course." White suggested that "[m]eetings could be held at their houses in such a way that one meeting devolved on each every 4–5 months. He proposes infrequent conversations lasting up to half an hour while driving in his automobile."

The decrypts further suggest that White's wife used her husband's position as a bargaining lever to benefit her family. According to a cable titled "FINANCIAL ASSISTANCE FOR 'RICHARD'" dated November 20, 1944, Terry Ann White told Silvermaster that her husband was looking for a job in the private sector "since this would relieve them of heavy expenses." Silvermaster took the hint, and "told [White's] wife, who knows about her husband's participation with us, that we would willingly have helped them and that in view of all the circumstances would not allow them to leave CARTHAGE"; that is, Washington. Silvermaster thought "that [White] would have refused a regular payment but might accept gifts as a mark of our gratitude." Akhmerov told Silvermaster "that in his opinion we would agree to provide for [White's] daughter's education," expenses for which "may come up to two thousand a year," but "definitively advised [Silvermaster, Ullmann] and the rest against attempting to offer [White] assistance" directly. White, the cable closed, "has taken the offer of assistance favourably."

In 1953, Whittaker Chambers had written that Harry White's "role as a Soviet agent was second in importance only to that of Alger Hiss—if, indeed, it was second." White, he said, had been "the perfect bureaucrat," rising under the radar to a position where he was able "to shape

U.S. Government policy in the Soviet government's interest."[92] Reviewing the Venona cables over fifty years after Chambers and Bentley made their startling espionage claims to the FBI, a U.S. Senate commission led by the late Daniel Patrick Moynihan (D-NY) concluded in 1997 that "the complicity of Alger Hiss of the State Department seems settled. As does that of Harry Dexter White of the Treasury Department."[93]

CHAPTER 11

Epilogue

The sterling crisis of 1947 summoned forth howls of execration in Britain against American dollar diplomacy and its immiserating effects. "Not many people in this country believe the Communist thesis that it is the deliberate and conscious aim of American policy to ruin Britain and everything that Britain stands for in the world," wrote the *Economist*. "But the evidence can certainly be read that way. And if every time that aid is extended, conditions are attached which make it impossible for Britain ever to escape the necessity of going back for still more aid, to be obtained with still more self-abasement and on still more crippling terms, then the result will certainly be what the Communists predict."[1]

The loan agreement, the terms of which had been imposed in accordance with the pre-Marshall American foreign economic policy objective of securing free multilateral trade at fixed exchange rates, had backfired. With sterling convertibility an abject failure, the United States abruptly discarded the diplomatic arsenal built up under White and Hull, which had been fashioned around the belief that Britain was a serious economic and political rival. This had been shown to be not only ridiculous, but a severe impediment to what was clearly now the critical objective: bolstering Britain, and western Europe, in the looming cold war with the Soviet Union. "The emergency in Britain has shocked this country," the *New York Times* wrote. "It has suddenly projected before our imagination the picture of a world without British power, without the balance wheel of British moderation, without the weight of Britain in the democratic scale. The consequences to us of such a void in the economic and political universe in which we live are as alarming as was the fear of British defeat which impelled us to help Britain long before we were forced into open war."[2]

The devastation of the war left the world starved of dollars, the only reliable surrogate for gold, and dangerously susceptible to whatever economic bug afflicted the United States at any given moment. In 1946, it was inflation in the wake of relaxed price controls, which drove up European import costs. In 1948 and '49, it was recession, which depressed U.S. import demand. In mid-1949, the IMF directors wrote a poignant epitaph to their wartime hopes: they had to confess that after four years of peace "dependence on bilateral trade and inconvertible currencies is far greater than before the war."[3]

Britain continued tightening currency controls, but could not stop the drain of gold and dollar reserves. On September 18, 1949, Britain devalued sterling by 30 percent; a pound would now buy only $2.80, rather than $4.03. The countless hours of debate between White and Keynes over the IMF's role in a country's exchange-parity change had in the end amounted to idle chatter; Britain gave the IMF a mere twenty-four hours notice of the devaluation. Twenty-three more countries devalued within a week; seven would follow soon after.

The devaluations helped attenuate the dollar shortage. In the case of Britain, reserve loss halted and reserves tripled over the next two years. Still, the United States continued to run a current account surplus; $3 billion annualized in the first half of 1950.[4] A European Payments Union was implemented that year, with U.S. blessing and financial support, to break down intra-European trade and payments barriers. In many ways, the eighteen-member EPU looked like a European IMF, though its purpose was to promote European trade by discriminating against the scarce dollar, rather than promoting global multilateral trade. Though launched with an initial two-year remit, the EPU carried on until 1958. The IMF in 1952 lamented that there had been "little secure or sustained progress toward the Fund objectives of unimpeded multilateral trade and the general convertibility of currencies," yet intra-European trade was now growing rapidly.[5]

The Suez crisis of 1956 served as a sharp and shocking reminder to the British that their formerly ample room for diplomatic and military maneuver on the world stage was now severely constrained by their need for dollars. In the wake of Egyptian President Gamal Abder

Nasser's nationalization of the Suez Canal on July 26, the British, French, and Israelis secretly conspired to invade Egypt and remove Nasser from power. The Israelis attacked the Sinai on October 29, with preorchestrated British and French support coming right behind. The assault was a military success, but a diplomatic disaster. An angry President Dwight Eisenhower and his cabinet, determined to slap down Britain's brazen and underhanded challenge to U.S. interests in the Middle East, at the center of which was keeping Soviet forces out of the region, applied dollar diplomacy with a ruthlessness that went well beyond anything ever tried by Harry White or Henry Morgenthau. The United States used its control of the IMF to deny Britain the dollars it needed to counter a run on sterling and blocked its efforts to secure emergency oil supplies. A disbelieving Britain, which was prepared to defy the United Nations, was in short order forced into a humiliating withdrawal by the prospect of an economic catastrophe inflicted on it by its most important ally.[6]

Though Britain, France, and Germany all experienced economic and political setbacks and crises over the course of the decade, growth resumed, trade soared, and—on the backs of large-scale American foreign aid and military expenditures—the dollar shortage dissipated. Fourteen EPU members declared current account convertibility on December 27, 1958. The quarter-century period from 1945 to 1971 is typically referred to as "the Bretton Woods era," yet the monetary regime called for in the agreements could not be said to have become operative until 1961, the year in which the first nine European countries, plus Peru and Saudi Arabia, formally adopted the convertibility commitments required by IMF Article VIII (bringing the global total to twenty countries). And by this time it had already come under pressure in ways that the broad mass of commentators had not envisioned.

Though in the immediate aftermath of the war the United States did indeed run the large balance-of-payments surpluses that most had feared, thereby worsening the global dollar shortage, those surpluses began falling away in short order. Excepting a brief period around the Suez crisis, the U.S. current account with western Europe was on a pronounced downward trend throughout most of the 1950s, falling into a large deficit at the end of the decade. U.S. exports of capital and economic aid were sustained throughout most of the decade at levels well in excess of the surpluses the country ran with the world as a whole, the gap showing up in two important places: rapidly rising foreign holdings of dollars, and huge U.S. gold losses as foreigners repatriated capital to take advantage of higher European interest rates. So as the United States solved one global problem, a global scarcity of dollars, it began creating another one—a scarcity of gold with which to pay back foreign holders of excess dollars.

Harry White, simply stated, had been wrong. The United States could not simultaneously keep the world adequately supplied with dollars *and* sustain the large gold reserves required by its gold-convertibility commitment. In fact, no country could perform such a feat with its national currency. The logic was laid bare by Belgian-born American economist Robert Triffin in his now-famous 1959 congressional testimony. There were, he explained, "absurdities associated with the use of *national* currencies as *international* reserves."[7] It constituted a "built-in de-stabilizer" in the world monetary system. The December 1958 European convertibility pledges, far from representing the final critical step into a new monetary era, "merely return[ed] the world to the unorganized and nationalistic gold exchange standard of the late 1920s."[8]

When the world accumulates dollars as reserves, rather than gold, it puts the United States in an impossible position. Foreigners lend the excess dollars back to the United States. This increases U.S. short-term liabilities, which implies that the United States should boost its gold reserves to maintain its convertibility pledge. But there's the rub: if it does so, the global dollar "shortage" persists; if it doesn't, the United States ultimately winds up hopelessly trying to guarantee more and more dollars with less and less gold. There is no stable, durable circumstance in which the United States can emit enough dollars to satisfy the world's trading needs *and* few enough to ensure that they can always be redeemed for a fixed amount of gold. The United States is ultimately damned if it meets the world's liquidity requirements and damned if it doesn't—as is the rest of the world. This became known as "the Triffin dilemma."

If concerted international action were not taken to change the system, Triffin explained, a deadly dynamic would set in. The United States would need to deflate, devalue, or impose trade and exchange restrictions to prevent the loss of all its gold reserves. This could cause a global financial panic and trigger protectionist measures around the world. Harry White's creation, in Triffin's rendering, was an economic apocalypse in the making.

What could prevent this? British Prime Minister Harold Macmillan told President John F. Kennedy in 1962 that "if the gold price were [doubled] to $70 an ounce, most of the difficulties would be over and done with."[9] Though not a solution to Triffin's dilemma, this might well have bought time for an orderly transition out of Harry White's system. But like Churchill in the early 1920s, Kennedy would not countenance devaluation; he viewed it as a crisis state. Austerity, likewise, was not in the cards. Instead, the United States resorted to plugging the dikes with taxes, regulations, gold market interventions, central bank swap arrangements, and moral suasion directed at banks and foreign governments—just as Triffin had anticipated.

Not every government was wholly cooperative. French President Charles de Gaulle blasted the "monumentally over-privileged position that the world had conceded to the American currency since the two world wars had left it standing alone amid the ruins of the others." The world, he said, had been given "no choice but to accept the international monetary system known as the 'gold-exchange standard,' according to which the dollar was automatically regarded as the equivalent of gold." The U.S. "reluctance to forgo its hegemony had led it continually . . . to issue dollars, which it used for lending to other countries, for paying its debts, or for buying goods, well in excess of the true value of its reserves." Moreover, the United States used its dominant position at the IMF to keep its trading partners from exercising their right to redeem excess dollars for gold. In September 1963, De Gaulle ordered the Bank of France "to demand from the Americans that eighty per cent of what they owed us by virtue of the balance of payments should henceforth be repaid in gold."[10]

De Gaulle gave a famous press conference on February 4, 1965, in which he elaborated the economic logic behind his conclusion that the dollar could never act as "an impartial and international trade medium . . . it is in fact a credit instrument reserved for one state only."[11] De Gaulle was no economist, so it was apparent that the acuity of his analysis owed to someone schooled in the art. Though he denied being "in any degree scriptwriter to General De Gaulle," this was unmistakably Keynes's old intellectual sparring partner over German World War One reparations, Jacques Rueff.[12] Rueff became, with Triffin, the most notable prophet of doom during the 1960s preaching the inevitable implosion of the dollar-based Bretton Woods system.[13] Though the diagnosis of the two was identical, their cures could not have been more different.

Triffin harked directly back to Keynes's "bancor" alternative to the White Plan: a new international reserve currency managed by the IMF. He suggested some bureaucratic safeguards against the potential inflationary bias of the scheme, but was otherwise satisfied simply to quote Keynes at length.[14] Rueff, in stark contrast, advocated a return to the pre-1914 classical gold standard. He was adamant that he had "no religious belief in gold"; other commodities might in principle do as well, even if gold had history on its side. It was rather the *mechanism* of a genuine gold standard that was needed to ensure that global imbalances were automatically restrained by credit expansion in the surplus country and contraction in the deficit country—or put alternatively, "to prevent the home population from consuming a part of domestic production that must be made available for export" in order to counteract a payments deficit.[15] Triffin's (and Keynes's) alternative of a new international reserve unit, in Rueff's view, represented a "purely arbitrary creation of means of foreign payment"; or put more bluntly, "nothingness dressed up as currency."[16] It had a built-in inflationary dynamic that no bureaucracy would be able to control. For his part, Triffin believed that Rueff's vision "impl[ied] the total surrender of national sovereignty . . . over all forms of trade and payment restrictions, and even over exchange rates. Such surrenders," he said, were "utterly inconceivable today in favor of a mere nineteenth century *laissez faire*, unconcerned with national levels of employment and economic activity."[17]

The political stage was now set for a reform to Bretton Woods that could mean all things to all governments, but nothing to the markets. This was the IMF's Special Drawing Right, or SDR, approved by the fund's board of governors in 1968.[18] For supporters of Keynes's bancor vision, the SDR was a first small step on the road to a truly international fiat currency. For France and opponents of the dollar-based Bretton Woods system, the new gold-linked instrument was a step toward dethroning the dollar and restoring gold as the primary international reserve. And it was for the United States a means of buying time to halt the drain on American gold reserves—an expedient to supplement the new policy of limiting gold transactions to monetary authorities, which could ostensibly be bullied into not converting dollars for gold.

By the time SDRs were activated the following year, the world was already well on its way to resolving one of the main problems that motivated their creation: a supposed shortage of international liquidity—in actuality, U.S. dollars. Inflation climbed rapidly under the Nixon administration, reaching nearly 6 percent in 1970, and world dollar reserves rose sharply. Few were any longer clamoring for SDR dollar surrogates; there was more than enough of the real stuff to go around. The problem was now whether an ever more abundant dollar could remain credibly moored to a fixed quantity of gold, American stocks of which had tumbled in recent years from over 50 percent of dollars held by foreign central banks to a mere 22 percent. As French Finance Minister Valéry Giscard d'Estaing would put it in 1970, the United States "could not eternally ask people to set their watches by a defective clock." The Nixon administration had either to sublimate its domestic economic agenda, and its pricey military prerogatives in places like Vietnam, to the needs of the Bretton Woods system, or to abandon the pretense that the dollar had an ordained privileged place in this architecture.

Fed officials warned that a dollar confidence crisis could break out at any time. But as Paul Volcker, then undersecretary for monetary affairs at Treasury, later reflected, "Presidents—certainly Johnson and Nixon—did not want to hear that their options were limited by the weakness of the dollar." Nixon certainly had no attachment to the arcane monetary contraptions fashioned by Harry White, whom he had long been convinced was a traitor.

By May 1971, pressure on the dollar had become too much for Germany to bear. The deutsche mark, revalued in 1961 and 1969, had been driven further upward by relentless capital inflows—$9.6 billion ($54 billion in today's dollars) since 1970. After a bruising internal debate, the German government floated the mark on May 10. While this succeeded in curbing speculative flows into Germany, it did not halt flows out of the United States. Nixon's Treasury Secretary John Connally, a self-proclaimed "bullyboy," angrily rejected suggestions from IMF managing director Pierre-Paul Schweitzer that the United States raise interest rates or devalue the dollar, instead blaming Japan, the newest destination for speculative capital in the wake of the mark's float, for its "controlled economy." Connally wanted the yen revalued. He argued publicly for greater access to foreign markets for U.S. goods, and privately that the United States "would have to revise its mutual security arrangements especially relating to Japan and Germany" to address its payments imbalance. Japan would not budge.

On August 6, a congressional subcommittee issued a report titled *Action Now to Strengthen the U.S. Dollar*, which, paradoxically, concluded that the dollar needed to be weakened. Dollar dumping accelerated. France sent a battleship to take home French gold from the New York Fed's vaults. Debate in Washington over how to respond was heated. Nixon opted for what Connally convinced him would be seen as a bold and decisive move. On August 15, the president went on national television to announce his New Economic Policy. In addition to tax cuts, a ninety-day wage and price freeze, and a 10 percent import surcharge, the gold window would be closed—the United States would no longer redeem foreign government dollar holdings. Schweitzer had been given a mere hour's advance warning—a clear breach of American IMF obligations.[19] Connally followed on by making the president's priorities brutally clear to a group of European officials, telling them that the dollar was "our currency, but your problem."

The Bretton Woods monetary system was finished. Though the bond between money and gold had been fraying for nearly sixty years, it had throughout most of the world and two and a half millennia of history been one that had only been severed as a temporary expedient in times of crisis.[20] This time was different. The dollar was in essence the last ship moored to gold, with all the rest of world's currencies on board, and the United States was cutting the anchor and sailing off for good. This should, Harry White had believed, have meant the end of the dollar's international hegemony. "There are some who believe that a universally accepted currency not redeemable in gold . . . is compatible with the existence of national sovereignties," he wrote in 1942. "A little thought should, however, reveal the impracticability of any such notion. Any foreign country is willing to accept dollars in payment of goods or services today because it is certain that it could convert those dollars in terms of gold at a fixed price."[21] The world would face rough waters before it would find out whether he was right. Would the world lapse into a 1930s-style spiral of protectionism? Or could an international monetary system of sorts be made to work without gold?

Schweitzer angered the administration by taking to the airwaves himself to argue that the system could be sustained through a general adjustment of the fixed exchange rates: "You might call it a devaluation of the dollar. You might call it a realignment of other currencies."[22] Following a difficult two days of bargaining among the Group of 10 ministers at Washington's Smithsonian Institution in December, Schweitzer got his wish. On average, the dollar was devalued by about 10 percent, with the deutsche mark appreciating 13.57 percent, the yen 16.9 percent, and gold 8.57 percent (to $38 an ounce). Permissible currency movements around the new parities were expanded from 1 percent to 2.25 percent. Nixon hailed the accord as "the most significant monetary agreement in the history of the world."[23]

The disappointing history of monetary agreements notwithstanding, this was nonsense. Nixon faced an election the following November, and was not about to tie his fortunes to the mast of new dollar parities. Appointed Treasury Secretary in June of 1972, George Shultz, an opponent of fixed exchange rates, continued his predecessor's blunt disownment of American obligations to the system: "Santa Claus is dead," he pronounced.[24] The president successfully bludgeoned Fed chairman Arthur Burns into cutting interest rates, which fueled monetary growth around the world. In January 1973, two months after his thumping defeat of Democratic challenger George McGovern, Nixon ended wage and price controls; dollar outflows resumed. Volcker secretly flew to Tokyo and Bonn to negotiate new parities, but Shultz opposed the administration undertaking any obligation to defend them, which would have interfered with his priority of eliminating capital controls. In tense multilateral discussions, the United States now took up the battle stance that Keynes and the British had adopted, and Harry White resolutely opposed, at Bretton Woods: surplus countries should be forced to reduce their surplus positions. Congressmen even demanded that the formerly hated scarce-currency clause be invoked against countries such as Germany and Japan. Whether

surplus countries were prudent and responsible, or obstinate and selfish, it seemed, depended on whether one's country was one. Such a
stance did not bode well for any sort of durable international monetary
cooperation.

In March 1973, the G-10 formally acknowledged the end of nearly
two years of tortuous efforts to reestablish a world of fixed exchange
parities. Not a single IMF member was any longer in conformity
with the Articles of Agreement. The United States refused to support Schweitzer for another term, and pushed him out in September, over vigorous European objection (which, in the case of France,
appeared to be more about bullying American form than the substance
of Schweitzer himself). The new managing director, former Dutch
Finance Minister Johannes Witteveen, initiated the IMF's historic
break from its founding principle of fixed (but adjustable) exchange
rates. "In the present situation," Witteveen said in January 1974, "a
large measure of floating is unavoidable and indeed desirable."[25] Germany and France, however, never abandoned their determination to
fix rates at the European level—the creation of the euro in 1999 marking the culmination of decades of painstaking political effort to make
such a system indelible, and moreover to establish a firmer foundation for deeper European political integration. By 2011, however, the
continental debt crisis had shown that monetary union did not itself
substitute for a viable political mechanism to orchestrate the mutual
accommodation of surplus and deficit countries; indeed, it made such
a mechanism a necessary condition for maintaining the union.

In the context of 1973, not everyone considered the political failure of the G-10 governments to agree on a new mechanism for stabilizing exchange rates to be a bad thing. Ten years prior, while Triffin
had been advocating a new international reserve currency and Rueff
a return to the classical gold standard, University of Chicago economist Milton Friedman had been preaching to Congress the benefits
of a floating dollar. Friedman shared Rueff's fondness for "a real gold
standard," in which economic "discipline was imposed by impersonal
forces which in turn reflected the realities of resources, tastes, and
technology," but considered the return to such discipline a political
pipe dream.[26] Instead, allowing the market to determine the level of
the dollar against other currencies would free U.S. policy makers to

pursue national economic objectives without having to obsess with balance-of-payments problems or having to appease foreign governments in endless negotiations.

Not all prominent economists who shared Friedman's moral and economic commitment to free enterprise, however, shared his sanguine view of floating exchange rates. Friedrich Hayek, who won the Nobel Prize in 1974, two years prior to Friedman, had argued as far back as 1937 that floating rates would lead to disastrously destabilizing capital flows. When rates were fixed on the classical gold standard, short-term capital movements "on the whole tended to relieve the strain set up by the original cause of a temporary adverse balance of payments."[27] This was because investors expected any deviations from exchange parities to be reversed in short order, creating profit opportunities for those who quickly bought low and sold high. If rates were variable, however, capital flows would tend to chase earlier flows, and thereby intensify exchange rate swings.[28]

"The frequency and increasing intensity of financial crises following the collapse of the Bretton Woods system suggests the costs of such a system to the world may have exceeded its benefits," observed Chinese central bank governor Zhou Xiaochuan in 2009. Supporters of Friedman would argue, however, that attempts to fix bilateral exchange rates under a fiat monetary system, with no gold anchor, do far more economic harm.[29] Both Friedman and Hayek despaired over the "stagflation"—low growth and high inflation—that overtook the world in the 1970s. Yet whereas Friedman blamed central banks for not restraining the growth of the money supply, Hayek argued that such indiscipline was inevitable when governments were unfettered by the sort of hard external constraints imposed by the gold standard; in 1976 he came out in favor of replacing monopoly central banks with competitive private currency issuers.[30]

Not surprisingly, Triffin's, Rueff's, and Hayek's radical alternatives to Bretton Woods—international money, a revived gold standard, and private money competition—were not congenial to governments, particularly that of the United States. But Friedman's monetarist ideas had legs; they did not threaten to make national central banks irrelevant. When President Jimmy Carter appointed Paul Volcker as Fed chairman in 1979, the time was ripe for the experiment. Inflation was soaring, reaching a high of 14.7 percent in 1980. Gold, which in many minds was still the ultimate store of value and means of payment, surged to a record $875 an ounce ($2,400 in today's dollars)—twenty-five times its official price a decade earlier. Oil-producing nations threatened to adopt dollar alternatives for pricing their product and denominating their monetary reserves.

A towering presence at six-foot-seven, Volcker set out to end inflation and the psychology that drove it by tightening the money supply and permitting market interest rates to rise to levels previously unimaginable in the United States. Though subjected to withering and sustained personal criticism, he allowed the Fed funds rate to soar to a high of 20 percent in June 1981. The country went into recession; unemployment mounted. The picture was worse abroad. A global dollar glut had fueled lending to poor countries in Latin America and elsewhere in the 1970s, underwritten by Citicorp chairman Walter Wriston's dictum that "countries don't go bankrupt." Yet with borrowing costs now soaring and commodity export prices plummeting, they did just that. The first major international debt crisis of the new fiat-money world was under way.

Keynes had famously remarked that "economists set themselves too easy, too useless a task if in tempestuous seasons they can only tell us that when the storm is past the ocean is flat again." Yet Volcker deliberately set sail into the storm, on the grounds that the tempest would only get worse if the government tried to avoid the choppy seas ahead. Inflation fell rapidly, down to an annualized 3.2 percent in 1983, a rate around which it began to stabilize, while economic growth resumed and jobs returned. Ultimate vindication would appear to have come in the form of the subsequent near-quarter-century stretch of relatively stable growth, underpinned by the Fed's mastery of consumer price inflation, mainly under the tutelage of Alan Greenspan.

A new age, dubbed "the Great Moderation," was declared by Greenspan's successor, Ben Bernanke, and others.[31] Harry White, it seemed, was wrong about gold; it was indeed, by all appearances, the barbarous relic that Keynes had tried to excise from man's monetary consciousness. Over the course of the 1990s, the world's central banks sold off large stocks of the relic, helping to drive its price down to $290 an ounce at the end of the millennium. The fiat dollar was king, as so many countries—from Korea to Russia to Brazil—would learn painfully at the hands of their foreign creditors, including the now widely reviled IMF. The answer, it seemed, was to accumulate more dollars. The method was to keep down the exchange rate and to generate trade surpluses.

China, the world's new rising economic power, began pegging its currency to the dollar in 1994. Voluntarily importing U.S. monetary policy had a compelling logic for a country rapidly integrating with the global economy, and conducting the vast bulk of its trade in dollars. It stuck with this policy even through the tumult of the Asian financial crisis of 1997 and 1998, in spite of widespread speculation that it would follow its neighbors and devalue. This earned it great praise from the United States government. "China, by maintaining its exchange rate policy," pronounced President Clinton's Treasury Secretary, Robert Rubin, in May of 1998, "has been an important island of stability in a turbulent region."[32]

The rising global trade imbalances of the past decade have been predominantly imbalances created by these two economic giants, today accounting for one-third of world GDP. As Triffin and Rueff would surely have anticipated, monetary troubles brewed. Dollars sent to China for merchandise came back overnight in the form of low-interest loans, and were then quickly recycled through the U.S. financial system to create more cheap credit. No force acted to reverse the growing Chinese trade surpluses or U.S. deficits—no dollar depreciation to make U.S. goods more competitive, and no gold outflow or Fed tightening to restrain the growth of U.S. credit. All forms of securitized credit—in particular, those related to housing—boomed. Gold prices also rose briskly, but these no longer held any meaning to policy makers.

China built up an astounding mountain of monetary reserves: $3.24 trillion in mid-2012, approximately 60 percent of which consisted of U.S. government securities. The United States, for its part, accumulated the world's largest international debt: $15.5 trillion. Each government eyes the size and trajectory of the two stockpiles with trepidation: the Chinese fear a collapse in the global purchasing power of their dollar hoard, the Americans a collapse in foreign funding. Larry Summers has called the standoff "a kind of balance of financial terror."[33] The two governments can find no cooperative means of reducing it.

In the 1940s, the United States pivoted from a stance of doggedly defending its creditor prerogatives under Morgenthau and White to one of cashing them in to revive global growth under Marshall and Clayton, partly because of a change in management, but mainly because of a rational recalibration of its interests in a changed geopolitical environment. In the here and now, the United States insists that the fault lies with its largest creditor, China, which continues to fix its exchange rate at an artificially low level. A practice praised by the U.S. Treasury Secretary in 1998, when the Chinese government was resisting downward market pressure on the renminbi, is now widely condemned as currency manipulation—as it was by Treasury Secretary nominee Timothy Geithner in 2009, when the Chinese government was resisting upward market pressure on its currency. Senators Charles Schumer and Lindsey Graham attacked the Chinese practice, declaring that "one of the fundamental tenets of free trade is that currencies should float." This contradicted not only the intellectual history of economics, but the tenet that guided the United States at Bretton Woods.[34]

There is a common thread running through White's blueprint for Bretton Woods in 1944, Nixon's closing of the gold window in 1971, Rubin's hailing of the Chinese currency peg in 1998, and Geithner's condemnation of it in 2009: whether the United States supports fixed or floating exchange rates at any given point in time is determined by which will give it a more competitive dollar. Whereas such elasticity of principle can be rationalized from a narrow perspective of U.S. national interest, it is more difficult to reconcile with enduring foreign confidence in a dollar-based global monetary system.

Not surprisingly, Chinese officials have rejected criticism of their policies and have pointed the finger at American profligacy and lax monetary controls. "The U.S. government has to come to terms with the painful fact that the good old days when it could just borrow its way out of messes of its own making are finally gone," thundered the state-run Xinhua news agency in August 2011. "China, the sole superpower's largest creditor, now has every right to demand that America address its structural debt problem and ensure the security of China's dollar denominated assets."[35] President Hu Jintao directed his concern at the Fed, though in more restrained terms: "The monetary policy of the United States has a major impact on global liquidity and capital flows and therefore the liquidity of the U.S. dollar should be kept at a reasonable and stable level." Hu noted, however, that the undesirable global repercussions of Fed actions derived from flaws in "the current international currency system," which was a "product of the past."[36] Governor Zhou, for his part, went further in explicitly recalling Triffin, whose analysis had suggested that no manner of American goodwill or prudence could rectify this fundamental problem.

Zhou called for a wholesale remaking of the international monetary system. "The acceptance of credit-based national currencies as major international reserve currencies, as is the case in the current system, is a rare special case in history," Zhou observed. But issuers of reserve currencies "cannot pursue different domestic and international objectives at the same time"; this is the heart of the Triffin critique of Bretton Woods. "Although crisis may not necessarily be an intended result of the issuing authorities," he argued, "it is an inevitable outcome of the institutional flaws." White's blueprint had failed. "The collapse of the Bretton Woods system, which was based on the White approach," he concluded, "indicates that the Keynesian approach may have been more farsighted." He called on the IMF to take the lead in boosting the all-but-forgotten SDR—to make it into a true "super-sovereign reserve currency," using the model of Keynes's bancor.[37] Xinhua, after blasting the United States for its "debt addiction" in 2011, repeated Zhou's call for a "new, stable, and secured global reserve currency."[38]

China, though a huge creditor of the United States, is, unlike the United States in the 1940s, in no position to orchestrate a Bretton Woods–type refashioning of the global monetary architecture. The United States today is hardly the supplicant Britain was in the 1940s. Britain had been bankrupted by two world wars; it could not pay for vital imports without foreign support in the form of dollars or gold. The United States, in contrast, still pays its bills in a currency it prints. In spite of its large and growing debt, it has sold record new issues of it at record low interest rates in a time of transatlantic financial crisis. The dollar still accounts for 60 percent of global foreign exchange reserves (down from 70 percent a decade ago), and even 75 percent of global imports from countries other than the United States.[39] During the 2008 financial crisis, the Fed was able to take extraordinary actions to support the domestic credit markets; in contrast, central banks from Sweden to Australia were obliged to sell foreign assets for dollars to do the same.[40] At present, the United States has no need to accommodate calls for it to sacrifice its exorbitant privilege to some vague vision of the global good. It will only waver when the market initiates a clear shift toward alternatives.

But credible alternatives are in short supply at present. The euro is in the midst of an existential crisis that has fueled grave doubts as to whether supranational fiat currencies of any sort are viable. As for SDRs, they currently represent less than 3 percent of global reserves, and there is no private trade invoicing, borrowing, or lending taking place in them.[41] Until that changes, there is little incentive for central banks to hold much more of them. Paradoxically, although it was Keynes who argued for, and White who fiercely resisted, a supranational reserve currency in the run-up to Bretton Woods, such a currency would have far greater viability in a world dominated by state trading—of the sort practiced by the former Soviet Union, and toward which White privately believed the world was moving.

Could the Chinese renminbi itself challenge the dominance of the U.S. dollar? Though China's economy could be larger than that of the United States by the end of the decade, its currency is subject to strict exchange controls, and its domestic capital market is state-directed and underdeveloped.[42] China is further boxed in by the reality that any successful moves to undermine the dominant reserve status of the dollar will involve the sacrifice of enormous amounts of purchasing power currently residing in its vast stash of American securities.

There is, finally, it is worth noting, a small but passionate constituency, curiously based mainly in the United States, for a return to some form of global gold standard. Though there is precious little evidence that any government would, or could, today live by its strictures, which require acceptance of deflation as a natural, and indeed necessary, periodic occurrence, a generalized loss of confidence in fiat currencies could provoke changes in public and private practice. Central banks around the world, in both rich and poor countries, have been reaccumulating gold reserves, reversing the trend of the 1990s, and governments could at some point seek to settle trade balances with it. Gold is used as collateral in derivatives transactions. Private gold "bank" accounts, though still a niche business, have also been proliferating, allowing depositors to make digital transfers across borders using gold as a means of payment. Electronic debit cards could someday be issued on such accounts.[43] It is therefore not science fiction to imagine that gold could regain an active monetary role without any sort of new system being proclaimed—indeed, the classical gold standard emerged without any international planning or agreement.

Brazilian Finance Minister Guido Mantega grabbed the headlines in September 2010 when he declared that "an international currency war" had broken out, with countries, most notably the United States, deliberately seeking to push down their currencies to boost exports and discourage imports in the midst of a severe economic slowdown. Switzerland, Japan, Brazil, and others intervened in the foreign exchange markets to counter what they saw as unacceptable upward pressure on their currencies. Though Mantega's observation may have been hyperbolic, its widespread repetition reflected a palpable growing sense in the markets that dangers lay in the passing of the Great Moderation.

Though the benign scenario of a gentle transition from a dollar-dominated world to one in which other developed and emerging market currencies play a much larger international role is plausible, precedent is lacking. When the dollar, pound, franc, and mark each played a reserve role in the early twentieth century, they were each surrogates for gold. When the dollar and pound shared reserve status in the middle of that century, the pound was largely inconvertible, and had mainly a captive clientele.

It is therefore at least as plausible that a marked shift away from the dollar will be disruptive and damaging; the 1930s, a decade in which global trade collapsed, offers a darker template. China's recent bilateral agreements with Japan, Brazil, Russia, and Turkey to pursue trade without dollars could be a worrisome harbinger, insofar as each would be more likely to undertake global trade discrimination to balance its bilateral trade than to stockpile other fiat currencies. The United States had sought to eliminate such discrimination permanently through Bretton Woods.

The creditor-debtor relationship between China and the United States today is very different from that between the United States and Britain in the 1940s and '50s. China and the United States are not allies, yet they are mutually economically dependent to a degree that political rupture would be dangerously costly to both. Whereas U.S. government holdings of British securities during the Suez crisis amounted to a mere $1 per resident, China's holdings of U.S. government securities today exceed $1,000 per resident.[44] The United States in the 1940s and '50s was therefore in a position to provoke a sterling crisis at any moment at little cost to itself; China, in contrast, cannot do the same with the dollar today. China believes that the U.S.-dominated international financial architecture is anachronistic and fails to provide adequate security for its economic interests. Yet it can identify no alternative blueprint that does not imply massive financial losses on its reserves, economic dislocation for its export industries and state-owned firms dependent on subsidized capital, and potential social unrest and political upheaval.

It is tempting to fall back on eighteenth-century Enlightenment thinking, of Immanuel Kant and David Hume in particular, and to imagine that commercial entanglement gives China and the United States sufficient interest in a stable international order that neither would risk provoking a rupture in order to change fundamentally the balance of geopolitical prerogatives between them. This would include the monetary order, and not just the geopolitics of territorial sovereignty in the South China Sea and control of global strategic resources such as energy.

Yet it is perhaps equally plausible that such a rupture is inevitable, in the same way that British Foreign Office official Eyre Crowe argued that it was between Britain and Germany back in 1907. Irrespective of Germany's intentions, or stated intentions, Crowe argued, Germany had an unmitigated interest in creating "as powerful a navy as she can afford," and the very existence of such a navy was "incompatible with the existence of the British Empire." Britain could not abide it; the risks were too great. Diplomacy therefore had its limits; war had become virtually a matter of time.[45] Though Britain emerged on the victorious side in the two world wars that followed, the financial strain ultimately brought about the liquidation of its empire.

In a 2005 *Foreign Affairs* article, longtime Chinese government policy adviser and Communist Party intellectual Zheng Bijian insisted that China "would not follow the path of Germany leading up to World

War I"; it was dedicated instead to a "peaceful rise."[46] Yet a modern-day Crowe might see the same dynamic at play today between a rising China and Britain's even more dominant successor, the United States. Whatever Zheng or others in the Chinese leadership might say, or even believe, China is going to expand its naval capacity in the Pacific dramatically in the coming years, and this is going to undermine the bedrock of America's security posture in the region and further afield. The United States will therefore be obliged to counter China's rise through new patterns of engagement with Pacific countries that China will inevitably find threatening. Deadly conflict, in this rendering, is unavoidable. Former U.S. Secretary of State Henry Kissinger, for one, believes that such a destructive dynamic is avoidable, but nonetheless deeply worrying.[47]

The Bretton Woods saga unfurled at a unique crossroads in modern history. An ascendant anticolonial superpower, the United States, used its economic leverage over an insolvent allied imperial power, Great Britain, to set the terms by which the latter would cede its dwindling dominion over the rules and norms of foreign trade and finance. Britain cooperated because the overriding aim of survival seemed to dictate the course. The monetary architecture that Harry White designed, and powered through an international gathering of dollar-starved allies, ultimately fell, its critics agree, of its own contradictions. The IMF, the institution through which it was launched, though, endures—however much its objectives have metamorphosed—and many hope that it can be a catalyst for a new and more enduring "Bretton Woods." Yet history suggests that a new cooperative monetary architecture will not emerge until the United States and China each comes to the conclusion that the consequences of muddling on, without the prospect of correcting the endemic imbalances between them, are too great. Even more daunting are the requirements for building an *enduring* system; monetary nationalism was the downfall of the last great effort in 1944.

APPENDIX 1: HARRY DEXTER WHITE
MANUSCRIPT PHOTOS

"Political Economic Int. of Future," manuscript by Harry Dexter White, undated. Page 1. (Princeton University Library. Harry Dexter White Papers, Public Policy Papers, Department of Rare Books and Special Collections, Princeton University Library)

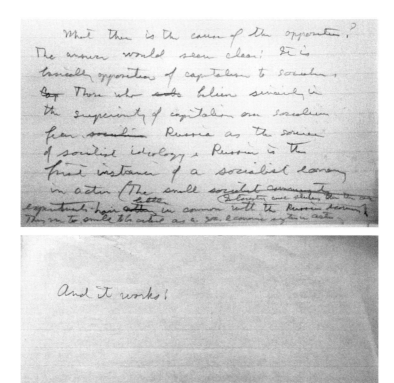

"Political Economic Int. of Future," manuscript by Harry Dexter White, undated. Pages 28–29. (Princeton University Library. Harry Dexter White Papers, Public Policy Papers, Department of Rare Books and Special Collections, Princeton University Library)

Transcript, pages 28–29:

What then is the cause of the opposition? The answer would seem clear: it is basically opposition of capitalism to socialism. Those who believe sincerely in the superiority of capitalism over socialism fear Russia as the source of socialist ideology. Russia is the first instance of a socialist economy in action. (The small socialist community experiments have little in common with the Russian economy. Interesting case studies though they are, they are too small to be [illegible] as a soc. economic system [illegible]).

And it works!

APPENDIX 2: STATEMENT OF HARRY S. TRUMAN ON HARRY DEXTER WHITE, 1953

New York Times. Nov. 17, 1953. "Text of Address by Truman Explaining to Nation His Actions in the White Case" (extract).

In late 1945, the FBI was engaged in a secret investigation of subversive activities in this country. In this investigation, the FBI was making an intensive effort to verify and corroborate certain accusations of espionage made by confidential informants.

A lengthy FBI report on this matter was sent to the White House in December, 1945. The report contained many names of persons in and out of Government service concerning whom there were then unverified accusations. Among the many names mentioned, I now find, was that of Harry Dexter White, who had been in the Treasury Department for many years and who was at that time an Assistant Secretary of the Treasury.

As best I can now determine, I first learned of the accusations against White early in February, 1946, when an FBI report specifically discussing activities of Harry Dexter White was brought to my attention. The February report was delivered to me by General Vaughan and was also brought to my personal attention by Secretary of State Byrnes.

This report showed that serious accusations had been made against White, but it pointed out that it would be practically impossible to prove these charges with the evidence then at hand.

Immediately after the matter was brought to my attention, I sent a copy of the report, with a covering note signed by me, to White's immediate superior, the Secretary of the Treasury, Fred Vinson. In this note dated February 6, 1946, I said:

"I am enclosing you a memorandum from the Secretary of State, which came to me this morning.

"I suggest that you read it, keeping it entirely confidential and then, I think, you, the Secretary of State, and myself should discuss the situation and find out what we should do." That's the end of the quotation from my note to Mr. Vinson.

Later—I believe it was the same day—I discussed the matter with Secretary Vinson as well as with Secretary Byrnes.

As I have mentioned, Mr. White was at that time an Assistant Secretary of the Treasury. It had been planned for some time that he should be transferred from that position to be the United States member on the board of executive directors of the International Monetary Fund, a new international organization then in process of being set up.

His appointment had been sent to the Senate for the new position, and it was confirmed on February 6, shortly before I saw Secretaries Byrnes and Vinson, and in this situation, I requested Secretary Vinson to consult with the appropriate officials of the Government and come back to me with recommendations.

Secretary of the Treasury Vinson consulted with Attorney General Tom Clark and other Government officials. When the results of these consultations were reported to me, the conclusion was reached that the appointment should be allowed to take its normal course.

The final responsibility for this decision was, of course, mine. The reason for this decision was that the charges which had been made to the FBI against Mr. White also involved many other persons. Hundreds of FBI agents were engaged in investigating the charges against all those who had been accused.

It was of great importance to the nation that this investigation be continued in order to prove or disprove these charges and to determine if still other persons were implicated.

Any unusual action with respect to Mr. White's appointment might well have alerted all the persons involved to the fact that the investigation was under way and thus endanger the success of the investigation.

It was originally planned that the United States would support Mr. White for election to the top managerial position in the International Monetary Fund—that of managing director—a more important post than that of a member of the board of executive directors.

But following the receipt of the FBI report and the consultations with members of my Cabinet, it was decided that he would be limited to membership on the board of directors.

With his duties thus restricted, he would be subject to the supervision of the Secretary of State, and his position would be less important and much less sensitive—if it were sensitive at all—than the position then held by him as Assistant Secretary of the Treasury.

CAST OF CHARACTERS

Acheson, Dean (1893–1971). American lawyer and statesman. Secretary of state, 1949–53. A highly intelligent patrician Anglophile, he represented the State Department at the Bretton Woods Conference, where he was the chief American delegate on Keynes's World Bank Commission.

Adler, Solomon ("Sol") (1909–1994). American economist. Department of the Treasury, 1936–50. Spent many years in China, during and after his government service. Identified by Whittaker Chambers and Elizabeth Bentley as a Soviet agent.

Akhmerov, Iskhak (1901–1975). Soviet NKVD intelligence official operating in the United States in the 1930s and '40s. Part of the group that initiated "Operation Snow," which allegedly used White to provoke Japan into attacking the United States.

Amery, Leopold (1873–1955). British Conservative politician. Secretary of state for India and Burma, 1940–45. A leading supporter of Churchill's policy of imperial preference.

Anderson, Sir John (1882–1958). British civil servant and politician. Chancellor of the exchequer, 1943–45.

Attlee, Clement (1883–1967). British Labour politician. Labour Party leader, 1935–55; prime minister, 1945–51. Promoted policies of increased state intervention and social protection. Presided over the decolonization of significant parts of the British Empire.

Bareau, Paul (1901–2000). Belgian-born British financial journalist. Member of the British Treasury delegation to Washington, 1945–46.

Barkley, Alben (1877–1956). American politician. Democratic Senate majority leader, 1937–47; Truman's vice president, 1949–53. As Senate majority leader, introduced to the chamber bill H.R. 1776—"Lend-Lease."

Baruch, Bernard (1870–1965). American financier and statesman. A talented businessman who was sought out as a political adviser by Presidents Wilson and Roosevelt.

Beaverbrook, Lord (William Maxwell Aitken) (1879–1964). Canadian-born British politician and press baron. One of only three British cabinet members to hold office during both World War I and II. Opposed the 1944 Anglo-American Joint Statement as well as Keynes's Clearing Union alternative.

Bentley, Elizabeth (1908–1963). American who spied for the Soviet Union from 1938 to 1945. Defected from the Communist Party in 1945. Exposed the Silvermaster and Perlo spy networks, revealing the names of more than eighty Americans working for the Soviet Union, including White.

Berle, Adolf (1895–1971). American lawyer and diplomat. Assistant secretary of state, 1938–44. One of FDR's trusted advisers.

Bernstein, Edward ("Eddie") (1904–1996). American economist. Principal economist, Department of the Treasury, 1940–46; director of research, IMF, 1946–58. Did not think White a strong economic technician, but considered him a fine crafter of policy.

Bevin, Ernest (1881–1951). British trade unionist and Labour politician. Minister of labour and national service, 1940–45; foreign secretary, 1945–51.

Beyen, Johan Willem (1897–1976). Dutch banker and civil servant. Leader of the Dutch delegation at Bretton Woods. President of the Bank for International Settlements, 1937–39.

Bidault, Georges (1899–1983). French politician. President, Provisional Government, 1946; foreign minister, 1947–48; prime minister, 1949–50.

Blum, John Morton (1921–2011). American political historian. Yale professor who authored the three-volume *From the Morgenthau Diaries*.

Blum, Léon (1872–1950). French Socialist politician. Prime minister, 1936–37, 1938; president, Provisional Government, 1946–47. A Jew, he was imprisoned and nearly executed by the Nazis during World War II.

Bolton, Sir George (1900–1982). British banker and Conservative politician. Member of Parliament, 1931–45, 1950–59; executive director of the Bank of England, 1948–57; director of the Bank of England, 1957–68. A member of the British delegation at Bretton Woods.

Boothby, Robert (1900–1986). British Conservative politician. Member of Parliament, 1924–58. A leading parliamentary opponent of the gold standard and critic of Bretton Woods.

Bradley, Omar (1893–1981). American army officer. Chairman of the Joint Chiefs of Staff, 1949–53. His concerns over White House press leaks may have been the reason why the Venona Project, which provided compelling evidence of White's espionage activities, was kept hidden from President Truman.

Brand, Robert (1878–1963). British civil servant and banker. British Treasury representative in Washington, 1944–46. A strong proponent of Anglo-American cooperation who shared Keynes's liberal sympathies.

Brown, Edward Eagle (1885–1959). American lawyer and banker. President of the First National Bank of Chicago. One of only two American delegates at Bretton Woods who was not from the government. Keynes remarked that it had been a long while since he had met "a more competent or distinguished banker."

Brownell, Herbert (1904–1996). American lawyer and politician. U.S. attorney general, 1953–57. Testified before Congress that Truman knew White was a "Communist agent" when he nominated him to be an IMF executive director.

Bullitt, William (1891–1967). American diplomat, journalist, and novelist. Ambassador to the Soviet Union, 1933–36; ambassador to France, 1936–40.

Burgess, Randolph (1889–1978). American banker and diplomat. Represented the interests of the New York banking community during the Bretton Woods negotiations. Opposed the IMF blueprint as unsound.

Bykov, Colonel Boris. Soviet Military Intelligence (GRU) agent. Whittaker Chambers claims to have introduced him to White in 1937.

Byrnes, James Francis (1882–1972). American politician. Democratic senator for South Carolina, 1931–41; justice of the Supreme Court, 1941–42; secretary of state, 1945–47. Confidant of FDR, and a mentor to Truman from the latter's earliest days in the Senate.

Cadogan, Sir Alexander (1884–1968). British civil servant. Ambassador to China, 1933–36; permanent under-secretary of state for foreign affairs, 1938–46. Participated in the Octagon meetings with FDR and Morgenthau in September 1944.

Catto, Lord (Thomas) (1879–1959). Scottish businessman and banker. Governor of the Bank of England, 1944–49. Born into a solidly working-class family, he still found common ground with Keynes, and the two became close friends.

Chamberlain, Neville (1869–1940). British Conservative politician. Chancellor of the exchequer, 1923–24, 1931–37; prime minister, 1937–40. Led the policy of German appeasement in the run-up to World War II. As chancellor, he opposed deficit spending. Keynes was relentlessly critical of him.

Chambers, Whittaker (1901–1961). American journalist. Communist Party member and Soviet agent who recruited White. Ultimately offered up the names of at least thirteen Americans operating in the United States as Soviet agents, including White.

Chechulin, Nikolai Fyodorovich (1908–1955). Russian banker. Vice-chairman of the board of the State Bank, 1940–55. Member of the Russian delegation at Bretton Woods.

Cherwell, Lord (Frederick Alexander Lindemann) (1886–1957). German-born British physicist. As head of the prime minister's statistical office, he was one of Churchill's most trusted advisers. Played an important role in Stage II Lend-Lease negotiations with the Americans.

Churchill, Winston (1874–1965). British Conservative politician. Chancellor of the exchequer, 1924–29; prime minister, 1940–45 and 1951–55. Keynes strongly opposed his returning Britain to the gold (or "gold-exchange") standard in 1925.

Clarke, Colonel Carter (1896–1987). American military official. As chief of the U.S. Army's Special Branch, he initiated the Venona Project in 1943 to intercept and decode Soviet wartime communications.

Clarke, Sir Richard ("Otto") (1910–1975). British civil servant. Served in various ministries before joining the Treasury in 1945. Though an admirer of Keynes, he was highly critical of his American loan negotiation strategy in 1945.

Clayton, William (1880–1966). American statesman. Assistant secretary of state for economic affairs, 1944–45; undersecretary of state for economic affairs, 1946–47. Signed the Anglo-American Loan Agreement in 1945. Was a strong proponent of open market-based free trade and laid the intellectual foundations of the Marshall Plan.

Coe, Frank (1907–1980). American economist and government official. Director of the Division of Monetary Research, Department of the Treasury, 1944–45; secretary of the IMF, 1946–52. Resigned his IMF post under pressure from Congress, owing to allegations by Whittaker Chambers and Elizabeth Bentley that he was a Soviet agent. Moved to China to work for Mao's government in 1958.

Collado, Emilio (1910–1995). American economist. Department of the Treasury, 1934–36; New York Federal Reserve Bank, 1936–38; Department of State, 1938–46; U.S. executive director of the World Bank, 1946–47. American technical adviser at Bretton Woods.

Connally, John (1917–1993). American politician. Democratic governor of Texas, 1963–69; secretary of the Treasury, 1971–2. After Nixon closed the gold window in 1971, Connally famously told European officials that the dollar was "our currency, but your problem."

Cripps, Sir Richard Stafford (1889–1952). British diplomat and politician. Ambassador to the Soviet Union, 1940–42; president of the Board of Trade, 1945–47; minister for economic affairs, 1947; chancellor of the exchequer, 1947–50. Involved in the American loan negotiations of 1945.

Crossman, Richard (1907–1974). British Labour politician. A cabinet minister under Harold Wilson in the 1960s. Initially pro-Arab, he became one of the Labour Party's leading Zionist supporters.

Crowley, Leo (1889–1972). American businessman and government official. Head of the Foreign Economic Administration, 1943–45. Helped negotiate the Lend-Lease agreements.

Cunliffe, Lord (Walter) (1855–1920). British banker. Governor of the Bank of England, 1913–18. Angered by Keynes's support of Treasury policy to defend the dollar-sterling exchange rate in 1917, he tried to have him fired.

Currie, Lauchlin (1902–1993). Canadian-born American economist. An adviser to FDR during World War II, he was later identified by Whittaker Chambers and Elizabeth Bentley as a Soviet agent working for the Silvermaster spy ring.

Dalton, Hugh (1887–1962). British economist and Labour politician. Chancellor of the exchequer, 1945–47. Became disenchanted with Keynes over his handling of the American loan negotiations in 1945.

de Gaulle, Charles (1890–1970). French military officer and politician. President, 1959–69. Led the Free French forces during World War II and founded the French Fifth Republic in 1958. Argued that the American dollar had a monumentally overprivileged position in the world economy. In 1963, demanded that the United States begin covering 80 percent of its payment deficit to France in gold.

Eady, Sir Wilfrid (1890–1962). British diplomat and Treasury official. Member of the British delegation at Bretton Woods. Opposed Keynes's conduct of the American loan negotiations in 1945.

Eccles, Marriner (1890–1977). American banker. Chairman of the Federal Reserve, 1934–48. Member of the American delegation at Bretton Woods. Tussled with White over his deference to Russian demands at the conference.

Eden, Anthony (1897–1977). British Conservative politician. Foreign secretary, 1935–38, 1940–45, and 1951–55; prime minister, 1955–57. Staunchly opposed the Morgenthau Plan for deindustrializing postwar Germany, and Churchill's acquiescence to it.

Eisenhower, Dwight David (1890–1969). American army officer and politician. President, 1953–61. Supreme Allied commander in western Europe during World War II.

Feis, Herbert (1893–1972). American statesman, author, and historian. Economic adviser for international affairs at the State Department under the Hoover and Roosevelt administrations.

Foley, Edward (1906–1982). American lawyer and government official. General counsel of the Department of the Treasury, 1939–42; assistant secretary of the Treasury, 1946–48; undersecretary of the Treasury, 1948–53. Drafted the original Lend-Lease bill.

Friedman, Milton (1912–2006). American economist. A renowned monetarist, he was also an early and articulate supporter of floating exchange rates. Awarded the Nobel Prize in Economic Sciences in 1976.

Funk, Walther (1890–1960). German economist and government official. Reich minister of economics, 1937–45; president of the Reichsbank, 1939–45. A staunch nationalist and anticommunist, he blasted the Bretton Woods monetary plans as a sop to the Soviets. Tried as a war criminal at Nuremburg.

Glasser, Harold (1905–1992). American economist. Department of the Treasury, 1936–47. Worked closely with White, who had helped bring him into the Treasury. Was later identified as a Soviet spy by Elizabeth Bentley.

Goldenweiser, Emanuel (1883–1953). Russian Ukrainian-born American economist. Director, Division of Research and Statistics, Federal Reserve Board, 1926–45. A member of the American delegation at Bretton Woods, he called Keynes "one of the brightest lights of mankind in both thinking and expression" and "the world's worst chairman."

Golos, Jacob (1890–1943). Russian Ukrainian-born member of the American Communist Party's three-man Control Commission and an NKVD agent. He became Elizabeth Bentley's first point of contact with Communist Party members; she became his assistant and lover.

Grant, Duncan (1885–1978). British painter and designer. Member of the Bloomsbury group of writers and artists, and Keynes's onetime lover.

Gromyko, Andrei (1909–1989). Russian diplomat and politician. Ambassador to the United States, 1943–46; foreign minister, 1957–85; president of the Presidium of the Supreme Soviet, 1985–88. In 1943, told future Russian Bretton Woods delegates, in front of White, that they were to be "observers" and were "not to give any opinion of any kind."

Halifax, Lord (Edward Wood) (1881–1959). British Conservative politician. Foreign secretary, 1938–40; ambassador to the United States, 1941–46. Had a close relationship with Keynes. Signed the Anglo-American Financial Agreement with Fred Vinson in Washington in December 1945.

Harriman, William Averell (1891–1986). American banker, diplomat, and politician. Ambassador to the Soviet Union, 1943–46; ambassador to the United Kingdom, 1946; secretary of commerce, 1946–48. Participated in World War II conferences at Placentia Bay (1941), Tehran (1943), and Yalta (1945).

Harrod, Sir Roy (1900–1978). British economist. Adviser, Prime Minister's Statistical Branch, 1940–42. Biographer of Keynes, with whom he maintained a long personal and professional correspondence.

Hayek, Friedrich (1899–1992). Austrian-born British economist. Widely known for his defense of free-market capitalism and classical liberalism. Though intellectually opposed to Keynesianism, he and Keynes maintained a warm and respectful relationship. Awarded the Nobel Prize in Economic Sciences in 1974.

Hébert, Felix Edward (1901–1979). American politician. Republican congressman for Louisiana, 1941–77. Member of the House Un-American Activities Committee, before which White famously testified in 1948.

Henderson, Sir Hubert (1890–1952). British economist. Adviser to the Treasury, 1939–44. A vocal opponent of Keynes's Clearing Union plan, which he thought even worse than the gold (or "gold-exchange") standard.

Hiss, Alger (1904–1996). American lawyer and government official. Director of the Office of Special Political Affairs, Department of State, 1944–46. Recruited as a Soviet agent by Whittaker Chambers, who later denounced him before the House Un-American Activities Committee. In 1950 was convicted of perjury in relation to his denial of involvement in Soviet espionage activities.

Hoover, John Edgar (1895–1972). American domestic intelligence official. Director of the Federal Bureau of Investigation, 1924–72. Alerted Truman, who distrusted him, to the existence of Soviet espionage networks at the highest levels of the U.S. government.

Hopkins, Harry (1890–1946). American government official. Director, Federal Emergency Relief Administration, 1933–35; director, Works Progress Administration, 1935–38; secretary of commerce, 1938–40. One of FDR's closest advisers, he helped formulate the New Deal and was a key architect of the Lend-Lease program.

Hull, Cordell (1871–1955). American statesman. Secretary of state, 1933–44. An ardent supporter of free trade who believed that the economic and political crises of the 1930s were largely attributable to protectionist policies. Was determined to eliminate the British system of imperial preference.

Kahn, Richard (1905–1989). British economist. Educated at King's College, Cambridge, where he was Keynes's favorite student. Fathered the concept of the fiscal multiplier, which Keynes adopted to great effect.

Kennan, George (1904–2005). American diplomat and historian. His 1946 "Long Telegram" laid the intellectual foundation for the postwar policy of Soviet containment. One of the architects of the Marshall Plan.

Kennedy, Joseph (1888–1969). American businessman, diplomat, and government official. Ambassador to the United Kingdom, 1938–40. Opposed American involvement in World War II. A hated figure in Downing Street, he was forced to resign from his position under pressure from FDR. Father of President John F. Kennedy.

Kung, Hsiang-hsi ("Daddy") (1880–1967). Chinese banker, businessman, and government official. Premier of the Republic, 1938–39. A larger-than-life character who claimed descent from Confucius. Headed the Chinese delegation at Bretton Woods.

Law, (Andrew) Bonar (1858–1923). British Conservative politician. Chancellor of the exchequer, 1916–19; prime minister, 1922–23. A rare Tory ally of Keynes.

Law, Richard (later Lord Coleraine) (1901–1980). British Conservative politician. Parliamentary under-secretary of state for foreign affairs, 1941–43; minister of state, 1943–45. The strongest, though still a tepid, cabinet supporter of the 1944 Anglo-American Joint Statement.

Lloyd George, David (1863–1945). British Liberal politician and statesman. Chancellor of the exchequer, 1908–15; prime minister, 1916–22. Thought Keynes impulsive and mercurial, and personally struck his name from the 1917 royal honors list. Keynes, for his part, detested Lloyd George through the course of World War I and the Paris Peace Conference, though his view later softened considerably.

Lodge, Henry Cabot (1850–1924). American politician. Republican senator for Massachusetts, 1893–1924. His "fourteen reservations" were instrumental in the Senate's rejection of the 1919 Treaty of Versailles.

Lopokova, Lydia (1892–1981). Russian ballerina and wife of Keynes.

Luxford, Ansel Frank (1911–1971). American lawyer and government official. Assistant secretary of the Treasury, 1944–46. Chief legal adviser to the American delegation at Bretton Woods.

Maletin, Pavel Andreyevich (1905–1969). Russian government official. Deputy people's commissar of finance, 1939–45. Member of the Russian delegation at Bretton Woods.

Marshall, Alfred (1842–1924). British economist. One of the great founders of the modern discipline of economics. Chose Keynes as a teaching assistant at King's College, Cambridge, in 1908, which was instrumental in Keynes's election to a life Fellowship at age twenty-six.

Marshall, George Catlett (1880–1959). American military leader and statesman. U.S. Army chief of staff, 1939–45; secretary of state, 1947–49; secretary of defense, 1950–51. His famed 1947 Harvard speech making the case for large-scale American assistance in a new European economic recovery program became the basis for the Marshall Plan. Awarded the Nobel Prize for Peace in 1953.

McAdoo, William Gibbs (1863–1941). American lawyer and politician. Secretary of the Treasury, 1913–18; chairman, Federal Reserve Board, 1914; Democratic senator for California, 1933–38. Keynes's painful experience appealing to McAdoo for British financial aid during World War I sensitized him to the geopolitical costs Britain would bear in having to beg in Washington again during World War II.

McKenna, Reginald (1863–1943). British banker and Liberal politician. Chancellor of the exchequer, 1915–16. Keynes was his most trusted adviser during World War I.

Meade, James (1907–1995). British economist. Director, Economic Section of the War Cabinet, 1946–47. He acknowledged Keynes's intellectual brilliance—regarding him as "God"—but considered his diplomatic skills poor. Awarded the Nobel Prize in Economic Sciences in 1977.

Mendès-France, Pierre (1907–1982). French politician. Prime minister, 1954–55. Headed the French delegation at Bretton Woods.

Mikesell, Raymond (1913–2006). American economist and government official. A member of the American technical staff at Bretton Woods, he was highly critical of the uncooperative approach of the Russian delegation.

Molotov, Vyacheslav (1890–1986). Russian diplomat. Minister of foreign affairs, 1939–49, 1953–56. Kept the Soviet delegates at Bretton Woods on the tightest possible leash, forbidding them from making the slightest concessions without authorization from Moscow. He painted any measure of Soviet cooperation as a personal gesture to Henry Morgenthau.

Morgenthau, Henry (1891–1967). American politician. Secretary of the Treasury, 1934–45. Longtime trusted friend of FDR. Had an important symbiotic political relationship with White, on whom he depended for policy formulation and who in turn depended on him for advancement and wider influence.

Newcomer, Mabel (1892–1983). American economist. A Vassar professor, she was the only female American delegate at Bretton Woods.

Nixon, Richard (1913–1994). American politician. President, 1969–74. As a member of the House Un-American Activities Committee, sparred with White in his August 1948 hearing. In 1950, publicly revealed an incriminating handwritten memo of White's, given to Nixon by Whittaker Chambers. Effectively ended the Bretton Woods monetary system by ceasing the dollar's fixed-rate gold convertibility in 1971.

Norman, Lord (Montagu Collet) (1871–1950). British banker. Governor of the Bank of England, 1920–44. He and Keynes were frequently and openly at odds intellectually, particularly over the gold standard.

Oliphant, Herman (1884–1939). American professor of law. General counsel of the Treasury, 1934–39.

Opie, Redvers (1900–1984). British economist. Counselor and economic adviser, British Embassy, Washington, 1939–46. Member of the British delegation at Bretton Woods.

Pasvolsky, Leo (1893–1953). Russian Ukrainian-born American economist. Special assistant to the secretary of state, 1936–38, 1939–46. Heavily involved in economic planning for the postwar period, working closely with the British.

Pavlov, Vitali (1914–2005). Soviet intelligence agent. Head of the American desk of the NKVD Intelligence Directorate. As described in his book *Operation Snow*, was sent to Washington in 1941 to reactivate "agent of influence" Harry Dexter White.

CAST OF CHARACTERS | 365

Peacock, Sir Edward (1871–1962). Canadian-born British banker. Director of the Bank of England, 1921–24, 1929–46. Enthusiastically endorsed Keynes's Clearing Union, while recognizing that it would have no chance of becoming reality for some decades.

Penrose, Ernest Francis (1895–1984). British economist. Adviser to the American ambassador to the United Kingdom, John Winant. Observed of White that he was "as much of a prima donna in his way as Keynes."

Perlo, Victor (1912–1999). American economist and member of the Communist Party USA. Held various positions within the American government, including the Treasury, until his exposure as a Soviet agent and leader of the so-called "Perlo Group." His ex-wife denounced White in an unsigned letter to FDR in 1944.

Phillips, Sir Frederick (1884–1943). British civil servant. Head of the Treasury Mission in Washington, 1940–43. Ably represented American views to Keynes and London, where they were not always grasped.

Pigou, Arthur Cecil (1877–1959). British economist. Fellow of King's College, Cambridge, 1902–59. He and Keynes had an intellectual falling-out in the 1930s. Stung by the manner of Keynes's criticisms, Pigou wrote a particularly cutting critique of Keynes's *General Theory*.

Pravdin, Vladimir (1905–1970). Russian KGB officer. Posed as a TASS news agency journalist in the United States, where he passed on intelligence from White to Moscow.

Reading, Lord (Rufus Isaacs) (1860–1935). British lawyer and Liberal politician. Lord chief justice of England, 1913–21; ambassador to the United States, 1918–19; foreign secretary, 1931. Led a begging mission to Washington in 1917, accompanied by Keynes.

Robbins, Lionel (1898–1984). British economist. Professor, London School of Economics, 1929–61; director, Economic Section of the War Cabinet Offices, 1941–45. Member of the British delegation at Bretton Woods. A non-Keynesian free trader, he eventually came to accept Keynes's thinking on public spending in slumps. Became an important ally at Bretton Woods.

Robertson, Sir Dennis Holme (1890–1963). British economist. A highly regarded classically liberal economic thinker in his time, he rejected Keynes's *General Theory* as a valid model of the market system. Member of the British delegation at Bretton Woods; inadvertently abetted White's subterfuge to establish the dollar as a global surrogate for gold.

Ronald, Nigel (1894–1973). British diplomat. Assistant undersecretary of state, 1942–47. Member of the British delegation at Bretton Woods.

Roosevelt, Franklin Delano (FDR) (1882–1945). American politician. President, 1933–45. Keynes admired Roosevelt for his bold economic policy interventions. Like Churchill, however, FDR had little interest in the details of foreign economic policy, and, in contrast to White, never embraced it as a geopolitical weapon.

Rueff, Jacques (1896–1978). French economist. Conservative, free-market thinker, and longtime adviser to the French government. Advocated a return to the pre-1914 classical gold standard.

Say, Jean-Baptiste (1767–1832). French economist. Best known for "Say's Law," an element of classical economic thinking that Keynes sought to demolish in his *General Theory*.

Schacht, Hjalmar (1877–1970). German banker. President of the Reichsbank, 1926–30; Reich minister of economics, 1934–37. Famous for creating the "Schachtian" system of national economic management. Transformed Germany from an open economy integrated with the West to a closed, autarkic one, imposing strict import controls and conducting foreign trade bilaterally on a barter basis.

Schumpeter, Joseph (1883–1950). Austrian-born American economist and political scientist. Famous for his focus on innovation and entrepreneurs as the critical drivers of the capitalist economic system. Was highly critical of Keynes's methods and "stagnationism."

Schweitzer, Pierre-Paul (1912–1994). French government official. Managing director of the IMF, 1963–73. Loathed by the Nixon administration.

Shultz, George (1920–). American economist and statesman. Secretary of the Treasury, 1972–74; secretary of state 1982–89. An outspoken critic of fixed exchange rates.

Silverman, Abraham George (1900–1973). American mathematician and government official. Identified by Elizabeth Bentley as a Soviet agent who was part of an American spy ring run by Nathan Gregory Silvermaster. Venona cables provide evidence that he was an intermediary between White and Soviet intelligence.

Silvermaster, Nathan Gregory (1898–1964). Russian Ukrainian-born American economist. Affiliated with the Department of the Treasury, and the War Assets Administration. Headed the Silvermaster spy ring from 1941 to 1945. Allegedly photographed large amounts of classified information in his basement, where White told the House Un-American Activities Committee that he played Ping-Pong.

Skidelsky, Lord (Robert) (1939–). British economic historian. Professor emeritus of political economy at Warwick University. Author of a three-volume prizewinning biography of Keynes.

Smith, Frederick Cleveland (1884–1956). American doctor and politician. Republican congressman for Ohio, 1939–51. Member of the House Committee on Banking and Currency. Opposed the Bretton Woods agreements.

Spence, Brent (1874–1967). American politician. Democratic congressman for Kentucky, 1931–63; chairman of the House Committee on Banking and Currency, 1943–47, 1949–53, 1955–63. Member of the American delegation at Bretton Woods.

Stepanov, Mikhail Stepanovich (1896–1966). Russian government official. Deputy commissar of foreign trade in the 1940s. Head of the Russian delegation at Bretton Woods. Enervated and impressed Henry Morgenthau, in equal order, with his polished obstructionism.

Stettinius, Edward Reilly, Jr. (1900–1949). American businessman and government official. Secretary of state, 1944–45.

Stimson, Henry (1867–1950). American lawyer and statesman. Secretary of state, 1929–33; secretary of war, 1940–45.

Sze, Alfred Sao-ke (1877–1958). Chinese politician and diplomat. Ambassador to the United States, 1935–37. After China announced that it was abandoning the silver standard in the 1930s, he negotiated silver sales to the United States with Henry Morgenthau.

Taft, Robert (1889–1953). American politician. Republican senator for Ohio, 1939–53. Staunch opponent of the IMF; considered it a scandalous scheme for the United States to bail out foreign debtors with its massive gold stock.

Thomas, John Parnell (1895–1970). American politician. Republican congressman for New Jersey, 1937–50. Chairman of the House Un-American Activities Committee, before which White famously testified in August 1948.

Tobey, Charles (1880–1953). American politician. Republican governor of New Hampshire, 1929–31; congressman for New Hampshire, 1933–39; senator for New Hampshire, 1939–53. Member of the American delegation at Bretton Woods.

Triffin, Robert (1911–1993). Belgian-born American economist. Famously testified before Congress in 1959, warning of fundamental flaws in the

Bretton Woods monetary system. His diagnosis came to be known as the "Triffin dilemma."

Truman, Harry S. (1884–1972). American politician. President, 1945–53. Signed the Bretton Woods Act into law in July 1945. Terminated Lend-Lease without warning a few weeks later, pushing Britain into a new phase of financial crisis. Transferred control of foreign economic policy from the Treasury to the State Department.

Ullmann, William Ludwig ("Lud") (1908–1993). American government official. Treasury colleague of White's. Accused by Elizabeth Bentley of being a Soviet agent and key member of the Silvermaster spy ring; corroborated in the Venona cables.

Vaughan, Brigadier General Harry (1893–1981). American army officer. Military aide to Vice President and then President Truman, 1945–53. White House FBI liaison in 1946, when J. Edgar Hoover was trying to prevent White's appointment as U.S. IMF executive director.

Viner, Jacob (1892–1970). Canadian-born American economist. Intellectual opponent of Keynes and teacher of Milton Friedman. As an adviser to Treasury Secretary Henry Morgenthau, brought White to Washington for his first government appointment.

Vinson, Frederick ("Judge") (1890–1953). American lawyer, judge, and government official. Democratic congressman for Kentucky, 1931–38; secretary of the Treasury, 1945–46; chief justice of the United States, 1946–53. Vice-chairman of the American delegation at Bretton Woods. Loathed White, and wanted him out of government after Hoover alleged he was a Soviet agent.

Volcker, Paul (1927–). American economist. Undersecretary of the Treasury for monetary affairs, 1969–74; president of the Federal Reserve Bank of New York, 1975–79; chairman of the Federal Reserve System, 1979–87. Renowned for dramatically reducing the high levels of inflation of the late 1970s and early 1980s.

Wagner, Robert (1877–1953). American politician. Democratic senator for New York, 1927–49; chairman of the Senate Committee on Banking and Currency, 1937–47. A prominent New Deal and pro-labor progressive, close to FDR. Member of the American delegation at Bretton Woods.

Waley, Sir David (Sigismund David Schloss) (1887–1962). British civil servant. Under-secretary, Treasury, 1939–46. Prescient with regard to the problems American monetary schemes posed for Britain in the postwar period, he urged Keynes to consider the possibility of Britain borrowing money privately as an alternative to cooperating with White and Morgenthau. Keynes emphatically rejected this advice.

Wallace, Henry (1888–1965). American politician. FDR's vice president, 1941–45; secretary of commerce, 1945–46. Ran for president as a Progressive in 1948, "dedicated to the proposition that the Russians earnestly wanted peace." Passionately supported by White, whom he wanted as his Treasury secretary.

Welles, (Benjamin) Sumner (1892–1961). American diplomat. Undersecretary of state, 1937–43. Fierce opponent of British imperial trade preferences.

White, Anne Terry (1896–1980). Russian Ukrainian-born American author of children's books. Wife of Harry Dexter White.

Wilson, Woodrow (1856–1924). American scholar and politician. President, 1913–21. Lampooned by Keynes in his book *The Economic Consequences of the Peace*. Wilson's losing fight with the Senate over the United States joining the League of Nations was influential in shaping FDR's Bretton Woods strategy.

Winant, John Gilbert (1889–1947). American politician and diplomat. Republican governor of New Hampshire, 1925–27 and 1931–35; ambassador to the United Kingdom, 1941–46. An Anglophile and friend of Keynes.

Witteveen, Johannes (1921–). Dutch economist and politician. Managing director of the IMF, 1973–78. Initiated the IMF's historic break from its founding principle of fixed (but adjustable) exchange rates.

Wolcott, Jesse (1893–1969). American politician. Republican congressman for Michigan, 1931–57. Member of the American delegation at Bretton Woods.

Wood, Sir (Howard) Kingsley (1881–1943). British Conservative politician. Chancellor of the exchequer, 1940–43.

Woolton, Lord (Frederick James Marquis) (1883–1964). British businessman and Conservative politician. Chairman of the Conservative Party, 1946–55. Opposed Bretton Woods, saying that it meant Britain "surrendering [its just rights] to the power of the dollar, because those responsible for the affairs of this country do not dare to retreat on the economic fastnesses of the Empire."

Zhou, Xiaochuan (1948–). Chinese economist and banker. Governor of the People's Bank of China, 2002–.

NOTES

CHAPTER 1: INTRODUCTION

1. James (1996:57).

2. The evacuation of the British Expeditionary Force from the French seaport of Dunkirk in 1940 marked the end of the disastrous Allied defense of the Low Countries. In Britain, the word Dunkirk itself subsequently became a synonym for disaster.

3. Gardner (1956 [1980]:xiii).

4. Howson and Moggridge (1990:133, 135).

5. Bareau (1951).

6. Keynes (1980) XXV, Oct. 3, 1943, p. 356.

7. Keynes (1980) XXV, Oct. 9, 1943, pp. 370–371.

8. White Archives (undated), "Political Economic Int. of Future." See appendix 1 for a photograph of the front and back pages.

CHAPTER 2: THE WORLD COMES
TO THE WHITE MOUNTAINS

1. *New York Times* (July 2, 1944:14). Treasury Secretary Henry Morgenthau said he regretted not having brought warm woolen socks. Well-wishers sent him seven pairs over the subsequent week (*Washington Post*, July 11, 1944:3).

2. American delegation Chief Technical Adviser and Executive Secretary Edward Bernstein quoted in Black (1991:47).

3. Robbins (1990:166).

4. Foreign Office (July 4, 1944).

5. Grant (1992).

6. Eckes (1975). Skidelsky (2000).

7. Grant (1992).

8. Eckes (1975:139).

9. *The New Yorker* (Aug. 5, 1944:12).

10. Skidelsky (2000:347).

11. *New York Times* (Feb. 20, 2009).

12. The hotel lists Keynes's room as 129, and even has a plaque on the door indicating his occupancy in 1944. Skidelsky (2000:347) and others repeat that room number, but it is almost certainly wrong. Morgenthau's account of noise from Lady Keynes's exercises above his ceiling (which would be room 219), rather than down the hall from him, is supported by that of another American delegation member, E. A. Goldenweiser, who wrote that "[Keynes's] function at Bretton Woods was primarily performed in a suite of rooms on the *second floor* to which everybody went for inspiration and guidance and compromise" (italics added) (Morgenthau, *Diaries*, Vol. 747, pp. 60A–C). Also, Morgenthau's son says that the Secretary "occupied [the suite] just below Lord and Lady Keynes" (Morgenthau III [1991:344–345]). Room 219 is almost identical to room 119, in which Morgenthau stayed, whereas room 129 is relatively small and modest. The Americans would surely not have housed the British delegation head there. It is therefore highly likely that 219 simply got mistyped as 129 in the hotel records at some point, perhaps during one of the changes of ownership.

13. Robbins (1990:167).

14. Italics added.

15. Harrod (1951:512).

CHAPTER 3: THE IMPROBABLE RISE
OF HARRY WHITE

1. *Time* (1953).

2. Interlocking Subversion in Government Departments Hearings, Aug. 30, 1955, p. 2647.

3. *Time* (1953). Rees (1973).

4. *Time* (1953).

5. *Time* (1953). Rees (1973).

6. Nathan White (1956:270–271).

7. Nathan White (1956:271).

8. Whipple (1953).

9. Interlocking Subversion in Government Departments Hearings, Aug. 30, 1955, pp. 2541–2542.

10. Zweig (1943 [2009]:1).

11. Harry Dexter White (1933:301–312).

12. Interlocking Subversion in Government Departments Hearings, Aug. 30, 1955, p. 2570.

13. White Archives (Jan. 22, 1934), p. 5.

14. White Archives (Jan. 22, 1934), pp. 7–8.

15. White Archives (Jan. 22, 1934), p. 245.

16. White Archives (Jan. 22, 1934), pp. 308, 310.

17. Bureau of Economic Analysis (2010).

18. United Nations Statistics Division (1962).

19. Lebergott (1957).

20. McJimsey (2003).

21. Blum (1959:141).

22. It was that same year, 1933, in which Keynes would famously write in the *Yale Review*, "Ideas, knowledge, science, hospitality, travel—these are the things which should of their nature be international. But let goods be homespun whenever it is reasonable and conveniently possible and, above all, let finance be primarily national."

23. Blum (1959:70).

24. Blum (1959:71).

25. Morgenthau (1947).

26. Levy (2010).

27. Morgenthau III (1991:272).

28. The first was Oscar Straus, Theodore Roosevelt's secretary of commerce and labor from 1906 to 1909.

29. Meltzer (2003).

30. White Archives (1935), "Deficit Spending" (underscore in original).

31. White Archives (1935), "Outline of Analysis."

32. White Archives (1935), "Deficit Spending."

33. "Outline Analysis of the Current Situation," Feb. 26 and Mar. 5, 1935, referenced in Rees (1973:56, f. 3).

34. White Archives (Mar. 15, 1935).

35. White Archives (Mar. 15, 1935), pp. 9–110.

36. Blum (1959:139).

37. Interlocking Subversion in Government Departments Hearings, June 1, 1955, pp. 2281–2282.

38. White Archives, (Jun. 13, 1935), "Personal Report on London Trip, April–May, 1935," p. 2.

39. White Archives (Jun. 13, 1935), "Summary of conversations with men interviewed in London," p. 1.

40. Feis (1966:107). Kimball (1969:5).

41. Rees (1973:63).

42. Blum (1959).

43. Blum (1959:145).

44. Blum (1959:162).

45. Blum (1959:178).

46. Blum (1967:90).

47. Morgenthau III (1991:310–311).

48. Morgenthau III (1991:313).

49. Blum (1967:90).

50. Rees (1973).

51. This account is in Chambers (1952:414–417). Rees (1973:454, f. 22) claims "There is no record of HDW's having owned such a rug," yet after White's death his widow told her lawyer that "she received a rug not later than the fall of 1937" (interview with A. George Silverman, Apr. 26, 1949, in Weinstein [1997:553, f. 40]). See Weinstein's comprehensive account of the rug story (Weinstein [1997:189–192]).

52. Chambers (1952:415–416). Silverman's maid recalled three rugs being delivered to the residence (see Sibley [2004:262, f. 127], also referring to Weinstein [1997:212–216]).

53. Weinstein (1997:189–190).

54. Chambers (1952:417).

55. See, for example, Chambers (1952:426, 419, 384, 430).

56. Chambers (1952:421–423).

57. Institute of Pacific Relations Hearings, Aug. 16, 1951, p. 492.

58. Chambers (1952:70, 383–384, 442).

59. Blum (1967:127).

60. Chambers (1952:419).

61. Chambers (1952:430).

62. Rees (1973).

63. Chambers (1952:430–431).

64. White Archives (Aug. 4, 1942), Section IV, p. 17 (note: the folder contains numerous duplicate page numbers).

65. Of the major published profiles of White, the most thorough and sober was written over two decades before the first critical public revelations of

secret 1940s Soviet communications with and about White (see chapter 10 of this book). David Rees's stolid work, published in 1973, therefore added little to public understanding of the controversy surrounding White, lacking as it did the most powerful corroborative evidence of his clandestine activities.

66. See in particular Schecter and Schecter (2002) and Romerstein and Breindel (2000).

67. See in particular Craig (2004) and Boughton (2000, 2004).

Craig's biography of White offers a blurry portrait of a man involved in what the author concludes obliquely was "a species of espionage." His unsteady take on his subject no doubt reflects a collision between the power of the Venona Soviet intelligence cable evidence (detailed in chapter 10 of this book) and the author's prior conviction that White had been a victim of a smear campaign by "right-wing extremists." Inaccuracies compound problems stemming from the book's contrived attempt at balance. "White's loyalties transcended any that he may have felt for his ancestral homeland, Mother Russia, the country of his birth," Craig writes in an awkward defense of White, who was actually born and raised in Boston. "That a potential employee had been (or even presently claimed to be) a Communist Party member was largely irrelevant to [White]," Craig insists, with no basis offered. "White simply did not care that a subordinate had past or even present ties with the Communist Party." Yet if this were true, then it would surely be notable that White was lying to a congressional committee when he told it "I would not have employed anybody I knew or suspected to be a Communist to [a high] government post." And this: "I can well understand and thoroughly sympathize with the view that if there is any slightest question of a man's being a Communist, he ought not to . . . hold a position where there was any confidential information passed . . . a mere suspicion was enough" (Craig [2004:263, 277, 275, 111]).

68. White Archives (undated), "Political Economic Int. of Future." See appendix 1 for a photo of the front and back pages of the manuscript.

69. Interlocking Subversion in Government Departments Hearings, Apr. 6, 1954, pp. 1421–1432.

70. Laski (1944:57).

71. Morgenthau III (1991:314).

72. Export Policy and Loyalty Hearings, July 30, 1948. See also May (1994:96); Sibley (2004:120).

73. Chambers (1952:432). In telling the story, Chambers refers to Harry Dexter White as "the Assistant Secretary of the Treasury," a post White only held briefly, from January 1945 to April 1946.

74. Chambers (1952:67–68).

75. Bentley (1951 [1988]:164–165).

76. Chambers (1952:426).

77. Much the same could be said about the Russian spy ring dismantled by the FBI in June 2010.

78. Chambers (1952:427).

79. Rees (1973:65).

80. White Archives (Mar. 22, 1938).

81. As White points out, however, silver prices began rising after countries began leaving the gold-exchange standard in 1931. Thus the Silver Purchase Act cannot be blamed for triggering the Chinese economic slump. See White Archives (1936).

82. White's demand looks curious in the context of the present monetary standoff between the United States and China, in which the United States persistently demands that the yuan be *unpegged* from the dollar. But today market pressure on China's currency is up, rather than down. The overarching American aim is the same: a more competitive dollar exchange rate.

83. Blum (1959:212).

84. Blum (1959:223).

85. White Archives (1936), pp. 40–41.

86. Blum (1959:524).

87. Blum (1959:524).

88. White Archives (Oct. 10, 1938).

89. Blum (1965:48).

90. Two untitled HDW memoranda, June 15 and Aug. 13, 1940, referenced in Rees (1973:109, f. 27).

91. White Archives, undated, referenced in Rees (1973:109, f. 7). Young (1963:193–194, 463).

92. White Archives (Mar. 31, 1939).

93. Two untitled HDW memoranda, June 15 and Aug. 13, 1940, referenced in Rees (1973:108, f. 27).

94. Sherwood (1948 [2008]:109).

95. Gilbert (1989:272–275).

96. Hastings (2009:181).

97. Schecter and Schecter (2002:45).

98. Rees (1973:121–125).

99. Karpov (2000:1). See also Schecter and Schecter (2002:43–44).

100. Pavlov (1996). I am grateful to Nikolai Krylov for his assistance in translating the relevant sections. Pavlov first told his story a year before the book was published, in the magazine *Novosti Razvedki I Kontrrazvedki* [News of Intelligence and Counterintelligence], 1995, nos. 9–10, 11–12.

101. Akhmerov was a Tatar who posed as a Turk to enroll in an American university in Peking, by way of which he was able to enter the United States under a false identity.

102. It is notable that historian Jonathan Utley, who knew nothing of Operation Snow and who thought highly of the "diplomatic revolution" White was proposing in U.S.-Japanese relations, still concluded that "[p]erhaps it was a naive plan that was too radical for Tokyo" (1985:170, 172).

103. "On its part, the Japanese Government proposes to do the following: 1. Withdraw all military, naval, air police forces from China (boundaries as of 1931) from Indo-China and from Thailand. 2. Withdraw all support—military, political, or economic—from any government in China other than that of the national government. 3. Replace the yen currency at a rate agreed upon among the Treasuries of China, Japan, England and United States all military scrip, yen and puppet notes circulating in China. 4. Give up all extra-territorial rights in China. 5. Extend to China a billion yen loan at 2 per cent to aid in reconstructing China (at a rate of 100 million yen a year)." Harry Dexter White (June 6, 1941).

104. Blum (1965:376).

105. White also expanded his portfolio in the Americas, both south and north of the border. He argued his case to Morgenthau for massive economic development loans to Latin America, which he considered "a remarkable opportunity," one that would bring the region closer "into the U.S. orbit" (Rees 1973:103). He represented the Treasury on a number of missions to the region, and was influential in technical matters such as reform of the Cuban central bank law (as passed in 1948). Critically, he was the lead author of the charter for a hemispheric development bank, which, though approved by an Inter-American Financial and Economic Advisory Committee in February 1940, subsequently failed to get the financial backing of key South American powers like Argentina and Chile, and ultimately suffered death by neglect in a U.S. Senate committee. But it did give White a valuable

trial run in fashioning multilateral financial institutions, which he put to good use a few years later in pushing through his far more ambitious Bretton Woods scheme.

In June 1941 White was appointed to the United States Canadian Joint Economic Committee, and in August he joined an interdepartmental committee on the use of the famous "Lend-Lease" program funds between the United States and Canada. U.S. Lend-Lease aid for the British war effort, with which White subsequently became intimately involved, became indelibly intermeshed with the Bretton Woods agenda.

106. Blum (1967:89).

CHAPTER 4: MAYNARD KEYNES AND THE MONETARY MENACE

1. Skidelsky (1983:13).

2. Keynes Papers (Mar. 11, 1906).

3. Skidelsky (1983:71).

4. Skidelsky (1994:496).

5. Keynes (1933 [1972]) X, p. 173.

6. Keynes (1933 [1972]) X, p. 446.

7. Skidelsky (1983:176).

8. Hubback (1985:77).

9. Keynes Papers (Sept. 13, 1907).

10. Skidelsky (1983:206). Keynes Papers (May 10, 1909).

11. Keynes Papers (Dec. 18, 1908).

12. Keynes (1913 [1971]) I, p. 51.

13. Keynes (1913 [1971]) I, p. 135.

14. Keynes (1983) XII, pp. 713–718.

15. Keynes (1983) XI, Dec. 1914, p. 320.

16. Skidelsky (1983:227).

17. Skidelsky (1983:57).

18. Keynes (1978) XVI, p. 296.

19. Keynes (1978) XVI, Feb. 28, 1916, p. 178.

20. Skidelsky (1983:315–327).

21. Skidelsky (1983:333).

22. Keynes (1978) XVI, Oct. 10, 1916, p. 198; Oct. 24, 1916, p. 201.

23. Keynes (1978) XVI, Sept. 24, 1939, p. 211.

24. Skidelsky (1983:335–336).

25. Hendrick (1928:269–270).

26. Spring-Rice (undated).

27. Keynes (1978) XVI, Jan. 1, 1918, p. 264.

28. Skidelsky (1983:342).

29. Keynes (1978) XVI, Apr. 19, 1918, p. 291. Keynes (1978) XVI, May 8, 1918, p. 287.

30. George (1938:684).

31. Keynes (1978) XVI, Dec. 24, 1917, p. 265.

32. Keynes (1919 [1971]) II, pp. 20–32. The words describing Lloyd George were left out of the final text, but can be found in Keynes (1933 [1972]) X, p. 23.

33. Keynes (1919 [1971]) II, p. 9.

34. Skidelsky (1983:359–360).

35. Keynes (1919 [1971]) II, p. 11.

36. Keynes (1978) XVI, p. 375.

37. Keynes (1978) XVI, p. 418.

38. MacMillan (2003:184).

39. See Rueff (Sept. 1929), which includes the reply by Keynes. See also Chivvis (2010:50–55).

40. Skidelsky (1983:352).

41. Keynes (1981) XX, Feb. 20, 1930, p. 64. Keynes (1981) XIX, Aug. 1, 1923, p. 112.

42. Keynes (1981) XIX, Nov. 24, 1923, p. 152.

43. Keynes (1981) XIX, Dec. 13, 1923, p. 160.

44. Keynes (1982) XXI, July 8 and 15, 1933, p. 244.

45. Keynes (1923 [1971]) IV, pp. 138, 139, 155.

46. Keynes (1923 [1971]) IV, p. 65.

47. Skidelsky (1994:161).

48. See, for example, the letter to *The Times* of London by Keynes's friend Henry Strakosch on July 31, 1925, to which Keynes replied the following day.

49. See, for example, Mundell (2000:331).

50. Keynes (1981) XX, Dec. 30, 1930, p. 263.

51. Skidelsky (1994:227–229).

52. Keynes (1931 [1972]) IX, Aug. 8 and 15, 1925, p. 297.

53. Keynes (1931 [1972]) IX, Aug. 8 and 15, 1925, p. 306.

54. Keynes Papers (1925–1926).

55. Keynes (1931 [1972]) IX, Oct. 11 and 18, 1930, p. 329.

56. Keynes Papers (Sept. 12, 1933) and (Oct. 2, 1933).

57. Keynes (1983) XII, p. 11.

58. Keynes (1981) XX, Mar. 7, 1930, p. 153.

59. Keynes (1930 [1971]) V, p. 152.

60. Keynes (1930 [1971]) V, p. 152.

61. Keynes (1930 [1971]) VI, p. 134.

62. Committee on Finance and Industry (1931:7653, 7836).

63. Skidelsky (1994:366). The rupture between Keynes and Henderson over how to generate economic recovery perfectly parallels the heated debates between economists today over the validity of Henderson's "Ricardian equivalence" arguments against fiscal stimulus.

64. Keynes (1981) XX, Feb. 20, 1930, p. 64.

65. Keynes (1981) XX, Feb. 26, 1930, p. 318.

66. Keynes (1981) XX, Feb. 28, 1930, p. 109.

67. Keynes (1987) XIII, Sept. 21, 1930, p. 186.

68. Keynes (1981) XX, Mar. 6, 1930, p. 147.

69. Keynes (1931 [1972]) IX, Oct. 11 and 18, 1930, p. 322.

70. Keynes (1931 [1972]) IX, Mar. 7, 1931, pp. 231–238.

71. Keynes (1981) XX, Mar. 16, 1931, pp. 496–497.

72. Keynes (1931 [1972]) IX, Jan. 14, 1931, pp. 135–136.

73. Keynes (1931 [1972]) IX, Sept. 10, 1931, pp. 238–242.

74. http://www.youtube.com/watch?v=U1S9F3agsUA&feature=related.

75. Rolph (1973:164).

76. Keynes (1931 [1972]) IX, Sept. 29, 1931, pp. 243–244.

77. Keynes Papers (Nov. 22, 1934).

78. Keynes (1978) XIV, Jan. 1, 1935, p. 492. The quote on Marx is from an earlier letter to Shaw dated Dec. 2, 1934.

79. Keynes (June 1933).

80. *Daily Mail* (Apr. 26, 1933).

81. Sefton and Weale (1995).

82. Keynes Papers (June 2, 1934).

83. Skidelsky (1994:481).

84. Skidelsky (1994:493).

85. Keynes (1982) XXI, July 8 and 15, 1933, pp. 233–246.

86. Skidelsky (1994:524).

87. Keynes (1978) XIV, Feb. 1947, p. 111.

88. Pigou (1936:115).

89. Clarke (2009:156–157).

90. Keynes (1936 [1973]) VII, p. 18.

91. Say (1880 [1971]:134–135).

92. Rymes (1989:92).

93. Barber (1990:114). Stein (1996:167).

94. Skidelsky (1994:543).

95. Joseph Schumpeter, Jacob Viner, Frank Knight, and Alvin Hansen were arguably the four most prominent U.S.-based reviewers of the *General Theory*; like Rueff, all of them focused on the importance of Keynes's conception of "liquidity preference."

96. Samuelson (1964:332).

97. Schumpeter (May 19, 1937).

98. Rueff (May 1947).

99. Sefton and Weale (1995).

100. Keynes (1982) XXVIII, Mar. 25, 1938, pp. 99–104.

101. Keynes Papers (Aug. 29, 1938). This letter is misdated by Keynes. It should read Sept. 29, 1938.

102. Clarke (1996:192).

103. Keynes (1982) XXII, Sept. 28, 1939, p. 31.

104. Keynes Papers (July 3, 1940). Keynes Papers (June 28, 1940).

105. Keynes (1982) XXII, pp. 353–354.

106. *The New Republic* (July 29, 1940).

107. Keynes Papers (Nov. 2, 1939).

108. Keynes Papers (Nov. 2, 1939).

109. Keynes (1979) XXIII, Mar. 11, 1941, p. 48.

110. Keynes (1979) XXIII, Oct. 27, 1940, pp. 13–26.

CHAPTER 5: "THE MOST UNSORDID ACT"

1. Sherwood (1948 [2008]:99).

2. Sherwood (1948 [2008]:117).

3. Sherwood (1948 [2008]).

4. Sherwood (1948 [2008]).

5. Sherwood (1948 [2008]).

6. Blum (1965:199–200).

7. Blum (1965:204).

8. Blum (1965:205–206).

9. Blum (1965).

10. Harriman and Abel (1975:5).

11. Lindbergh (1940).

12. Gilbert (1989:156).

13. Howard (Oct. 1977).

14. Gilbert (1989:162).

15. Clarke (2008:11).

16. Churchill (Nov. 10, 1941).

17. Cuthbert Headlam, quoted by Hastings (2009:161).

18. Black (2003:595).

19. Quoted in the *Daily Cleveland Herald* (Mar. 29, 1869). Variations on the quotation began to be attributed to Otto von Bismarck in the 1930s.

20. Blum (1967:122–123).

21. Blum (1967:123).

22. Blum (1967:124).

23. Blum (1967:136).

24. White Archives (Oct. 21, 1938), p. 1.

25. White Archives (Aug. 31, 1938), pp. 12–13.

26. White Archives (Feb. 2, 1939), p. 6.

27. White Archives (Sept. 6, 1938).

28. Keynes (1979) XXIII, Mar. 11, 1941, pp. 46–48.

29. Skidelsky (2000).

30. Keynes (1979) XXIII, Apr. 7, 1941, pp. 62–63.

31. Skidelsky (2000:106).

32. Keynes (1979) XXIV, Dec. 12, 1944, p. 212.

33. Treasury Papers (May 8–11, 1941).

34. Keynes (1979) XXIII, June 2, 1941, and July 13, 1941, pp. 107, 154–155.

35. Skidelsky (2000:111).

36. Treasury Papers (May 22, 1941).

37. Morgenthau, *Diaries*, Vol. 410, June 19, 1941, p. 103.

38. Keynes (1979) XXIII, May 19, 1941, pp. 87–88.

39. Treasury Papers (May 24 and 26, 1941).

40. Halifax, *Diary*, July 7, 1941.

41. Culbertson (1925:192).

42. Skidelsky (2000).

43. Skidelsky (2000).

44. Harrod (1951:512).

45. London Chamber of Commerce (1942).

46. Acheson (1969:28).

47. Keynes (1933:769).

48. *Foreign Relations of the United States, 1941* (1941:21–22); Kimball (1971:252–253); Dobson (1986:52).

49. Hastings (2009:162–163).

50. Hastings (2009:164).

51. Gilbert (1989:222).

52. Hastings (2009:171).

53. Memorandum between Welles and Cadogan, cited in Gardner (1956 [1980]:42).

54. Churchill (1950 [2005]:385).

55. Welles (1946:7–8).

56. Welles (1946:12–13).

57. Welles (1946:12–15).

58. Churchill (1950 [2005]:397).

59. *Congressional Record*, Senate (Aug. 19, 1941).

60. Gardner (1956 [1980]:51).

61. Sherwood (1948 [2008]:298).

62. Roosevelt (1942).

63. Hull (1948:1152).

64. House of Commons Debates (1944).

65. Skidelsky (2000:180).

66. Skidelsky (2000).

67. Morgenthau, *Diaries*, Vol. 753, July 13, 1944, p. 162.

CHAPTER 6: THE BEST-LAID PLANS OF WHITE AND KEYNES

1. *Proceedings and Documents* (1948), pp. 1107–1126.

2. *New York Herald Tribune* (Mar. 31, 1946).

3. Blum (1967:92, 123).

4. Hastings (2009:204).

5. Sherwood (1948 [2008]:394).

6. White Archives (Mar. 1942), "United Nations Stabilization Fund."

7. The WTO was only created in 1995. It was preceded by the General Agreement on Tariffs and Trade (GATT).

8. Hastings (2009:212–213).

9. White Archives (Mar. 1942), "Suggested Plan," pp. 1–3, 9.

10. Hastings (2009:214, 217).

11. Sherwood (1948 [2008]:402).

12. "[Gold] constitutes the best medium in which general purchasing power may be stored or saved. . . . [E]very country in the world will sell goods for gold and no country will refuse gold in settlement of debt or in payment for services rendered. . . . With adequate gold holdings, a country can permit its outpayments to be greater than its inpayments for a long period of time without being forced to attempt to raise foreign funds by borrowing abroad or by liquidating the foreign assets of its nationals, and to do so without being forced to curtail imports, depreciate its currency, subsidize exports, or resort to complicated multiple currency devices in order to help balance its international accounts. Gold holdings constitute one of the effective cushions for insulating the domestic economy from the adverse repercussions of economic changes abroad." White Archives (Aug. 4, 1942), pp. 4–5, 12 (note: the folder contains numerous duplicate page numbers).

13. White Archives (Aug. 4, 1942), pp. 13–14 (note: the folder contains numerous duplicate page numbers).

14. Simmel (1900 [1978]:181–182).

15. White Archives (Aug. 4, 1942), pp. 13–14 (note: the folder contains numerous duplicate page numbers).

16. White Archives (Aug. 4, 1942), Section IV, p. 12 (note: the folder contains numerous duplicate page numbers).

17. White Archives (Aug. 4, 1942), Section IV, p. 16 (note: the folder contains numerous duplicate page numbers).

18. "Sweden, Switzerland and Argentina may keep part of their reserves of international payments in the form of dollar balances or even in the form of United States Government securities, but they feel safe to do so only because they know they can convert those dollars into gold if and when necessary. . . . No country is going to elect to pile up balances in a foreign country . . . unless there is confidence that the foreign currency will be no less valuable . . . under all conditions, and for all time." White Archives (Aug. 4, 1942), Section IV, pp. 1, 3, 13 (note: the folder contains numerous duplicate page numbers).

19. White Archives (Aug. 4, 1942), Section IV, p. 20 (note: the folder contains numerous duplicate page numbers).

20. White Archives (Aug. 4, 1942), Section IV, p. 7 (note: the folder contains numerous duplicate page numbers).

21. "The gold standard, as the text books described it and in the semi-automatic manner in which it sometimes operated, died in 1914. Its painful and chequered resurrection between 1925 and 1931 was perhaps part of the price which had to be paid for the understanding of economic realities. The lesson which should have derived from this interlude was not a distrust of gold as such, but a distrust of false parities, of the barren masses of international indebtedness created by the last war, of economic nationalism, of the whole crazy pattern of economic contradictions which doomed the new gold standard—and would have made equally short work of any international monetary system. . . .

"[S]ome international standard of value and means of payment is essential. The national currency units must be expressed in terms of some uniform standard. That standard must in turn be related to the means chosen to pay uncleared balances of international indebtedness; and strong arguments support the claims of gold to fulfil these twin functions. The most important, if at the same time the most imponderable, of these arguments is the reverence in which gold is still held over the greater part of the world. That feeling goes back to the birth of civilization. It cannot be killed in a day. At this moment, gold is quoted in the free market in Bombay and in all the black markets of the world at levels ranging to twice the official dollar and sterling prices. There is no country in the world where it is not acceptable.

"The alternative to gold or to some international unit of account based on gold would be one or other of the existing currencies—inevitably the dollar, in the post-war economic set-up—as the standard of international values and payments. There might well be grave political objections to such an appointment. However dominant the dollar may become in the post-war currency world, and however complete may be the dependence of gold on the readiness of the United States to buy it at a fixed price in terms of dollars, there are solid reasons why gold should act as the cloak under the cover of which the strong currencies play their part." *The Economist* (Nov. 28, 1942:655–656).

22. White Archives (Jan. 8, 1943).

23. White Archives (Aug. 4, 1942), p. 18 (note: the folder contains numerous duplicate page numbers).

24. White Archives (Aug. 4, 1942), Section IV, p. 22 (note: the folder contains numerous duplicate page numbers).

25. "Inflows can be impounded in the fund instead of being added to the credit base, while outflows can be released from the fund instead of being deducted from the credit base. Further, a fund can be employed either to ease or to tighten the money market, or to reduce or increase fluctuations in government bond prices. It can help stimulate or curb a credit expansion. It can be employed to strengthen and weaken foreign exchanges, to peg exchanges for short or long periods and to increase or reduce fluctuations in foreign exchange." White Archives (undated), "Stabilization," p. 1.

26. White Archives (undated), "Stabilization," pp. 5–6.

27. White Archives (Mar. 1942), "Suggested Plan," Section I, p. 7.

28. White Archives (Mar. 1942), "Suggested Plan," Section II, pp. 49–50.

29. White Archives (Mar. 1942), "Suggested Plan," Section II, pp. 55–56.

30. "Russia, despite her socialist economy could both contribute and profit by participation. To deny her the privileges of joining in this cooperative effort to improve world economic relations would be to repeat the tragic errors of the last generation, and introduce a very discordant note in the new era millions everywhere are hoping for. If the Russian Government is willing to participate, her counsel in the preliminary negotiations should be as eagerly sought as that of any other country, and her membership in both Fund and Bank equally as welcome.

"A socialist economy like a capitalistic economy engages in international trade and financial transactions which can be either beneficial or harmful to other countries. In fact, because the conduct of foreign trade and international financial transactions are exclusively the creature of the government in a socialist economy, there is all the more reason to attempt to get them to join in a cooperative attempt to introduce stability in international economic relationships and a higher level of trade. If for no other reason than that there are no limits to which a powerful socialist economy could go if it sought to disrupt trade. It would be extremely shortsighted not to welcome Russia to participate." White Archives (Mar. 1942), "Suggested Plan," Section II, pp. 62–63.

31. Hastings (2009:238).

32. White Archives (undated), "Political Economic Int. of Future."

33. White Archives, (Mar. 1942), "Suggested Plan," Section II, pp. 62–63.

34. Skidelsky (2000:191).

35. Keynes (1980) XXV, Aug. 8, 1941, p. 28.

36. Keynes (1980) XXV, Jan. 22, 1942, p. 107.

37. Goodhart and Delargy (1998).

38. Keynes (1983) XI, Oct. 13, 1936, p. 501.

39. Keynes (1980) XXV, Apr. 25, 1941, pp. 16–19.

40. Keynes (1980) XXV, Jan. 22, 1942, pp. 106–107.

41. Schumpeter (1952:274).

42. Keynes (1980) XXV, Apr. 25, 1941, pp. 16–19.

43. Keynes (1980) XXV, Dec. 1, 1940, pp. 8–9.

44. Henderson (Jan. 26, 1951).

45. See Ahamed (2009) for a vivid portrait of Schacht, his thinking, and his system.

46. Keynes (1980) XXV, Apr. 25, 1941, pp. 16–19.

47. Skidelsky (2000:202–204).

48. Keynes (1943).

49. Keynes (1980) XXV, Dec. 15, 1941, pp. 74–75.

50. Keynes (1943).

51. Keynes (1980) XXV, Apr. 19, 1942, p. 148.

52. Keynes (1980) XXV, Dec. 15, 1941, pp. 86–87.

53. Keynes (1980) XXV, Nov. 18, 1941, p. 54.

54. Keynes (1980) XXV, May 4, 1943, p. 258.

55. Keynes (1980) XXV, Nov. 18, 1941, p. 55.

56. Keynes (1980) XXV, May 18, 1943, p. 279.

57. Keynes (1980) XXV, Nov. 18, 1941, p. 60.

58. See minutes of British and U.S. negotiating delegations, Keynes (1980) XXV, Sept. 24, 1943, p. 348.

59. White Archives (Mar. 1942), "United Nations Stabilization Fund."

60. Keynes (1980) XXV, Aug. 3, 1942, p. 161.

61. Keynes (1980) XXV, Apr. 16, 1943, p. 246.

62. White proposed that the contribution of each country would consist of (1) 25 percent up-front in cash, at least half of which in the form of gold, (2) 25 percent up-front in interest-bearing government securities, and (3) 50 percent via subsequent installments in a form to be determined by the fund.

63. White Archives (Sept. 3, 1942).

64. Keynes (1980) XXV, July 2, 1943, pp. 330–331.

65. Keynes (1980) XXV, May 8, 1942, p. 152.

66. Treasury Papers (May 16, 1944), Waley to Keynes, Brand, and Eady.

CHAPTER 7: WHITEWASH

1. Morgenthau eventually accepted a British proposal for separate invasion currencies: a special "yellow seal dollar" for the American forces and a "military authority pound" for the British (Blum [1967:141–142, 158]).

2. Morgenthau, *Diaries*, Vol. 526, p. 111.

3. Morgenthau, *Diaries*, Vol. 527, pp. 235–236.

4. *Foreign Relations of the United States, 1942* (1942:171–172).

5. Morgenthau, *Diaries*, Vol. 545, pp. 35–37.

6. Morgenthau, *Diaries*, Vol. 529, pp. 115–117.

7. Morgenthau, *Diaries*, Vol. 750, July 5, 1944, p. 125.

8. Morgenthau, *Diaries*, Vol. 545, pp. 90–114.

9. Treasury Papers (July 8, 1942).

10. Treasury Papers (July 14, 1942).

11. Treasury Papers (Aug. 4, 1942).

12. Van Dormael (1978:60).

13. Keynes (1980) XXV, Aug. 3, 1942, pp. 158–159.

14. Keynes (1980) XXV, Aug. 3, 1942, p. 160.

15. Keynes (1980) XXV, Apr. 16, 1943, p. 245.

16. Keynes (1980) XXV, Aug. 3, 1942, pp. 160–166.

17. Treasury Papers (Oct. 7, 1942). Brand could well have been describing the European Central Bank in 2010–2011, as it conjured new euros to buy up Greek, Irish, Portuguese, Spanish, and Italian debt that private investors would not touch.

18. Penrose (1953:48–49).

19. Keynes (1980) XXV, Dec. 16, 1942, p. 201.

20. Harry Dexter White (Mar. 1943:382–387).

21. Keynes (1980) XXV, Jan. 8, 1943, pp. 204–205.

22. White Archives (Aug. 28, 1942).

23. Treasury Papers (Jan. 21, 1943).

24. Treasury Papers (Feb. 19, 1943).

25. Treasury Papers (Feb. 16, 1943).

26. Foreign Office (Feb. 17, 1943).

27. Treasury Papers (Feb. 18, 1943).

28. Treasury Papers (Feb. 19, 1943).

29. Foreign Office (Mar. 24, 1943).

30. Van Dormael (1978:72).

31. Keynes (1980) XXV, Feb. 26, 1943, p. 208.

32. Keynes (1980) XXV, Apr. 22, 1943, p. 251.

33. Keynes (1980) XXV, May 5, 1943, p. 266.

34. Keynes (1980) XXV, Apr. 16, 1943, p. 240.

35. Morgenthau, *Diaries*, Vol. 622, pp. 8–9.

36. Morgenthau, *Diaries*, Vol. 622, pp. 242–246.

37. *New York Times* (Mar. 30, 1943).

38. *New York World-Telegram* (1943).

39. *The Times* (London) (Apr. 8, 1943).

40. *Daily Herald* (Apr. 8, 1943).

41. Keynes (1980) XXV, Apr. 16, 1943, p. 242.

42. Keynes (1980) XXV, Apr. 21, 1943, p. 236.

43. Keynes (1980) XXV, Apr. 16, 1943, p. 242.

44. Keynes (1980) XXV, Apr. 22, 1943, p. 253.

45. Keynes (1980) XXV, Apr. 16, 1943, p. 245.

46. Keynes (1980) XXV, May 18, 1943, p. 278.

47. Keynes (1980) XXV, May 18, 1943, p. 269.

48. Keynes (1980) XXV, May 18, 1943, p. 269.

49. Treasury Papers (Jan. 21, 1943).

50. Keynes (1980) XXV, Apr. 22, 1943, p. 252.

51. Van Dormael (1978:86).

52. Van Dormael (1978:83).

53. Van Dormael (1978:88).

54. Keynes (1980) XXV, Mar. 2, 1943, p. 227.

55. Keynes (1980) XXV, Mar. 4, 1943, p. 230.

56. Keynes (1980) XXV, Apr. 12, 1943, p. 238.

57. Foreign Office (May 20, 1943).

58. Foreign Office (June 18, 1943).

59. Foreign Office (July 19, 1943; July 1, 1943).

60. Foreign Office (June 13, 1943).

61. *Foreign Relations of the United States, 1943* (1943:1081–1082).

62. Gilbert (1989:447).

63. Keynes (1980) XXV, July 24, 1943, and Sept. 21, 1943, pp. 335–338, 341–342.

64. Harrod (1951:558–559).

65. Van Dormael (1978:101).

66. Keynes (1980) XXV, Oct. 3, 1943, p. 356, 361.

67. Keynes (1980) XXV, Oct. 3, 1943, p. 363.

68. Keynes (1980) XXV, Oct. 4, 1943, p. 364.

69. Keynes (1980) XXV, Oct. 3, 1943, p. 364.

70. Keynes (1980) XXV, Oct. 9, 1943, pp. 370–371.

71. Keynes (1980) XXV, Oct. 10, 1943, pp. 372–373.

72. Foreign Office (Jan. 7, 1944).

73. Treasury Papers (Jan. 26, 1944).

74. *Congressional Record*, House (Nov. 1, 1943), pp. 8964–8975.

75. Treasury Papers (Feb. 3, 1944).

76. Treasury Papers (Jan. 14, 1944).

77. Treasury Papers (Dec. 14, 1943).

78. War Cabinet Minutes, Cab. 66/47.

79. War Cabinet Minutes, Cab. 66/47, WP(44)129; Foreign Office (undated).

80. War Cabinet Minutes, Cab. 66/46, WP(44)75.

81. Blum (1967).

82. Keynes (1979) XXIV, p. 63.

83. Hastings (2009:244).

84. Keynes (1980) XXV, Feb. 23, 1944, p. 412.

85. Keynes (1980) XXV, Mar. 8, 1944, p. 417.

86. Keynes (1980) XXV, Mar. 11, 1944, pp. 417–418.

87. Morgenthau, *Diaries*, Vol. 719, pp. 208–209.

88. Treasury Papers (Apr. 13, 1944).

89. Van Dormael (1978:124).

90. Morgenthau, *Diaries*, Vol. 723, pp. 37–38.

91. Treasury Papers (Apr. 16, 1944).

92. Treasury Papers (Apr. 25, 1944).

93. Foreign Office (Apr. 30, 1944).

94. Harrod (1951:573).

95. Keynes (1980) XXVI, May 16, 1944, p. 5.

96. Keynes (1980) XXVI, May 18, 1944, pp. 8–9.

97. Keynes (1980) XXVI, May 23, 1944, p. 10.

98. Keynes (1980) XXVI, May 23, 1944, pp. 9–21.

99. Keynes (1980) XXV, Aug. 3, 1942, p. 160.

100. Keynes (1980) XXVI, May 23, 1944, pp. 9–21.

101. Keynes (1980) XXVI, May 22, 1944, p. 24.

102. Keynes (1980) XXVI, May 31, 1944, p. 25.

103. Keynes (1980) XXVI, May 23, 1944, p. 14.

104. *Deutsche Bergwerks-Zeitung* (June 8, 1944). See Van Dormael (1978:150).

105. *Kölnische Zeitung* (May 26, 1944). See Van Dormael (1978:150).

106. National Archives, RG59.800.515–BWA/6–2444.

107. Treasury Papers (May 16, 1944), Waley to Keynes, Brand, and Eady.

108. Treasury Papers (May 16, 1944), Keynes memorandum.

109. Foreign Office (May 9, 1944).

110. Blum (1967:253).

111. Keynes (1980) XXVI, May 24, 1944, p. 27.

112. Keynes (1980) XXVI, May 30, 1944, pp. 41–42.

113. Foreign Office (May 24, 1944).

114. Keynes (1979) XXIV, pp. 34–65, 93.

115. See, for example, Wapshott (2011).

116. Keynes (1980) XXVI, June 25, 1944, p. 56.

117. Keynes (1980) XXVI, June 25, 1944, p. 61.

118. Keynes (1980) XXVI, June 25, 1944, pp. 61, 63.

119. Keynes (1980) XXVI, June 26, 1944, p. 65.

120. National Archives, RG59.800.515–BWA/6–2444, Collado Notes.

121. Van Dormael (1978).

122. National Archives, RG59.800.515/6–2844.

123. Keynes (1980) XXVI, June 30, 1944, pp. 67–68.

124. Morgenthau, *Diaries*, Vol. 747, pp. 60A–C.

125. Board of Governors of the Federal Reserve System, American meeting (June 26, 1944).

126. Van Dormael (1978:166).

127. The exact number of foreign delegations is in dispute, with different sources offering numbers from thirteen to seventeen. The World Bank indicates that it was fifteen: http://jolis.worldbankimflib.org/Bwf/60panel2.htm.

128. Board of Governors of the Federal Reserve System (June 26, 1944).

129. Van Dormael (1978).

130. Morgenthau, *Diaries*, Vol. 746, pp. 133–139.

131. Blum (1967:253).

CHAPTER 8: HISTORY IS MADE

1. Gilbert (1989).

2. Morgenthau, *Diaries*, Vol. 748, June 30, 1944, pp. 228–229.

3. *Christian Science Monitor* (July 3, 1944:1).

4. Morgenthau, *Diaries*, Vol. 748, June 30, 1944, pp. 228–229.

5. Keynes (1980) XXV, Dec. 15, 1941, p. 71.

6. Robbins (1990:167). Skidelsky (2000:347) and Morgenthau's son (Morgenthau III, 1991:339) write that Keynes skipped the opening ceremonies, which might have made sense given the American snub. But there is no evidence that Keynes did not attend, which would certainly have caused a diplomatic kerfuffle. Moggridge, editor of Keynes's *Collected Writings*, writes only that "Keynes took no formal part in the opening preliminaries and speeches," which clearly is not the same thing as failing to attend (Keynes [1980] XXV, p. 71). Morgenthau's son strangely manufactures a quote from Moggridge indicating that Keynes "chose instead [of attending the ceremonies] to give a small dinner party." Not only did Moggridge not write this, but we know from the conference *Proceedings and Documents* (1948, Vol. 1, p. 3) that the opening event began at 3:00 p.m. and ended before 5:00 p.m., well before Keynes's dinner.

7. *Time* (July 3, 1944).

8. Robbins (1990:168).

9. *Christian Science Monitor* (July 1, 1944:1).

10. *Chicago Tribune* (July 23, 1944:G9).

11. *Chicago Tribune* (July 3, 1944:13).

12. *Chicago Tribune* (July 9, 1944:10), "Good Money For Bad."

13. *Wall Street Journal* (July 5, 1944:6).

14. *Time* (July 10, 1944).

15. Morgenthau, *Diaries*, Vol. 756, July 21, 1944, pp. 251–252.

16. Bernstein quoted in Black (1991:45).

17. Tenkotte and Claypool (2009). Kenton County Historical Society (Feb. 1997).

18. Blum (1967:252).

19. *Biographical Directory of the United States Congress*.

20. Blum (1967:251).

21. *Chicago Tribune* (June 12, 1944:12).

22. *Chicago Tribune* (July 2, 1944:6).

23. *Time* (July 17, 1944).

24. Keynes Papers (July 22, 1944).

25. *Vassar Encyclopedia*.

26. *New York Times* (July 5, 1944:20), "Monetary Conference Keeps Dr. Newcomer Too Busy for Her Mountain-Climbing Hobby."

27. Morgenthau, *Diaries*, Vol. 749, July 1, 1944, pp. 22–23.

28. Morgenthau, *Diaries*, Vol. 749, July 1, 1944, p. 24.

29. Morgenthau, *Diaries*, Vol. 749, July 1, 1944, p. 25.

30. Morgenthau, *Diaries*, Vol. 749, July 1, 1944, p. 30.

31. Morgenthau, *Diaries*, Vol. 753, July 13, 1944, p. 125.

32. *Christian Science Monitor* (July 15, 1944:16).

33. *Washington Post* (July 8, 1944:4).

34. Lippmann (July 13, 1944:7).

35. *The Times* (London) (July 17, 1944:3).

36. Gilbert (1989:551).

37. Morgenthau, *Diaries*, Vol. 749, July 3, 1944, pp. 284–286.

38. Goldenweiser, Papers, Bretton Woods Conference, Box 4.

39. Morgenthau, *Diaries*, Vol. 753, July 13, 1944, pp. 90–91.

40. Morgenthau, *Diaries*, Vol. 749, July 2 or 3, 1944, pp. 210–211.

41. *Washington Post* (July 12, 1944:1).

42. Morgenthau, *Diaries*, Vol. 752, July 10, 1944, pp. 58–78.

43. *Chicago Tribune* (July 7, 1944:10).

44. *Wall Street Journal* (July 3, 1944:4).

45. *Wall Street Journal* (July 7, 1944:2).

46. *Christian Science Monitor* (July 12, 1944:17).

47. Robbins (1990:174, 184).

48. Robbins (1990:179).

49. *Chicago Tribune* (July 9, 1944:A5), "Study Means to Balk Hiding of Axis Assets."

50. Bourneuf (July 6, 1944:3–4). Van Dormael (1978:201–202).

51. Morgenthau, *Diaries*, Vol. 753, July 13, 1944, p. 85.

52. The terms "gold-convertible currency" and "gold-convertible exchange" were used interchangeably in the discussions.

53. See Rosenberg and Schuler (2012: page numbers unavailable), transcript of the fourth meeting of Commission One, July 13, 1944, 2:30 p.m. See also Bourneuf (July 13, 1944:3).

At the 10:00 a.m. Commission One meeting the following morning, July 14, Robertson raised the issue again in a different context. "I want to be assured that the correction suggested last time is being duly embodied in Article III now," he said. "On page 3, in place of the phrase 'ten percent of its official holdings [of gold and gold convertible] exchange,' read 'ten percent of its net official holdings of gold and U.S. dollars.'"

Bernstein responded: "It has been my intention to refer to this change when the question of definition arises. I think, however, that it is the thought of those who have considered this question that the change 'gold convertible exchange' into 'U.S. dollars' would be in effect a restatement of the same principle. There are few, if any, currencies other than U.S. dollars which would now meet this definition, and if we may insert it this point, it would facilitate progress."

"Then the alteration is suggesting replacing 'gold convertible exchange' with 'U.S. dollars,'" White concluded, to no objections (Rosenberg and Schuler [2012]).

54. Morgenthau, *Diaries*, Vol. 754, July 14, 1944, p. 3.

55. Gilbert (1989:552–553).

56. *New York Times* (July 7, 1944:7), "Britain is 'Broke,' Two Ministers Say."

57. Keynes (1980) XXVI, July 4, 1944, pp. 78–79, 81.

58. *New York Times* (July 7, 1944:9), "Keynes Attacks Fund Plan Critics."

59. *New York Times* (July 5, 1944:19), "Quota Issues Split World Fund Talks."

60. Robbins (1990:168).

61. *New York Times* (July 9, 1944:E6).

62. Robbins (1990:179).

63. Foreign Office (July 1944 [day unclear]).

64. Foreign Office (July 10, 1944).

65. Foreign Office (July 11, 1944).

66. Robbins (1990:174).

67. Goldenweiser, Papers, Bretton Woods Conference, Box 4.

68. Morgenthau, *Diaries*, Vol. 753, pp. 143–144.

69. Morgenthau, *Diaries*, Vol. 753, July 13, 1944, pp. 133–164.

70. Robbins (1990:174).

71. Morgenthau, *Diaries*, Vol. 752, pp. 33–36; Vol. 753, pp. 122–132.

72. Morgenthau, *Diaries*, Vol. 752, July 10, 1944, pp. 34–38.

73. Morgenthau, *Diaries*, Vol. 753, July 13, 1944, pp. 89.

74. Morgenthau, *Diaries*, Vol. 754, July 14, 1944, pp. 4–5.

75. Blum (1967:269–270).

76. Keynes (1980) XXVI, July 14, 1944, p. 92.

77. Morgenthau, *Diaries*, Vol. 754, July 15, 1944, p. 6.

78. Keynes (1980) XXVI, July 17, 1944, p. 94–95.

79. *New York Times* (July 19, 1944:5).

80. Morgenthau, *Diaries*, Vol. 756, July 20, 1944, p. 120.

81. Robbins (1990:168).

82. Robbins (1990:183–184, 192).

83. Acheson (1969:81–82).

84. Morgenthau, *Diaries*, Vol. 753, July 13, 1944, pp. 133–164.

85. Robbins (1990:181).

86. Robbins (1990:190).

87. Skidelsky (2000:354).

88. Robbins (1990:190).

89. Morgenthau, *Diaries*, Vol. 756, July 20, 1944, pp. 137–169.

90. Morgenthau, *Diaries*, Vol. 756, July 20, 1944, p. 144.

91. Morgenthau, *Diaries*, Vol. 756, July 20, 1944, p. 120.

92. Skidelsky (2000:355).

93. Robbins (1990:191).

94. Foreign Office, July 20, 1944.

95. Morgenthau, *Diaries*, Vol. 756, July 20, 1944, p. 119.

96. Morgenthau, *Diaries*, Vol. 756, July 20, 1944, p. 151.

97. Robbins (1990:182).

98. *The Times* (London) (July 10, 1944:3).

99. *New York Times* (July 17, 1944:19).

100. Bernstein quoted in Black (1991:47).

101. *New York Times* (July 19, 1944:18).

102. *New York Times* (July 18, 1944).

103. *New York Times* (July 18, 1944:18).

104. *Chicago Tribune* (July 9, 1944:10), "Good Money For Bad."

105. *Chicago Tribune* (July 15, 1944:6).

106. White Archives (undated), "Political Economic Int. of Future."

107. Morgenthau, *Diaries*, Vol. 751, July 9, 1944, pp. 272–291.

108. Morgenthau, *Diaries*, Vol. 754, July 15, 1944, pp. 164–176.

109. Robbins (1990:172).

110. Mikesell (1951:104–105).

111. Bernstein quoted in Black (1991:43).

112. Robbins (1990:172).

113. *New York Times* (July 8, 1944:20).

114. *New York Times* (July 14, 1944:28).

115. Morgenthau, *Diaries*, Vol. 750, July 5, 1944, pp. 87–124.

116. Mikesell (1951:108).

117. Morgenthau, *Diaries*, Vol. 750, July 5, 1944, pp. 87–124.

118. Mikesell (1951:103).

119. Morgenthau, *Diaries*, Vol. 750, July 5, 1944, pp. 87–124.

120. *Christian Science Monitor* (July 6, 1944:15).

121. Morgenthau, *Diaries*, Vol. 750, July 5, 1944, pp. 87–124.

122. *New York Times* (July 9, 1944:E6).

123. Mikesell (1951:104).

124. *Chicago Tribune* (July 15, 1944:6).

125. Morgenthau, *Diaries*, Vol. 752, July 11, 1944, pp. 203–216.

126. Morgenthau, *Diaries*, Vol. 754, July 14, 1944, pp. 14–20.

127. Robbins (1990:185).

128. Morgenthau, *Diaries*, Vol. 754, July 15, 1944, pp. 115–139.

129. Robbins (1990:186).

130. Morgenthau, *Diaries*, Vol. 755, July 17, 1944, pp. 69–86.

131. *New York Times* (July 18, 1944:1).

132. *New York Times* (July 20, 1944:24).

133. Robbins (1990:192).

134. Mikesell (1951:104).

135. Morgenthau, *Diaries*, Vol. 756, July 21, 1944, p. 255.

136. Morgenthau, *Diaries*, Vol. 756, July 21, 1944, pp. 258–260.

137. Keynes Papers (July 22, 1944).

138. Bernstein quoted in Black (1991:104).

139. Bernstein quoted in Black (1991:47).

140. Morgenthau, *Diaries*, Vol. 757, July 22, 1944, pp. 1–13.

141. Bernstein quoted in Black (1991:48).

142. Bareau (1951).

143. Skidelsky (2000:357).

144. Black (1991:57).

145. *Proceedings and Documents* (1948), Vol. 1, pp. 1107–1126.

146. Robbins (1990:193).

147. Morgenthau, *Diaries*, Vol. 757, July 22, 1944, pp. 13A–13B.

148. Morgenthau, *Diaries*, Vol. 723, pp. 37–38.

149. Morgenthau, *Diaries*, Vol. 757, July 22, 1944, pp. 13A–13B.

150. Zlobin (Oct. 15, 1944).

151. Grand Jury Testimony in the Alger Hiss Case, 1947–1949, HDW, Mar. 24–25, 1948, pp. 2740–2741.

152. Mikesell (1951:104).

153. Zlobin (Oct. 15, 1944).

CHAPTER 9: BEGGING LIKE FALA

1. Foreign Office (Dec. 29, 1944).

Ghost:

> Thus was I, sleeping, by a brother's hand
> Of life, of crown, of queen, at once dispatch'd
> Cut off even in the blossoms of my sin,
> Unhousel'd, disappointed, unaneled;
> No reckoning made, but sent to my account
> With all my imperfections on my head
> (*Hamlet*, Act 1, Scene 5, Lines 74–79)

2. Foreign Office (Apr. 5, 1945).

3. Skidelsky (2000:358).

4. Foreign Office (Dec. 29, 1944).

5. Morgenthau, *Diaries*, Vol. 805, p. 163.

6. Morgenthau, *Diaries*, Vol. 807, pp. 151–156.

7. *Commercial and Financial Chronicle* (Sept. 14, 1944).

8. Morgenthau, *Diaries*, Vol. 816, pp. 108–118.

9. Morgenthau, *Diaries*, Vol. 752, p. 279.

10. Morgenthau, *Diaries*, Vol. 763, pp. 219–220.

11. Morgenthau *Diaries*, Vol. 657, p. 6.

12. Van Dormael (1978:246).

13. *Wall Street Journal* (Apr. 13, 1945).

14. Foreign Office (Dec. 1944).

15. *The Economist* (July 21, 1945).

16. Skidelsky (2000:361).

17. Blum (1967:314).

18. Blum (1967:315).

19. Morgenthau, *Diaries*, Vol. 780, pp. 1–13.

20. Skidelsky (2000:367–368).

21. Keynes (1979) XXIV, Dec. 12, 1944, p. 217.

22. Blum (1967:314).

23. Herring Jr. (1971:271).

24. Blum (1967:320).

25. Blum (1967:323).

26. Herring Jr. (1971:269).

27. Gilbert (1989:683–686).

28. Herring Jr. (1971:274).

29. Blum (1967:448–449).

30. Blum (1967:463–464).

31. Blum (1967:327, 332–333).

32. Blum (1967:342).

33. Blum (1967:343).

34. Skidelsky (2000).

35. Blum (1967:344, 350).

36. Blum (1967:338).

37. Blum (1967:338–339).

38. Dietrich (2002:17).

39. Morgenthau III (1991:164).

40. Rees (1973).

41. Blum (1967:355).

42. Blum (1967:369).

43. Churchill (1953:158).

44. Blum (1967:371).

45. Rees (1973:278).

46. Blum (1967:374). Rees (1973:277).

47. Rees (1973:279).

48. Blum (1967:373).

49. Hull (1948:1614).

50. Rees (1973:282).

51. Dietrich (2002:71).

52. Dietrich (2002:70–72).

53. Rees (1973:284–286).

54. Rees (1973:177).

55. Petrov (1967:122–123).

56. Blum (1967:180–181).

57. Parts of Bentley's conspiratorial account of White's actions with regard to the Allied military marks are at best confused, and possibly just wrong. She claimed that, following orders from Soviet Intelligence, she used intermediaries to procure samples of the currency from White, which the Soviets had hoped, but failed, to use to create counterfeits. Yet White had

actually openly sent copies to Soviet Ambassador Gromyko on February 9, 1944, and so such shadowy dealings were unnecessary.

58. Rees (1973:189).

59. Petrov (1967).

60. Dietrich (2002).

61. Blum (1967:469–473).

62. Skidelsky (2000:381–383).

63. Keynes (1979) XXIV, June 23, 1945, p. 369.

64. Clarke (2008:393).

65. Skidelsky (2000:413).

66. Skidelsky (2000:410).

67. Skidelsky (2000:407).

68. Skidelsky (2000:416).

69. Skidelsky (2000:420).

70. Keynes (1979) XXIV, Oct. 12, 1945, p. 541.

71. Keynes (1979) XXIV, Oct. 12, 1945, p. 540.

72. Keynes (1979) XXIV, Oct. 5, 1945, p. 535.

73. Skidelsky (2000:421).

74. Skidelsky (2000:425–427).

75. Skidelsky (2000:432).

76. This is one variation of the exchange, which British negotiator Paul Bareau related to Skidelsky (2000:434). Gardner (1956 [1980]:201) has a slightly different version.

77. Skidelsky (2000:434–444).

78. Van Dormael (1978:276–280).

79. House of Commons Debates (Dec. 13, 1945).

80. Keynes (1979) XXIV, Jan. 1, 1946, p. 627.

81. Keynes (1979) XXIV, May 15, 1945, p. 278.

82. Skidelsky (2000:451–452).

83. Clarke (1982:57).

84. Mikesell (1951).

85. James (1996:69–70).

86. Kennan (1946).

87. For example, a cable dated January 18, 1945, indicates that "RICH-ARD" was about to be appointed assistant secretary in "NABOB'S" [Morgenthau's] department (National Security Agency, Venona Files, T247 [Reissue], Jan. 18, 1945). White was appointed assistant secretary on January 23.

CHAPTER 10: OUT WITH THE OLD ORDER,
IN WITH THE NEW

1. Chambers (1952:453–470).

2. Haynes and Klehr (1999:90–92).

3. Tanenhaus (1997:203); Rees (1973:408).

4. Hayden B. Peake, afterword to Bentley (1951 [1988]).

5. Sibley (2004:120–121).

6. Bentley (1951 [1988]:113–114); Rees (1973:207); Haynes and Klehr (1999:133).

7. Bentley (1951 [1988]:113–114).

8. Packer (1962:117).

9. Haynes and Klehr (1999:150).

10. "It was originally planned that the United States would support Mr. White for election to the top managerial position in the International Monetary Fund. . . . But following the receipt of the FBI report and consultations with members of my Cabinet, it was decided that he would be limited to membership on the board of directors" (*New York Times*, Nov. 17, 1953).

11. Truman's full account is reprinted in appendix 2.

12. Rees (1973:377–390). Interlocking Subversion in Government Departments Hearings, Dec. 3, 1953, and Dec. 16, 1953, p. 1219, 1247.

13. See the testimony of J. Edgar Hoover, Interlocking Subversion in Government Departments Hearings, Nov. 17, 1953, pp. 1143, 1145–1147.

14. Keynes (1980) XXVI, Mar. 7, 1946, pp. 210–214. See also memoranda by W. M. Tomlinson, Jan. 19, 1946, and William H. Taylor, Jan. 24, 1946, referenced in Rees (1973:367). Horsefield's (1969:135) account of why White was passed over for the IMF managing director position is identical to Keynes's summary of Vinson's account. See also Mason and Asher (1973:40).

15. Skidelsky (2000:464–465).

16. Skidelsky (2000:465).

17. Gardner (1956 [1980]:266).

18. Bareau (1951).

19. Memo dated March 27, 1946, reprinted in Harrod (1951:630).

20. Keynes (1980) XXVI, Mar. 27, 1946, p. 222.

21. Keynes (1980) XXVI, Mar. 13, 1946, p. 217.

22. Van Dormael (1978:299–300).

23. Bareau (1951).

24. Skidelsky (2000:467–468).

25. Skidelsky (2000:468–469).

26. Keynes (1980) XXVI, Mar. 27, 1946, p. 234.

27. Keynes (1946:172–187).

28. Skidelsky (2000:470).

29. Rees (1973:371).

30. Keynes (1980) XXVII, Feb. 11, 1946, p. 480.

31. Clarke (2008:409, 413–415).

32. Clarke (2008:417).

33. Gardner (1956 [1980]:237).

34. Keynes (1980) XXVII, Feb. 11, 1946, p. 466.

35. Keynes (1980) XXVII, Jan. 29, 1946, pp. 464–465.

36. Clarke (2008:460–462).

37. Clarke (2008:474–487).

38. Reproduced in Clarke (1982:156–157).

39. Reproduced in Clarke (1982:159–166).

40. Memorandum dated July 23, 1947, reproduced in Clarke (1982:168–176).

41. Gardner (1956 [1980]).

42. Nitze (1989:51–52). Fossedal and Mikhail (1997:195–199).

43. Fossedal (1993:225).

44. See Fossedal (1993:228–229). Many were involved in the drafting, of course, and the contributions of Acheson, Kennan, fellow Soviet expert Charles ("Chip") Bohlen, and Benjamin Cohen should certainly be highlighted.

45. Acheson (1969:234–235).

46. Clarke (2008:492–493).

47. Fossedal (1993:240).

48. Gardner (1956 [1980]).

49. Fossedal (1993:252–253).

50. *New York Times* (Oct. 15, 1947:1).

51. Fossedal (1993:258).

52. See, for example, Robert Lovett's memorandum to Clayton, *Foreign Relations of the United States, 1947* (Aug. 26, 1947): http://digicoll.library.wisc.edu/cgi-bin/FRUS/FRUS-idx?type=turn&entity=FRUS.FRUS1947v03.p0404&id=FRUS.FRUS1947v03&isize=M.

53. These include the establishment of the European Payments Union in 1950 and the European Coal and Steel Community in 1951.

54. Acheson (1969:231). See also Healy (Apr. 2011).

55. Clayton (Jan. 5, 1958).

56. Fossedal (1993:286).

57. Published in Harry Dexter White (July 1947:21–29).

58. Rees (1973:401).

59. White Archives (May 19, 1948), "Rough Draft."

60. White Archives (undated), "Political Economic Int. of Future."

61. White Archives (May 19, 1948), "Rough Draft."

62. Draft letter from White to Henry Wallace, dated Jan. 17, 1948, quoted in Rees (1973:407).

63. Rees (1973:407). Interlocking Subversion in Government Departments Hearings, Aug. 3, 1955, pp. 2529–2530. Craig (2004:204).

64. Kennan (1967:292).

65. Nathan White (1956:71).

66. Craig (2004:208).

67. HUAC Hearings, July 31, 1948, pp. 511, 553.

68. *Sunday Globe* (Aug. 1, 1948).

69. HUAC Hearings, Aug. 3, 1948, pp. 574, 580.

70. Tanenhaus (1997:214).

71. HUAC Hearings, Aug. 13, 1948, pp. 877–906.

72. *New York Times* (Aug. 14, 1948).

73. HUAC Hearings, Aug. 13, 1948, p. 891.

74. Tanenhaus (1997:438).

75. Chambers (1952:38, 40–41).

76. *Congressional Record*, House (Jan. 26, 1950).

77. Chambers (1952:40).

78. The initial analysis was performed by the FBI on December 6, 1948 (Craig [2004:299–300, f. 82]). See "Report by Harold Gesell, Handwriting Expert of the Veterans' Administration, on the 'White Memorandum,' March 2, 1949," reprinted in Rees (1973:435–436).

79. Haynes and Klehr (1999:1–15).

80. Haynes and Klehr (1999). Romerstein and Breindel (2000). Andrew and Mitrokhin (1999).

81. Haynes and Klehr (1999:15).

82. Federal Bureau of Investigation (Oct. 16, 1950). I am indebted to Harvey Klehr for a copy of this memo.

83. This assumes that White was one of the eight named by Chambers, as suggested by Isaac Don Levine's and Adolf Berle's accounts.

84. Haynes and Klehr (1999:91).

85. These cables can be found on the Web site of the National Security Agency: http://www.nsa.gov/public_info/declass/venona/.

86. Andrew and Mitrokhin (1999:xxi, 106, 109).

87. Haynes and Klehr (1999:142).

88. Romerstein and Breindel (2000) write that Akhmerov was given these orders, but the actual cable decrypt references only "ALBERT" without identifying him.

89. See Haynes, Klehr, and Vassiliev (2009:260, 592, f. 118).

90. Craig (2004:257).

91. Weinstein and Vassiliev (2000:169).

92. Chambers (Dec. 2, 1953).

93. Commission on Protecting and Reducing Government Secrecy (1997). For White's most persistent and stalwart defender, IMF historian James Boughton, the Venona cable decrypts only "confirm that White was indiscreet in discussing policy issues with the Soviets." Yet this is implausible, as the cables not only indicate that White was acutely conscious of the dangers of his activities, but that he was operating *through American intermediaries*. The minor sin of "indiscretion" can, logically, only be applicable where White was dealing with his Soviet contacts directly.

With regard to the FDR administration's internal debates about wartime financial assistance to the Soviets, Boughton writes that for White "to keep his Soviet contacts apprised of the progress of that effort would have been consistent with his usual working habits" (2004:234–235). To Boughton, then, White was innocently keeping Soviet diplomats informed of the status of his efforts to get them better loan terms. Boughton does not see a problem with White providing the Soviets with confidential information that would materially affect their negotiating tactics; more importantly, however, he mischaracterizes how White transmitted the information. The Soviets learned about White's efforts not through White, but through an American government official, Nathan Gregory Silvermaster, head of a Soviet espionage network in the United States, who regularly relayed information to Moscow provided to him by White. The cables also indicate that White was aware of where his information was going.

CHAPTER 11: EPILOGUE

1. *The Economist* (Aug. 23, 1947).

2. *New York Times* (Feb. 14, 1947).

3. Gardner (1956 [1980]:298).

4. Eichengreen (2008:104).

5. James (1996:97).

6. See the excellent account of Kunz (1991).

7. Triffin (Oct. 28, 1959).

8. Triffin (1960:87, 145).

9. James (1996:158).

10. De Gaulle (1970:372–375).

11. Reprinted in Rueff (1972:72).

12. Rueff (1972:76).

13. Rueff and Triffin gave a joint interview on the inevitability of a dollar crisis that was published in the London *Sunday Times* on July 3, 1966, and the Paris *l'Aurore* the following day (reprinted in Rueff [1972:107–114]).

14. Triffin (1960:91–93).

15. Rueff (1972:41).

16. Rueff (1972:95, 143). Rueff was referring specifically to the IMF's later Special Drawing Right in his "nothingness" reference, but the term certainly applied in his mind to Keynes's bancor, Edward Bernstein's composite reserve units (CRU), and other variations on fiat international reserve issues.

17. Triffin (1960:146).

18. For an up-to-date historical account of SDRs, albeit one with an atypically positive gloss, see Wilkie (2012).

19. James (1996:211–220).

20. Silver too had played an important monetary role throughout history, as in China until the 1930s (see chapter 3).

21. White Archives (Aug. 4, 1942), Section IV, pp. 1, 3, 13 (note: the folder contains numerous duplicate page numbers).

22. James (1996:222).

23. Dale Jr. (Dec. 19, 1971:1).

24. Cohen (1974:129).

25. Witteveen (Jan. 15, 1974).

26. Friedman (Nov. 14, 1963).

27. Hayek (1937 [1989]:64).

28. The Hayek-Friedman split on fixed versus floating exchange rates largely reprised that between two influential League of Nations economists in the 1930s, Ragnar Nurske and Gottfried Haberler. See James (1996:38, 89).

29. Zhou (Mar. 23, 2009).

30. Hayek (1976).

31. Stock and Watson (2002). Bernanke (Feb. 20, 2004).

32. Rubin (May 26, 1998).

33. Summers (Mar. 23, 2004).

34. Schumer and Graham (Sept. 25, 2006).

35. Xinhua News Agency (Aug. 6, 2011).

36. *Wall Street Journal* (Jan. 18, 2011).

37. Zhou (Mar. 23, 2009).

38. *Wall Street Journal* (Aug. 8, 2011).

39. International Monetary Fund (2011). Goldberg and Tille (2009).

40. Steil (July 11, 2011).

41. International Monetary Fund (2012).

42. For a broader perspective on the challenges China faces in internationalizing its currency, see Mallaby and Wethington (2012).

43. Steil (2007).

44. Eichengreen (2011:159).

45. Kissinger (2011:518–519).

46. Zheng (2005).

47. Kissinger (2011:520–530).

REFERENCES

Acheson, Dean. 1969. *Present at the Creation: My Years in the State Department*. New York: W. W. Norton.

Ahamed, Liaquat. 2009. *Lords of Finance: The Bankers Who Broke the World*. New York: Penguin.

Andrew, Christopher, and Vasili Mitrokhin. 1999. *The Sword and the Shield: The Mitrokhin Archives and the Secret History of the KGB*. New York: Basic Books.

Barber, William J. 1990. "Government as a Laboratory Under Roosevelt." In *The State and Economic Knowledge: The American and British Experience*, ed. Mary Furner and Barry Supple. Cambridge: Cambridge University Press.

Bareau, Paul. 1951. "Anglo-American Financial Relations during and since the War." Four lectures delivered at the London School of Economics. In the possession of Peter Bareau.

Bentley, Elizabeth. 1951 [1988]. *Out of Bondage: The Story of Elizabeth Bentley*. New York: Ballantine.

Bernanke, Ben S. Feb. 20, 2004. "The Great Moderation." Remarks by Governor Ben S. Bernanke at the meetings of the Easter Economic Association, Washington, D.C.

Biographical Directory of the United States Congress. "Wolcott, Jesse Paine (1893–1969)." Available at http://bioguide.congress.gov/scripts/biodisplay.pl?index=W000668.

Black, Conrad. 2003. *Franklin Delano Roosevelt: Champion of Freedom*. New York: PublicAffairs.

Black, Stanley W. 1991. *A Levite among the Priests*. Boulder: Westview Press.

Blum, John Morton. 1959. *From the Morgenthau Diaries: Years of Crisis, 1928–1938*. Boston: Houghton Mifflin.

———. 1965. *From the Morgenthau Diaries: Years of Urgency, 1938–1941*. Boston: Houghton Mifflin.

———. 1967. *From the Morgenthau Diaries: Years of War, 1941–1945*. Boston: Houghton Mifflin.

Board of Governors of the Federal Reserve System. June 26, 1944. American meeting. Washington, D.C.

Boughton, James M. 2000. "The Case Against Harry Dexter White: Still Not Proven." International Monetary Fund Working Paper 00/149. International Monetary Fund, Washington, D.C.

———. June 2004. "New Light on Harry Dexter White." *Journal of the History of Economic Thought* 26:179–195.

Bourneuf, Alice. July 6, 1944. Notes on Bretton Woods Conference. Bretton Woods Conference Collection, International Monetary Fund, Box 15.

———. July 13, 1944. Notes on Bretton Woods Conference. Bretton Woods Conference Collection, International Monetary Fund, Box 15.

Bureau of Economic Analysis. Aug. 2010. *GDP and Other Major NIPA Series, 1929–2010: II*. Available at http://www.bea.gov/scb/pdf/2010/08%20August/0810_gdp_nipa_series.pdf.

Chambers, Whittaker. 1952. *Witness*. New York: Random House.

———. Dec. 2, 1953. "The Herring and the Thing." *Look*.

Chicago Tribune. June 12, 1944. "Babes in Bretton Woods."

———. July 2, 1944. "Among Those Absent."

———. July. 3 1944. "White Admits Bankers Fight Money Scheme."

———. July 7, 1944. "Front Views & Profiles."

———. July 9, 1944. "Good Money for Bad."

———. July 9, 1944. "Study Means to Balk Hiding of Axis Assets."

———. July 15, 1944. "Skin Game."

———. July 23, 1944. "The Englishman Who Rules America."

Chivvis, Christopher S. 2010. *The Monetary Conservative: Jacques Rueff and Twentieth-Century Free Market Thought*. Dekalb: Northern Illinois Press.

Christian Science Monitor. July 1, 1944. "Monetary World Looks to Bretton Woods Parley."

———. July 3, 1944. "Money Experts Start on Draft of World Plan."

———. July 6, 1944. "Money Parley Pace Is Slowed; Fund Transactions Major Topic."

———. July 12, 1944. "Fund Quotas Still Unsettled; Final Russian Answer Asked."

———. July 15, 1944. "Mimsy Were the Borogoves."

Churchill, Winston. Nov. 10, 1941. Mansion House speech. Available at http://www.ibiblio.org/pha/policy/1941/411110a.html.

———. 1950 [2005]. *The Second World War, Volume 3: The Grand Alliance*. London: Penguin.

———. 1953. *Triumph and Tragedy*. Boston: Houghton Mifflin.

Clarke, Peter. 1996. *Hope and Glory: Britain, 1900–2000*. London: Penguin.

———. 2008. *The Last Thousand Days of the British Empire: Churchill, Roosevelt, and the Birth of the Pax Americana*. New York: Bloomsbury Press.

———. 2009. *Keynes: The Rise, Fall, and Return of the 20th Century's Most Influential Economist*. New York: Bloomsbury Press.

Clarke, Sir Richard. 1982. *Anglo-American Economic Collaboration in War and Peace, 1942–1949*. Oxford: Oxford University Press.

Clayton, William, L. Jan. 5, 1958. "Removing Trade Barriers." *New York Times*.

Cohen, Benjamin J. 1974. "The Revolution in Atlantic Economic Relations: A Bargain Comes Unstuck." In *The United States and Western Europe: Political, Economic and Strategic Perspectives*, ed. Wolfram F. Hanrieder. Cambridge: Winthrop.

Commercial and Financial Chronicle. Sept 14, 1944. Reprint from the National Economic Council.

Commission on Protecting and Reducing Government Secrecy. 1997. *Report of the Commission on Protecting and Reducing Government Secrecy*. Washington, D.C.: United States Government Printing Office. Available at http://www.fas.org/sgp/library/moynihan/.

Committee on Finance and Industry [Macmillan Committee]. 1931. *Minutes of Evidence*. Vols. I and II. London: HMSO.

Congressional Record, House. Nov. 1, 1943. 78th Congress, 1st Session.

———, House. Jan. 26, 1950. 81st Congress, 2nd Session.

———, Senate. Aug. 19, 1941. 77th Congress, 1st Session.

Craig, R. Bruce. 2004. *Treasonable Doubt: The Harry Dexter White Spy Case.* Lawrence: University Press of Kansas.

Culbertson, William S. 1925. *International Economic Policies: A Survey of the Economics of Diplomacy.* New York: Appleton and Company.

Daily Cleveland Herald. Mar. 29, 1869.

Daily Herald. Apr. 8, 1943.

Daily Mail. Apr. 26, 1933.

Dale, Edwin L., Jr. Dec. 19, 1971. "Nixon Hails Pact." *New York Times.*

De Gaulle, Charles. 1970. *Memoirs of Hope: Renewal and Endeavor.* New York: Simon and Schuster.

Dietrich, John. 2002. *The Morgenthau Plan: Soviet Influence on American Postwar Policy.* New York: Algora Publishing.

Dobson, Alan P. 1986. *US Wartime Aid to Britain.* London: Croom Helm.

Eckes, Alfred E., Jr. 1975. *A Search for Solvency: Bretton Woods and the International Monetary System, 1941–1971.* Austin: University of Texas Press.

The Economist. Nov. 28, 1942. "The Future of Gold."

———. July 21, 1945.

———. Aug. 23, 1947.

Eichengreen, Barry. 1992. *Golden Fetters: The Gold Standard and the Great Depression, 1919–1939.* Oxford: Oxford University Press.

———. 2008. *Globalizing Capital: A History of the International Monetary System.* Princeton: Princeton University Press.

———. 2011. *Exorbitant Privilege: The Rise and Fall of the Dollar and the Future of the International Monetary System.* New York: Oxford University Press.

Export Policy and Loyalty Hearings. July 30–Aug. 6, 1948. Hearings Before the Investigations Subcommittee of the Committee on Expenditures in the Executive Departments. United States Senate.

Federal Bureau of Investigation. Oct. 16, 1950. Memorandum, Ladd to Director.

Feis, Herbert. 1966. *1933: Characters in Crisis.* Boston/Toronto: Little, Brown.

Foreign Office (National Archives, Kew, UK). Feb. 17, 1943. FO371/35330, Phillips to Treasury.

———. Mar. 24, 1943. FO371/35331, Casaday to Waley.

———. May 20, 1943. FO371/35334, Phillips to Keynes.

————. June 13, 1943. FO371/35334, Halifax to Foreign Office.

————. June. 18, 1943. FO371/35335, Halifax to Foreign Office.

————. July 1, 1943. FO371/35335, Keynes to Jebb.

————. July 19, 1943. FO371/35335, Keynes to Eady.

————. Jan. 7, 1944. FO371/40583, Halifax to Foreign Office.

————. Apr. 30, 1944. FO371/40587, Halifax to Foreign Office.

————. May 9, 1944. FO371/40588, Opie to Ronald.

————. May 24, 1944. FO371/40588, Opie to Foreign Office.

————. July 1944 (day unclear). FO371/40918, Response from Bretton Woods to telegrams No. 68 and 69.

————. July 4, 1944. FO371/40918, Richard Miles memorandum.

————. July 10, 1944. FO371/40916, No. 51.

————. July 11, 1944. FO371/40917, Response to telegram No. 37.

————. July 20, 1944. FO371/40918.

————. Dec. 1944. FO371/45662, Report.

————. Dec. 29, 1944. FO371/45662, Keynes memorandum.

————. Apr. 5, 1945. FO371/45664, Keynes to Brand.

————. Undated. FO371/40585.

Foreign Relations of the United States, 1941. 1941. *Volume III, The British Commonwealth; the Near East and Africa.* Washington, D.C.: United States Department of State.

————, *1942*. 1942. *Volume I, General; the British Commonwealth; the Far East.* Washington, D.C.: United States Department of State.

————, *1943*. 1943. *Volume I, General.* Washington, D.C.: United States Department of State.

————, *1947*. 1947. *The British Commonwealth; Europe.* Washington, D.C.: United States Department of State.

Fossedal, Gregory. 1993. *Our Finest Hour: Will Clayton, the Marshall Plan, and the Triumph of Democracy.* Stanford: Hoover Institution Press.

Fossedal, Gregory, and Bill Mikhail. May/June 1997. "A Modest Magician: Will Clayton and the Rebuilding of Europe." *Foreign Affairs* 76 (3): 195–199.

Friedman, Milton. Nov. 14, 1963. "Using the Free Market to Resolve the Balance of Payments Problem." Statement to the congressional Joint Economic Committee. Reprinted Mar./Apr. 1964. *Financial Analysts Journal* 20 (2): 21–25.

Gardner, Richard N. 1956 [1980]. *Sterling-Dollar Diplomacy: Anglo-American Collaboration in the Reconstruction of Multilateral Trade.* New York: Columbia University Press.

George, David Lloyd. 1938. *War Memoirs.* London: Oldhams Press.

Gilbert, Martin. 1989. *The Second World War: A Complete History.* New York: Henry Holt and Company.

Goldberg, Linda, and Cedric Tille. Nov. 2009. "Micro, Macro, and Strategic Choices in International Trade Invoicing." CEPR Discussion Paper No. 7534. London: Centre for Economic Policy Research.

Goldenweiser, Emanuel. Goldenweiser Papers, Bretton Woods Conference, Library of Congress.

Goodhart, Charles, and P.J.R. Delargy. 1998. "Financial Crises: Plus ça Change, plus c'est la Même Chose." *International Finance* 1 (2): 261–287.

Grand Jury Testimony in the Alger Hiss Case. 1947–1949. Record Group 118. New York, National Archives.

Grant, James. 1992. *Money of the Mind: Borrowing and Lending in America from the Civil War to Michael Milken.* New York: Noonday Press.

Halifax, Edward Frederick Lindley Wood. *Diary.*

Harriman, W. Averell, and Elie Abel. 1975. *Special Envoy to Churchill and Stalin, 1941–1946.* New York: Random House.

Harrod, Roy. 1951. *The Life of John Maynard Keynes.* New York: W. W. Norton.

Hastings, Max. 2009. *Winston's War: Churchill, 1940–1945.* New York: Alfred A. Knopf.

Hayek, Friedrich. 1937 [1989]. *Monetary Nationalism and International Stability.* New Jersey: Augustus M. Kelley.

―――. 1976. *Denationalisation of Money—the Argument Refined: An Analysis of the Theory and Practice of Concurrent Currencies.* London: Institute of Economic Affairs.

Haynes, John Earl, and Harvey Klehr. 1999. *Venona: Decoding Soviet Espionage in America.* New Haven: Yale University Press.

―――. 2003. *In Denial.* San Francisco: Encounter Books.

Haynes, John Earl, Harvey Klehr, and Alexander Vassiliev. 2009. *Spies: The Rise and Fall of the KGB in America.* New Haven: Yale University Press.

Healy, Timothy. Apr. 2011. "Will Clayton, Negotiating the Marshall Plan, and European Economic Integration." *Diplomatic History* 35 (2).

Henderson, Hubert. Jan. 26, 1951. *The Spectator*. Review of Roy Harrod's *The Life of John Maynard Keynes*.

Hendrick, Burton Jesse. 1928. *The Training of an American: The Earlier Life and Letters of Walter H. Page*. London: Heinemann.

Herring, George C., Jr. June 1971. "The United States and British Bankruptcy, 1944–1945: Responsibilities Deferred." *Political Science Quarterly* 86 (2): 260–280.

Horsefield, J. Keith. 1969. *The International Monetary Fund, 1945–1965: Twenty Years of International Monetary Cooperation. Volume I: Chronicle*. Washington, D.C.: International Monetary Fund.

House of Commons Debates. Apr. 21, 1944. "Orders of the Day—Empire and Commonwealth Unity." Available at http://www.theyworkforyou.com/debates/?id=1944-04-21a.495.4.

———. Dec. 13, 1945. "Anglo-American Financial and Economic Discussions." Available at http://hansard.millbanksystems.com/commons/1945/dec/13/anglo-american-financial-and-economic.

House of Lords Debates. May 18, 1943. "International Clearing Union." Available at http://hansard.millbanksystems.com/lords/1943/may/18/international-clearing-union.

Howard, Michael. Oct. 1977. "It Is Never Very Easy for the British." *Books & Bookmen*, in a review of Joseph P. Lash's *Roosevelt and Churchill, 1939–41*.

Howson, Susan, and Donald Moggridge (eds.). 1990. *The Wartime Diaries of Lionel Robbins and James Meade, 1943–45*. New York: St. Martin's Press.

HUAC Hearings. Hearings Before the Committee on Un-American Activities. House of Representatives, 80th Congress.

Hubback, David. 1985. *No Ordinary Press Baron: A Life of Walter Layton*. Worthing, West Sussex: Littlehampton Book Services.

Hull, Cordell. 1948. *The Memoirs of Cordell Hull*. New York: Macmillan.

Institute of Pacific Relations Hearings. Hearings Before the Subcommittee to Investigate the Administration of the Internal Security Act and Other Internal Security Laws. United States Senate, 82nd Congress.

Interlocking Subversion in Government Departments Hearings. Hearings Before the Subcommittee to Investigate the Administration of the Internal Security Act and Other Internal Security Laws. United States Senate, 83rd and 84th Congress.

International Monetary Fund. 2011. "Currency Composition of Official Foreign Exchange Reserves (COFER)." Available at http://www.imf.org/external/np/sta/cofer/eng/index.htm.

———. 2012. International Financial Statistics Database. Available at http://elibrary-data.imf.org/DataExplorer.aspx.

James, Harold. 1996. *International Monetary Cooperation since Bretton Woods*. New York: Oxford University Press.

Karpov, Vladimir. Jan. 21, 2000. "Notes from the Archive." *Independent Military Review*. Moscow.

Kennan, George F. 1946. Telegram from George Kennan Charge d'Affaires at United States Embassy in Moscow to the Secretary of State: The Long Telegram, 02/22/1946. College Park, Md., National Archives.

———. 1967. *Memoirs: 1925–1950*. Boston: Atlantic, Little, Brown.

Kenton County Historical Society. Feb. 1997. *Bulletin*. Available at http://www.nku.edu/~myerssh/KCHS/scans/99.pdf.

Keynes, John Maynard. Mar. 11, 1906. JMK to Lytton Strachey. Keynes Papers. King's College Archive Centre, University of Cambridge.

———. Sept. 13, 1907. JMK to Lytton Strachey. Keynes Papers. King's College Archive Centre, University of Cambridge.

———. Dec. 18, 1908. JMK to Duncan Grant. Keynes Papers. King's College Archive Centre, University of Cambridge.

———. May 10, 1909. JMK to Duncan Grant. Keynes Papers. King's College Archive Centre, University of Cambridge.

———. 1913 [1971]. *The Collected Writings of John Maynard Keynes: Volume I, Indian Currency and Finance*. Cambridge: Cambridge University Press.

———. 1919 [1971]. *The Collected Writings of John Maynard Keynes: Volume II, The Economic Consequences of the Peace*. Cambridge: Cambridge University Press.

———. 1923 [1971]. *The Collected Writings of John Maynard Keynes: Volume IV, A Tract on Monetary Reform*. Cambridge: Cambridge University Press.

———. 1925–1926. Unpublished fragment. Keynes Papers, PS/6. King's College Archive Centre, University of Cambridge.

———. 1930 [1971]. *The Collected Writings of John Maynard Keynes: Volume V, A Treatise on Money in Two Volumes: 1 The Pure Theory of Money*. Cambridge: Cambridge University Press.

———. 1930 [1971]. *The Collected Writings of John Maynard Keynes: Volume VI, A Treatise on Money in Two Volumes: 2 The Applied Theory of Money.* Cambridge: Cambridge University Press.

———. 1931 [1972]. *The Collected Writings of John Maynard Keynes: Volume IX, Essays in Persuasion.* Cambridge: Cambridge University Press.

———. Oct. 1931. Filmed monologue. Available at http://www.youtube .com/watch?v=U1S9F3agsUA&feature=related.

———. 1933 [1972]. *The Collected Writings of John Maynard Keynes: Volume X, Essays in Biography.* Cambridge: Cambridge University Press.

———. 1933. *The Means to Prosperity.* London: Macmillan. Available at http://gutenberg.ca/ebooks/keynes-means/keynes-means-00-h.html.

———. June 1933. "National Self-Sufficiency." *The Yale Review* 22 (4): 755–769.

———. Sept. 12, 1933. Max Radin to JMK. Keynes Papers, L/33. King's College Archive Centre, University of Cambridge.

———. Oct. 2, 1933. JMK to Max Radin. Keynes Papers, L/33. King's College Archive Centre, University of Cambridge.

———. June 2, 1934. JMK to Victor Szeliski. Keynes Papers, AV/1. King's College Archive Centre, University of Cambridge.

———. Nov. 22, 1934. JMK to Alick de Jeune. Keynes Papers, A/34. King's College Archive Centre, University of Cambridge.

———. 1936 [1973]. *The Collected Writings of John Maynard Keynes: Volume VII, The General Theory of Employment, Interest and Money.* Cambridge: Cambridge University Press.

———. Aug. 29, 1938. JMK to Florence Keynes. Keynes Papers. King's College Archive Centre, University of Cambridge.

———. Nov. 2, 1939. Notes on the War for the President. Keynes Papers, W/2. King's College Archive Centre, University of Cambridge.

———. June 28, 1940. JMK to Florence Keynes. Keynes Papers. King's College Archive Centre, University of Cambridge.

———. July 3, 1940. JMK to Arthur C. Pigou. Keynes Papers, PP/45. King's College Archive Centre, University of Cambridge.

———. Apr. 1943. "Proposals for an International Clearing Union." British Government White Paper Cmd. 6437.

———. July 22, 1944. JMK to Lord Catto. Keynes Papers, W/1. King's College Archive Centre, University of Cambridge.

———. June 1946. "The Balance of Payments in the United States." *Economic Journal* LVI, No. 222: 172–187.

———. 1978. *The Collected Writings of John Maynard Keynes: Volume XIV, The General Theory and After: Defence and Development.* Cambridge: Cambridge University Press.

———. 1978. *The Collected Writings of John Maynard Keynes: Volume XVI, Activities 1914–19: The Treasury and Versailles.* Cambridge: Cambridge University Press.

———. 1978. *The Collected Writings of John Maynard Keynes: Volume XXII, Activities 1939–45: Internal War Finance.* Cambridge: Cambridge University Press.

———. 1979. *The Collected Writings of John Maynard Keynes: Volume XXIII, Activities 1940–43: External War Finance.* Cambridge: Cambridge University Press.

———. 1979. *The Collected Writings of John Maynard Keynes: Volume XXIV, Activities 1944–46: The Transition to Peace.* Cambridge: Cambridge University Press.

———. 1980. *The Collected Writings of John Maynard Keynes: Volume XXV, Activities 1940–44: Shaping the Post-war World: The Clearing Union.* Cambridge: Cambridge University Press.

———. 1980. *The Collected Writings of John Maynard Keynes: Volume XXVI, Activities 1943–46: Shaping the Post-war World: Bretton Woods and Reparation.* Cambridge: Cambridge University Press.

———. 1980. *The Collected Writings of John Maynard Keynes: Volume XXVII, Activities 1940–46: Shaping the Post-war World: Employment and Commodities.* Cambridge: Cambridge University Press.

———. 1981. *The Collected Writings of John Maynard Keynes: Volume XIX, Activities 1924–29: The Return to Gold and Industrial Policy: Part I and II.* Cambridge: Cambridge University Press.

———. 1981. *The Collected Writings of John Maynard Keynes: Volume XX, Activities 1929–31: Rethinking Employment and Unemployment Policies.* Cambridge: Cambridge University Press.

———. 1982. *The Collected Writings of John Maynard Keynes: Volume XXI, Activities 1931–39: World Crises and Policies in Britain and America.* Cambridge: Cambridge University Press.

———. 1982. *The Collected Writings of John Maynard Keynes: Volume XXVIII, Social, Political, and Literary Writings.* Cambridge: Cambridge University Press.

———. 1983. *The Collected Writings of John Maynard Keynes: Volume XI, Economic Articles and Correspondence: Academic.* Cambridge: Cambridge University Press.

———. 1983. *The Collected Writings of John Maynard Keynes: Volume XII, Economic Articles and Correspondence: Investment and Editorial.* Cambridge: Cambridge University Press.

———. 1987. *The Collected Writings of John Maynard Keynes: Volume XIII, The General Theory and After: Part 1. Preparation.* Cambridge: Cambridge University Press.

Keynes Papers: See individual items, listed by date, under Keynes, John Maynard.

Kimball, Warren F. 1969. *The Most Unsordid Act: Lend-Lease, 1939–1941.* Baltimore: Johns Hopkins University Press.

———. 1971. "Lend-Lease and the Open Door: The Temptation of British Opulence 1937-42." *Political Science Quarterly* 86 (2): 232–259.

Kissinger, Henry. 2011. *On China.* New York: Penguin.

Kunz, Diane B. 1991. *The Economic Diplomacy of the Suez Crisis.* University of North Carolina Press.

Laski, Harold J. 1944. *Faith, Reason, and Civilisation: An Essay in Historical Analysis.* London: Gollancz.

Lebergott, Stanley. 1957. "Annual Estimates of Unemployment in the United States, 1900–1954." *The Measurement and Behavior of Unemployment.* Cambridge, Mass.: National Bureau of Economic Research. Available at http://www.nber.org/chapters/c2644.pdf.

Levy, Herbert. 2010. *Henry Morgenthau, Jr.: The Remarkable Life of FDR's Secretary of the Treasury.* New York: Skyhorse Publishing.

Lindbergh, Charles Augustus. May 19, 1940. "The Air Defense of America." Speech.

Lippmann, Walter. July 13, 1944. "Bretton Woods and Senator Taft." *Washington Post.*

London Chamber of Commerce. 1942. *Report on General Principles of a Post-war Economy.*

MacMillan, Margaret. 2003. *Paris 1919: Six Months That Changed the World.* New York: Random House.

Mallaby, Sebastian, and Olin Wethington. Jan./Feb. 2012. "The Future of the Yuan." *Foreign Affairs* 91 (1): 135–146.

Mason, Edward S., and Robert E. Asher. 1973. *The World Bank since Bretton Woods.* Washington, D.C.: The Brookings Institution.

May, Gary. 1994. *Un-American Activities: The Trials of William Remington*. New York: Oxford University Press.

McJimsey, George (ed.). 2003. "Document 80, Papers as President: President's Secretary's File." *Documentary History of the Franklin D. Roosevelt Presidency, Volume 17, FDR and the London Economic Conference*. New York: LexisNexis.

Meltzer, Allan H. 2003. *A History of the Federal Reserve, Volume 1: 1913–1951*. Chicago: University of Chicago Press.

Mikesell, Raymond F. 1951. "Negotiating at Bretton Woods, 1944." In *Negotiating with the Russians*, ed. Raymond Dennett and Joseph E. Johnson. Boston: World Peace Foundation.

Morgenthau, Henry, Jr. *The Morgenthau Diaries*.

———. Oct. 25, 1947. "The Morgenthau Diaries: the Paradox of Poverty and Plenty." *Collier's*.

Morgenthau, Henry, III. 1991. *Mostly Morgenthaus: A Family History*. New York: Ticknor & Fields.

Mundell, Robert A. June 2000. "A Reconsideration of the Twentieth Century." *The American Economic Review* 90 (3): 327–340.

National Archives, Washington, D.C. State Decimal File 1940–44, RG59.800.515–BWA/6–2444.

———. RG59.800.515/6–2844.

National Security Agency. Venona Files. Available at http://www.nsa.gov/public_info/declass/venona/.

The New Republic. July 29, 1940. "The United States and The Keynes Plan."

New York Herald Tribune. Mar. 31, 1946. "Morgenthau 'Shocked' by News Douglas May Head World Bank."

New York Times. Mar. 30, 1943. "A 'New' World Currency?"

———. July 2, 1944. "Delegates Search for Warm Clothes."

———. July 5, 1944. "Monetary Conference Keeps Dr. Newcomer Too Busy for Her Mountain-Climbing Hobby."

———. July 5, 1944. "Quota Issues Split World Fund Talks."

———. July 7, 1944. "Britain is 'Broke,' Two Ministers Say."

———. July 7, 1944. "Keynes Attacks Fund Plan Critics."

———. July 8, 1944. "Funk Denounces Currency Parley."

———. July 9, 1944. "Fund Talks Reveal Post-war Attitude."

———. July 14, 1944. "Five Snags Delay Monetary Accord."

———. July 17, 1944. "Expect Early Pact on a World Bank."

———. July 18, 1944.

———. July 18, 1944. "Conference Adds 3 Days to Talks: Snarled on Bank."

———. July 18, 1944. "Results at Bretton Woods."

———. July 19, 1944.

———. July 19, 1944. "An International Bank?"

———. July 20, 1944.

———. Feb. 14, 1947. "We Stand By Britain."

———. Oct. 15, 1947. "Europe Will Feel Loss."

———. Aug. 14, 1948. "Currie and White Deny under Oath They Aided Spies."

———. Nov. 17, 1953.

———. Feb. 20, 2009. "An Economic Bright Spot in New Hampshire."

New York World-Telegram. 1943.

The New Yorker. Aug. 5, 1944. "Host."

Nitze, Paul H. 1989. *From Hiroshima to Glasnost: At the Center of Decision; A Memoir of Five Perilous Decades*. New York: Weidenfeld & Nicolson.

Obsfeld, Maurice, and Alan M. Taylor. 2004. *Global Capital Markets: Integration, Crisis, and Growth*. New York: Cambridge University Press.

Packer, Herbert L. 1962. *Ex-Communist Witnesses: Four Studies in Fact Finding—a Challenging Examination of the Testimony of Whittaker Chambers, Elizabeth Bentley, Louis Budenz, and John Lautner*. Stanford: Stanford University Press.

Pavlov, Vitali. 1995. *Novosti Razvedki I Kontrrazvedki* [News of Intelligence and Counterintelligence]. Nos. 9–10, 11–12.

———. 1996. *Operatsia Sneg*. Moscow: Gaia Iterum.

Penrose, Ernest Francis. 1953. *Economic Planning for the Peace*. Princeton: Princeton University Press.

Petrov, Vladimir. 1967. *Money and Conquest: Allied Occupation Currencies in World War II*. Baltimore: Johns Hopkins Press.

Pigou, Arthur C. 1936. "Mr. J. M. Keynes' General Theory of Employment, Interest and Money." *Economica* 3 (10): 115–132.

Proceedings and Documents of United Nations Monetary and Financial Conference, Bretton Woods NH, July 1–22, 1944. 1948. Washington, D.C.: United States Department of State.

Rees, David. 1973. *Harry Dexter White: A Study in Paradox*. New York: Coward, McCann & Geoghegan.

Robbins, Lionel. 1990. "Bretton Woods, June–August 1944." In *The Wartime Diaries of Lionel Robbins and James Meade, 1943–45*, eds. Susan Howson and Donald E. Moggridge. New York: St. Martin's Press.

Rolph, C. H. 1973. *Kingsley: The Life, Letters & Diaries of Kingsley Martin*. London: Gollancz.

Romerstein, Herbert, and Eric Breindel. 2000. *The Venona Secrets: Exposing Soviet Espionage and America's Traitors*. Washington, D.C.: Regnery History.

Roosevelt, Franklin D., President. Mar. 11, 1942. *Message from the President of the United States Transmitting a Report on the First Year of Lend-Lease Operations*. Washington, D.C.: Government Printing Office.

Rosenberg, Andrew, and Kurt Schuler (eds.). 2012. *The Bretton Woods Transcripts*. New York: Center for Financial Stability.

Rubin, Robert E. May 26, 1998. "Remarks for Opening Plenary China–U.S. Joint Economic Committee—Eleventh Session." Office of Public Affairs, United States Treasury, Washington, D.C.

Rueff, Jacques. Sept. 1929. "Mr. Keynes on the Transfer Problem." *The Economic Journal* 39 (155): 388–408.

———. May 1947. "The Fallacies of Lord Keynes' General Theory." *Quarterly Journal of Economics* 61 (3): 343–367.

———. 1972. *The Monetary Sin of the West*. New York: Macmillan.

Rymes, Thomas K. (ed.). 1989. *Keynes's Lectures, 1932–1935: Notes of a Representative Student*. London: Macmillan.

Samuelson, Paul A. 1964. "A Brief Survey of Post-Keynesian Developments [1963]." In *Keynes' General Theory: Reports of Three Decades*, ed. Robert Lekachman. New York: St. Martin's Press.

Say, Jean-Baptiste. 1880 [1971]. *A Treatise on Political Economy*, trans. C. R. Prinsep. New York: Augustus M. Kelley.

Schecter, Jerrold L., and Leona P. Schecter. 2002. *Sacred Secrets*. Washington, D.C.: Brassey's.

Schumer, Charles E., and Lindsey O. Graham. Sept. 25, 2006. "Play by the Rules." *Wall Street Journal*.

Schumpeter, Joseph A. May 19, 1937. JAS to K. Bode. Schumpeter Papers, 4.8, Box 2, Harvard University Archives.

———. 1952. *Ten Great Economists*. Sydney: Allen & Unwin.

Sefton, James, and Martin Weale. 1995. *Reconciliation of National Income and Expenditure: Balanced Estimates of National Income for the United Kingdom, 1920–1990*. Cambridge: Cambridge University Press.

Sherwood, Robert E. 1948 [2008]. *Roosevelt and Hopkins: An Intimate History*. New York: Enigma Books.

Sibley, Katherine A. S. 2004. *Red Spies in America: Stolen Secrets and the Dawn of the Cold War*. Lawrence: University Press of Kansas.

Simmel, Georg. 1900 [1978]. *The Philosophy of Money*. London: Routledge & Kegan Paul.

Skidelsky, Robert. 1983. *John Maynard Keynes: Hopes Betrayed, 1883–1920*. London: Macmillan.

———. 1994. *John Maynard Keynes: The Economist as Saviour, 1920–1937*. New York: Penguin.

———. 2000. *John Maynard Keynes: Fighting for Britain, 1937–1946*. London: Macmillan.

Spring-Rice, Cecil. Undated. Cecil Spring-Rice to Florence Spring-Rice. Spring-Rice Papers. Churchill Archives Centre, University of Cambridge.

Steil, Benn. May/June 2007. "The End of National Currency." *Foreign Affairs* 86 (3).

———. July 11, 2011. "Central Banks Can't Paper Over the Economy." *Financial News*.

Stein, Herbert. 1996. *The Fiscal Revolution in America: Policy in Pursuit of Reality*. Washington, D.C.: American Enterprise Institute.

Stock, James H., and Mark W. Watson. 2002. "Has the Business Cycle Changed and Why?" In *NBER Macroeconomics Annual 2002, Volume 17*, ed. Mark Gertler and Kenneth Rogoff. Cambridge, Mass.: MIT Press.

Summers, Lawrence H. Mar. 23, 2004. "The United States and the Global Adjustment Process." Speech at the Third Annual Stavros S. Niarchos Lecture, Peterson Institute for International Economics, Washington, D.C. Available at http://www.iie.com/publications/papers/paper.cfm?researchid=200.

Sunday Globe. Aug. 1, 1948. "White Denies He Gave Secret Information."

Tanenhaus, Sam. 1997. *Whittaker Chambers: A Biography*. New York: Random House.

Tenkotte, Paul A., and James C. Claypool (eds.). 2009. *The Encyclopedia of Northern Kentucky*. Lexington: University Press of Kentucky.

Time. July 3, 1944. "U.S. At War: The Mission of Daddy Kung."

———. July 10, 1944. "Exchange: Money Talks."

———. July 17, 1944. "Exchange: 1,300 Men with a Mission."

———. Nov. 23, 1953. "Investigations: One Man's Greed."

The Times (London). July 31, 1925.

———. Apr. 8, 1943.

———. July 10, 1944. "Fixing the Quotas."

———. July 17, 1944. "Monetary Fund Quota: Contributions Fixed."

Treasury Papers (National Archives, Kew, UK). May 8–11, 1941. T247/113, Lucius Thompson's diary.

———. May 22, 1941. T175/121, E. Playfair to S. D. Waley.

———. May 24 and 26, 1941. T247/113, JMK to Lord Halifax, May 24, 1941; Lord Halifax to JMK, May 26, 1941.

———. July 8, 1942. T160/1281/F18885/1, Phillips to Foreign Office.

———. July 14, 1942. T160/1281/F18885/1, Waley to Hopkins.

———. Aug. 4, 1942. T160/1281/F18885/1, The International Clearing Union.

———. Oct. 7, 1942. T160/1281/F18885/1, note by Brand.

———. Jan. 21, 1943. T160/1281/F18885/1, Keynes to Eady.

———. Feb. 16, 1943. T160/1281/F18885/1, Keynes to Waley.

———. Feb. 18, 1943. T160/1281/F18885/1, Keynes memorandum.

———. Feb. 19, 1943. T160/1281/F18885/1, Waley to Chancellor.

———. Dec. 14, 1943. T160/1281/F18885/7, Waley to Padmore.

———. Jan. 14, 1944. T160/1281/F18885/7, The Monetary Plan.

———. Jan. 26, 1944. T160/1281/F18885/7, Keynes, Draft Section on Monetary Policy.

———. Feb. 3, 1944. T160/1281/F18885/8, White to Keynes.

———. Apr. 13, 1944. T160/1281/F18885/10, Opie to Keynes.

———. Apr. 16, 1944. T160/1281/F18885/10, Keynes to Chancellor.

———. Apr. 13, 1944. T160/1281/F18885/10, Opie to Keynes.

———. Apr. 25, 1944. T160/1281/F18885/11, Newsletter.

———. May 16, 1944. T160/1281/F18885/11, Keynes memorandum.

———. May 16, 1944. T160/1281/F18885/11, Waley to Keynes, Brand, and Eady.

Triffin, Robert. Oct. 28, 1959. "Statement to the Joint Economic Committee of the 87th Congress." Reprinted 1960. *Gold and the Dollar Crisis*. New Haven: Yale University Press.

———. 1960. *Gold and the Dollar Crisis*. New Haven: Yale University Press.

United Nations Statistics Division. May 1962. International Trade Statistics, 1900–1960. Available at http://unstats.un.org/unsd/trade/imts/Historical%20data%201900-1960.pdf.

Utley, Jonathan G. 1985. *Going to War with Japan, 1937–1941*. Knoxville: University of Tennessee Press.

Van Dormael, Armand. 1978. *Bretton Woods: Birth of a Monetary System*. New York: Holmes and Meier.

Vassar Encyclopedia. "Mabel Newcomer." Available at http://vcencyclopedia .vassar.edu/faculty/prominent-faculty/mabel-newcomer.html.

Wall Street Journal. July 3, 1944. "Treasury Finds Most Bankers Are Opposed to Stabilization Fund, White Discloses."

———. July 5, 1944. "Right Names Would Help."

———. July 7, 1944. "Russia Asks Stabilization Fund Quote Equaling or Exceeding That of England."

———. Apr. 13, 1945.

———. Jan. 18, 2011. "Q&A with Hu Jintao."

———. Aug. 8, 2011. "China Takes Aim at U.S. 'Debt Addiction.'"

Wapshott, Nicholas. 2011. *Keynes Hayek: The Clash That Defined Modern Economics*. New York: W. W. Norton.

War Cabinet Minutes. Cab. 66/46, WP(44)75. National Archives, Kew, UK.

———. Cab. 66/47. National Archives, Kew, UK.

———. Cab. 66/47, WP(44)129. National Archives, Kew, UK.

Washington Post. July 8, 1944. "At Bretton Woods."

———. July 11, 1944. "The Federal Diary."

———. July 12, 1944. "Taft Predicts Nations' Bank Will Be Rejected by Congress."

Weinstein, Allen. 1997. *Perjury: The Hiss-Chambers Case*. New York: Random House.

Weinstein, Allen, and Alexander Vassiliev. 2000. *The Haunted Wood: Soviet Espionage in America—the Stalin Era*. New York: Modern Library.

Welles, Sumner. 1946. *Where Are We Heading?* New York: Harper & Brothers.

Whipple, Charles L. Nov. 18, 1953. "An Instructor at Harvard." *Boston Globe*.

White, Harry Dexter. 1933. *The French International Accounts, 1880–1913*. Cambridge, Mass.: Harvard University Press.

———. Jan. 22, 1934. Selection of a Monetary Standard for the United States. Harry Dexter White Archives, Princeton University, Box 4, Folder 3.

———. 1935 (underscore in original). Deficit Spending Policy in 1935. Harry Dexter White Archives, Princeton University, Box 4, Folder 12.

———. 1935. Outline of Analysis of Current Situation. Harry Dexter White Archives, Princeton University, Box 4, Folder 9.

———. Feb. 26, Mar. 5, 1935. Outline Analysis of the Current Situation. Referenced in Rees (1973:56, f. 3).

———. Mar. 15, 1935. Recovery Program: The International Monetary Aspect. Harry Dexter White Archives, Princeton University, Box 3, Folder 13.

———. June 13, 1935. Personal Report on London Trip, April–May, 1935. Harry Dexter White Archives, Princeton University, Box 1, Folder 6.

———. June 13, 1935. Summary of conversations with men interviewed in London. Harry Dexter White Archives, Princeton University, Box 1, Folder 6.

———. 1936. Memo to Secretary Morgenthau on China. Harry Dexter White Archives, Princeton University, Box 1, Folder 3.

———. Mar. 22, 1938. Monetary Possibilities. Harry Dexter White Archives, Princeton University, Box 4, Folder 10.

———. Aug. 31, 1938. The Sterling Situation. Harry Dexter White Archives, Princeton University, Box 1, Folder 7.

———. Sept. 6, 1938. The Sterling Decline and the Tripartite Accord. Harry Dexter White Archives, Princeton University, Box 1, Folder 7.

———. Oct. 10, 1938. Memo to Secretary Morgenthau. Harry Dexter White Archives, Princeton University, Box 1, Folder 4.

———. Oct. 21, 1938. The Dollar-Sterling Situation. Harry Dexter White Archives, Princeton University, Box 1, Folder 7.

———. Feb. 2, 1939. Economic Factors Relating to the Appropriateness of the Sterling-Dollar Rate. Harry Dexter White Archives, Princeton University, Box 1, Folder 7.

———. Mar. 31, 1939. Proposal for Economic Aid to Latin America, China, and Russia. Harry Dexter White Archives, Princeton University, Box 5, Folder 5.

———. June 15, Aug. 13, 1940. Two untitled memoranda, referenced in Rees (1973:109, f. 27).

———. June 6, 1941. Memorandum to Secretary Morgenthau. In *The Morgenthau Diaries*, Vol. 405, p. 470.

———. Mar. 1942. Suggested Plan for a United Nations Stabilization Fund and a Bank for Reconstruction of the United and Associated Nations. Harry Dexter White Archives, Princeton University, Box 6, Folder 6.

———. Mar. 1942. United Nations Stabilization Fund and a Bank for Reconstruction and Development of the United and Associated Nations (preliminary draft). Harry Dexter White Archives, Princeton University, Box 6, Folder 16.

———. Aug. 4, 1942. The Future of Gold: An Unpublished Study. Harry Dexter White Archives, Princeton University, Box 1, Folder 9.

———. Aug. 28, 1942. Letter from Sir Frederick Phillips, UK Treasury Representative at the British Embassy in Washington, to Harry White. Harry Dexter White Archives, Princeton University, Box 7, Folder 1.

———. Sept. 3, 1942. U.S. Treasury memorandum. Harry Dexter White Archives, Princeton University, Box 7, Folder 2.

———. Jan. 8, 1943. Memo from John W. Gunter on "The Future of Gold," *The Economist*, Nov. 28, 1942. Harry Dexter White Archives, Princeton University, Box 1, Folder 9.

———. Mar. 1943. "Postwar Currency Stabilization." *The American Economic Review* 33 (1) Part 2, Supplement, Papers and Proceeding of the Fifty-fifth Annual Meeting of the American Economic Association: 382–387.

———. Nov. 30, 1945. Maintaining Peace. Harry Dexter White Archives, Princeton University, Box 6, Folder 5.

———. July 1947. "The International Monetary Fund: The First Year." *The Annals of the American Academy of Political and Social Science* 252 (1): 21–29.

———. May 19, 1948. Proposed Amendments to the Articles of Agreement of the International Monetary Fund. Harry Dexter White Archives, Princeton University, Box 9, Folder 16.

———. May 19, 1948. Rough Draft of a Statement that Might Be Used to Introduce the Proposed Amendments on the Agenda. Harry Dexter White Archives, Princeton University, Box 11, Folder 27.

———. Undated. Political Economic Int. of Future. Harry Dexter White Archives, Princeton University, Box 9, Folder 18.

———. Undated. Stabilization and International Trade. Harry Dexter White Archives, Princeton University, Box 4, Folder 1.

White, Nathan I. 1956. *Harry D. White—Loyal American*. (Privately printed by Bessie White) Bloom, Waban, Mass.

White Archives: See individual items, listed by date, under White, Harry Dexter.

Wilkie, Christopher. 2012. *Special Drawing Rights: The First International Money.* New York: Oxford University Press.

Witteveen, Johannes. Jan. 15, 1974. "The Role of the International Monetary Fund." Address to the World Banking Conference, London.

Xinhua News Agency. Aug. 6, 2011. "After Historic Downgrade, U.S. Must Address Its Chronic Debt Problems."

Young, Arthur N. 1963. *China and the Helping Hand, 1937–1945.* Cambridge, Mass: Harvard University Press.

Zheng, Bijian. Sept./Oct. 2005. "China's 'Peaceful Rise' to Great-Power Status." *Foreign Affairs* 84 (5).

Zhou, Xiaochuan. Mar. 23, 2009. "Statement on Reforming the International Monetary System". Available at http://www.cfr.org/china/zhou-xiaochuans-statement-reforming-international-monetary-system/p18916.

Zlobin, I. D. Oct. 15, 1944. "Meetings in America." *The War and the Working Class*, No. 20. Translation in FBI files (WFO 65-5428) by John Dorosh, curator of the Slovak Room of the Library of Congress.

Zweig, Stefan. 1943. *The World of Yesterday: An Autobiography.* New York: Viking Press.

INDEX